D0983519

RESEARCH IN PERSONNEL AND HUMAN RESOURCES MANAGEMENT

RESEARCH IN PERSONNEL AND HUMAN RESOURCES MANAGEMENT

Series Editor: Joseph J. Martocchio

Volumes 1–10:   Edited by Kendrith M. Rowland and Gerald R. Ferris

Volumes 11–20:   Edited by Gerald R. Ferris

Supplement 1:   International Human Resources Management
Edited by Albert Nedd

Supplement 2:   International Human Resources Management
Edited by James B. Shaw and John E. Beck

Supplement 3:   International Human Resources Management
Edited by James B. Shaw, Paul S. Kirkbridge and Kendrith M. Rowland

Supplement 4:   International Human Resources Management in the Twenty-First Century
Edited by Patrick M. Wright, Lee D. Dyer, John W. Boudreau and George T. Milkovich

Volume 21:   Edited by Joseph J. Martocchio and Gerald R. Ferris

Volume 22:   Edited by Joseph J. Martocchio and Gerald R. Ferris

Volumes 23–25:   Edited by Joseph J. Martocchio

RESEARCH IN PERSONNEL AND HUMAN RESOURCES
MANAGEMENT VOLUME 26

RESEARCH IN PERSONNEL AND HUMAN RESOURCES MANAGEMENT

EDITED BY

JOSEPH J. MARTOCCHIO

University of Illinois, USA

ELSEVIER
JAI

Amsterdam – Boston – Heidelberg – London – New York – Oxford
Paris – San Diego – San Francisco – Singapore – Sydney – Tokyo
JAI Press is an imprint of Elsevier

JAI Press is an imprint of Elsevier
Linacre House, Jordan Hill, Oxford OX2 8DP, UK
Radarweg 29, PO Box 211, 1000 AE Amsterdam, The Netherlands
525 B Street, Suite 1900, San Diego, CA 92101-4495, USA

First edition 2007

British Library Cataloguing in Publication Data
A catalogue record for this book is available from the British Library

ISBN: 978-0-7623-1432-4
ISSN: 0742-7301 (Series)

For information on all JAI Press publications
visit our website at books.elsevier.com

Printed and bound in the United Kingdom

07 08 09 10 11 10 9 8 7 6 5 4 3 2 1

Working together to grow
libraries in developing countries

www.elsevier.com | www.bookaid.org | www.sabre.org

ELSEVIER   BOOK AID International   Sabre Foundation

6560990

CONTENTS

LIST OF CONTRIBUTORS

Fred R. Blass	Department of Management, College of Business, Florida State University, Tallahassee, FL, USA
Donald E. Conlon	The Eli Broad Graduate School of Management, Michigan State University, East Lansing, MI, USA
Russell Cropanzano	Department of Management and Policy, Eller College of Business and Public Administration, University of Arizona, Tucson, AZ, USA
Gerald R. Ferris	Department of Management, College of Business, Florida State University, Tallahassee, FL, USA
Aparna Joshi	Institute of Labor and Industrial Relations, University of Illinois at Urbana-Champaign, Champaign, IL, USA
Mary Dana Laird	Department of Management, College of Business, Florida State University, Tallahassee, FL, USA
Anne L. Lytle	The Australian Graduate School of Management, University of New South Wales, Sydney, NSW, Australia
Christopher J. Meyer	Hankamer School of Business, Baylor University, Waco, TX, USA

Christopher Robert   Department of Management and
                             Department of Psychological Sciences,
                             University of Missouri-Columbia,
                             Columbia, MO, USA

Hyuntak Roh   Institute of Labor and Industrial
                             Relations, University of Illinois at
                             Urbana-Champaign, IL, USA

Dianna L. Stone   Department of Management, College of
                             Business, University of Texas at San
                             Antonio, San Antonio, TX, USA

Eugene F. Stone-   Department of Management, College of
Romero   Business, University of Texas at San
                             Antonio, San Antonio, TX, USA

Michael C. Sturman   545F Statler Hall, School of Hotel
                             Administration, Cornell University,
                             Ithaca, NY, USA

Harold W. Willaby   School of Psychology, The University of
                             Sydney, Sydney, NSW, Australia

Thomas A. Wright   Management Department, Kansas State
                             University, KS, USA

Wan Yan   Department of Management, University
                             of Missouri-Columbia, Columbia,
                             MO, USA

Robert Zinko   Department of Management, College of
                             Business, East Carolina University,
                             Greenville, NC, USA

OVERVIEW

Volume 26 of *Research in Personnel and Human Resources Management* continues the tradition of publishing papers that contain an eclectic mix of ideas from economics, psychology, and sociology written to illuminate our understanding of the HRM field and to capture the multidisciplinary spirit of the field. This volume contains seven engaging papers on important HRM topics such as the notion of diversity context, dynamic performance research, and the role of humor in promoting creativity and other positive outcomes.

In the first paper, Joshi and Roh consider the context of workplace diversity to help shed light on the mixed research findings on work team diversity. They discuss how diversity context may be conceptualized, specify various aspects of this context at multiple levels of analysis, and consider how contextual variables can shape the outcomes of work team diversity. These researchers present findings from a literature review (1999–2006) to identify key trends and patterns of results reported in recent research as well as contextual factors that have received attention to date. Joshi and Roh also consider how the non-significant, positive, negative, and curvilinear effects of diversity found reported in studies can be explained by the contextual factors outlined. Implications for future research are also discussed.

In the second paper, Sturman reviews the extensive history of dynamic performance research, with the goal of providing a clear picture of where the field has been, where it is now, and where it needs to go. Past research has established that job performance does indeed change, but the implications of this dynamism and the predictability of performance trends remain unresolved. From this review, Sturman proposes research questions to bridge the theoretical and methodological gaps of this area. Answering these questions can advance both research involving job performance prediction and our understanding of the effects of human resource interventions.

In the third paper, Stone-Romero and Stone remind us how individuals are often stigmatized by virtue of their status on various dimensions and that they are often the targets of both access and treatment discrimination in organizations. The authors present a model of the cognitive, affective, and cultural influences on stigmatization in organizations, detail how stigmatization affects human resource management processes and practices, and consider strategies that can be used to reduce the problems faced by stigmatized individuals in organizations.

In the fourth paper, Zinko, Ferris, Blass, and Laird maintain that in work organizations, we engage in frequent discourse about the nature of reputations, and we also see personal reputation used as a basis for important human resources decisions; however, there has been very little theory and research on personal reputation in organizations published in the organizational sciences. The authors address this need by proposing a conceptualization of personal reputation in organizations. In this conceptualization, reputation is presented as an agreed upon, collective perception by others, and involves behavior calibration derived from social comparisons with referent others that results in a deviation from the behavioral norms in one's environment, as observed and evaluated by others. Implications of this conceptualization are discussed, as are directions for future research.

In the fifth paper, Robert and Yan address the topic of humor in organizations. They tell us that the study of humor has a long tradition in philosophy, sociology, psychology, anthropology, and communications. Evidence from these fields suggests that humor can have effects on creativity, cohesiveness, and performance, but organizational scholars have paid it relatively little attention. The authors first outline the theoretical rationale underlying the production and appreciation of humor, namely, its motivational, cognitive, and emotional mechanisms. Next, they review the literature linking humor to creativity, cohesiveness, and other performance-relevant outcomes. Finally, the authors venture beyond the current humor literature by developing specific predictions about how culture might interact with humor in organizational contexts. Throughout the paper, they discuss possible research directions and methodological issues relevant to the study of humor in organizations.

In the sixth paper, Wright and Cropanzano address the happy/productive worker thesis. They point out that since at least the famous Hawthorne studies, the happy/productive worker thesis has forcefully captured the imagination of management scholars and human resource professionals alike. According to this "Holy Grail" of management research, workers who are happy on the job will have higher job performance, and possibly higher job retention, than those who are less happy. But what is happiness? Most typically, happiness has been measured in the management sciences as job satisfaction. They argue that this viewpoint is unnecessarily limiting and suggest a twofold, expanded view of this thesis. First, they consider worker happiness as psychological well-being. Second, incorporating Fredrickson's (1998, 2001) broaden-and-build model of positive emotions as the theoretical base, the authors suggest that the job satisfaction to job performance and job satisfaction to employee retention relationships may be better explained by controlling for the moderating effect of psychological well-being. Future research directions for human resource professionals are introduced.

In the seventh paper, Conlon, Meyer, Lytle, and Willaby focus on alternative dispute resolution procedures, in particular third party procedures and how these procedures are used in different cultural contexts. Next, the authors evaluate the procedures in terms of how they impact four key criteria that have been noted in the literature related to negotiation: process criteria, settlement criteria, issue-related criteria, and relationship criteria. Then, they subsequently explore the potential impact of culture on evaluations of these criteria. The authors conclude with a discussion of future directions for research and practice, emphasizing that procedural recommendations should be made carefully when the criteria for effectiveness and applicability are derived from US-centric research.

In sum, the authors offer interesting takes on essential topics in the HRM field. The more I read, the more I want to know. Altogether, I hope these papers inspire your work in the field.

Joseph J. Martocchio
Series Editor

CONTEXT MATTERS: A MULTILEVEL FRAMEWORK FOR WORK TEAM DIVERSITY RESEARCH

Aparna Joshi and Hyuntak Roh

ABSTRACT

Several comprehensive reviews are united in drawing the conclusion that the cumulative research evidence on work team diversity is equivocal. Rather than review the extant state of diversity research, in this paper we redirect attention to the context of workplace diversity as a possible explanation for these mixed findings. We discuss how diversity context may be conceptualized, specify various aspects of this context at multiple levels of analysis, and consider how contextual variables can shape the outcomes of work team diversity. We present findings from a literature review (1999–2006) to identify key trends and patterns of results reported in recent research as well as contextual factors that have received attention to date. This paper also considers how the non-significant, positive, negative, and curvilinear effects of diversity reported in studies can be explained by the contextual factors outlined. Implications for future research are also discussed.

Research in Personnel and Human Resources Management, Volume 26, 1–48
ISSN: 0742-7301/doi:10.1016/S0742-7301(07)26001-3

1

INTRODUCTION

Over the past two decades the call for a business case for diversity has gained momentum in the US workplace. Yet, several comprehensive reviews on this topic are united in drawing the conclusion that research evidence demonstrating a business case for diversity is by and large equivocal (Harrison & Klein, 2007; Jackson, Joshi, & Erhardt, 2003; Milliken & Martins, 1996; Van Knippenberg & Schippers, 2007; Williams & O'Reilly, 1998). The lack of scientific evidence supporting the benefits of diversity has not dimmed corporate investments in diversity management efforts. Nearly 95% of *Fortune* 1000 companies have diversity training initiatives in place (Grensing-Pophal, 2002) and diversity consultants generate annual revenues estimated to be between $400 million and $600 million (Hansen, 2003). We believe that this apparent mismatch between practitioner zeal and academic uncertainty has serious implications for future research on workplace diversity and can threaten future theory building in this area. To the extent that organizations are "customers" or "end-users" of the products of diversity research, the lack of a clear message hampers the market-orientation of this research. A market-orientation is vital for applied research in general and specifically for further theory building in the area of diversity for a number of reasons (cf. Dubin, 1976). Without a market orientation, the application of diversity research to the workplace may be called into question and the overall mandate for diversity in organizations may come under threat. After all, if researchers are unable to provide definitive answers regarding the benefits and overall performance gains from diversity, why would companies continue to invest in and implement diversity management practices? The lack of a market orientation also implies that when the practical implications of past research are unclear, companies may be even less amenable to serve as research sites for field researchers, thereby stymieing future empirical extensions of theory.

In this paper we propose that in order to resolve this dilemma, researchers need to reframe current approaches to diversity research by engaging in more comprehensive considerations of the *context* of diversity. Focusing only on the outcomes of work group level diversity without accounting for the environment in which these work groups are nested does not allow us to fully appreciate the complexity of diversity in organizations. Only a detailed consideration of the diversity context will allow researchers to gain an understanding of the mechanisms and boundary conditions under which diversity can translate into positive organizational outcomes. Such an approach also enhances the practical relevance of diversity research. We define diversity as an aggregate group level construct that represents differences among members of an interdependent work group with respect to a specific personal attribute (Harrison & Klein, 2007; Jackson et al., 2003). In the broader domain of management literature, context is defined as the situational setting in which workplace phenomena occur (Cappelli & Sherer, 1991). This paper aims at providing a template for future research that might consider how various aspects of the situational setting can shape the outcomes of diversity in work groups.

Current theoretical perspectives framing diversity research, such as social identity theory, social categorization theory, or the attraction-selection-attrition framework, offer explanations for *why* differences within work groups may manifest in specific attitudinal outcomes such as conflict or cohesion or behavioral outcomes such as turnover or absenteeism (see Jackson et al., 2003). In general, current applications of these theoretical perspectives in diversity research have been a – contextual, that is, they have been applied to offer broad generalizations across various dimensions of diversity and across a wide array of work group and organizational outcomes. However, without considering the boundary conditions that may be relevant to these theoretical perspectives, they provide only insufficient explanations for the diversity dynamics under consideration. In addition to "why" diversity manifests in specific outcomes, a careful examination of the situational setting would also incorporate "what", "when", "where", and "how", diversity dynamics unfold in the workplace; these contextual considerations are not often captured in studies (see Johns, 2006) and are pertinent for reconciling the mixed findings from past research.

To illustrate the role of context in explaining the mixed findings of past research, let us consider a recent set of studies that examined the effects of team demographic diversity on performance outcomes in field settings. Kochan et al. (2003) recently published a report on four field studies that considered various aspects of diversity in relation to performance outcomes. All four studies were conducted in organizations that had implemented diversity management practices for several years. Consistently, across these four studies, the authors reported few significant main effects of diversity on team performance. Overall, gender diversity had either a weak positive effect or a non-significant relationship with objective indicators of performance. Racial diversity had a weak negative relationship with team performance. In general, findings were stronger for the effects of diversity on process outcomes rather than performance outcomes. Other field research also reports similar mixed findings (e.g., Kirkman, Tesluk, & Rosen, 2004; Pelled, Eisenhardt, & Xin, 1999).

Based on current theoretical applications of attraction-selection-attrition theory or social identity theory, researchers would surmise that race or gender diversity would manifest in similar organizational outcomes. Yet, why does racial diversity emerge as a significant predictor of negative outcomes while gender diversity is either non-significant or positively associated with group process outcomes? Researchers have proposed various answers to this question. Kochan et al. (2003) concluded that gender diversity is less problematic than race diversity because white women tend to have better representation in organizations than minority men or women. The positive effects of gender diversity reflected more conducive relationships between white men and women in gender balanced groups. In a similar vein, Kirkman et al. (2004) explained their non-significant findings for gender diversity and negative outcomes for racial diversity by noting that there is relatively less gender bias than racial bias in companies. These explanations offer preliminary leads, but also beg a fuller inquiry into the boundary conditions shaping diversity dynamics in teams. A contextualized response to the question posed above would draw attention to organizational and even extra-organizational factors that may shape the outcomes of gender and racial diversity. Such a response would draw attention to specific socio-political trends in the US workplace that might shape race and gender-based diversity dynamics differentially. Indeed, some researchers have argued that gender discrimination has become more insidious rather than overt, but is certainly alive and well in the US workplace (see Meyerson & Fletcher, 2000). At the same time, recent developments in immigration laws and media attention on immigration issues may trigger race or ethnicity-based identities in the workplace and manifest in the salience of race or ethnic diversity relative to gender diversity in teams. Thus, societal level history, culture, or legal developments as well as organizational level structures, strategy, and practices could trigger a series of effects that could trickle down into the diversity dynamics within work groups and have implications for research findings. Cumulatively, these contextual considerations might lead researchers to very different conclusions than arguments borne out of various theoretical perspectives applied in current research.

This paper delves deeper into the contextual considerations highlighted above. In the next section, we discuss in detail how diversity context may be conceptualized, outline various aspects of this context at various levels, and present the implications of these contextual factors for the outcomes of work team diversity. Next, we present the findings from a review of field research conducted between 1999 through 2006. We identify specific trends in terms of diversity attributes and outcomes considered in research as well as the pattern of results reported. We also aim at identifying various aspects of the context that have been considered in research in this period. In the third section, we consider how the non-significant, positive, negative, and curvilinear effects of diversity found in research to date can be explained by these contextual features. Finally, we consider the implications of these contextual considerations for future research on work team diversity.

WHAT IS THE CONTEXT OF DIVERSITY?

Several researchers acknowledge that contextual considerations are critical in diversity research (e.g., Jackson et al., 2003; Martins, Miliken, Wiesenfeld, & Salgado, 2003). However, a detailed description and conceptualization of diversity context has been less forthcoming. Recently, Johns (2006) offered a welcome and comprehensive framework for defining the many facets of context in the study of organizational phenomena. In outlining a framework for the contextual antecedents of work team diversity, we draw on and extend this conceptualization of context (see Fig. 1). Broadly, drawing on Johns' terminology, we consider two main dimensions of context – an omnibus diversity context and a discrete diversity context.

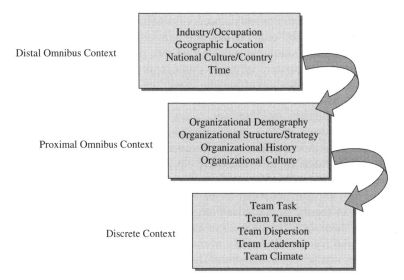

Fig. 1. Aspects of Diversity Context.

Omnibus diversity context is defined as the overall environment relevant to all types of work groups and interactions between organizational members. This type of context sets the overall constraints within which diversity phenomena are likely to occur. Omnibus context may also be viewed as the domain of macro theoretical perspectives that highlight the role of the organizational environment, labor market characteristics, technology, structure, and strategy in shaping organizational phenomena (House, Rousseau, & Thomas-Hunt, 1995). In the omnibus contextual domain, sociological and political perspectives would suggest that interactional processes within the work group are shaped by differential access to resources and power which are also reflected in organizational and occupational demographics as well as managerial practices (for a review see Skaggs & DiTomaso, 2004). These perspectives would draw attention to both organizational characteristics such as history, demography, culture, and strategy that reflect differential access of demographic groups to power and resources as well as extra-organizational factors such as occupational demographics, and societal trends and events that may shape these organizational attributes (House et al., 1995; Skaggs & DiTomaso, 2004). In this paper, we further categorize omnibus contextual factors in terms of whether these variables would exert distal or proximal influences on work group outcomes. Distal omnibus factors would shape the outcomes of diversity in work groups through intermediate organizational level variables. We consider the following distal aspects of context: the industry/occupation, geographic location, national culture, and temporal factors including societal and organizational trends and events that can potentially shape diversity-related outcomes. Proximal omnibus context incorporates variables within the organizational domain that may be shaped by distal factors and serves to filter the effects of distal omnibus context on the discrete diversity context. These factors include but are not necessarily limited to organizational demography, culture, history, and business strategy.

The *discrete diversity context* may be an outcome of the overall omnibus context and pertains to the immediate environment in which interpersonal interactions between diverse team members occur. Micro-theoretical perspectives that explain behavior *within* the work group entity such as social categorization theory or the attraction-selection-attrition framework would be relevant theoretical perspectives at the discrete level. Following an input-process-output framework, a bulk of diversity research has focused on team demographic composition as an input that manifests in specific processes such as communication, cohesion, or conflict that, in turn, manifest in performance outcomes (Jackson et al., 2003; Williams & O'Reilly, 1998). Based on extant theoretical perspectives as well as empirical research that has taken an input-process-output approach to understanding the outcomes of diversity, we focus on specific aspects of the discrete context that can potentially influence process and performance outcomes (see also Van Knippenberg & Schippers, 2007). Specifically, we examine the following aspects of discrete context: team task, team tenure, team dispersion, team leadership, and team climate. Below we consider each of these aspects of context in greater detail. We first discuss how each of these aspects of context can shape the outcomes of work group diversity. We then present findings from the literature review to get an indication of the extent to which these contextual factors have been taken into consideration in team diversity research.

Distal Omnibus Context

Industry/Occupation

A significant body of sociological research on the demographics of occupations and industry shows that industry or occupation level demographics can have important implications for gender and ethnicity or race-based diversity in organizations (for a review see Reskin, McBrier, & Kmec, 1999). Prior research in this area has shown that occupational demography can influence earning and rewards. For example, the degree to which occupations are female-dominated is predictive of occupational wage levels; as the degree of female representation increases, averages wages decrease for both men and women in the occupation (O'Neill, 2003; Pfeffer & Davis-Blake, 1987). This "feminization" effect persists even when human capital requirements of different occupations and jobs are taken into account (Elvira & Graham, 2002). In other words, it appears as if feminization of occupations results in the occupations themselves being devalued (Blau, 1977). Ostroff and Atwater (2003) found that increasing proportions of female peers, subordinates, and managers had negative effects on managerial compensation. Elvira and Graham (2002) also found that the negative effects of feminization were evident in both base pay and contingent pay. Research on occupational demography typically focuses on gender rather than ethnicity, in part because racial typing of occupations is less prevalent than occupational feminization (Tomaskovic-Devey, 1993). Nevertheless, the dynamics of feminization may be generalizable to other demographic attributes as well and may influence interactional processes within work groups (Skaggs & DiTomaso, 2004).

A recent study by Frink et al. (2003) highlights the importance of acknowledging industry level gender segregation on the outcomes of diversity in organizations. The study examined the effects of gender diversity on firm performance in two organizations and found support for an inverted U-shaped relationship between firm level gender composition and performance. However, the authors noted that in some industries it may not be possible to fully utilize the potential value of gender diversity. Specifically, they pointed out that the inverted U-shaped relationship between gender composition and performance was only observed in service/wholesale/retail industries which, in comparison with manufacturing/utilities and finance industries, are comprised of a higher proportion of women in general. The fact that the level of gender segregation is higher in the latter set of industries may reflect the inability of organizations in male-dominated industries to capitalize on the benefits of gender diversity. Within work groups, gender segregation in the workplace may also reinforce status distinction between male and female work group members (Skaggs & DiTomaso, 2004), thereby influencing work group processes such as communications and information sharing, and ultimately group performance.

Geographic Location
Communities in which organizations are located can also be a relevant contextual factor shaping the outcomes of diversity. As Brief et al. (2005) recently noted that community researchers have considered the role of proximity between minority and white individuals on inter-group relationships (Blalock, 1956; Giles, 1977). This research is based on the premise that perceptions of resource scarcity enhance the threat perceived from out-group members. As a result, dominant in-group members view increasing proportions of out-group members as a threat and respond by forming prejudicial attitudes towards them (Sherif, 1966; Sherif, Harvey, White, Hood, & Sherif, 1961). Based on this premise, researchers have looked at both the effect of the demographic composition of communities on the attitudes of white and minority individuals. At the community level of analysis, research suggests that the metropolitan concentrations of blacks was associated with occupational and income inequality in some geographic locations (Taylor, 1998). The proportion of blacks in communities has also been associated with higher levels of prejudice among white individuals (Blalock, 1956; Pettigrew, 1959; Taylor, 1998). Corroborating this research in an organizational setting, Brief et al. (2005) found that the closer whites lived to blacks, the more likely they were to perceive inter-ethnic conflict in their communities and respond negatively to black co-workers.

The inter-group contact perspective also suggests that the nature of interactions with diverse individuals outside the organization can shape the nature of interactions within organizations and work groups. Pettigrew (1998) noted that "optimal contact" requires sustained long-term interactions with out-group members and highlights the role of individual's past experiences with the out-group members and their value differences may shape the manner in which they approach inter-group contact situations. Further, using the strife in Northern Ireland and Quebec as illustrations, Pettigrew noted that the level of inter-group conflict in the immediate community might play a role in shaping the manner in which individuals approach inter-group contact situations. These perspectives suggest that individuals' past experiences and encounters in the non-work domain can shape their interactions with out-group members within the work group.

Another approach to understanding the effects of community demographics takes a very different view of how these demographics could shape group diversity outcomes. This approach, characterized as the customer-match perspective, views the community as a source of customers rather than employees' social relationships. Studies taking this approach have found little support for the often-cited business case that assumes that firms are more likely to reap financial benefits when employee demographics match the demographics of the community. For example, Leonard, Levine, and Joshi (2004) examined whether the match between employee–customer demographics across 700 retail stores (including gender, race, and age) in a two mile radius around the stores predicted store financial performance. Results indicated that store-community demographic match did not predict store performance. More recently, Sacco and Schmitt (2005) also did not find support for this relationship in a large sample of quick service restaurants.

Together, these various approaches to understanding the effects of community demographics on the relationship between work group demographics and performance suggest that, while important, community demographics may have somewhat different implications for the outcomes of diversity than is conveyed by the customer matching perspective (that is also often the basis for the business case for diversity). These studies reviewed above suggest that community demographics may have a more immediate impact on interpersonal relationships in organizations rather than the organizational bottom-line and may therefore be an important consideration while examining the impact of diversity on interactional processes in the team.

National Culture/Country
In a global economy, trends in worker migration and immigration have made diversity-related considerations fairly prevalent. In countries like South Africa, India, Japan, and the European Union, various aspects of

culture and history can shape specific aspects of diversity (Mor-Barak, 2005). These considerations have prompted some scholars to consider how the nature and meaning of diversity may be driven by the country context. Ferner, Almond, and Colling (2005) examined the transfer of diversity management practices from US parent companies to UK subsidiaries. They found that the transfer and implementation of diversity management practices was complicated by the differing meanings of diversity within the US and UK. These findings raise questions regarding the role that country context plays in shaping diversity-related phenomena in non-US workplaces and call into question the somewhat US-centric conceptualization of diversity (Ferner et al., 2005). The growing internationalization of management research community has resulted in several studies that are being conducted in non-US contexts. For instance, in a Dutch context, Schippers, Den Hartog, Koopman, and Wienk (2003) examined the effects of an overall diversity measure (including age, gender, education, and team tenure) on outcomes including team reflexivity, satisfaction, commitment, and performance. Neither the overall diversity measure nor each aspect of diversity considered in this study had a direct impact on the outcomes considered. We surmise that at least a partial explanation for these non-significant findings may be the nature of the Dutch context in which the study was conducted. Other research on the meaning of diversity in the Netherlands suggests that the Dutch associate the term "diversity" with "ethnic differences" or "immigrants" (see Mor-Barak, 2005). The diversity attributes considered by Schippers and colleagues may be less salient in the Dutch setting than perhaps national origin or ethnicity-based diversity.

In addition to the ways in which country location can shape the meaning of diversity, national culture may also shape the manner in which diversity dynamics play out in organizations. Culture is defined as "the human-made part of the environment (Herskovits, 1955). It has both objective elements – tools, roads, and appliances – and subjective elements – categories, associations, beliefs, attitudes, norms, roles, and values" (Triandis, 1994, p. 113). Cultural values shape work-related attitudes and behaviors (Triandis, 1994). Hofstede's fourfold framework of cultural dimensions has been considered a major landmark in the area of cross-cultural research (Triandis, 1994) and has provided an enduring framework for understanding cultural differences in employee attitudes and behaviors. The four dimensions of culture, power distance, masculinity (femininity), uncertainty avoidance, and individualism (collectivism) have been widely applied in cross-cultural research for over two decades (Hofstede, 1980; for a review see Triandis, 1994). These dimensions have been useful in revising current theories of motivation, leadership, and work values in organizations (Hofstede, 1980; Meindl, Hunt, & Lee, 1989).

Recently, there have been some studies that have incorporated the effects of culture on the outcomes of diversity in organizations. Van Der Vegt, Van De Vliert, and Huang (2005) examined the effects of Hofstede's power distance dimension on the impact of demographic diversity on organization level innovative climates. The authors argued that since demographic diversity is associated with status differences, the effects of demographic diversity would differ in high versus low power distance cultures. Supporting these propositions the study found that, in low power distance cultures, tenure and functional diversity were positively associated with innovative climates, while in high power distance cultures diversity was negatively associated with innovative climates. These effects were not, however, found for age or gender diversity. The study raises important issues regarding the role of culture in shaping the outcomes of diversity. The extent to which equality or inequality is emphasized in a culture may shape the diversity dynamics within work groups. Other aspects of culture that emphasize the extent to which individuals feel interdependent on group members may also shape the extent to which diversity plays out in group settings. Kirkman and Shapiro (2001) examined the extent to which national culture moderated the effects of individual team members' cultural values on resistance to self-managing teams. Their results indicated that, in high power distance and collectivistic contexts, individual employees are less likely to express disagreements or discomfort with employment practices such as self-managing teams. In these contexts, the relationship between employee cultural orientation and resistance to teams was weaker than in low power distance and individualistic settings. Together, the studies reviewed above suggest that country location as well as national culture can play an important role in shaping the outcomes of diversity. With the growing internationalization of diversity research as well as the increasing multiculturalism of the US workplace, the role of national culture in shaping the effects of diversity is likely to increase in relevance.

Time
Research on time-related influences on diversity dynamics has focused primarily on the role of team tenure in shaping diversity dynamics. We will discuss team tenure as a contextual influence in a subsequent section. For the present, we consider how omnibus temporal factors can shape the environment in which team diversity might unfold. Johns (2006) describes time as an omnibus contextual variable that "affects the web of social and

economic relationships that surrounds any aspect of organizational behavior" (p. 392). Considering temporal effects as environmental stimuli shaping diversity-related outcomes raises interesting questions for diversity research. In the broader management research, some studies have examined how time may shape the meaning and relevance of employee behavior (e.g., absenteeism, see Martocchio, Harrison, & Berkson, 2000) and work group processes (e.g., Gersick, 1988). One approach to understanding the effects of time is to consider how significant events can shape behaviors in organizations. This event-based perspective on time (see Ancona, Okhuysen, & Perlow, 2001) would suggest that societal and organizational events can shape the meaning and outcomes of diversity in organizations. Consider, for instance, the salience of an African American racial identity in Xerox Corporation in the late 1960s that was triggered by local events such as race riots in Rochester, New York (where the corporate headquarters is located) as well national events such as the passing of the Civil Rights legislation. These events played a role in highlighting the distinctive African American experience outside the organization and mobilized the formation of an African American identity within the company ultimately leading the development of one of the first caucus groups in the US employment history (Friedman, 1996). More recent national events such as the September 11th 2001 terrorist attacks may also have the power to shape diversity dynamics in organizations. While, intuitively, one might expect that inter-religious conflict would increase in the workplace there is some research to suggest the contrary. Studies in educational settings conducted in the aftermath of the 9/11 attacks found an increase in levels of inclusion and inter-group cooperation along with renewed institutional efforts to address bias and prejudice in campus communities (e.g., Miele, 2004). Thus it is possible that certain significant events such as a war or a national catastrophe might have an "inclusivity effect" and serve to minimize inter-group conflict and shape the outcomes of diversity within teams. Further research might help us understand in more detail how these events would shape inter-group relations in the workplace. In addition, events within organizations such as the appointment of a new CEO, restructuring and lay offs, corporate scandals, or a discrimination law suit can possibly trigger inter-group dynamics that shape team diversity outcomes.

Event-based perspectives on time suggest that significant events such as those discussed above can exert a powerful influence on the outcomes of diversity in teams. Clock-time or cyclical time-based perspectives (see Ancona et al., 2001 for a detailed discussion) would suggest that broader trends in society and in the organization can also be an influence on diversity dynamics. For example, over the past three decades, age-related trends in the US workforce have heightened the age diversity within organizations. For the first time in employment history, four generational groups are working alongside each other. It is possible that these age-based trends change the nature of inter- and intra-generational interactions within work groups which, in turn, can shape the outcomes of age diversity in teams (see Dencker, Joshi, & Martocchio, 2007). As evidenced in the 2001 *Academy of Management Review*'s special issue on the effects of time in organizations, the broader domain of management research has acknowledged the relevance of considering temporal factors in research. We propose that a similar effort be made in diversity research.

Proximal Omnibus Context

Organizational Demography

In previous sections, we considered how occupational or industry level demographics can influence diversity-related outcomes in organizations. While acknowledging that demographics of the occupation or industry sets limits on the available skilled labor pool for the organization, in this section we consider the contextual influences of demographics within the organization on the outcomes of work group. In the management literature, a significant body of research pioneered by Pfeffer (1983) has considered how organizational demography can shape diversity-related outcomes.

The demography of an organization provides a roadmap for understanding the impact of status and relative proportions on interactional processes between demographic groups. Two objective characteristics of organization's demographic composition can influence these factors – the overall heterogeneity of the organization (in terms of the representation of demographic groups in the organization) and the level of structural integration (the representation of minority groups at higher levels in the organization) (see Cox, 1991; Joshi, 2006). The degree to which an organization is structurally segregated can be a powerful influence on social category-based identification and conflict among demographic groups (Cox, 1993; Ely, 1994; Wharton, 1992). In structurally segregated organizations, the balance of power and status is skewed in favor of the dominant demographic group; these status and power differentials in this context can undermine inter-group harmony and cooperation within the work group (Cox, 1993).

Ely's (1994, 1995) definitive work on the social construction of gender identity in organizations highlights the powerful influence that organizational demography can have on perceptual processes related to gender-based identification. These studies and others (e.g., Ridgeway, 1997) show that, in organizations where subordinate groups are under-represented, negative stereotypes and biases toward these groups are higher. A more recent study by Joshi, Liao, and Jackson (2006) examined how organizational unit management demography and work group demographic composition influence pay differences based on ethnicity and gender in a large sales organization. Commensurate with Ely's research, Joshi and colleagues' study demonstrated that, in sales units with a greater number of female managers, the pay gap between male and female employees reduced and women were able to perform at higher levels. In a similar vein, Martins et al. (2003) compared the effects of racio-ethnic diversity in a homogeneous and a heterogeneous organization. Results suggest that the outcomes of racio-ethnic diversity were more negative in racio-ethnically homogeneous contexts than in more heterogeneous contexts. While organizational demography has received considerable attention in diversity research, we call more cross-level research that considers the specific impact of organizational level variables on interpersonal diversity dynamics within teams.

Organizational Strategy

The nature and extent of internal and external pressures that firms face to adopt diversity management practices may be determined by organization's business strategy. External pressures include industry wide trends such as increased competition from new entrants or changing consumer demands. Internal pressures include resources available within the firm and the resources and capabilities of the top management team (see Dass & Parker, 1999). The manner in which a firm reacts to these pressures may often be a reflection of the firm's strategy. Miles and Snow (1984) distinguished between "prospector" firms that actively seek out new opportunities and are more likely to view these pressures as opportunities and "reactor" firms that may view the same set of pressures as threats. Depending on the firm's strategy, external and internal pressures to adopt diversity management practices may be addressed differentially and have consequences for diversity-related outcomes.

In a series of studies, Richard and colleagues examined the effects of firm business strategy on the relationship between firm diversity and performance. Richard, Barnett, Dwyer, and Chadwick (2004) examined if a curvilinear relationship between firm's cultural diversity and performance was moderated by firm-level entrepreneurial orientation. The study found that firm-level entrepreneurial orientation, defined as propensity to take risks and act proactively and innovatively, did indeed moderate the U-shaped relationship proposed between management diversity and performance. In high innovativeness firms, there was a positive relationship between management racial diversity and firm productivity. In low innovativeness firms, this relationship was non-significant. The results followed a different pattern with regard to gender diversity. The study found an inverted U-shaped relationship for gender diversity and firm performance in high risk taking firms. In low-risk taking firms, this relationship was positive. These results suggest that the *type* of firm entrepreneurial strategy (i.e., one focused on innovativeness versus risk taking) as well as the nature of management diversity considered (i.e., gender versus race) matter for firm performance. In another study, Richard, McMillan, Chadwick, and Dwyer (2003) found that firms that followed an innovation strategy benefited to a greater degree from racial diversity than firms low in innovation. In an earlier study, Richard (2000) also found that racial diversity was positively associated with firm performance in firms that followed a growth strategy and negatively associated in firms that followed a downsizing strategy. Together, these studies indicate that firms' business strategy is a key contextual factor that shapes the value that can be derived from diversity. In general, commensurate with resource-based perspectives of firms, more growth-oriented and innovative firms may be in a better position to harness the value of diversity in comparison with firms that are efficiency-oriented (Richard, 2000; Richard et al., 2004). These findings also suggest that the diversity within teams may also be shaped by firm-level strategy. In firms that are growth-oriented, diversity within the team may have the potential to contribute to greater levels of creativity and innovation (e.g., Bantel & Jackson, 1989). However, in firms that follow risk-averse and efficiency-oriented strategies, diversity in teams may be associated with "process losses" that impede performance.

Organizational History
An organization's history with regard to diversity-related issues can be viewed as a "blueprint" for current and future diversity management practices. Recently, applying a genealogical perspective, Phillips (2005) examined whether gender inequality is transferred from parent law firms to progeny law firms through the replication of routines engendered by the movement of founding partners. The study examined how organizational routines and structures are replicated by founders in the progeny firms, so that founders from parent firms characterized by gender inequality tended to replicate a similar inequality in the progeny firm. The study findings suggest that organizational routines related to inequality can be transferred across generations of employees and the extent of transfer depends on the degree of

institutionalization of gender inequality in the founding firms (Phillips, 2005). Thus, organizational history can be viewed as a replication of routines across generations of employees and extent to which organizational founders focused on rectifying inequality and discrimination may be replicated across generations of employees. In organizations where historically women and minorities have had a voice and access to resources, gender or race-based diversity may have more positive outcomes in comparison with organizations where women and minorities have historically been in subordinate positions. From an institutional perspective, in organizations where historically women and minorities have held leadership positions, their equal status in the organization is legitimized; these organizations may also be able to mine the value of diversity within the work group more effectively (Ridgeway, 1997). These perspectives suggest that organizational history with diversity-related issues may shed light on the specific dynamics of diversity within work groups and merit closer attention in future research.

Organizational Culture

Like organizational history, organizational culture also sends signals regarding the organization's approach to diversity. Organizational culture is defined as the shared values, beliefs, expectations, and norms prevalent in an organization and manifests itself in organizational rituals, practices, and managerial behavior (Cox, 1993; Schneider, 2000). Cox (1993) discusses the role of two aspects of organizational culture that can shape the employee behavior and employment outcomes – culture strength and culture content. Culture *strength* refers to the extent to which organizational norms and values are explicit and enforced. Organizations with strong cultures are characterized by uniform expectations and responses. In organizations with weak cultures, there is less agreement about appropriate behaviors and expectations. To the extent that diversity management practices are supported by a strong organizational culture, they are more likely to be implemented successfully in organizations (Cox, 1993).

Organizational culture *content* refers to the specific norms, values, and beliefs that are prevalent in organizations (Cox, 1993). Chatman and colleagues have examined the extent to which individualistic versus collectivistic organizations shape the outcomes of diversity in work groups. Chatman and Spataro (2005) argued that work group processes would be shaped by the extent to which organizations emphasize independence versus interdependence. In organizations that emphasize independence, demographic dissimilarity to the work group is more likely to be negatively associated with work group cooperation. In more collectivistic settings, however, individuals are more likely to pick up cues that emphasize cooperation in the face of demographic dissimilarity. In an earlier study, Chatman, Polzer, Barsade, and Neale (1998) found that the positive effects of demographic diversity are more likely to emerge in organizations that emphasize organizational membership through a collectivistic orientation rather than in organizations that emphasize individualism and distinctiveness. In a recent study, Ely and Thomas (2001) found that employees in bank branches that emphasized a learning perspective were more likely to view their racial diversity as a valuable resource even while performing race-neutral tasks. Together, these studies suggest that organizational culture can be a powerful influence on the extent to which the positive outcomes of diversity can materialize in work groups.

Discrete Context

Team Task

The nature of a team's task can have a significant influence on the extent to which team members are interdependent in terms of goals and task outcomes and on the utilization of cognitive resources represented by team members; team task is therefore an important consideration in theoretical models of team effectiveness (see Ilgen, Hollenbeck, Johnson, & Jundt, 2005; LePine, Hanson, Borman, & Motowidlo, 2000). Not surprisingly, several researchers have argued that task characteristics such as the nature of task complexity and task interdependence can influence the manner in which diversity shapes team processes and outcomes.

For example, Schippers et al. (2003) argued that team outcome interdependence "buffers" the negative effects of diversity on team process outcomes. The authors propose that outcome interdependence reinforces common group goals that can counteract the negative effects of diversity, such that highly outcome interdependent teams with high levels of diversity would show more positive outcomes (i.e., team reflexivity) than highly diverse teams with low outcome interdependence. Highly outcome inter-dependent teams with low levels of diversity would be less reflexive than highly diverse teams with low outcome interdependence. Findings suggested that for the overall diversity measure, gender diversity and tenure diversity, high levels of diversity and outcome interdependence predicted higher levels of reflexivity than the other three conditions.

Researchers have also considered other aspects of team task such as task complexity and routineness as moderators of the relationship between diversity and key outcomes. For example, Pelled et al. (1999) posed contradictory hypotheses, proposing that task routineness could either enhance or diminish the positive relationship between team diversity and task conflict. The authors also proposed that task routines would reduce the positive relationship between diversity and emotional conflict; because complex tasks impose greater levels of stress on employees and group members, they may be more likely to feel frustration with dissimilar others in groups. Results indicated that task routineness enhanced the positive relationship between diversity and task conflict and reduced the negative relationship between team diversity and emotional conflict. Based on sensation-seeking theory, the authors suggested that the level of stimulation provided by team tasks could determine the way team members respond to dissimilar team members. When team members are "bored" by routine tasks, they may want to engage in task-oriented debates with team members but not in "unpleasant arousing experiences" that would characterize emotional conflict. These studies suggest that team tasks, in terms of the level of challenge they offer employees as well as the extent to which they reinforce common goals, can shape important process outcomes of team diversity. Together, these studies suggest that rather than a simple linear relationship between team composition-process-performance, studies that account for team task and consider more complex team level interactive effects are more likely to offer a comprehensive understanding of the outcomes of team diversity.

Team Tenure
At the discrete level, team tenure (length of time team members have spent in the team) as well as group longevity (length of time the team has existed) have been viewed as relevant temporal influences on team diversity outcomes. This body of research has been informed by Harrison and colleagues' work on the effects of time on the outcome of diversity (Harrison, Price, & Bell, 1998; Harrison, Price, Gavin, & Florey, 2002). This research shows that over a length of time, the effects of surface-level aspects of diversity (that are related to social categorization effects) may diminish in salience and deep-level aspects of diversity (that reflect differences in attitudes or values) can become more salient in teams.

Some studies have corroborated Harrison et al.'s study findings (Chatman & Flynn, 2001; Earley & Mosakowski, 2000; Pelled et al., 1999), while others have shown mixed support for the effects of time on diversity outcomes. For example, Schippers et al. (2003) distinguished between team tenure and group longevity and argue that team members expectations regarding the life of a group are also likely to influence the way they respond to and interact with dissimilar group members. Their findings indicate that diversity was negatively associated with processes under conditions of *higher* group longevity. Diversity was positively associated with group processes among "younger" teams. This result is contradictory to the general pattern of results reported by Harrison and colleagues and suggests that the manner in which time is measured at the discrete level may influence the nature of the moderating effect. Further in the present business context, where teams are constantly being reconfigured and individuals work on multiple teams simultaneously, it may be pertinent to also examine other aspects of team tenure such as tenure volatility which captures the variation (rather than the central tendency) in team members' tenure in the team.

Team Dispersion
Organizations are increasingly implementing geographically dispersed teams to cut costs and increase efficiency and customer responsiveness (Apgar, 1998). Given the growing prevalence of these teams, the role of team dispersion as a contextual antecedent of diversity-related outcomes is becoming increasingly relevant. Based on the premise that status and social influence are more likely to pervade face-to-face interactions than computer-mediated settings (which are considered more depersonalized), researchers have contrasted face-to-face groups with computer-mediated groups to examine whether the nature of participation varied in these two settings. In general, these studies find that the use of computer-mediated communications in groups reduces social inhibitions and equalizes participation (Sproull & Kiesler, 1986). In comparing gender diverse face-to-face versus computer-mediated groups, Bhappu, Griffith, and Northcraft (1997) also found that inter-group bias was lower in computer-mediated settings. In contrast, other research shows that the medium of communication itself did not alter social influence processes; status and social influence-based effects were as likely to occur in face-to-face groups as in computer-mediated groups (e.g., Weisband, Schneider, & Connolly, 1995). In this study, the authors' findings suggest that "even in the relatively impoverished social context of anonymous computer interaction, when high-status members were aware that a low-status member was in their group, the former made assumptions about the (latter's) identity" (Weisband et al., 1995, p. 1146). The study suggests that the specific mechanisms by which status manifests in computer-mediated and dispersed settings needs further investigation. In light of these research findings, we propose that dispersion may be considered a critical aspect of context raising several interesting research questions for future investigation.

Team Leadership
The role of leadership as a contextual influence on team diversity-related outcomes could be considered either in terms of specific leader attributes or leadership styles. Some researchers have considered whether leaders' demographic attributes influenced the relationship between team demographic composition and outcomes. Drawing on leader-member exchange theory and "similar-to-me" effects found in performance appraisal literature, Kirkman et al. (2004) argued that when leader demographic attributes do not match team demographic composition, there is likely to be lower levels trust and higher levels of bias among team members regarding their leaders. In this situation, team members may also view themselves as members of the out-group with lesser access to organizational resources. In support of these arguments, the study found that leader's racial fit with the team was associated with higher levels of team empowerment and leader rated team effectiveness (Kirkman et al., 2004).

Apart from leader attributes, leadership style can also be a moderating influence on the relationship between team diversity and outcomes. Recently, Somech (2006) considered the effects of participative versus directive leadership styles on the relationship between functional heterogeneity and team performance and innovation. Results indicated that participative leadership styles enhanced the positive relationship between team functional heterogeneity and innovation but not team performance. The findings suggested that the style of leadership may be important to consider depending on whether innovation and creativity-based outcomes or efficiency and effectiveness-based outcomes of diversity are desired. Others have argued that external leaders set the stage for positive team processes, psychological safety, and clear goals and objectives for the team (Gibson & Vermeulen, 2003; Mohrman, 1995; Nembhard & Edmondson, 2006). These perspectives suggest that by paving the way for favorable group processes, leaders may be able to mitigate process losses associated with team diversity.

Theoretical developments in the area of leadership and social identity theory also suggest that motivational leadership styles are conducive to developing greater levels of collective identification in groups. A growing body of research examines the effects of leader behaviors on identification with collective entities (see Howell & Shamir, 2005; Shamir, House, & Arthur, 1993). Drawing on social identity theory, researchers have suggested that motivational leaders, who can build enduring linkages between an individual's self-concept and a social group, thereby can enhance identification with the social group (Ellemers, De Gilder, & Haslam, 2004;

Turner & Haslam, 2001). By emphasizing the team's mission, shared values and ideology, and the link between followers' individual interests with team interests, these leaders can provide team members with opportunities to appreciate team accomplishments and other team members' contributions, and build a broad basis for identification with the team (Kark & Shamir, 2002). Drawing on Brewer and Gardner's (1996) work on self-identity, Kark and Shamir (2002) theorize that these leaders may be viewed as prototypic members of the team and representatives of the team's identity and values and, hence, elicit identification with the team as a collective (Howell & Shamir, 2005). Based on these theoretical perspectives, we propose that future research might consider the role of motivational leadership styles in influencing the outcomes of diversity in teams.

Team Climate
The overall climate in the team has been considered as a relevant contextual variable by a number of researchers. Some researchers have focused on aspects of climate that relate to the orientation of team members to work in groups (e.g., Eby & Dobbins, 1997; Mohammed & Angell, 2004). Mohammed and Angell (2004) proposed that the levels of team orientation (defined as team members' preference for working as a group) moderated the relationship between demographic diversity and relationship conflict. The study did not find any direct effects of team diversity on task or relationship conflict, but found that, in support of the moderating propositions, team orientation mitigated the negative effects of diversity on conflict. Other aspects of team climate such as psychological safety and empowerment have also been considered relevant moderating variables influencing the relationship between team diversity and outcomes. Gibson and Vermeulen (2003) argued that to the extent that the team context reflects psychological safety and empowerment, team members would be more likely to engage in information seeking behaviors and look toward continuously improving work processes. Their findings indicated that contextual influences such as the climate for empowerment in the team can influence team learning behavior differentially depending on the strength of demographic sub-groups (i.e., degree of overlap in demographic characteristics) within the team. Results suggested that empowerment has a negative influence on learning behavior in teams with either no sub-groups or very strong sub-groups. Empowerment had a positive influence on learning behavior only in teams with moderate sub-group strength.

Conclusion

In conclusion, we argued above that various aspects of omnibus and discrete contextual variables can have potentially important implications for the outcomes of diversity in organizations. We propose that the mixed findings from diversity research can be better explicated through a careful analysis of the context in which these studies were undertaken. In the subsequent sections, we present the findings of a literature review that we undertook to answer three main questions:

1. Are there specific trends in diversity research that help us articulate the importance of considering diversity context?
2. Which aspects of the context have received attention in diversity research either as moderator or as control variables?
3. What are the various research contexts in which diversity research has been undertaken and can these research contexts account for the varied findings reported in studies?

Overview and Findings of Literature Search

A literature search was conducted in September/November 2006 by an electronic search (utilizing computerized sources such as ABI/INFORM, Psyc INFO, and EBSCO Academic) for the years 1999–2006 using numerous key terms including work team diversity, work group/team demographic composition, and work group/team demography. In addition, a manual search was conducted for articles that might not yet have been published or not available electronically. Researchers were also contacted by email and copies of unpublished papers were requested when necessary. Targeted for the review were 19 major journals including *Academy of Management Journal, Administrative Science Quarterly, Journal of Applied Psychology, Group and Organization Management,* and *Journal of Organizational Behavior* among others that have been considered the most highly cited journals in the field of management (see Gomez-Meija & Balkin, 1992). Given the time frame for this review, we used the same database used by Jackson et al.'s (2003) recent review for an initial search. Additional searches were conducted to identify more recent studies in the period 2002–2006. Studies were included if they (a) were conducted at the team or organization level, (b) included a work outcome variable of performance, process, or affect/attitude, and (c) provided the necessary quantitative information to gain statistical results of diversity effects. Table 1 summarizes overall findings of diversity effects from our literature search. Eighty-eight studies were selected for inclusion and, specifically, in all 487 reported relationships were investigated for the analysis. The findings we discuss below are expressed as a percentage of the total number of diversity effects that we included in our analysis.

Key Trends in Research

We found that race/ethnic diversity and gender diversity were the most often considered diversity attributes in extant research (16 and 15%, respectively). Other diversity attributes considered were functional and educational background (16%), age (10%), and tenure (9%). Together, these easily detected or surface-level attributes accounted for about 70% of the diversity effects reported in our analysis. A number of studies have also focused on deep-level diversity attributes such as cognitive and cultural aspects of team composition. In the current review, 10% of relationships reported the effects of cognitive diversity on various work outcomes and 7% addressed the influence of different cultural values. Compared with Jackson et al.'s (2003) review, we found that there had been an 11.5% increase in research attention given to these deeper level diversity attributes (from 5.5% to 17%). We also found that a small percentage of studies relied on faultline measures of team diversity (4%).

Among three categories of work outcome variables, researchers showed a preference for studying performance outcomes (44%) as opposed to affective/attitudinal (30%) or process (27%) outcomes. Typical measures for performance outcomes included both financial (i.e., ROA, ROE, sales growth, labor productivity) and non-financial (i.e., strategic change, technology/process innovation) results at the firm level. At the work group level, outcome measures included team's objective performance (i.e., goal achievement, productivity, effectiveness/efficiency, project grades), subjective performance ratings by team members or supervisors, and team innovation. Attitudinal outcomes considered in the studies were – conflict (task, relational, or emotional), job satisfaction, and organizational commitment. Process outcomes examined in the studies we reviewed included – group integration/cohesion, information sharing, and learning behavior. Also, several studies incorporated these process or affect/attitude outcome variables as mediators in addressing the effects of diversity on performance outcomes. Of the 88 studies we reviewed, 20 studies examined process and attitudinal measures as mediators.

Table 1. Overview of Past Findings by Types of Diversity Attributes.

Type of Diversity[a]	Outcome Type[b]		
	Performance	Process	Affect/Attitude
Race/ethnicity (16%)			
Curvilinear	0	0	0
Positive	7	5	3
Negative	8	5	4
Null	20	13	11
	35 (46%)	23 (30%)	18 (24%)
Gender (15%)			
Curvilinear	3	1	1
Positive	5	1	6
Negative	3	7	5
Null	20	9	14
	31 (41%)	18 (24%)	26 (35%)
Functional background (11%)			
Curvilinear	2	3	0
Positive	7	5	1
Negative	6	5	1
Null	16	7	5
	31 (54%)	20 (35%)	7 (12%)
Age (10%)			
Curvilinear	2	0	0
Positive	2	0	2
Negative	6	1	4
Null	15	6	12
	25 (50%)	7 (14%)	18 (36%)
Cognitive/mental model (10%)			
Curvilinear	0	0	0
Positive	3	1	1
Negative	6	10	4
Null	10	8	6
	19 (39%)	19 (39%)	11 (22%)
Tenure (9%)			
Curvilinear	1	0	0
Positive	6	2	3
Negative	6	3	1
Null	7	3	10
	20 (48%)	8 (19%)	14 (33%)
Cultural values (7%)			
Curvilinear	0	0	0
Positive	2	5	4
Negative	1	2	7
Null	1	4	6
	4 (13%)	11 (34%)	17 (53%)

Table 1. (*Continued*)

Type of Diversity[a]	Outcome Type[b]		
	Performance	Process	Affect/Attitude
Education level (5%)			
Curvilinear	0	0	0
Positive	5	0	2
Negative	2	0	1
Null	3	2	10
	10 (40%)	2 (8%)	13 (52%)
Composite measure (4%)			
Curvilinear	0	1	0
Positive	1	0	0
Negative	4	2	1
Null	6	5	0
	11 (55%)	8 (40%)	1 (5%)
Faultlines (4%)			
Curvilinear	1	3	1
Positive	0	0	6
Negative	0	0	2
Null	1	2	3
	2 (11%)	5 (26%)	12 (63%)
Nationality (3%)			
Curvilinear	1	3	0
Positive	3	0	0
Negative	0	2	1
Null	4	1	1
	8 (50%)	6 (38%)	2 (13%)
Personality (3%)			
Curvilinear	0	0	0
Positive	5	0	1
Negative	0	1	0
Null	4	2	1
	9 (64%)	3 (21%)	2 (14%)
Others (2%)[c]			
Curvilinear	1	0	0
Positive	3	0	1
Negative	2	1	2
Null	1	0	0
	7 (64%)	1 (9%)	3 (27%)
Total (N = 487)[d]	212 (44%)	131 (27%)	144 (30%)

[a]Proportion (%) of each diversity attribute studied among total relationships (in parenthesis)
[b]Proportion (%) of each outcome type considered within each diversity attribute (in parenthesis)
[c]Marital status based diversity, network density, geographic diversity, experience diversity
[d]Total 88 studies were selected for a review. Specifically, 487 reported effects were coded in the analysis above; total proportion (%) of each outcome type considered among total 487 relationships was reported in parenthesis.

Directly pertinent to our opening remarks, with regard to consequences of diversity effects, we found that more than a half of studies reported null effects of diversity variables. Among the total 487 diversity effects examined in this review, only 20% of the cases provided evidence for a significant relationship between diversity and positive outcomes, 24% of the cases provided evidence for a significant relationship between diversity and negative outcomes, and 5% of reported curvilinear relationships. Despite some exceptions (e.g., when diversity was measured in terms of cultural values, personality, or faultlines), we generally found evidence empirical findings regarding the effects of diversity on various work outcomes were predominantly non-significant. More specifically, in the studies we reviewed 51% of diversity effects reported were non-significant.

Contextual Variables Considered in Past Research
Next, we turn our attention to contextual variables that have received attention in extant research either as moderator or as control variables.

Table 2a summarizes findings of contextual variables investigated in past diversity research. As described in the previous section, various aspects of diversity context were examined at multiple levels of analysis. In general, of those three distinct levels of analysis we discussed earlier, we found that the research attention had been predominantly focused on discrete level contextual variables (72% of contextual variables considered were at the discrete level). Among discrete level moderating variables, those that received the most attention were – team climate (22%), task characteristics (e.g., task interdependence, task complexity/routineness) (21%), team leader characteristics (17%), and various team processes (e.g., communication) (15%). Together, these variables accounted for a large proportion of discrete contextual moderators considered in past research (75%). A promising trend indicated by our review was a growing emphasis on temporal factors at the discrete level. In our review, we found a total of 8 effects across three studies incorporated team tenure/group longevity as a moderator variable. Other discrete level variables such as team size or team affect/attitudinal composition were predominantly considered as control variables rather than moderators.

Among the distal omnibus level contextual influences, those that received attention were the demographic composition of the geographic location in which teams were embedded; specifically these diversity effects accounted for community or customer demographics as moderator variables (5% of all moderating variables considered). Other distal omnibus factors such as industry/occupation (2% of all control variables considered), country/

Table 2a. Contextual Variables Studied in Diversity Research.

Level[a]	Contextual Variables Measured	Moderator		Control	
		Cases	Percentage (%)	Cases	Percentage (%)
Distal omnibus (8.4%)	Industry/occupations	0	0	8	23
	Geographic location[b]	10	67	0	0
	Country/region	2	13	12	34
	National culture	1	7	1	3
	Business environment[c]	2	13	14	40
		15	30	35	70
Proximal omnibus (19.4%)	Organizational demography	21	55	9	12
	Organizational structure/strategy	8	21	7	9
	Organizational culture	5	13	0	0
	Organizational age	1	3	12	15
	Organizational performance[d]	3	8	6	8
	Organizational size	0	0	28	36
	Other organizational characteristics[e]	0	0	16	21
		38	33	78	67
Discrete (72.2%)	Team task interdependence	15	15	2	1
	Team task complexity/routineness	6	6	14	4
	Team tenure/group longevity	8	8	36	11
	Team communication	12	12	10	3

Table 2a. (Continued)

Level[a]	Contextual Variables Measured	Moderator		Control	
		Cases	Percentage (%)	Cases	Percentage (%)
	Other team processes[f]	3	3	0	0
	Team climate[g]	22	22	0	0
	Team leadership style	8	8	0	0
	Team leader attributes[h]	9	9	0	0
	Team dispersion	4	4	0	0
	Team affect/attitude[i]	0	0	8	2
	Team cognitive factors[j]	0	0	17	5
	Team size	0	0	94	28
	Team demography	0	0	113	34
	Other team diversity attributes	12	12	2	1
	Other experimental controls[k]	0	0	36	11
		99	23	332	77

[a]Proportion (%) of overall contextual variables measured at each level (in parenthesis).
[b]Community, customer demographic fit.
[c]Environmental uncertainty, technical environment, market competition, labor market condition.
[d]Prior firm performance, financial capability, market share, product market power.
[e]Company type, ownership type, organizational hierarchy, resource type, unionization, compensation level.
[f]Decision-making, conflict resolution.
[g]Team orientation, collaboration, integration, collective team identity.
[h]Leader demographic attributes, leader creativity.
[i]Team tenure, longitudinal effects on teams.
[j]Conflict (task, relationship, emotion), commitment, job satisfaction.
[j]Perception of group norm, agreement on time urgency, knowledge consistency.
[k]Prior mean GPA, instructor, class type, project stage, day of experiments.

region (3%), or business environment (3%) were mostly incorporated as control variables in research. At the proximal omnibus level, organizational demography received the most attention as a moderator variable (11% of all moderating effects examined). Other proximal omnibus variables that received attention as moderators were organizational structure (4%) and culture (3%).

Our findings indicate that, overwhelmingly, both discrete and omnibus contextual variables were considered as control variables rather than directly incorporated in study hypotheses. As noted by Johns (2006) "controlling away" contextual variables rather than directly and explicitly accounting for their influence on the outcomes of diversity may undermine the cumulative contributions of diversity research and offer only a disjointed perspective on the various boundary conditions shaping diversity dynamics in the workplace. In the studies we reviewed, often the non-significant effects of diversity emerged as significant when some aspects of the context were explicitly included as moderators. For example, Richard et al.'s (2004) study examined the effect of cultural diversity (e.g., race, gender) of management teams on firm performance in a banking industry. Main effects were initially found non-significant, but emerged as significant when specific strategic organizational contexts were considered. Specifically, in highly entrepreneurial organizational contexts, race diversity emerged as a positive influence on firm performance and gender diversity had an inverted U-shape relationship with firm performance. Table 2b lists some illustrative study examples incorporating the various contextual factors discussed above.

In addition, we propose that other aspects of context not directly measured in studies may also account for the mixed findings from past research. For example, in a household goods moving firm, Jehn, Northcraft and Neale (1999) found that gender and race diversity was associated with negative affective outcomes such as emotional conflict in the team. In the context of a public university, Mohammed and Angell (2004) found that these aspects of diversity had no significant effect on relationship-based conflict at the work group level. It is possible that the varied nature of these two research settings accounted for these contradictory findings. To explore this idea further, we also coded different research settings in which past diversity research has been conducted. As shown in Table 3 below, studies have been conducted across a wide range of industries, geographic locations, and using varied types of teams. We propose that these aspects of the research context might possibly either magnify, nullify, or even reverse effects of diversity attributes on various work outcomes.

Table 2b. Summary of Illustrative Studies Measuring Diversity Context.

Level	Authors	Diversity Attributes	Work Outcomes	Moderators	Results
Distal omnibus	Frink et al. (2003)	Gender composition	Firm (financial and perceptual) performance	Industry/occupation	$N = 722$ firms; an inverted U-shaped relationship was found; the relationship was observed only in industries with high proportions of women in general (i.e., service, wholesale, retail)
	Brief et al. (2005)	Ethnicity	Quality of work relationships, organizational attractiveness	Community demographics (proximity to blacks), perceived ethnic conflict	$N = 236$ whites; the closer whites lived to blacks and the more interethnic conflict whites perceived in their communities, the more negatively they responded to diverse workplaces
	Van Der Vegt et al. (2005)	Task-oriented (tenure, functional background), relation-oriented (age, gender)	Innovative climates (organization unit level)	National culture (power distance)	$N = 248$ organization units of multinational firms in 24 countries; task-oriented diversity was negatively related to innovative climates in high power distance countries but positively related in low power distance countries; no such interactions were found for relation-oriented diversity

Proximal omnibus	Joshi et al. (2006)	Gender, ethnicity	Pay (inequality), sales performance	Organization demography (team demographic composition, unit management composition)	$N = 3,318$ employees in 437 sales teams; ethnicity-based earning inequalities were smaller in teams with more people of color, and gender- and ethnicity-based inequalities were smaller in units with more women and people of color as managers
	Richard et al. (2004)	Cultural diversity (race, gender)	Firm performance (productivity, ROE)	Organizational strategy (entrepreneurial orientation)	$N = 153$ banks; main effects were initially found non-significant but emerged as significant when organizational strategic contexts were considered; in high entrepreneurial orientations, race diversity was positively related to firm performance and gender diversity had an inverted U-shape relationship with firm performance
Discrete	Schippers et al. (2003)	Diversity index (age, gender, education, team tenure)	Team process (reflexivity), team performance, commitment, satisfaction	Group longevity, team outcome interdependence	$N = 54$ teams in 13 organizations; neither the overall diversity measure nor the individual diversity aspect had a direct impact on the outcomes; instead, interaction effects were found: outcome interdependence buffered the negative effects of

Table 2b. (Continued)

Level	Authors	Diversity Attributes	Work Outcomes	Moderators	Results
					diversity on process outcomes; diversity became positively associated with process outcomes among younger teams
	Somech (2006)	Functional heterogeneity	Team performance, team innovation	Leadership style (directive versus participative)	$N = 136$ primary care teams; participative leadership styles enhanced the positive relationship between team functional heterogeneity and innovation but not team performance
	Mohammed and Angell (2004)	Surface level (gender, race), deep level (time urgency, extraversion)	Relationship conflict	Team orientation (working as a group), team process (leadership, communication, coordination)	$N = 45$ student project teams; no direct effects were found; however, in support of moderating propositions, team orientation neutralized the negative effects of gender diversity on relationship conflict; team process weakened the negative effects of time urgency

Table 3. Research Settings Across Studies.

Research Settings	Number of Studies[a]	Percentage (%)
Industry		
Manufacturing	18	17.6
High-technology[b]	14	13.7
Banking/finance	10	9.8
Service[c]	10	9.8
Government/non-profit/military	6	5.9
Healthcare	5	4.9
Education	2	2.0
Sports team	1	1.0
Multi-industries	9	8.8
Student experiment	23	22.5
Not-specified	4	3.9
	102	100
Type of team		
Work teams[d]	26	25.2
TMT	24	23.3
Student (laboratory setting)	22	21.4
R&D	7	6.8
Service	7	6.8
Sales	3	2.9
Production	3	2.9
Not-specified	11	10.7
	103	100
Geographic location		
US/Canada	54	56.8
Europe[e]	7	7.4
Israel	4	4.2
Australia/New Zealand	2	2.1
Asia[f]	1	1.1
Globally dispersed[g]	6	6.3
Not-specified	21	22.1
	103	100
Study design		
Longitudinal	14	15.2
Cross-sectional	78	84.8
	92	100

[a]Numbers do not add up to 88 (total number of studies) because some contain multiple industries, teams, or locations; four studies have two sub-studies within them.
[b]Information technology, semiconductor, biotechnology, e-commerce.
[c]General service industry (e.g., moving service, retail, restaurant, professional service) unless categorized as banking/finance, healthcare, education, or government/non-profit.
[d]Generic work teams (e.g., project teams, multifunctional teams) unless categorized as production, service, sales, R&D, or TMT.
[e]UK, The Netherlands, Belgium, Finland, Ireland.
[f]The Philippines.
[g]Subsidiaries of multinational companies.

Integrating our framework for diversity context presented in the previous section with the various types of diversity-related effects uncovered in past research and discussed in this section, we consider next how various aspects of diversity context can influence the range of diversity effects in past research.

TAKING STOCK OF CONTEXTUAL INFLUENCES ON DIVERSITY RESEARCH: FROM "BLACK BOX" TO "PANDORA'S BOX"?

We started out by noting that the discrepant findings of past research may to some extent be resolved by a closer scrutiny of the context that shapes diversity dynamics. The process of identifying and discussing many aspects of context in this paper was daunting and the issues we discussed above raise more challenging questions than the ones we hoped to answer, leaving us wondering if we had opened a "Pandora's Box" of moderator variables for future research consideration. The studies we reviewed revealed that in response to calls to open the "black box" of organizational demography (Lawrence, 1997), in the past decade researchers were playing closer attention to possible mediating mechanisms linking diversity variables to process and performance outcomes. In the more recent research we reviewed, we also found a growing emphasis on moderating influences on diversity dynamics, albeit at the discrete level. This is certainly a fruitful development in the field and we hope this trend continues to evolve as researchers engage in and expand contextual considerations to fully appreciate the complex outcomes of workplace diversity.

Our purpose in this paper was to open an initial line of inquiry that takes into consideration various contextual influences relevant to diversity research and attempts to resolve the contradictory findings from past research. Below we consider how context may produce some of the contradictory results that we discussed in the previous section. Fig. 2 summarizes how various aspects of context could play a role in engendering the mixed pattern represented in Table 1.

Contextual Explanations for the Non-Significant Effects of Diversity

As discussed by Johns (2006), context can influence the organizational behavior by restricting observable range as well as affecting the base rate of

	Negative Outcomes	Positive Outcomes	Null Effects	Curvilinear Effects
Distal Omnibus	Time	Time	Industry/Occupation Geographic Location National Culture	Industry/Occupation
Proximal Omnibus	Organization History Organizational Culture	Organization History Organization Demography Organization Strategy Organization Culture	Organization Demography Organization Culture	Organization Demography
Discrete	Team Task	Team Task Team Leadership Team Climate	Team Task Team Dispersion	Team Climate Team Tenure

Fig. 2. Taking Stock of Context Effects in Diversity Research.

organizational variables. Both these factors can render the effects of diversity non-significant. A number of diversity studies we reviewed were conducted in white male dominated settings (e.g., Jackson & Joshi, 2004; Kochan et al., 2003). In these settings we are unlikely to find a full range of team diversity attributes. Not surprisingly, these studies do not yield significant relationships between team gender or race diversity and process or performance outcomes. Thus, aspects of the research context such as the demographics of the occupation represented in the sample could set limits on the range of gender or ethnic diversity that we might find in teams, leading to the possibility of null findings. As indicated in Table 3, the top two industries in which field research has been conducted are – manufacturing (18%) and information processing and technology (14%). These are both male-dominated settings restricting the range as well as the base rates of team diversity variables. Like occupational demo graphy, organizational demography can also restrict the range of diversity variables within teams. In white male dominated organizations, the possibility of finding a full range of gender and ethnic diversity within the team would be low, thereby rendering the effects of team diversity non-significant.

Country location may also pose similar constraints. Although a bulk of research we reviewed was conducted in the North American context (57% of the studies reviewed and possibly more studies that did not specify location were also conducted in the US), the small percentage of studies that were conducted outside the US in Europe (7%) or in Asia (1%) showed non-significant relationships for certain aspects of diversity. As the frontiers of management research cross North American boundaries understanding whether certain diversity variables would be salient in particular cultural contexts would be an important consideration. Diversity attributes that are important in a US setting may not be relevant in certain national contexts and field studies that examine these diversity attributes in certain cultures may not find significant relationships between diversity and team outcomes (Schippers et al., 2003).

At the discrete level, the nature of the tasks that teams perform could explain non-significant relationships. To the extent that the "teams" included in study samples are administrative units and team members tasks are additive and do not involve goal or outcome interdependence may serve to minimize the possible negative or positive effects of diversity. Twenty five percent of studies we reviewed were conducted in settings where the nature of the teams were unspecified and included various departments or were generically classified as "management teams". Although as indicated in Table 2a, a number of studies do account for team interdependence (measured using a perceptual scale) in their research design, the nature of tasks and associated rewards may be more complex than can be accounted for by a single task interdependence measure. Indeed, Mowday and Sutton (1993) have argued that relying on perceptual measures of context from the sample that is also included in the study may provide inaccurate and incomplete assessments of context. They suggest that context be measured more directly by using samples that display systematic variation in the contextual variable or include objective measures of the context.

As we discussed earlier, the growing implementation of virtual teams and reliance on electronic technology for communicating across distances can be another important factor influencing the relationship between team diversity and outcomes. Researchers have argued that, in dispersed settings that may be characterized as a depersonalized context, surface level diversity can have less significant consequences. It is possible that in these settings, aspects of diversity that are more closely tied to nature of communication both spoken and written may play a more significant role and other aspects of diversity may be less salient. Even in co-located settings, team members may rely on electronic communications for day-to-day communications (Kirkman & Mathieu, 2005). Therefore, physical dispersion as well as level of reliance on technology enabled communications may be important contextual considerations that can potentially mitigate the effects of diversity on outcomes. Since an overwhelming number of diversity effects that we uncovered in our literature search were non-significant, we suggest that the contextual considerations described above merit closer scrutiny in future research.

Contextual Explanations for the Negative Outcomes of Diversity

Researchers have considered conflict and lack of cohesion or cooperation as the negative outcomes of diversity (Williams & O'Reilly, 1998; Van Knippenberg & Schippers, 2007). Several aspects of the diversity context considered earlier can also serve to exacerbate these negative outcomes of diversity. At the distal omnibus level, aspects of cyclical time such as socio-economic trends could serve to highlight perceptions regarding availability of public resources and increase inter-group competition over perceived or real scarcity. As we discussed earlier, trends such as the aging workforce or increasing levels of immigration could enhance these negative perceptions.

At the proximal omnibus level, organizational demography as well as culture could also exacerbate negative outcomes. Research on organizational demography suggests that in demographically segregated organizations characterized by the presence of minorities at lower levels and a token presence in upper management, out-group salience and in-group solidarity may be enhanced (Ashforth & Mael, 1989; Cox, 1993; Joshi, 2006). Majority members may view minorities as a threat to the status quo (Ashforth & Mael, 1989). At the same time minority members may also mobilize collective action that can increase inter-group conflict (Cox, 1993). Even in organizations that have incorporated diversity management practices over several years, differing perceptions of these diversity practices by majority and minority groups may induce negative outcomes in teams. In a detailed analysis of a corporation with a history of progressive actions in promoting race relations, Alderfer, Tucker, Morgan, and Drasgow (1983) examined the manner in which black and white managers viewed race relations programs varied. They found that blacks viewed progressive policies as efforts to rectify white advantage with no specific losses to whites. White employees, on the other hand, viewed these efforts as resource reallocation that inherently implied loss of privilege and greater competition over scarce organizational resources. These findings suggest that an organization's history with implementing diversity practices may serve to exacerbate conflict between racial groups and have implications for work group diversity. Overall, organizational factors, such as demography, culture/climate, or history with diversity-related issues could amplify negative outcomes.

At the discrete level, task characteristics that enhance time and resource pressures on team members may also serve to enhance negative outcomes of conflict. Recent meta-analytic findings suggest that higher levels of task complexity enhanced the negative correlation between diversity and performance (De Dreu & Weingart, 2003). The increased difficulties with managing diverse perspectives in complex task situations may bring negative attitudes and perceptions regarding team members to the surface and manifest in negative outcomes.

Contextual Explanations for the Positive Outcomes of Diversity

Context can also shape the positive outcomes of diversity such as creativity, innovativeness, and performance. At the omnibus level, aspects of diversity such as significant events could foster positive outcomes by creating an inclusivity effect across various demographic groups. As we discussed earlier, significant crises or catastrophes may serve to reduce the salience of social identity-based grouping and generate a more collective identity orientation. Such events may pave the way for facilitating the positive outcomes of diversity within work groups. Organizational events may also serve similar purpose. For example, the appointment of a minority female CEO (consider the appointment of Indira Nooyi, an Indian-born female, as the new CEO of Pepsico) may influence the status cues associated with this particular demographic within work groups so that their opinions hold greater value within work groups. Overall, these events may foster conditions for positive inter-group contact within diverse teams that can facilitate positive team outcomes.

Organizational strategy, history, culture, and demography can also jointly or independently influence positive outcomes. As we discussed earlier, organizations that have an innovation and growth-oriented strategy are more likely to value diverse perspective as well as ensure that policies and practices are in place to allow the full utilization of diverse perspectives. As we also discussed above, organizational demography and culture can reduce the salience of demographic-based social categorization and as a result reduce the negative effects of social category-based diversity in organizations. This contextual factor may also lead to the expression of positive outcomes of task-based diversity such as functional or educational diversity. At the organizational level, in "multicultural" organizations, which are characterized by formal and informal integration, demographic attributes such as race or gender would not be associated with employment outcomes (Cox, 1993). In these settings, demographic diversity may not be predictive of process losses and provide a context wherein the positive outcomes of diversity of perspectives can be realized.

At the discrete level, team leadership can have an influence on the positive outcomes of diversity. As we discussed earlier, recent extensions of social identity theory and leadership research suggest that leaders can forge a common ground for identification among diverse team members. Thus leadership styles particularly motivational forms of leadership may be particularly suited to this outcome. In addition, leader-team demographic fit may influence the leader-member exchange and facilitate more positive interactions between the leader and team members thereby facilitating positive outcomes for teams. Finally, team climate can also be a contextual factor facilitating positive outcomes. To the extent that climate either reflects the propensity of team members to collaborate (i.e., a collectivistic orientation), to trust team members, and to feel empowered and psychologically safe to voice differences and learn from different perspectives, team climate may serve to reverse the negative effects of diversity considered earlier or strengthen the positive outcomes of diversity such as learning behavior, creativity, and innovation.

Contextual Explanations for the Curvilinear Effects of Diversity

Curvilinear effects are viewed as a manifestation of contextual influences particularly in instances where the level of independent variable depends on the nature of the context (Johns, 1991, 2006; Rousseau & Fried, 2001). From this standpoint, our arguments in the preceding sections cumulatively suggest that curvilinear effects are germane to diversity research because the level of diversity within the team is a function of the organizational and occupational context discussed earlier. However, even within specific omnibus and discrete contexts, some aspects of diversity may have U-shaped effects on process or performance outcomes. As discussed earlier, Frink et al. (2003) observed that an inverted curvilinear relationship between percentage of women in the firm and firm performance was only observable in industries that had lower levels of gender segregation. Organizational demography may exert a similar influence so that in particular organizational contexts, for example, demographically segregated settings, moderately diverse teams may be most likely to experience negative effects in comparison with homogeneous or extremely diverse teams. Team tenure may also trigger curvilinear effects. Based on the logic that highly tenured teams are less likely to display the effects of team diversity, curvilinear diversity effects are more likely in teams that are less tenured. Understanding the curvilinearity of diversity effects greatly enhances the complexity of diversity research. Acknowledging the boundary conditions shaping the nature of this curvilinearity may be a fruitful course of action for the future.

NEXT STEPS: CONSIDERATIONS FOR
FUTURE RESEARCH

From a research standpoint, several areas remain for further enhancing our understanding of the multi-faceted and complex nature of diversity context. Our review suggests that while there has been a greater focus on the discrete level context, this is only one layer of the overall contextual framework that can impinge upon the outcomes of diversity. Our discussion above reveals that other layers of context can also act as powerful influences on the outcomes of work group diversity. In our opening remarks, we proposed that while current theory and empirical research in the area of diversity has focused on "why", diversity may manifest in process or performance outcomes contextual considerations allow us to take into account "when", "where", "what", and "how" diversity matters (cf. Johns, 2006). In this section we return to this heuristic to pose contextual considerations in future diversity research:

1. *"What" aspects of diversity context should researchers focus on?* Given the long list of contextual factors listed in this paper deciding which aspects of context to focus on appears daunting. We propose that the decision to focus on certain aspects of context be driven by the specific conceptualization of diversity in a study. Recently, Harrison and Klein (2007) offered a typology that considers three conceptualizations of diversity – *disparity*, *variety*, and *separation*. Diversity as *disparity* refers to inequality among work group members in terms of status and access to resources. Diversity as *separation* refers to actual differences among team members with regard to a specific continuous attribute (as embodied in research on similarity-attraction or social categorization within work groups). Diversity as *variety* refers to within-team differences in terms of perspectives and expertise and is reflected in research that views the team as an information-processing unit (Harrison & Klein, 2007). Based on the discussion above with regard to omnibus and discrete contexts, we propose that the nature of diversity may inform the choice of contextual variables. For example, diversity conceptualized in terms of disparity may be influenced by omnibus contextual factors such as the demography of the occupation or organization. Sociological studies suggest that the demography of occupations and organizations reflects inequality among demographic groups (see Ridgeway, 1997). Within work teams these omnibus contextual factors are likely to influence inequality among demographic groups in terms of access to resources and power in the organization and will have consequences for process or performance

outcomes. Other forms of diversity such as diversity as variety or separation are more likely to be influenced by discrete context. For example, contextual factors such as the nature of the task, technology or climate in the team may influence the extent to which team members are likely to identify and utilize each others varied expertise (i.e., diversity as variety) or communicate with each other based on perceived similarity (i.e., diversity as separation). Overall, we suggest that the nature and conceptualization of diversity in a study should inform the specific aspects of context that are more likely to be salient.

2. *"How" does context influence diversity outcomes?* Answering how contextual variables at higher levels of aggregation such as the organization or society can shape work group diversity outcomes remains a challenge from a theoretical standpoint. While there is growing appreciation and demand for cross-level research, there is less theoretical guidance on possible mechanisms that can link the various levels at which diversity context was discussed in this paper. We call for greater integration between sociological, political and psychological disciplines to examine the interplay between various levels of diversity considered in this study. Skaggs and DiTomaso (2004) presented an extremely comprehensive and multidisciplinary review of research on the effects of organizational demographics on workplace outcomes such as pay, career progression, job satisfaction and performance. The authors integrated sociological, psychological, and management literatures to argue that status inequalities are perpetuated in organizations through managerial practices and can have implications for interactional processes between group members. We call for similar integrations of macro–micro perspectives to understand how other omnibus level factors can influence within team dynamics.

3. *"When" is diversity likely to impact a given set of team outcomes?* As discussed in this paper, temporal factors both at omnibus and discrete levels can have a powerful impact on the outcomes of diversity. The emphasis on longitudinal team diversity research that we found in our review has been extremely valuable for understanding how the dynamics of diversity unfolds within the team. In the current review, 14 longitudinal studies were identified which accounted for 15% of total studies included. However, omnibus time is also an important contextual consideration for future research. Understanding the role that societal and organizational events in shaping diversity outcomes would enable us to account for why specific aspects of diversity would be more important to consider in certain situations versus others. As noted by Johns (2006), temporal considerations would also influence the type of dependent variables that

are considered in research. For example, events such as race riots in the surrounding community may lead to greater focus on race diversity in teams in relation to emotional conflict and other affective outcomes.

4. *"Where" are we likely to see specific outcomes of diversity?* We believe that location-specific contextual factors are extremely relevant for informing our choice of diversity variables as well as the outcomes of diversity. Our review of diversity research suggests that, to date, the research has taken a US-centric perspective both in the conceptualization of diversity leading to the inclusion of certain diversity variables over others, as well as in terms of the type of dependent variables considered. The choice of diversity attributes and outcome variables would vary in other national contexts. For example, in the Indian context, age diversity may not translate into conflict at the team level because prevalent age-related cultural norms that dictate deferential inter-generational interactions. In fact, age diverse teams in India would represent greater cohesion and fewer process losses than team that are homogeneous in terms of age. In age-based homogeneous teams in India, it is possible that team members are more likely to engage in social comparison and competition that may be detrimental to team functioning. With the growing internationalization of the management research community taking into account the unique aspects and outcomes of diversity in non-US settings may change the nature of the debate around the pros and cons of diversity that has evolved in the US.

CONCLUSION

In conclusion, we proposed that the mixed findings of past diversity research necessitate an explicit consideration of contextual variables. While several researchers have called for the inclusion of contextual variables in diversity research, there remains less of an understanding of the overall scope and nature of the diversity context. Contextual considerations in diversity research are critical for maintaining the market orientation of our research and demand innovative theoretical and methodological tools. From a theoretical standpoint, greater efforts to link micro–macro theory would be valuable to take into consideration how omnibus as well as discrete contextual factors could independently as well as jointly shape diversity-related outcomes. Methodologically, qualitative research would enhance the sensitivity of diversity research to omnibus and discrete contextual variables. We join others (e.g., Johns, 2006; Rousseau & Fried, 2001) to propose that qualitative techniques can greatly inform the choice of diversity variables measured as well as the dependent variables considered in a study. Our discussion provides as a preliminary framework for considering contextual variables that may be further extended in future research. The future of contextualized diversity research promises to be a challenging and exciting journey – a journey, we hope, researchers will increasingly undertake.

REFERENCES

Alderfer, C. P., Tucker, R. C., Morgan, D. R., & Drasgow, F. (1983). Black and white cognitions of changing race relations in management. *Journal of Occupational Behavior, 4*, 105–136.

Ancona, D. G., Okhuysen, G. A., & Perlow, L. A. (2001). Taking time to integrate temporal research. *Academy of Management Review, 26*, 512–529.

Apgar, M. (1998). The alternative workplace: Changing where and how people work. *Harvard Business Review, 76*, 121–137.

Ashforth, B., & Mael, F. (1989). Social identity theory and the organization. *Academy of Management Review, 14*, 20–39.

Bantel, K., & Jackson, S. (1989). Top management and innovations in banking: Does the composition of the team make a difference? *Strategic Management Journal, 10*, 107–124.

Bhappu, A. D., Griffith, T. L., & Northcraft, G. B. (1997). Media effects and communication bias in diverse groups. *Organizational Behavior and Human Decision Processes, 70*, 199–205.

Blalock, H. M. (1956). Economic discrimination and Negro increase. *American Sociological Review, 21*, 584–588.

Blau, P. M. (1977). *Inequality and heterogeneity: A primitive theory of social structure*. New York: Free Press.

Brewer, M. B., & Gardner, W. L. (1996). Who is this "we"? Levels of collective identity and self-representation. *Journal of Personal and Social Psychology, 50*, 543–549.

Brief, A., Umphress, E., Dietz, J., Burrows, J., Butz, R., & Scholen, L. (2005). Community matters: Realistic group conflict theory and the impact of diversity. *Academy of Management Journal, 48*, 830–844.

Cappelli, P., & Sherer, P. (1991). The missing role of context in OB: The need for a meso-level approach. In: L. L. Cummings & B. M. Staw (Eds), *Research in organizational behavior* (Vol. 13, pp. 55–110). Greenwich, CT: JAI Press.

Chatman, J. A., & Flynn, F. (2001). The influence of demographic heterogeneity on the emergence and consequences of cooperative norms in work teams. *Academy of Management Journal, 44*, 956–974.

Chatman, J. A., Polzer, J. T., Barsade, S. G., & Neale, M. A. (1998). Being different yet feeling similar: The influence of demographic composition and organizational culture on work processes and outcomes. *Administrative Science Quarterly, 43*, 749–780.

Chatman, J. A., & Spataro, S. E. (2005). Using self-categorization theory to understand relational demography-based variations in people's responsiveness to organizational culture. *Academy of Management Journal, 48*, 321–331.

Cox, T. (1991). The multicultural organization. *Academy of Management Executive, 5*, 34–47.

Cox, T. (1993). *Cultural diversity in organizations: Theory, research and practice.* San Francisco, CA: Berrett-Koehler Publishers.

Dass, P., & Parker, B. (1999). Strategies for managing human resource diversity: From resistance to learning. *Academy of Management Executive, 13,* 68–80.

De Dreu, C. K. W., & Weingart, L. R. (2003). Task and relationship conflict, team performance, and team member satisfaction: A meta-analysis. *Journal of Applied Psychology, 88,* 741–749.

Dencker, J. C., Joshi, A., & Martocchio, J. J. (2007). Employee benefits as context for intergenerational conflict. *Human Resource Management Review,* Forthcoming.

Dubin, R. (1976). Theory building in applied areas. In: M. D. Dunnette (Ed.), *Handbook of industrial and organizational psychology* (pp. 17–39). Chicago, IL: Rand McNally.

Earley, P. C., & Mosakowski, E. M. (2000). Creating hybrid team cultures: An empirical test of international team functioning. *Academy of Management Journal, 43,* 26–49.

Eby, L. T., & Dobbins, G. H. (1997). Collectivistic orientation in teams: An individual and group-level analysis. *Journal of Organizational Behavior, 18,* 275–295.

Ellemers, N., De Gilder, D., & Haslam, S. A. (2004). Motivating individuals and groups at work: A social identity perspective on leadership and group performance. *Academy of Management Review, 29,* 459–478.

Elvira, M. M., & Graham, M. E. (2002). Not just formality: Pay system formalization and sex-related earnings effects. *Organization Science, 13,* 601–617.

Ely, R. (1994). The effects of organizational demographics and social identity on relationships among professional women. *Administrative Science Quarterly, 39,* 203–238.

Ely, R. (1995). The power in demography: Women's social constructions of gender identity at work. *Academy of Management Journal, 38,* 589–634.

Ely, R., & Thomas, D. (2001). Cultural diversity at work: The effects of diversity perspectives on wok group processes and outcomes. *Administrative Science Quarterly, 46,* 229–273.

Ferner, A., Almond, P., & Colling, T. (2005). Institutional theory and the cross-national transfer of employment policy: The case of 'workforce diversity' in US multinationals. *Journal of International Business Studies, 36,* 304–321.

Friedman, R. (1996). Defining the scope and logic of minority and female network groups: Can separation enhance integration? In: K. M. Rowland & G. R. Ferris (Eds), *Research in personnel and human resource management* (Vol. 9, pp. 307–349). Greenwich, CT: JAI Press.

Frink, D. D., Robinson, R. K., Reithel, B., Arthur, M. M., Ferris, G. R., Kaplan, D. M., et al. (2003). Gender demography and organizational performance: A two study investigation with convergence. *Group and Organization Management, 28,* 127–147.

Gersick, C. (1988). Time and transition in work teams: Toward a new model of group development. *Academy of Management Journal, 31,* 9–41.

Gibson, C. B., & Vermeulen, F. (2003). A healthy divide: Subgroups as a stimulus for team learning behavior. *Administrative Science Quarterly, 48,* 202–239.

Giles, M. W. (1977). Percent black and racial hostility: An old assumption reexamined. *Social Science Quarterly, 58,* 412–417.

Gomez-Meija, L., & Balkin, D. (1992). Determinants of faculty pay: An agency theory perspective. *Academy of Management Journal, 35,* 921–955.

Grensing-Pophal, L. (2002). Reaching for diversity. *HR Magazine, May,* 53–56.

Hansen, F. (2003). Diversity's business case doesn't add up. *Workforce, April,* 28–32.

Harrison, D. A., & Klein, K. J. (2007). What's the difference? Diversity constructs as separation, variety, or disparity in organizations. *Academy of Management Review*, Forthcoming.

Harrison, D. A., Price, K. H., & Bell, M. P. (1998). Beyond relational demography: Time and the effects of surface- and deep-level diversity on work group cohesion. *Academy of Management Journal*, *41*, 96–107.

Harrison, D. A., Price, K. H., Gavin, J. H., & Florey, A. T. (2002). Time, teams, and task performance: Changing effects of surface- and deep-level diversity on group functioning. *Academy of Management Journal*, *45*, 1029–1045.

Herskovits, M. J. (1955). *Cultural anthropology*. New York: Alfred A. Knopf.

Hofstede, G. (1980). *Culture's consequences: International differences in work-related values*. Newbury Park, CA: Sage.

House, R., Rousseau, D., & Thomas-Hunt, M. (1995). The meso paradigm: A framework for the integration of micro and macro organizational behavior. In: L. L. Cummings & B. M. Staw (Eds), *Research in organizational behavior* (Vol. 17, pp. 71–114). Greenwich, CT: JAI Press.

Howell, J. M., & Shamir, B. (2005). The role of followers in the charismatic leadership process: Relationships and their consequences. *Academy of Management Review*, *1*, 96–112.

Ilgen, D. R., Hollenbeck, J. R., Johnson, M., & Jundt, D. (2005). Teams in organization: From input-process-output models to IMOI models. *Annual Review of Psychology*, *56*, 517–543.

Jackson, S. E., & Joshi, A. (2004). Diversity in social context: A multi-attribute, multi-level analysis of team diversity and sales performance. *Journal of Organizational Behavior*, *25*, 675–702.

Jackson, S. E., Joshi, A., & Erhardt, N. L. (2003). Recent research on team and organizational diversity: SWOT analysis and implications. *Journal of Management*, *29*, 801–830.

Jehn, K. A., Northcraft, G. B., & Neale, M. A. (1999). Why differences make a difference: A field study of diversity, conflict, and performance in workgroups. *Administrative Science Quarterly*, *44*, 741–763.

Johns, G. (1991). Substantive and methodological constraints on behavior and attitudes in organizational research. *Organizational Behavior and Human Decision Processes*, *49*, 80–104.

Johns, G. (2006). The essential impact of context on organizational behavior. *Academy of Management Review*, *31*, 386–408.

Joshi, A. (2006). The influence of organizational demography on the external networking behavior of teams. *Academy of Management Review*, *31*, 583–595.

Joshi, A., Liao, H., & Jackson, S. E. (2006). Cross-level effects of workplace diversity on sales performance and pay. *Academy of Management Journal*, *49*, 459–481.

Kark, R., & Shamir, B. (2002). The dual effect of transformational leadership: Priming relational and collective selves and further effects on follower. In: B. J. Avolio & ?F. J. Yammarino (Eds), *Transformational and charismatic leadership: The road ahead*. Oxford: Elsevier Science.

Kirkman, B. L., & Mathieu, J. E. (2005). The dimensions and antecedents of team virtuality. *Journal of Management*, *31*, 700–718.

Kirkman, B. L., & Shapiro, D. L. (2001). The impact of cultural values on job satisfaction and organizational commitment in self-managing work teams: The mediating role of employee resistance. *Academy of Management Journal*, *44*, 557–569.

Kirkman, B. L., Tesluk, P. E., & Rosen, B. (2004). The impact of demographic heterogeneity and team leader-team member demographic fit on team empowerment and effectiveness. *Group and Organization Management, 29*, 334–368.

Kochan, T., Bezrukova, K., Ely, R., Jackson, S., Joshi, A., Jehn, K., et al. (2003). The effects of diversity on business performance: Report of the diversity research network. *Human Resource Management, 42*, 3–21.

Lawrence, B. S. (1997). The black box of organizational demography. *Organization Science, 8*, 1–22.

Leonard, J. S., Levine, D. I., & Joshi, A. (2004). Do birds of a feather shop together? The effects on performance of employees' similarity with one another and with customers. *Journal of Organizational Behavior, 25*, 731–754.

LePine, J. A., Hanson, M. A., Borman, W. C., & Motowidlo, S. J. (2000). Contextual performance and teamwork: Implications for staffing. In: G. R. Ferris & K. M. Rowland (Eds), *Research in personnel and human resources management* (Vol.19, pp. 53–90). Greenwich, CT: JAI Press.

Martins, L. L., Miliken, F. J., Wiesenfeld, B. M., & Salgado, S. R. (2003). Racioethnic diversity and group member's experience. *Group and Organization Management, 28*, 75–106.

Martocchio, J. J., Harrison, D. A., & Berkson, H. (2000). Connections between lower back pain, interventions, and absence from work: A time-based meta-analysis. *Personnel Psychology, 53*, 595–624.

Meindl, J. R., Hunt, R. G., & Lee, W. (1989). Individualism-collectivism and work values: Data from the United States, China, Taiwan, Korea, and Hong Kong. In: G. R. Ferris & K. M. Rowland (Eds), *Research in personnel and human resources management* (Suppl. 1, pp. 59–77). Greenwich, CT: JAI Press.

Meyerson, D. E., & Fletcher, J. K. (2000). A modest manifesto for shattering the glass ceiling. *Harvard Business Review, 78*, 126–136.

Miele, C. (2004). Building community by embracing diversity. *Community College Journal of Research and Practice, 28*, 133–140.

Miles, R. E., & Snow, C. C. (1984). Designing strategic human resources systems. *Organizational Dynamics, 13*, 36–52.

Miliken, F. J., & Martins, L. L. (1996). Searching for common threads: Understanding the multiple effects of diversity in organizational groups. *Academy of Management Review, 21*, 402–433.

Mohammed, S., & Angell, L. C. (2004). Surface- and deep-level diversity in workgroups: Examining the moderating effects of team orientation and team process on relationship conflict. *Journal of Organizational Behavior, 25*, 1015–1039.

Mohrman, S. A. (1995). Designing work teams. In: H. Richard & C. Fay (Eds), *Enhancing workplace effectiveness* (pp. 257–276). San Francisco, CA: Jossey-Bass.

Mor-Barak, M. E. (2005). *Managing diversity: Toward a globally inclusive workplace*. Thousand Oaks, CA: Sage Publications.

Mowday, R. T., & Sutton, R. I. (1993). Organizational behavior: Linking individuals and groups to organizational contexts. *Annual Review of Psychology, 44*, 195–229.

Nembhard, I. M., & Edmondson, A. C. (2006). Making it safe: The effects of leader inclusiveness and professional status on psychological safety and improvement efforts in health care teams. *Journal of Organizational Behavior, 27*, 941–966.

O'Neill, J. (2003). The gender gap in wages, circa 2000. *American Economic Review, 93*, 309–314.

Ostroff, C., & Atwater, L. (2003). Does whom you work with matter? Effects of referent group gender and age composition on managers' compensation. *Journal of Applied Psychology*, *88*, 725–740.

Pelled, L. H., Eisenhardt, K. M., & Xin, K. R. (1999). Exploring the black box: An analysis of work group diversity, conflict, and performance. *Administrative Science Quarterly*, *44*, 1–28.

Pettigrew, T. F. (1959). Regional differences in anti-negro prejudices. *Journal of Abnormal and Social Psychology*, *49*, 28–36.

Pettigrew, T. F. (1998). Intergroup contact theory. *Annual Review of Psychology*, *49*, 65–85.

Pfeffer, J. (1983). Organizational demography. In: L. L. Cummings & B. M. Staw (Eds), *Research in organizational behavior* (Vol. 5, pp. 299–357). Greenwich, CT: JAI Press.

Pfeffer, J., & Davis-Blake, A. (1987). The effects of the proportion of women on salaries: The case of college administrators. *Administrative Science Quarterly*, *32*, 1–24.

Phillips, D. J. (2005). Organizational genealogies and the persistence of gender inequality: The case of Silicon Valley law firms. *Administrative Science Quarterly*, *50*, 440–472.

Reskin, B. F., McBrier, D. B., & Kmec, J. (1999). The determinants and consequences of workplace sex and race composition. *Annual Review of Sociology*, *25*, 355–361.

Richard, O. C. (2000). Racial diversity, business strategy, and firm performance: A resource-based view. *Academy of Management Journal*, *43*, 164–177.

Richard, O. C., Barnett, T., Dwyer, S., & Chadwick, K. (2004). Cultural diversity in management, firm performance, and the moderating role of entrepreneurial orientation dimensions. *Academy of Management Journal*, *47*, 255–266.

Richard, O. C., McMillan, A., Chadwick, K., & Dwyer, S. (2003). Employing an innovation strategy in radically diverse workforce. *Group and Organization Management*, *28*, 107–126.

Ridgeway, C. (1997). Interaction and the conservation of gender inequality: Considering employment. *American Sociological Review*, *62*, 218–235.

Rousseau, D. M., & Fried, Y. (2001). Location, location, location: Contextualizing organizational research. *Journal of Organizational Behavior*, *22*, 1–13.

Sacco, J. M., & Schmitt, N. A. (2005). A dynamic multilevel model of demographic diversity and misfit effects. *Journal of Applied Psychology*, *90*, 203–231.

Schippers, M. C., Den Hartog, D. N., Koopman, P. L., & Wienk, J. A. (2003). Diversity and team outcomes: The moderating effects of outcome interdependence and group longevity and the mediating effect of reflexivity. *Journal of Organizational Behavior*, *24*, 779–802.

Schneider, B. (2000). The psychological life of organizations. In: N. M. Ashkanasy, C. Wilderom & M. F. Peterson (Eds), *Handbook of organizational culture and climate*. Thousand Oaks, CA: Sage.

Shamir, B., House, R. J., & Arthur, M. B. (1993). The motivational effects of charismatic leadership: A self-concept based theory. *Organization Science*, *4*, 577–594.

Sherif, M. (1966). *Group conflict and co-operation: Their social psychology*. London: Routledge & Kegan Paul.

Sherif, M., Harvey, O., White, B. J., Hood, W. R., & Sherif, C. W. (1961). *The robber's cave experiment: Intergroup conflict and cooperation*. Middletown, CT: Wesleyan University Press.

Skaggs, S., & DiTomaso, N. (2004). Understanding the effects of workforce diversity on employment outcomes: A multidisciplinary and comprehensive framework. In: N. DiTomaso & C. Post (Eds), *Research in the sociology of work* (pp. 279–306). New York: Elsevier.

Somech, A. (2006). The effects of leadership style and team process on performance and innovation in functionally heterogeneous teams. *Journal of Management*, *32*, 132–157.

Sproull, L., & Kiesler, S. (1986). Reducing social context cues: Electronic mail in organizational communication. *Management Science, 32*, 1492–1512.

Taylor, M. C. (1998). How white attitudes vary with the racial composition of local populations: Numbers count. *American Sociological Review, 63*, 512–535.

Tomaskovic-Devey, D. (1993). The gender and race composition of jobs and the male/female, white/black pay gaps. *Social Forces, 72*, 45–76.

Triandis, H. C. (1994). *Culture and social behavior*. New York: McGraw-Hill.

Turner, J. C., & Haslam, A. (2001). Social identity, organizations and leadership. In: M. Turner (Ed.), *Groups at work: Theory and research* (pp. 25–65). Mahwah, NJ: Lawrence Erlbaum.

Van Der Vegt, G. S., Van De Vliert, E., & Huang, X. (2005). Location-level links between diversity and innovative climate depend on national power distance. *Academy of Management Journal, 48*, 1171–1182.

Van Knippenberg, D., & Schippers, M. C. (2007). Workgroup diversity. *Annual Review of Psychology, 58*, 2.1–2.27.

Weisband, S. P., Schneider, S. K., & Connolly, T. (1995). Computer-mediated communication and social information: Status salience and status differences. *Academy of Management Journal, 38*, 1124–1151.

Wharton, A. (1992). The social construction of gender and race in organizations: A social identity and group mobilization perspective. In: P. Tolbert & S. Bacharach (Eds), *Research in the sociology of organizations* (Vol. 10, pp. 55–84). Greenwich, CT: JAI Press.

Williams, K., & O'Reilly, C. A. (1998). Demography and diversity in organizations: A review of 40 years of research. In: B. M. Staw & L. L. Cummings (Eds), *Research in organizational behavior* (Vol. 20, pp. 77–140). Greenwich, CT: JAI Press.

THE PAST, PRESENT, AND FUTURE OF DYNAMIC PERFORMANCE RESEARCH

Michael C. Sturman

ABSTRACT

This article reviews the extensive history of dynamic performance research, with the goal of providing a clear picture of where the field has been, where it is now, and where it needs to go. Past research has established that job performance does indeed change, but the implications of this dynamism and the predictability of performance trends remain unresolved. Theories are available to help explain dynamic performance, and although far from providing an unambiguous understanding of the phenomenon, they offer direction for future theoretical development. Dynamic performance research does suffer from a number of methodological difficulties, but new techniques have emerged that present even more opportunities to advance knowledge in this area. From this review, I propose research questions to bridge the theoretical and methodological gaps of this area. Answering these questions can advance both research involving job performance prediction and our understanding of the effects of human resource interventions.

Research in Personnel and Human Resources Management, Volume 26, 49–110
ISSN: 0742-7301/doi:10.1016/S0742-7301(07)26002-5

INTRODUCTION

The extensive history to the study of employee job performance is filled with research that is predominantly static in nature. That is, most of this research examines the correlates of various sorts of job performance ratings, with the often implicit assumption that the results would generalize to the same population of subjects at any other point in time. Yet there is abundant, and as I will argue in this paper overwhelming, evidence that indeed individuals' job performance does change with time. Accepting that an individual's job performance changes, also known as dynamic performance or dynamic criteria, requires research on job performance to consider the effects associated with the passage of time (Hulin, Henry, & Noon, 1990). Sometimes, time-related issues seem to receive some acknowledgment, such as demonstrated by the extensive use of variables such as age, organizational tenure, or job experience as controls (Sturman, 2003), yet job performance research still primarily focuses on the cross-sectional prediction of what is commonly called *the criterion* (Austin & Villanova, 1992; Campbell, 1990; Dunnette, 1963).

Even though the examination of job performance at a given point in time is most common, job performance, perhaps more than any other individual-level variable in organizational research, has been examined in conjunction with time. Research has considered job performance longitudinally since at least the 1940s (e.g., Kunst, 1941; Rothe, 1946, 1947), and effects associated with time have long been recognized as important when measuring job performance (e.g., Ghiselli, 1956; Ghiselli & Haire, 1960). Research on dynamic performance has most often been framed as a critical issue for selection (e.g., Ghiselli & Haire, 1960; Henry & Hulin, 1989; Prien, 1966; Steele-Johnson, Osburn, & Pieper, 2000). If performance changes over time, then the validity of selection devices for predicting job performance obtained from an original validation study may not be stable over time. But the impact of a dynamic criteria reaches far beyond just selection. Human resource researchers investigate how employees are selected, placed, developed, trained, appraised, and compensated within their organizations, processes all intended to affect job performance and all inherently involving the passage of time. For our field to understand employee job performance we require an understanding of what happens to this performance with the passage of time. Nevertheless, despite the time that has passed since issues related to dynamic performance were first raised, there has been less progress in this area than its long history might suggest.

The study of dynamic performance is also complicated by a wide array of methodological issues. First, although time is inherently a longitudinal issue, cross-sectional research can be used to address questions related to the effects of time. It is important to understand where cross-sectional research can and cannot help explain the effects on performance associated with time. Second, recent advances in analytical methods are providing new means to analyze longitudinal data. These methods open up a wide range of possibilities for examining job performance as it relates to time, with each method possessing different assumptions, advantages, and weaknesses. Third, the very nature of studying job performance over time gives rise to a variety of methodological problems that will confront all research on the topic. These issues cause any longitudinal analysis of performance ratings to be at least somewhat flawed, and so it is important to understand the implications of these necessary data limitations. To advance our knowledge about dynamic performance, it is important to have a good understanding of the methodological issues facing those who study the effects associated with time on job performance.

The purpose of this article is to review the current state of knowledge about dynamic performance, discuss the relevant analytical methods and issues, and provide some structure to emerging research in this area. The alignment of past work, past theories, new theories, and methodological advances provides an exciting opportunity for research of both applied and theoretical value. It is my hope that not only will this review clarify the current state of knowledge regarding job performance considered within the context of time, but also will inspire more research on the phenomenon.

DEFINING JOB PERFORMANCE AND DYNAMIC PERFORMANCE

Before reviewing research and theory on dynamic performance, it is critical first to articulate both how job performance itself and the phenomenon of dynamic performance have been defined. Past research in this area has used a variety of measures and definitions of both. My goal here is to review past practices and provide clear definitions that I will employ for the rest of this paper.

Defining Job Performance

Past research on job performance has most commonly defined the construct as behaviors that are under the control of the individual and that contribute to the goals of the organization (Dunnette, 1963; Campbell, 1990; Campbell, McCloy, Oppler, & Sager, 1993; Motowidlo, Borman, & Schmitt, 1997;

Rotundo & Sackett, 2002). A key issue here is that job performance is defined as behavior, and hence distinguishable from the results of such behavior. While this definition is applicable to the performance of work in any role within any form of organization (Campbell, 1990), I will assume here that this behavior is within the context of an employment relationship. The employing organization is also assumed to have goals, with the job performance in some way (directly or indirectly) being able to contribute to those goals.

Past research focused on understanding the definition and conceptualization of job performance has usually employed this definition. Other research, and particularly research involving performance over time, has also considered job performance in different ways. Previous longitudinal job performance research often uses results-based measures, such as sales or output rates (Sturman, Cheramie, & Cashen, 2005). It is also important to note that job performance has been considered as the organizational value associated with employees' behaviors (Brogden & Taylor, 1950; Schmidt & Kaplan, 1971). Papers taking this perspective are based on the idea that employees' behaviors and the results of their behaviors have a direct or indirect association with organizational value, and this value can be approximated and studied as a substantive outcome. This performance value, often referred to as utility, relates to the particular monetary value associated job performance behaviors (Boudreau, 1991). From this perspective, research has estimated the value of various human resource programs by considering the stream of costs and benefits associated with employee performance, often in a longitudinal context (e.g., Boudreau & Berger, 1985; Sturman, 2000; Sturman, Trevor, Boudreau, & Gerhart, 2003).

Any review of the research on job performance and time must therefore be careful to distinguish between, but still consider, the various forms of performance that have been examined. It is important (1) to note that these conceptualizations of job performance are very different and (2) to make a distinction between the theoretical and methodological issues relevant to understanding each. For this paper, I specifically distinguish between *job performance*$_{(behaviors)}$, *job performance*$_{(results)}$, *and job performance*$_{(utility)}$. Unless otherwise noted, for simplicity and space, references to "job performance" will refer to job performance$_{(behaviors)}$.

Defining Dynamic Performance

Past Definitions

Research considering job performance over time has also devoted energy to the definition of what it means for performance to be dynamic. For much of the history of the literature, three definitions generally prevailed. Two definitions involve evidence from the individual-level of analysis; the third about changes at the group-level.

First, performance dynamism may be defined as occurring when the rank-ordering of scores on the criterion change over time (Barrett, Caldwell, & Alexander, 1985; Deadrick & Madigan, 1990; Hanges, Schneider, & Niles, 1990). This definition of dynamic performance has most often led to the examination of correlations between criterion scores at multiple points in time. Such studies have been framed as considering the test–retest reliability or the stability of performance ratings.

Second, performance dynamism has been defined as occurring when predictor validities change over time (Austin, Humphreys, & Hulin, 1989; Barrett et al., 1985; Ghiselli, 1956; MacKinney, 1967; Prien, 1966; Smith, 1976; Steele-Johnson et al., 2000). Research using this definition has focused on examinations of the validity of selection devices for predicting job performance of employees over multiple time periods. Some have argued that a dynamic criterion would lead to a decrease in validity over time (Austin et al., 1989); others have suggested that simply the fluctuation of validity is evidence of a dynamic criterion (Barrett et al., 1985); still others have argued that dynamic criteria could lead to predictors becoming more valid with time (Ackerman, 1987; Murphy, 1989).

Third, performance dynamism has been defined as changes over time in the average level of group performance (Barrett et al., 1985; Hanges et al., 1990). This definition has been criticized as the weakest conceptually and operationally (Barrett et al., 1985). In part, average performance curves may not reflect the shape of the individual performance curves comprising them. Group-level performance could even change when individuals' performance remains constant if the performance level of those leaving the organization were different than the performance level of those entering (Boudreau & Berger, 1985).

Proposed Definition of Dynamic Performance
The three definitions for dynamic performance present an interesting divergent set of ways of considering performance over time, and the use of any single definition has often led to very different research tasks. The problem with these definitions is that they do not present a logically consistent set of classifications. That is, it is possible for the first condition to be met without meeting the second or third definitions. Similarly, the third definition could be met without meeting the first two. The reason this occurs is that the second and third definitions consider the potential consequences of dynamic

performance. For this reason, the definition of dynamic performance should be based on the first definition – changes in the rank-order (or correlations) of job performance over multiple time periods – because it is the only definition that directly addresses the issue of stability (Hanges et al., 1990). Moreover, this dynamism should occur specifically for job performance$_{(behaviors)}$. While the same definition (i.e., changes in the rank-order) can be applied to any outcome, the definition of job performance should be consistent with the view that job performance connotes behaviors. Environmental changes that affect performance results or utility (such as changes in situational constraints), while potentially related to job performance$_{(behaviors)}$, should be recognized as a different phenomenon and not direct evidence of dynamic performance. With this perspective, research can easily distinguish between dynamic performance and the consequences of this dynamism, such as changes in the validity of selection devices (i.e., the second definition), changes in job performance ratings aggregated to a group-level (i.e., the third definition), changes in job performance$_{(results)}$, or changes in job performance$_{(utility)}$.

The first definition, though, needs to be considered carefully. A correlation less than one between performance measures is not necessarily indicative of performance dynamism. Rather, correlations between performance measures over time may be affected by measurement error rather than actual changes in job performance (Barrett et al., 1985; Hanges et al., 1990; Sturman et al., 2005), and it is important to distinguish between temporal consistency, stability, and test–retest reliability (Sturman et al., 2005). Temporal consistency is the correlation between performance measures at different points of time (Heise, 1969; Sturman et al., 2005). It captures the relationship between measures of job performance but not necessarily of the true construct of performance. Test–retest reliability refers to the amount of transient error that effects ratings of job performance at different points in time (Sturman et al., 2005). For performance to be dynamic, changes must occur to the construct of performance. This has been defined as stability: the extent to which the true value of a construct remains constant over time (Carmines & Zeller, 1979; Sturman et al., 2005). I thus define dynamic performance as a lack of stability in job performance$_{(behaviors)}$ over time.

THE PAST: THREE STREAMS OF DYNAMIC PERFORMANCE RESEARCH

When one looks at the body of research related to performance and time, three streams of work emerge. All three lines of research involve the prediction of job performance, yet the way these goals are pursued are markedly differently, thereby involving notably different theoretical and methodological issues. These three areas of research are (1) the search for evidence of the dynamic performance phenomenon, (2) the prediction of changes in job performance, and (3) the prediction of job performance trends.

Evidence of Dynamic Performance

The earliest work on dynamic performance primarily focused on measuring job performance over time and the implications of any inconsistency for the validation of selection devices. Much of this early research addressed the question of "is performance dynamic?" That is, does job performance satisfy the earlier definitions of dynamic performance articulated above.

This work on dynamic performance was concerned with describing the nature of performance consistency. Essentially, this research challenged the assumption of a criterion that is reliable across time. While psychological research often insists on a highly reliable measure of job performance (or for that matter, any criterion) assessed at a point in time, scant attention was paid to whether the criterion had reliability from one time-period to the next. Consequently, a body of research emerged examining the reliability of performance ratings at various time lags (e.g., Ghiselli, 1956; Prien, 1966; Rambo, Chomiak, & Price, 1983; Rambo, Chomiak, & Rountree, 1987; Rothe, 1946, 1978; Rothe & Nye, 1958, 1959, 1961).

Other work in this area sought to determine the prevalence of simplex (or quasi-simplex) patterns in measures of job performance (e.g., Bass, 1962; Deadrick & Madigan, 1990; Dennis, 1954, 1956; Ghiselli & Haire, 1960; Hanges et al., 1990; Henry & Hulin, 1987). For job performance, the simplex pattern of correlations (Guttman, 1955; Humphreys, 1960) is a systematic decrease in the magnitude of correlations between measures of job performance as the time-span between performance measures increases. A perfect simplex is based on a model with no or negligible measurement error; a quasi-simplex model includes a measurement model (Jöreskog, 1970). If job performance follows a simplex or quasi-simplex pattern, and especially if that led to correlations between measures of performance approaching zero, then this would suggest that the validity of selection devices could not be generalized across time. If true, then the utility (economic and practical) of selection devices would be much lower than cross-sectional research has suggested (Henry & Hulin, 1987).

In all, this body of research resulted in strong, arguably undeniable, support of a lack of performance consistency. Empirically reviewing the research, Sturman et al. (2005) attempted to partial out unreliability from stability, and thus present information on the extent to which performance truly is dynamic. The results of their study showed that while there is evidence of test–retest unreliability (and other measurement error) causing some of the observed inconsistency in job performance ratings over time, job performance ratings (both job performance$_{(behaviors)}$ and job performance$_{(results)}$) are dynamic. While there remains debate in the literature as to the pervasiveness and extent of performance changes (e.g., Austin et al., 1989; Barrett & Alexander, 1989; Barrett et al., 1985), and there does appear to be at least some portion of job performance that is stable over time (Hanges et al., 1990; Sturman et al., 2005), there is now abundant research and general consensus that job performance does change over time (Deadrick & Madigan, 1990; Deadrick, Bennett, & Russell, 1997; Henry & Hulin, 1987; Hofmann, Jacobs, & Baratta, 1993; Hofmann, Jacobs, & Gerras, 1992; Hulin et al., 1990; Ployhart & Hakel, 1998; Sturman & Trevor, 2001; Sturman et al., 2005). Still in question, though, are the implications of performance dynamism and the causes and correlates of individual job performance changes over time.

Changing Predictability of Job Performance

Explicitly stated in some research on dynamic performance, and implicit in others, is that the presence of dynamic criteria poses a significant problem for the prediction of job performance over time (i.e., reviewed earlier as the formerly second definition of dynamic criteria). Indeed, this was a concern raised by a number of researchers examining dynamic criteria (e.g., Ghiselli, 1956; Hanges et al., 1990; Henry & Hulin, 1987; MacKinney, 1967; Prien, 1966; Rambo et al., 1983; Smith, 1976). Some argued that the existence of dynamic criteria does not necessarily mean a lack of predictability (Ackerman, 1988, 1989; Barrett, Caldwell, & Alexander, 1989, 1992; Hanges et al., 1990). This led to an extensive debate in the literature on the effect of time on the validity of job performance predictors.

In their examination of validities examined longitudinally, Barrett et al. (1985) found examples of both stable and instable validities. They concluded that, "factors such as temporal unreliability and restriction of range serve as viable explanations in the few instances where significant change over time was found" (Barrett et al., 1985, p. 53). Overall, they argued that evidence of dynamic criteria (as specified by the second definition) was relatively rare. Other researchers took an opposing view, arguing that the same evidence reviewed in Barrett et al. (1985) was not as dismissive of a dynamic criterion as Barrett et al. suggest (Austin et al., 1989). A similar debate emerged soon thereafter. A paper by Henry and Hulin (1987) argued that "instability and change in nearly all areas of human performance, skills, and measures of general ability are more to be expected than is stability" (p. 461) and therefore the long-term predictability of performance is questionable. This paper was criticized by Ackerman (1989), who argued that while job performance ratings may follow a simplex patter, "ability measures *can* maintain levels of predictive validity over time and, when chosen properly, may actually increase" (Ackerman, 1989, p. 364), followed by a rejoinder by Henry and Hulin (1989) countering some of the criticisms. The point here is not specifically to weigh in on these debates, but their review shows that there are divergent opinions on the matter, and the evidence had not yielded definitive conclusions for the field.

In one of the most comprehensive examinations of performance predictors over time, Keil and Cortina (2001) examined the validity of cognitive ability, perceptual speed ability, and psychomotor ability to predict job performance. They found that the validities deteriorate with time. This deterioration occurred for all three predictors, and for both consistent and inconsistent tasks. Although they argued that this deterioration is pervasive, there are still examples from other research of selection devices maintaining their predictability over time.

Published in the same year, Farrell and McDaniel (2001) examined how well general mental ability, perceptual speed, and psychomotor ability predicted job performance at various experience levels in a large cross-sectional sample of employees. They found that the correlation between the various abilities and performance did differ when the model was divided by job consistency. They also found some instances of correlations increasing with experience, decreasing with experience, and fluctuating (decreasing and then increasing again) with experience.

Other studies can be found that also show that there is no definitive answer to this research question. For example, McEvoy and Beatty (1989) examined the validity of an assessment center over seven years. While the correlations varied (from 0.19 to 0.41 for supervisory ratings of performance), the authors demonstrated that the selection device had validity over an extended period of time. Tziner, Ronen, and Hacohen (1993) also demonstrated the long-term validity of an assessment center. Similarly, Deadrick and Madigan (1990) examined the validity of psychomotor ability, cognitive ability, and experience over a six-month period. They found that psychomotor ability predicted initial performance, and cognitive ability predicted performance growth. In conclusion, while it appears that Keil and Cortina (2001) provide strong evidence that the validities of ability measures decrease with greater time lags, conflicting (but albeit cross-sectional) findings of Farrell and McDaniel (2001), along with the presence of some other exceptions from longitudinal studies and the contradictory findings with regard to assessment centers, keeps alive the question about what happens to the validity of selection devices over time.

The long history of research and debate in this area might suggest that issues of dynamic performance would be salient in the staffing literature. However, selection research still often ignores the dimension of time. For example, in recent studies on staffing and selection tools, time is not considered (e.g., Behling, 1998; Carlson, Connerley, & Mecham, 2002; Chait, Carraher, & Buckley, 2000; Stevens & Campion, 1999; Ryan, McFarland, Baron, & Page, 1999; Ryan & Tippings, 2004). Similarly, current texts on selection tend to devote little space to the role of time. Time may be mentioned with regard to estimating test–retest reliability (e.g., Heneman, Heneman, & Judge, 1997). The text by Gatewood and Feild (2001) does briefly mention Hulin et al.'s (1990) conclusion that the validity of some measures decay with time, although the concern is quickly dismissed and there is no real discussion of the implications of performance changes. In an exception, Ployhart, Schneider, and Schmidt (2006) explicitly state that performance is dynamic, and that this has implications for validity, but that there is enough stability in performance for it to be predicted. Nonetheless, the attention devoted to the role of time remains minimal, despite that the goals of staffing are to *"improve* organizational functioning and effectiveness by attracting, selecting, and *retaining* people who will facilitate the accomplishments of organizational goals. ..."* (Ployhart et al., 2006, p. 2, emphasis added). Inherent in this definition is the passage of time. If performance is defined as the behaviors that contribute to the goals of organizations, and if these behaviors change over time, then the passage of time is critical to the issue of selection.

Researchers studying job performance and time have often disagreed as to the proper interpretation of past evidence, but they all seem to agree that more research is needed into the implications and consequences of its instability (Ackerman, 1989; Barrett et al., 1985, 1989; Hanges et al., 1990) or inconsistency (Austin et al., 1989). This research should involve better conceptualizations of the outcomes being predicted (Austin et al., 1989) and the identification and removal of intrinsic and extrinsic source of criterion unreliability in measures of job performance over time (Barrett et al., 1985; Sturman et al., 2005).

Nonetheless, the question of "is performance dynamic?" as defined in this paper, is resolved. There is no need for future research specifically to address this question. However, the field is still far off from a clear understanding of what happens to job performance over time, what causes it to be dynamic, how effectively selection devices work over time, and how human resource interventions can be used to affect job performance when considered in a longitudinal context.

Predicting Performance Trends

The most recent development in the dynamic performance literature has been the examination of employee performance trends. This new line of research presents a shift in the focus of dynamic performance research to investigations of individual change patterns (Hofmann et al., 1993).

The goal of this line of research is to model within-person patterns of performance and to understand what affects these patterns. By its nature, this research is interested in the prediction of job performance at more than one point in time (Ployhart, Holtz, & Bliese, 2002). The early work in this area simply demonstrated that modeling individual performance trends was possible. Performance trends were shown to be systematic, and hence predictable (Hofmann et al., 1992, 1993). Research in this area then expanded on this finding by similarly modeling performance trends, but also considering individual-level characteristics which predict the level and slope of these trends (Deadrick et al., 1997). Later research expanded both the complexity of the performance trend model (to non-linear patterns) and the types of predictors used to explain the trends (Day, Sin, & Chen, 2004; Ployhart & Hakel, 1998; Stewart & Nandkeolyar, 2006; Thoresen, Bradley, Bliese, & Thoresen, 2004).

Related to this stream of research has been the work examining the consequences of performance trends. Some research has examined how performance trends influence the likelihood of turnover (Harrison, Virick, & William, 1996; Sturman & Trevor, 2001). Both studies found that changes in subsequent performance scores affected the likelihood of turnover, and Sturman and Trevor (2001) showed that even after controlling for this change, long-term performance trends also predicted turnover. This research shows that performance changes (short-term and long-term) may be valuable predictors in other longitudinal phenomena, even though work on the implications of performance trends is still in its early stages.

Investigations in this third stream of dynamic performance research show that performance trends are both predictable and related to outcomes of interest. As a result, it seems clear that, consistent with the conclusions of many in the second stream of research reviewed above, selection devices need to be considered not just in terms of their validity at a point in time (or even validity at several points in time), but in terms of how well they predict performance trends. Furthermore, the dynamic nature of performance and the predictability of performance trends suggest that for essentially all areas of human resource research interested in the prediction of job performance ratings, it would provide a more accurate understanding of performance to consider the predictability of performance levels and trajectories.

THE PRESENT: CURRENT THEORY RELEVANT TO DYNAMIC PERFORMANCE

Over the history of research on dynamic performance, repeated calls have been made for more theoretical development (e.g., Austin et al., 1989; Campbell, 1990; Deadrick & Madigan, 1990; Deadrick et al., 1997; Henry & Hulin, 1987; Hofmann et al., 1992, 1993; Hulin et al., 1990; Steele-Johnson et al., 2000). While more theoretical progress is certainly desired, there are some notable works that have considered the issue of what happens to performance over time that provide a useful framework for research in this area. Some of this research has been widely cited in the dynamic performance literature. Others are relevant but have not been extensively applied or developed within the literature. The purpose of this section is to review theoretical perspectives that are applicable for studying performance over time, hopefully presenting opportunities for greater clarification and demonstrating where future research is most needed.

Changing Subjects and Changing Tasks Models

Two models have emerged directly from the literature on dynamic performance to help explain why the relationship between predictors and performance changes over time: the changing tasks model and the changing subjects model. While, as reviewed above, there is debate as to the extensiveness and rapidity of decreases in validity, both models are valuable for understanding why performance changes over time.

The Changing Subjects Model
The changing subjects model (also referred to as the changing-person model; e.g., Keil & Cortina, 2001) posits that individuals possess various characteristics which result in (i.e., cause) performance (be it performance on a task or performance on a job; I will be focusing exclusively on job performance). While most uses of this model have considered abilities, it may also refer to characteristics such as motivation and job knowledge. Because these performance-causing characteristics change over time, performance levels change even if the contribution of these characteristics to performance remains constant (Adams, 1957; Alvares & Hulin, 1973; Deadrick & Madigan, 1990; Humphreys, 1960; Keil & Cortina, 2001).

While employed in an organization, a multitude of changes occur to an individual than can affect performance. For example, while holding a given job, an employee accumulates experience that then affects performance levels (e.g., McDaniel, Schmidt, & Hunter, 1988; Schmidt, Hunter, & Outerbridge, 1986; Sturman, 2003). Simultaneously, aging may affect performance (e.g., Lawrence, 1988; Rhodes, 1983; Salthouse, 1979; Sterns & Doverspike, 1989; Sturman, 2003; Waldman & Avolio, 1993). Because experience and age are related to job performance, the changes in the individual's characteristics cause job performance to change with the passage of time. Although other models (discussed below) provide additional explanations as to why performance changes over time, research supports the changing subjects model as at least a partial explanation as to why performance changes over time (Deadrick & Madigan, 1990; Dunham, 1974). Indeed, much of the field of training is based on the idea that individual characteristics which cause performance can be changed, so performance can be improved through effective training (e.g., Noe, 2005). The logic behind changing compensation plans is also similarly based on the idea that incentives can cause individuals to change in ways that affects their performance levels (e.g., Milkovich & Newman, 2005).

Certainly, there has been debate regarding the validity of the changing subjects model, but much of this debate was caused by issues related to the definition of abilities. If one considers an ability to be a relatively static trait, then there are definitional flaws with the changing subjects model if one defines it as changes in abilities causing performance changes. However, by broadening the model to consider abilities and skills (e.g., Keil & Cortina, 2001), or broadening it even further as I do above by considering all individual-level performance-causing characteristics (including abilities, skills, knowledge, and motivation), then the focus of the model is wider and more consistent with static models of job performance (e.g., Campbell, 1990; Motowidlo et al., 1997; Schmidt et al., 1986). Additionally, with a broader focus, the changing-subjects model can be seen as complementary to the changing tasks model rather than as a competing alternative explanation (Keil & Cortina, 2001).

The Changing Tasks Model
In addition to changes in individual characteristics, performance changes may be attributable to job changes, new job roles, or revised organizational requirements. The changing tasks model predicts that an individual's performance changes because the determinants of performance change (Alvares & Hulin, 1972; Deadrick & Madigan, 1990; Fleishman & Hempel, 1954). Changes in job requirements – such as after a promotion, transfer, the introduction of new technology, or other change in job duties – may lead to the need for new sets of abilities while reducing the impact of current abilities on job performance (Alvares & Hulin, 1972; Fleishman, 1953, 1960; Fleishman & Hempel, 1954; Fleishman & Rich, 1963; Murphy, 1989; Steele-Johnson et al., 2000). For example, a scientist may be promoted to a management position (e.g., Boudreau & Berger, 1985). In this circumstance, the company might lose a high performing scientist while gaining a poor performing manager. When an employee changes jobs, individual characteristics may remain the same, but the changes in the job duties may cause different individual characteristics (e.g., managerial experience and knowledge rather than scientific experience and knowledge) to become determinants of job performance.

By drawing attention to how the requirements of individual performance change over time, the changing tasks model may also explain variance in performance remaining after controlling for prior performance (e.g., Sturman et al., 2005). The effect of task changes on performance dynamism depends on the similarity between the old job and the new job. The greater the similarity, the more that past performance should be able to predict future performance.

The logic behind the changing tasks model is consistent with the underlying assumption behind such organizational actions such as work redesign (e.g., Hackman & Oldham, 1976) and empowerment (e.g., Lawler, 1986). That is, by changing the nature of the job, environment, or organization, employee job performance can be improved.

Static Models of Job Performance and their Implications for Time

A common approach for conceptualizing the determinants of job performance is some form of static model, such as

Performance $= f$ (motivation, ability),
Performance $= f$ (motivation, ability, opportunity),
Performance $= f$ (declarative knowledge, procedural knowledge and skill, motivation).

As noted by Campbell (1990), determining the precise functional form of such a model is likely impossible; however, considering this sort of model does provide insights for understanding the nature of performance changes over time, particularly if one builds upon the changing subjects and changing tasks models discussed above.

Even if not determining all the specific causes of performance, one can generally specify that performance is a function of certain characteristics, some of whom are stable and some of which change with time. For example, cognitive ability is generally shown to be highly correlated with job performance (e.g., Hunter, 1986; Hunter & Hunter, 1984; Ree & Earles, 1992; Schmitt, Gooding, Noe, & Kirsch, 1984; Schmidt & Hunter, 1998) and is also shown to be relatively stable for adults over their careers (Bayley, 1949, 1955; Charles, 1953; Hertzog & Schaie, 1986, 1988; Jensen, 1980; Owens, 1953; Schaie, 1994; Thorndike, 1940). Similarly, personality has been shown to be related to performance (e.g., Barrick & Mount, 1991; Dudley, Orvis, Lebiecki, & Cortina, 2006; Hurtz & Donovan, 2000; Salgado, 1997; Tett, Jackson, & Rothstein, 1991) and also is a relatively stable individual characteristic (Costa & McCrae, 1988, 1992). Other individual characteristics related to performance change with time, such as job knowledge (e.g., Schmidt et al., 1986), job experience (e.g., Schmidt et al., 1986; Sturman, 2003), leadership (e.g., Day et al., 2004), and motivation (e.g., Kanfer, 1991, 1992). Based on any static performance model, at any point in time, job performance is at least partly determined by a function of these characteristics. This perspective incorporates aspects of the changing subjects model, as any longitudinal application of this model will show that performance over time changes because some of the causes of performance change with time. At the same time, the changing tasks model suggests that some predictors of performance change over time.

For both stable and dynamic characteristics, the functional relationship of predictors of performance can be either stable or dynamic. This leads to the following general model:

$$P_t = B_0 + B_1 \times \textbf{(Stable characteristics)}$$
$$+ B_{2(t)} \times \textbf{(Stable characteristics)}$$
$$+ B_3 \times \textbf{(Dynamic characteristics}_t\textbf{)}$$
$$+ B_{4(t)} \times \textbf{(Dynamic characteristics}_t\textbf{)} + e \qquad (1)$$

Where B_1 and B_3 are stable coefficients over time, and B_2 and B_4 change over time (as signified above with the addition of (t) in the subscript; the bold indicates matrices of characteristics and coefficients).

The above model shows the problem associated with using cross-sectional data to consider longitudinal phenomena. Specifically, in any sort of cross-sectional analysis, one cannot observe changes within subjects across time. This means that when examining the results of any analysis, one will be unable to distinguish between the stable and dynamic betas or between stable and dynamic characteristics. As such, the coefficients derived from any model may be accurate, but may not generalize to even the same subjects at a different point in time. This condition limits the potential value of cross-sectional analyses when considering longitudinal phenomena. As will be discussed later, though, this does not mean that cross-sectional research is of no value. Nonetheless, the above model cannot be explicitly tested as shown. One may be able to employ other research to distinguish between the stable and dynamic characteristics, but it remains impossible to know the functional form of the dynamic betas.

To help understand where time plays a role in the prediction of job performance, perhaps the easiest adjustment to the above model is to consider lagged measures of job performance. By using a lagged measure of job performance, one can derive a simpler model that can help focus attention on the dynamic factors associated with job performance. That is, if one is modeling $P_{(t)}$, and subtracts $P_{(t-1)}$ from each side of the equation, one gets the following:

$$P_t - P_{(t-1)} = B_{0t} + B_1 \times S + B_{2(t)} \times S + B_3 \times D_{(t)}$$
$$+ B_{4(t)} \times D_{(t)} - P_{(t-1)} + e_{(t)} \qquad (2)$$

With substitution, this becomes

$$P_t - P_{(t-1)} = B_{0t} + B_1 \times S + B_{2(t)} \times S + B_3 \times D_{(t)} + B_{4(t)} \times D_{(t)} + e_{(t)}$$
$$- (B_{0(t-1)} + B_1 \times S + B_{2(t-1)} \times S + B_3 \times D_{(t-1)} + B_{4(t-1)}$$
$$\times D_{(t-1)} + e_{(t-1)}) \qquad (3)$$

or

$$\Delta(P) = B_0' + B_{2(t-1)} \times S + B_{2(t)} \times S + B_3 \times (D_t - D_{(t-1)})$$
$$+ B_{4(t)} \times D_{(t)} - B_4 \times D_{(t-1)} + e' \tag{4}$$

To help with explanation, this can be simplified as follows:

$$\Delta(P) = B_I + B_A \times S + B_B \times \Delta D + B_C \times D_t + B_D \times D_{(t-1)} + e \tag{5}$$

Note that by using a lagged variable, the stable effects associated with stable characteristics are eliminated from the model. Also in this model, B_A represents evidence of the changing tasks model. If stable characteristics are related to performance after controlling for prior performance, then this can only occur if it is because the way in which the stable characteristics relate to performance change with time. Significant coefficients within B_c presents evidence of the changing subjects model, and significant coefficients of B_D presents evidence of the simultaneous effects of both changing subjects and changing tasks.

A flaw with the above model, though, is that the analysis of change scores is not always desirable (e.g., Edwards, 1994, 2001). While there are a number of issues related to difference in scores, most salient here is that modeling the change score above is equivalent to the following:

$$P_t = B_I + B_A \times S + B_B \times \Delta D + B_C \times D_t - B_D \times D_{(t-1)} + (1.0) \times P_{(t-1)} + e \tag{6}$$

That is, it assumes that the effect associated with lagged performance is 1.0. If one is able to model performance longitudinally, there is little advantage to making this assumption. Rather, one should allow the model to estimate the effect of the lagged performance measure, as its interpretation can be quite useful. Hence, one should model

$$P_t = B_I + B_A \times S + B_B \times \Delta D + B_C \times D_t - B_D \times D_{(t-1)} + B_{\text{Lag}} \times P_{(t-1)} + e \tag{7}$$

If the performance model being used is fully specified, then B_{Lag} should be equal to one, an assumption that can be tested empirically.

The theoretical value of such a test, though, is not likely to be large. This is because research has already shown that performance trends tend to be non-linear (Deadrick et al., 1997; Ployhart & Hakel, 1998; Sturman et al., 2005). This means that, because job performance tends to follow a negatively accelerating curve, controlling for the linear effects of prior performance will not fully capture the extent to which past performance can predict future performance.

The non-linear trends of job performance will cause the above model to be under specified in a way that could affect the interpretation of the independent variables of interest. That is, although lagged performance may be in the model, this coefficient does not partial out all of the effects associated with past performance. The potential for this problem can be seen by comparing the results of Harrison et al. (1996) and Sturman and Trevor (2001). In their studies of turnover, both papers showed that changes in performance were associated with the probability of turnover. However, Sturman and Trevor (2001) extended the work by Harrison et al. (1996) by demonstrating that even after controlling for the most recent change in turnover, long-term trends of performance also affected the probability of turnover. Hypothetically, in another study of turnover that controlled only for the most recent change in performance, it is possible that some independent variable under investigation would be correlated with these performance trends. If so, the variable may falsely appear to relate to the dependent variable because the effects of the long-term trends were not controlled for in the model.

At the present, this is only a hypothetical. With few exceptions (Harrison et al., 1996; Sturman & Trevor, 2001), there is little research looking at the consequences of performance trends. When using some sort of lagged performance model, researchers need to give careful consideration to the potential effects associated with performance trends. This is a potential concern in many areas of human resource research, but perhaps most so in the areas of compensation and training. In compensation, rewards are commonly associated with more than just the most recent performance evaluation; if estimating the effects of a training program, controlling for the trajectory of performance scores may be essential for isolating the effects associated with the training intervention. Ideally, one should control for multiple measures of prior job performance to more fully specify any performance model, thereby gaining confidence in any potential effects associated with an independent variable of interest (e.g., earning a certain bonus in time $[t-1]$, participating in a given training program at $[t-1]$).

The question thus arises: how many prior performance scores should be controlled for in longitudinal analytical models? Unfortunately, the existing research on dynamic performance does not have a definitive answer. Simply put, more is better. If one can control for one instance of prior performance, the analyses will control the linear effects associated with job performance on the dependent variable, but it will not partial out the known non-linear effects on the dependent variable of interest. If one controls for two instances of prior performance, one is then controlling for the linear effects of prior performance and the effects of performance changes. Controlling for three prior measures of performance controls for the linear effects associated with performance in addition to the effects associated with change and the effects associated with which the rate of change is itself changing. Obviously, using more measures of performance is more specified. More measures also presents a more conservative test if trying to show that some other independent variable (e.g., a bonus, a training program) has an effect on performance over time.

Research examining performance trends has generally examined no more than cubic trends (i.e., the rate in which the change in performance is changing) (e.g., Hofmann et al., 1992, 1993; Keil & Cortina, 2001; Ployhart & Hakel, 1998). Although it would be desirable to test the assumption that performance slopes can be described with up to cubic parameters, controlling for three measures of prior job performance may fully capture the effects associated with performance trends. Of course, longitudinal research is often rare, and adding the extra demand that longitudinal studies of job performance have at least four waves of data would only make such research less feasible. Researchers should be aware of the potential effects of non-linear (cubic) performance trends when considering longitudinal models of performance. However, given the current lack of research in this area, potential specification error of effects associated with prior performance is a limitation that is worth accepting until the quantity of knowledge in this area is sufficiently expanded.

Employment Stage Models

Another key theoretical development in the area of dynamic performance research is the employment stage models developed by Ackerman (1987, 1988, 1992) and Murphy (1989). Ackerman's work is focused on skill development; Murphy's model applied Ackerman's work to job performance. Both are obviously related, and both are pertinent and have been applied to the study of job performance over time.

Ackerman proposed a theory of skill acquisition, predicting that task performance becomes automatic through practice. His theory posits that the importance of certain abilities to task performance change during skill acquisition. Furthermore, the nature of this change depends on the particular ability and the nature of the task.

The theory postulates that individuals proceed through three phases of skill acquisition. The first phase (the cognitive phase) involves a strong demand on the general mental ability of the performer as performance strategies are formulated and tested. During this phase, performance speed and accuracy increase quickly, and the demands on cognitive ability are reduced. The second phase (the associative phase) involves the refinement of the stimulus–response connections developed in the first phase. Here, "perceptual speed ability" refers to abilities that are associated with "an individual's facility in solving items of increasing complexity ...[and] the speed of processing" (Ackerman, 1988, p. 290). Ultimately, the third and final stage of performance is characterized as automatic. In this phase, tasks can be completed competently even without the full attention of the performer. Performance in this phase is less dependent on perceptual speed ability and more so on psychomotor ability (defined as processing speed and accuracy independent of information processing per se; Ackerman, 1988).

Although described as distinct, Ackerman postulates that individuals proceed through the three phases in a continuous manner. The effects of the various abilities on task performance change continuously with practice. The effect of general mental ability begins high and decreases; the effect of perceptual speed ability begins low, increases to a peak in Phase two, and ultimately decreases again; the effect of psychomotor ability begins low and increases with practice.

Ackerman also predicts that progression through stages is affected by the complexity and consistency of the task. Complexity refers to the cognitive demands of the task, including memory load, amount of information to process, number of responses, amount of information to be learned, and the amount of stimulus–response compatibility. Greater complexity changes the importance of the various abilities on performance. For example, in tasks with a weak compatibility between stimulus and response, the task will place higher cognitive demands on the learner to determine and execute the appropriate response. This places a greater emphasis on perceptual speed ability and delays the emphasis on general mental ability until further into the skill acquisition process (Ackerman, 1988).

Task consistency effects the rate in which tasks can be mastered. Initially, it has no effect on skill acquisition, as the task being learned is novel to all performers. However, the inconsistency in the task slows the rate in which practice allows for skill acquisition. As a result, inconsistent tasks require performers to depend on cognitive processing (i.e., Phase one) for longer periods of time.

A limitation of Ackerman's work is that the theory is focused on task performance. While task performance is obviously related to job performance, the contexts and constructs are distinct. For example, Ackerman's work generally examined tasks where skills acquisition can be completed in fewer than 20 hours of training. For job performance, even the simplest of jobs generally involves performance of multiple tasks (Borman, 1991). Second, while tests of task performance employ relatively simple measures of performance, the construct of job performance is recognized to be far more difficult to measure, complex, and multidimensional (e.g., Motowidlo et al., 1997; Murphy & Schiarella, 1997; Rotundo & Sackett, 2002; Viswesvaran, Ones, & Schmidt, 2005; Welbourne, Johnson, & Erez, 1998). Third, tests of Ackerman's model generally frame time in terms of minutes or hours (e.g., Ackerman, 1988, 1992; Kanfer & Ackerman, 1989) whereas studies of job performance over time generally describe performance in terms of months or years (e.g., Deadrick et al., 1997; Ployhart & Hakel, 1998; Sturman, 2003; Sturman et al., 2005; Sturman & Trevor, 2001).

Recognizing the substantive differences between task performance and job performance, Murphy (1989) applied Ackerman's theory to the job performance context. Murphy's application is in many ways similar to Ackerman's work, but with some notable differences. First, because of the different nature of tasks (as examined by Ackerman) and the elements comprising job performance, Murphy does not distinguish between complexity and consistency. Rather, complexity "is used as a gross index of a job's cognitive demands" (Murphy, 1989, p. 195).

Murphy's application also results in a model with two phases instead of three: the transition and maintenance stages. The transition stage occurs when an employee is new to a job or when the major duties associated with a job change. Similar to the first phase of Ackerman's model, this phase places high cognitive demands on workers who must acquire new information and cannot rely on past experience. The maintenance stage occurs when jobs are well-learned. Murphy predicts that in this stage, cognitive ability is less important and personality and motivational factors play a more important role in the determination of job performance (note that Ackerman's model does not consider personality or motivational factors). Although Murphy recognizes that "predicting the length of transition stages may be particularly difficult" (p. 191), his model predicts that there are "distinct stages that characterize a worker's performance on the job" (p. 192).

Subsequent relevant empirical tests using job performance as a dependent variable have not distinguished between Ackerman's and Murphy's models. For example, papers by both Farrell and McDaniel (2001) and Keil and

Cortina (2001) present tests of Ackerman's model but examine job performance ratings over time frames that are consistent with research on jobs but not the earlier work on task performance. Specifically, Keil and Cortina (2001) considered both short-term (< 1 day) and long-term outcome measures; Farrell and McDaniel (2001) exclusively employed supervisor ratings of job performance.

Although these studies purport to investigate Ackerman's model, they actually provide useful evidence for comparing and contrasting the predictions of Murphy with Ackerman. The results from Keil and Cortina (2001) actually provide support of Murphy's model as it is differentiated from Ackerman's. For example, Keil and Cortina (having examined cognitive ability, perpetual speed ability, and psychomotor ability) concluded that "the most pervasive finding of the present study was that validities deteriorate over time" (p. 687). While Ackerman had predicted different functional forms for the relationships between these abilities and task performance over time, Keil and Cortina found that the relationship between these abilities and performance began to deteriorate in the early stages of task performance for both consistent and inconsistent tasks. Note that while this is inconsistent with Ackerman's predictions, they are perfectly consistent with Murphy's prediction that abilities (in general, and including all three studied here) would initially predict performance and then decrease in validity in the transition stage.

Keil and Cortina also support what they labeled a "Eureka effect" which is increases in experience tend to produce insights that lead to sudden jumps in performance. Recall that Ackerman predicted continuous development through stages, whereas Murphy called for "distinct" stages. This finding is also consistent with Murphy but contrary to Ackerman's task-based model.

On the other hand, Farrell and McDaniel's study is in some ways more consistent with the predictions of Ackerman's model, and in other ways contradictory to both models. The effects of general mental ability, perceptual speed ability, and psychomotor speed were of different functional forms. There were also notable differences in these relationships for consistent and inconsistent jobs. However, contrary to both models, the effect of abilities on performance for consistent jobs appeared to increase with experience. It should be noted, though, that Farrell and McDaniel's study suffer from the limitations of cross-sectional research of longitudinal phenomena. That is, the authors did show a significant (negative) correlation between their temporal variable (experience) and all of their ability measures. This suggests that the cohorts in their sample were not equivalent. This could mean that hiring standards have increased over time (and therefore newer people have entered the population who have higher levels of the abilities), that higher performers (or at least those with higher levels of abilities) were more likely to leave the organization, that abilities under consideration were not static as has been assumed, or some combination of these explanations. It is simply not possible to determine the cause of these correlations or to know the consequences of them in a cross-sectional study. Nonetheless, their findings do have value when considering the validity of stage models.

In all, both Ackerman's and Murphy's models are valuable in that they provide a theory for understanding why performance changes with time, and how the relationship between predictors and performance should change over this time. Although it has not received much direct explicit attention, Murphy's approach to differentiating task performance from individual job performance is a critical theoretical advance for understanding individual job performance. The contradictory predictions of Ackerman and Murphy, and the contrary findings of Keil and Cortina (2001) and Farrell and McDaniel (2001) demonstrate that more work in this area is needed. Even if not building upon Murphy's contribution, other work considering Ackerman's model of task performance needs to be specifically adapted to understanding the construct of job performance. Murphy's work is a good demonstration of this, but the model is far from resolved.

Learning Curve Theory

A potentially fruitful theoretical perspective generally unexplored in the dynamic performance literature for modeling job performance over time comes from Learning Curve Theory. While the dynamic performance literature has described performance trends as following a learning curve (e.g., Farrell & McDaniel, 2001; Ployhart & Hakel, 1998), little use has been made of Learning Curve Theory to make specific predictions. Despite its origins in psychological research (e.g., Kjerstad, 1919; Thurstone, 1919), Learning Curve Theory has received scant research attention focused on individual employees. Instead, Learning Curve Theory remains a staple of operations research, and has been dominated by a macro-organizational perspective, describing the collective efforts of many employees (Hirschmann, 1964).

Learning Curve Theory predicts that organizational productivity improves based on the accumulation of experience. The learning curve phenomenon is the graphical representation of the learning-by-doing phenomenon observed in people performing manual tasks. The theory, supported by empirical evidence, suggests that with the repetition of a task, the performance of that task improves predictably. The advances to this domain of literature have been in the analytical methods used to represent the functional form of the relationship, methods to estimate the required parameters, and applications of these methods in industrial settings.

The value of Learning Curve Theory for the dynamic performance literature is that it posits a specific functional form that performance should follow. Essentially, the literature related to Learning Curve theory describes the nature of aggregated employee performance over time. Although based on considering performance at an aggregated level, my purpose of reviewing Learning Curve Theory is to demonstrate its value of (re)applying it to the individual-level of analysis.

At its core, Learning Curve Theory stipulates that people learn by doing (Teplitz, 1991). It was originally developed in the psychological literature to describe the rate in which individuals learn how to perform a repetitive, manual task (Kjerstad, 1919; Thurstone, 1919), but it was soon applied to the task of predicting production rates and production costs in manufacturing settings (e.g., Wright, 1936). The theory posits, with repeated examples of empirical support, that as experience with a task increases, the resources required to complete the task (usually labor hours or price per unit) decreases. More specifically, it is held that as the quantity of production doubles, the resources needed to complete the production will be reduced by a constant percentage (called the learning rate; Yelle, 1979). Additionally, this learning rate is expected to be consistent for every doubling of production, a phenomenon known as the "doubling effect." Much of the research and use of Learning Curve Theory has been involved in the estimation of this learning rate, or the development of methods to estimate the learning rate more accurately.

Because of the strong emphasis on the mathematics of the theory's premise, methodological representations of the learning curve have played a very important role in the Learning Curve Theory literature. The most common representation of the learning curve is the log-linear model, also called the Wright model, represented as follows:

$$P_X = I \times X^N \tag{8}$$

P_X = measure of performance (usually either the number of labor hours required to produce the Xth unit or the cost to produce the Xth unit, see Yelle, 1979).

I = The number of units required to produce the first unit (e.g., labor hours), or the expected initial performance level.
X = The cumulative unit number.
N = The learning index; log Φ/log 2.
Φ = The learning rate.
$1-\Phi$ = The progress ratio.

Other learning curve models include the plateau model (Guibert, 1945), the Sigmoid S Curve (Carr, 1946), the Prior-Learning Model (Stanford Research Institute, 1949), the asymptotic model (DeJong, 1957), the adaptation function (Levy, 1965), the exponential function (Pegels, 1969); time-rate models (Bemis, 1981), and cost-rate models (Smith, 1981). It is not my purpose here to provide a comprehensive review of all modifications of the learning curve model; this is a task best left for texts specifically on this topic (see, Belkaoui, 1986 and Teplitz, 1991). Nonetheless, it is important to at least bring up that a variety of mathematical functions exist, as the use of one of these specific models may be more appropriate when modeling individual job performance scores.

Even with the variety of possible approaches to modeling learning curves that have been created, the Wright model is the basis for all other developments, and remains the most popular approach. While abundant research has worked at improving, extending, and applying Learning Curve Theory and learning curve models, it is unquestionable that the basic premise of the theory has received extensive support, and the application of the theory has proven extremely valuable to many different industries (Belkaoui, 1986; Muth, 1986; Teplitz, 1991; Yelle, 1979).

The work on Learning Curve Theory from the operations literature has shown that organizational productivity tends to follow a specific functional form over time. As reviewed earlier, the dynamic performance literature similarly has suggested that there exist systematic and predictable relationships between individual-level job performance measures and time (e.g., Day et al., 2004; Deadrick et al., 1997; Ployhart & Hakel, 1998; Stewart & Nandkeolyar, 2006; Thoresen et al., 2004), but has not sought to propose a basic theoretical form for this relationship. My purpose of reviewing Learning Curve Theory in this article is that it may prove useful for the dynamic performance literature. Although individual-level performance curves of interest to dynamic performance researchers and the aggregated results-based performance curves from the operations literature are not the same, if the two are related such that evaluative performance is an unbiased indicator of results-based performance, then aggregation of evaluative performance measures should follow the same functional form as the aggregation of results-based performance. Common to such macro perspectives, the key assumption behind a model of aggregated job performance is that there are substantial consistencies in the behavior of individuals, hence making it is possible to focus on aggregate responses and ignore variation across individuals (Klein & Kozlowski, 2000; Kozlowski & Klein, 2000). As Learning Curve Theory describes the aggregated productivity of an organization, the applicability of the theory to evaluative performance measures would be confirmed when evaluative measures of job performance are well-modeled by Learning Curve Theory functions.

While so far I have argued that Learning Curve Theory, in principle, may be valuable for understanding individual evaluative measures of job performance over time, specific adaptation of the theory is necessary before it is possible to confirm or falsify this proposition. This application will require three issues to adapt Learning Curve Theory (back) to understanding individual job performance.

First, the correct functional form needs to be identified. The Wright model (Eq. (8)) does not specifically lend itself to modeling job performance ratings. The Wright model is most applicable for modeling costs, with the functional form showing a decrease in costs with the accumulation of experience. With performance ratings, we expect job performance to increase with the accumulation of experience (Sturman, 2003), and other research has suggested a quadratic form to performance trends (e.g., Hofmann et al., 1992, 1993; Keil & Cortina, 2001; Ployhart & Hakel, 1998). The literature on performance trends and Learning Curve Theory can be combined to yield an appropriate functional form for modeling job performance over time.

Second, another assumption of Learning Curve Theory is that it is used to model repetitive tasks, and its applications have been predominantly in the manufacturing sector. Although this is not a flaw in the theory, it does limit its potential generalizability to a wider array of jobs and the modeling of individual performance scores. Job complexity has been shown to moderate relationships with job performance, particularly with regard to temporal issues (Farrell & McDaniel, 2001; Sturman, 2003; Sturman et al., 2005). Because job complexity affects the relationship between time and performance (Sturman, 2003) and the stability of job performance ratings over time (Sturman et al., 2005), it will affect the functional form of performance over time. The resultant functional form of learning to represent job performance over time should be explicitly capable of incorporating the effects associated with job complexity.

Third, a fundamental problem with the premise of the Learning Curve Theory, particularly in light of the SHRM literature, is that the theory seems to imply that managers can simply sit back and await guaranteed productivity gains (Teplitz, 1991). This is inconsistent with the fundamental premise of the SHRM literature, which is based on the idea that HR programs can influence organizational performance through effects on individuals within the organization (Wright & Boswell, 2002). It is also inconsistent with the notable different "learning rates" found in many applications of Learning Curve Theory (Adler & Clark, 1991). Therefore, just as Learning Curve Theory can be of value to the dynamic performance literature, the theory itself can incorporate the potential effects of human resource interventions (e.g., Adler & Clark, 1991) which can then affect organizational performance. In other words, the methods behind the functional form must be capable of representing organizational-level effects on the individual-level phenomenon (i.e., job performance) being modeled.

In sum, Learning Curve Theory has potential applicability to modeling performance over time. The success of the theory in the operations literature suggests it has merit, but its applicability to helping understand behaviorally based performance measures needs explicit testing. Before such testing can occur, though, the functional forms must be adapted to this sort of measure, identifying the necessary parameters, and developing the model to be tested.

The primary benefit of applying Learning Curve Theory to the dynamic performance literature is that it provides a theory and related methodology for explicitly modeling the shape of individual job performance over time. Specific functional forms can be hypothesized and tested. With a theoretical basis for predicting the shape of individual job performance, research could then focus more attention on the factors influencing this shape. Currently, research on dynamic performance is ad hoc in terms of specifying its functional form. Some studies consider linear effects, others quadratic, and others cubic. Little rationale is given for any form, and there is certainly no consensus regarding which functional form is most appropriate. Learning Curve Theory provides the opportunity to develop theory regarding the nature of this functional form.

THE PRESENT: ANALYTICAL TECHNIQUES AND METHODOLOGICAL ISSUES

Dynamic performance research has employed a wide variety of methodologies. These have included the use of cross-sectional methodologies with temporal variables (e.g., Farrell & McDaniel, 2001; Sturman, 2003), the examination of correlations between performance measures for various time lags (e.g., Deadrick & Madigan, 1990; Keil & Cortina, 2001; Sturman et al., 2005), and the application of new advances in research methods – latent growth curve modeling (LGCM) and hierarchical linear modeling – to analyze performance trends (Deadrick et al., 1997; Hofmann et al., 1992, 1993; Ployhart & Hakel, 1998; Sturman & Trevor, 2001). While research methodologies play an important role in any field, there are particular conditions in the study of job performance and time that make it crucial to discuss certain methodological issues and problems. These include research design, analytical techniques, and the sort of statistical problems that necessarily accompany research in this area.

Research Design

A critical issue for research on performance that must be addressed early in the research process is the development of a study's methodology. Most basically, the study must employ either a cross-sectional or longitudinal design. While calls for longitudinal research are the norm, it is often difficult to get extensive longitudinal data. What's more, studies involving time do not necessarily need longitudinal data to test their hypotheses. Although it may at first seem that any sort of hypothesis involving time must be studied with longitudinal data, one must first consider the nature of what is being studied to best determine the study design.

The nature of the research design dictates the sort of research question that can be tested. Cross-sectional research provides no opportunity for examining within-person changes (Hulin et al., 1990), whereas longitudinal studies provide the potential to consider both within-person and across-person effects. Below I will discuss issues related to both research designs.

Cross-Sectional Designs

Cross-sectional data are still useful when considering performance over time if one is interested in modeling across-person relationships. Essentially, if one is examining how the relationship between some predictor (X) and some rating of job performance (Y) changes with time, then cross-sectional data can yield useful hypothesis tests.

This design is useful for applications (explicitly or implicitly) of the changing tasks model. In such models, cross-sectional data can be used to consider if the relationship between X and Y changes by testing if time moderates the relationship between X and Y. Fortunately, time-related variables are frequently available in organizational research. Specifically, age, organizational tenure, and job experience are often available and used as control variables, but seldom are the complexities of the dynamic performance literature drawn upon to appropriately integrate such temporal variables in meaningful ways (Sturman, 2003). One way to consider potential dynamic effects is by looking for interactions associated with temporal variables. For example, if a given characteristic, say cognitive ability, is interacted with job experience, and this interaction is shown to be associated with job performance, a logical conclusion is that the effect of cognitive ability on job performance changes with time. Similarly, dividing employees into cohorts by experience (e.g., Farrell & McDaniel, 2001; Schmidt et al., 1986) allows one to consider longitudinal issues with cross-sectional data. For example, if the coefficients associated with an independent variable varies systematically across cohorts (like for cognitive ability as shown in Farrell & McDaniel, 2001), this evidence would support the conclusion that the effect of cognitive ability changes with the passage of time. Given we have prior reason to believe that cognitive ability is a stable characteristic, the presence of the type of significant effects described above would suggest support for the changing tasks model. In terms of the static and dynamic model reviewed earlier, the effect of cognitive ability (B) is contained within $B_{2(t)}$.

Certainly, cross-sectional analysis has its limitations when considering job performance over time. The disadvantage of this approach is that conclusions must be based on two critical assumptions. First, one must assume that the mean level of the characteristic does not vary with time. For the example above, cognitive ability should not be lower for individuals with less experience than for those with more experience. Unfortunately, in the study of job performance, it is likely that this assumption will be violated. One reason this may occur is because of the demonstrated relationship between job performance and turnover (Trevor, Gerhart, & Boudreau, 1997; Salamin & Hom, 2005; Williams & Livingstone, 1994). If the characteristics under investigation are associated with performance, and if performance is related to turnover, then the distribution of the characteristic will likely change over time. Because of the negative relationship between performance and turnover (Williams & Livingstone, 1994), those with low levels of the characteristic would be expected to leave the company over time, and a cross-sectional representation would have a wider range of the characteristic for newer employees and a restricted distribution of the characteristics for those with more tenure. If high performers are also leaving (Trevor et al., 1997; Salamin & Hom, 2005), this would further restrict the distribution. Methodologically, this creates heteroskedasticity. More generally, it limits any potential causal implications that can be made when interpreting the interaction or differences across cohorts. Of course, this assumption can be tested in any given sample, such as by examining the distribution of the characteristic at various experience levels (e.g., using a median split). If not statistically significantly different, one may have some confidence that this first assumption holds.

Even if the independent variable included in the model does not specifically cause turnover, a second reason that the mean levels of a predictor may change with time is that the distribution of an independent variable may become restricted because of selection processes. The Attraction-Selection-Attrition (ASA) model (Schneider, 1987) suggests that through the process of recruitment, selection, and turnover, individuals self-select and are selected in ways that increase the similarity of individuals within the organization. This filtering process may create the appearance of a relationship between these characteristics and performance. For example, even if a given characteristic, say a dimension of personality, is not related to performance, the simultaneous effects of learning for individuals who remain in the company in conjunction with the increase in homogeneity of individuals within the company over time could cause an interaction of the characteristic and time to appear significant. Again, this concern may be tested by examining the distribution of the characteristic in question for various levels of the temporal variable.

The second key assumption when using cross-sectional data to consider effects associated with time is that characteristics of the hiring process (or internal selection or turnover processes) remained stable over time. If this is not true, specification error may cause variables to appear to have an interaction with time. For example, if the hiring process has changed, resulting in employees with a different distribution of characteristics than those hired earlier, other correlated characteristics may falsely appear to be significant if the model is not appropriately specified. Researchers can try to minimize this risk by having well-developed theoretical models which identify the variables to be measured and by ruling out alternative explanations for their findings. Nonetheless, this is a concern that in all likelihood cannot be fully mitigated.

Despite these limitations, though, cross-sectional research can play an important role for considering dynamic phenomena. Any longitudinal model of job performance that can be used to make predictions about job performance over time should also have implications if a "snap-shot" of the employees is taken during any point of their development. Cross-sectional research, when using interactions with temporal variables or samples divided into cohorts by some temporal variable, can be of use when considering the implications of such models. While clearly not ideal for studying longitudinal phenomena and its limitations must be explicitly recognized, the information provided in cross-sectional research should not be dismissed or ignored. Furthermore, any study that examines job experience, job tenure, organizational tenure, or age is already implicitly involving the modeling of effects that are associated with time. Research on performance, even if intended to be static and using cross-sectional data, needs at least to recognize where the literature on dynamic performance may be relevant to their proposed models, and perhaps may even necessitate that variables of interest be interacted with temporal variables to provide at least some test of the stability of the beta-coefficient of interest.

Longitudinal Designs
For studying job performance over time, longitudinal designs have obvious benefits. With longitudinal data, one can look at both within-person and across-person differences. This allows the examination of how performance changes, how individual characteristics change, and how the effects of individual characteristics on performance change. With these benefits, though, come both practical and methodological problems.

The most practical problems are associated with data collection, but it is more than a convenience problem. Difficulties of longitudinal research in general are compounded by the specific needs of research on dynamic performance. First, the collection of data from multiple time periods already can be practically difficult, but for modeling within-person relationships this difficulty is compounded because more than two waves of data are highly preferable. As discussed earlier, we know job performance trends are non-linear, and that controlling for simply the last instance of job performance will yield an underspecified model. Given the evidence (so far) that job performance actually follows (at least) a cubic form (e.g., Hofmann et al., 1992, 1993; Keil & Cortina, 2001; Ployhart & Hakel, 1998), this means that a highly specified model requires data from at least four waves, and more would be preferable to test this assumption (although applications of Learning Curve Theory could provide a model with a different specification).

Second, dynamic performance research has frequently used sales as a measure of performance. This is convenient because the data is often available on a monthly basis, thereby making the data demands of dynamic performance research more easily satisfied; however, this is counter to most theoretical work on job performance that defines individual job performance as behaviors. Most typically, behavioral measures of job performance are based on ratings by a supervisor. Sometimes specific research tools are created for that purpose, but other times researchers rely on the supervisory ratings employed by an organization. With such ratings typically performed annually, the desired longitudinal study would require at least four years of data. The practical difficulties of soliciting this sort of data from an organization only increases the difficulty of performing the sort of research on job performance over time that the existing literature suggests is preferable.

Third, as has been discussed, research on dynamic performance has moved beyond the simple question of "is performance dynamic?" Research is needed into the functional form of performance trends, and more importantly, on the causes and consequences of these trends. Not only does this necessitate multiple years of supervisory evaluations, but other variables of interest must also be available. While companies may possess records of employee performance, the data required to advance the literature on performance over time make studies involving attitudinal data very difficult.

Fourth, longitudinal research designs require the use of methodologies that are more complex than most cross-sectional analyses. These issues will be discussed below, but may require complex treatments of error terms, methods more complex than OLS regression, methods for handling missing data, corrections for range restriction, and more.

The nature of any research involving time makes it highly desirable to use longitudinal data. Unfortunately, it is far easier to call for such research than it is to perform. So, while longitudinal designs are preferable for studying dynamic performance, they are no panacea.

Analytical Tools

The research needs of the dynamic performance literature combined with the practical difficulties of collecting and analyzing the requisite data presents a daunting research problem. Many of these negatives, though, are counterbalanced by new methodological developments that provide exciting opportunities for research in this area. New (or relatively new) techniques that allow modeling within-person relationships are providing valuable opportunities for analyzing the trends of individual scores over time and the correlates of these trends. Adding some confusion to this area is the fact that there are even more names to represent these techniques.

The techniques to which I am referring have been called covariance components models, hierarchical linear models, hierarchical models, latent curve analysis, latent growth models, mixed models, mixed linear models, multilevel models, multilevel linear models, random effects models, and random coefficient models (Raudenbush, 2001). In actuality, these many names essentially represent two approaches, which I will review below. Furthermore, although there are different approaches to estimate these models, fortunately there are common characteristics that make a general framework applicable to understanding the modeling of individual performance trends (Raudenbush, 2001).

For all these approaches, job performance over time is now typically thought of as a multilevel problem, with individuals' performance scores over time nested within individuals. Typically, the within-person scores are referred to as the first-level (i.e., Level-1), whereas individual-characteristics are at the second-level (i.e., Level-2). Conceivable, more levels are possible, including dyads, teams, departments, organizations, industries, and nations (cf., Ployhart, 2004); however, research on dynamic performance has yet to expand to such domains.

A simple Level-1 model capturing the linear effects of time would appear as follows:

$$\text{Job Performance}_{it} = B_{0i} + B_{1i} \times \text{time}_{it} + e_{it} \qquad (9)$$

A more complex model, capturing demonstrated cubic effects would be

$$\text{Job Performance}_{it} = B_{0i} + B_{1i} \times \text{time}_{it} + B_{2i} \times \text{time}_{it}^2 + B_{3i} \times \text{time}_{it}^3 + e_{it} \qquad (10)$$

Each beta coefficient is computed for each individual. If the betas are modeled with error, it is a random effects model; otherwise, it is a fixed effects model.

Time may be entered simply as the raw variable (e.g., months, years), or may be transformed. As one employs a higher order model, centering becomes a greater issue (Hofmann & Gavin, 1998). When using polynomials, and specifically wanting to isolate linear from quadratic from cubic effects, orthogonal polynomials for time can be used because such a process allows one to decompose the various time elements (linear, quadratic, and cubic) and avoid potential multicollinearity (Ployhart & Hakel, 1998; Willett & Sayer, 1994).

There are different ways to estimate this sort of multilevel model. A criticism of research employing these methods, though, is that software choice often influences, or even precedes the analytical strategy. One common approach is hierarchical linear modeling (HLM), often associated with the package "HLM" or "mixed models" from SAS Proc Mixed. The other most common approach, often referred to as a latent growth curve model, or LGCM, is performed using structural equations modeling software such as AMOS, EQS, or LISREL (Raudenbush, 2001). In actuality, both approaches are special cases of the General Linear Mixed Model (GLMM) (Rovine & Molenaar, 2001), although they have divergent structures and assumptions which make them different in application. I will briefly review the principles behind the GLMM, highlighting the difficulties with this approach and why the other approaches ultimately become more practical alternatives. I will then discuss both HLM and LGCM in turn, including their relative advantages and disadvantages.

The General Linear Mixed Model
The GLMM (Laird & Ware, 1982) is an expanded case of the general linear model. The model is as follows:

$$y_i = \beta X_i + Z_{i\gamma_i} + \varepsilon_i \qquad (11)$$

where y_i is a $1 \times n_i$ vector of outcomes (i.e., job performance) for individual i, X_i is a $b \times n_i$ matrix of fixed effects, Z_i is a $g \times n_i$ matrix for the random effects, γ_i is a $1 \times g$ vector of random effects, and β is a $1 \times b$ vector of fixed effects parameters. Residuals between any two individuals are assumed to be uncorrelated, but residuals within an individual have a particular covariance structure. The fixed effects component (β) are constant across individuals; the random effects component (Z_i) are different across individuals, hence the indexing subscript i. The random effects (γ_i) are assumed to be distributed independently across individuals, with the following distribution:

$$\gamma_i \sim N(0, \sigma^2 D) \qquad (12)$$

where D is an arbitrary "between subjects" covariance matrix (Rovine & Molenaar, 2001)

The within-subjects errors (ε_i) have the distribution

$$\varepsilon_i \sim N(0, \sigma_\varepsilon^2 W_i) \qquad (13)$$

Note that the general static model of job performance discussed earlier is actually a form of the GLMM. Examining Eq. (1), the stable coefficients

(B_1 and B_3) are both parameters within β from Eq. (11). Similarly, $B_{2(t)}$ and $B_{4(t)}$ are parameters within Z_i. The individual characteristics (both stable and dynamic) are individual observations, taken at each point in time, within X_i and γ_i. Thus, one can immediately see that there is a high degree of potential synergy between the analytical methods emerging from the GLMM and the study of job performance over time.

The problem with such a general model is that it is statistically impossible to estimate in its most general form (Laird & Ware, 1982; Rovine & Molenaar, 2001). Constraints must be placed on the model. HLM and structural equations approaches (i.e., LGCM) use different constraints, giving each advantages and disadvantages.

Hierarchical Linear Modeling
HLM is a methodological technique designed to analyze multilevel data, where data is nested hierarchically in groups. For the study of performance over time, this methodology has immediate relevance, as individual job performance ratings are gathered on a set of people, and the repeated measures contain information about each individual's performance trends (Hofmann, 1997; Raudenbush & Bryk, 2002). The approach recognizes that an individual's performance scores (i.e., the within-individual data) may be more similar to each other than data from other individuals, which is in contrast to an OLS approach where within-and across-individual residuals are not estimated separately (Hofmann, 1997).

As is typically employed, HLM approaches model employee performance by using two levels of analysis. The within-person analysis, labeled Level-1, is modeled as specified above in Eq. (9), or with greater complexity as in Eq. (10). In HLM, the second-level of analysis is used to model the parameters from the first level. The Level-2 model (for Eq. (9)) may appear as follows:

$$B_{0i} = \gamma_{00} + \gamma_{01}X_1 + \gamma_{02}X_2 + \ldots + U_{0i} \qquad (14)$$

$$B_{1i} = \gamma_{10} + \gamma_{11}X_1 + \gamma_{12}X_2 + \ldots + U_{1i} \qquad (15)$$

Here, each individual's intercept (B_{0i}) is modeled as a function of an overall average (γ_{00}), some covariates (X), and across-person error (U_{0i}). Simultaneously, the individual's performance slope (B_{1i}) is estimated by an intercept (γ_{10}), some covariates (not necessarily the same ones as in Eq. (14)), and error (U_{1i}). If estimating a two-level model, the effects of the Level-2 covariates are fixed effects (i.e., they are estimated without estimating an error term specifically for those coefficients). However, the model can be expanded to possess more levels, where each parameter is estimated as a function of higher-order characteristics (e.g., job characteristics if studying employees in multiple jobs, organizational characteristic is studying employees from multiple organizations, and so on). Applications of HLM, though, have rarely gone beyond the second-level of analysis, and popular software like the "HLM" package only allow up to three-level models.

The primary advantages for using an HLM approach for modeling individual performance trends are that it does not require equal observations per person, it does not require that the observations be spaced in the same way across subjects (Raudenbush, 2001; Raudenbush & Bryk, 2002), and there are well-articulated series of tests to determine the adequacy of using the full model (called the slopes-as-outcomes models, shown above as Eqs. (14) and (15)) (Deadrick et al., 1997; Hofmann, 1997; Raudenbush, 2001; Raudenbush & Bryk, 2002). The primary disadvantage of HLM is that it places a number of restrictions on how the data is modeled (Raudenbush, 2001). Specifically, the nature of the error structures is fixed, making it impossible to model alternative error structures such as autocorrelation. HLM approaches have nonetheless proven to be a useful means for helping understand the nature of job performance over time (e.g., Deadrick et al., 1997; Hofmann et al., 1993; Sturman & Trevor, 2001).

Latent Growth Curve Modeling

LGCM provides another means for modeling development, represented as different latent factors which capture the growth function. The LGCM approach involves testing the effect of latent constructs representing the growth parameters that define the shape of the performance function over time. At its simplest, the model includes an intercept and a linear construct. With sufficient information, the model can be expanded to include quadratic, cubic, or higher order functions if desired.

Like HLM, LGCM requires restrictions of the GLMM. Whereas HLM required restrictions with regard to how error and covariates are modeled, LGCM has restrictions on the structure of the data to be analyzed. When using a structural equations approach (SEM) to modeling, a key constraint is that the covariance matrices of within subjects errors must be the same for each individual (Raudenbush, 2001). Expressed mathematically (and referring back to Eq. (13)), $W_i = W$. Note that this is not a limitation of SEM software, but is an inherent characteristic to the method (Raudenbush, 2001). It is this constraint that most differentiates LGCM from HLM. That is, this assumption requires that when performing LGCM there are the same number of observations per individual. It also requires that all the observations be spaced at the same temporal intervals. If the number of observations or the spacing between observations differ, such models cannot be estimated with LGCM (Raudenbush, 2001). (Note, however, that I will discuss below missing data techniques that may ultimately allow LGCM to use unbalanced data.)

While the requirement of equal within-subjects error covariance matrices limits the nature of the type of data that can be analyzed with LGCM, the approach allows for far greater sophistication with regard to modeling the error structure. The relationship between the errors associated with the separate observations of job performance can be modeled in a variety of ways.

The simplest approach is to assume that the residuals are independent. The residuals would then have the following pattern:

$$\sigma^2 \begin{bmatrix} 1 & & & \\ 0 & 1 & & \\ 0 & 0 & 1 & \\ 0 & 0 & 0 & 1 \end{bmatrix}$$

Note that this is the error covariance structure assumed by HLM (i.e., the variance is computed from the sum squared residuals from Level-1 of the analysis). The problem with this pattern, and the advantage of LGCM, is that when modeling longitudinal data, the residuals may not be independent. A common approach to modeling longitudinal data is to assume that the residuals are correlated, such that $\varepsilon_{it} = \rho \times \varepsilon_{i(t-1)} + v_i$, where ρ is the autocorrelation coefficient and $v_i \sim N(0, \sigma^2)$. This is a first-order autoregressive model (AR[1]), yielding the following structure:

$$\sigma^2 \begin{bmatrix} 1 & & & \\ \rho & 1 & & \\ \rho^2 & \rho & 1 & \\ \rho^3 & \rho^2 & \rho & 1 \end{bmatrix}$$

An even more flexible option would be a general autoregressive pattern:

$$\begin{bmatrix} \sigma_1 & & & \\ \sigma_2 & \sigma_1 & & \\ \sigma_3 & \sigma_2 & \sigma_1 & \\ \sigma_4 & \sigma_3 & \sigma_2 & \sigma_1 \end{bmatrix}$$

The advantage of this approach is that it allows non-linear error variances, which may be most appropriate for modeling job performance over time.

The disadvantage is that such an approach requires the estimation of additional parameters, potentially decreasing the chance of being able to estimate the desired model. The flexibility of the LGCM approach is quite appealing, but at the cost of greater information demands which may not be feasible and the requirement of an equal data structure which may not reflect the realities of collecting job performance data.

Contrasting HLM and LGCM

As discussed earlier, HLM and LGCM are special cases of the GLMM. In many ways, the approaches are very similar. Looking at the HLM equations, the coefficients at Level-1 can be seen as latent variables: unobservable parameters that are approximated with error at Level-2 of the model (Raudenbush, 2001). For LGCM, these models are multilevel (or hierarchical) because they describe data that varies at two levels: within and across persons; they are random coefficients model because each within-person observation is modeled with error, and the latent growth variables (i.e., the Level-2 across-person parameters) are also modeled with error (Raudenbush, 2001). In fact, for certain instances, HLM and LGCM are equal. If the longitudinal data has the same number of observations per person, if all observations are spaced with the same temporal intervals, and if the individual-level residuals are assumed to be uncorrelated, then HLM and LGCM will yield the exact same parameter estimates.

Some have also suggested the utility of second-order latent growth models (Sayer & Cumsille, 2001). While the specifics of this analysis are best described in detail elsewhere (e.g., Duncan, Duncan, Strycker, Li, & Alpert, 1999; Sayer & Cumsille, 2001; Williams, Edwards, & Vandenberg, 2003), this approach allows one to distinguish between the variance attributable to potentially different factors (Sayer & Cumsille, 2001) like group membership (e.g., if different jobs cause different performance slopes). This approach is again similar to (or potentially equal to) an HLM model, but a three-level model where the first level represents within-person performance scores, the second level represents individual-level characteristics, and the third level captures representation within groups (e.g., jobs, and perhaps characteristics associated with specific jobs).

Power Issues for HLM and LCGM

A concern for all empirical research methods is that of power, and some research has begun to pay attention to power issues with regard to longitudinal modeling. One such work examining the power of LCGM to detect individual differences in change, as well as correlations among changes between two variable, showed its power to be quite low (Hertzog, Lindenberger, Ghisletta, & von Oertzen, 2006). Most salient for research on job performance over time, a simulation study revealed that power did not exceed .80 for a sample size of 200 until reliability was nearly perfect (e.g., >0.96) for designs of 6 or fewer occasions (Hertzog et al., 2006). While studies of performance results, like monthly sales over a multiyear period may appear well suited for LGCMs, realities of data collection may make them less appropriate when using annual ratings of job performance behaviors.

Power for HLM is somewhat harder to determine because of the likely potential of unbalanced data. If the data is balanced, then the power would be the same as in the equivalent LGCM, suggesting that HLM too suffers from the power concerns discussed by Hertzog et al. (2006). Other research also suggests that HLM has power concerns. Zhang and Willson (2006) showed that HLM needs large sample sizes to have adequate power – upwards of 35 observations at Level-1, a size unlikely to be reached in longitudinal studies of job performance. They also showed that HLM models are more sensitive to changes in the Level-2 coefficients than SEM approaches.

These empirical investigations into the power of HLM and LGCM give cause for some concern; however, research measuring performance trends has generally been quite successful in finding significant effects. In models of job performance trends using just an intercept and slope, significance has been found quite frequently (e.g., Deadrick et al., 1997; Stewart & Nandkeolyar, 2006; Sturman & Trevor, 2001). Hofmann et al. (1993) found significant effects for their hypothesized quadratic and cubic growth terms (although not linear). Therefore, power does not seem to be a major hindrance for modeling growth trends, although power for detecting moderators of these trends still remains in question. Applicants of LGCM are less common in management research (Williams et al., 2003), and particularly for modeling individual job performance over time. In one example, Ployhart and Hakel (1998) using LGCM found the linear, quadratic, and cubic effects that they hypothesized. Thus, while power is always a concern in empirical research and has the potential to be particularly limiting for studies of dynamic performance, it does not appear to have been a significant issue in applications of job performance trend modeling.

Choosing between HLM and LGCM
As specific applications of the GLMM, HLM and LGCM each have advantages and disadvantages. The choice of HLM and LGCM approaches depends on the nature of the data structure and the desired treatment of error terms (Raudenbush, 2001). In short, HLM allows for greater flexibility

with regard to the form of the data, but limited flexibility with regard to the error structure. In contrast, LGCM allows for more choices for modeling the error, but less flexibility in terms of the data's structure (Raudenbush, 2001).

If one has unbalanced data, the LCGM is simply not an option (unless missing data techniques can make the data balanced, but this will be discussed later). HLM provides the flexibility to model this sort of data structure and determine the nature of employee trends. On the other hand, if one is testing or otherwise cannot accept the assumptions regarding the error structure (or other factors that can be manipulated in the SEM-base LCGM method that cannot be changed in HLM), then the flexibility of LCGM makes it a more desirable option. Ideally, this choice should not simply be guided by the convenience of data availability, but be driven by a strong theoretical rationale or the need for specific hypothesis testing.

Methodological Issues

While characteristics of the data and the nature of the desired analyses must be considered to choose a research design and a technique for analyzing the subsequent job performance data, there are also methodological issues that are inevitable when studying dynamic performance. All of these issues will influence research on job performance over time in at least some way regardless of analytical choice. I will briefly review the types of issues and their likely consequences for research on this topic.

The Measurement of Job Performance

Research examining performance over time has generally examined either job performance ratings from supervisors or measures of performance results (Sturman et al., 2005). While research on job performance has acknowledged that the two measures are different (e.g., Bommer, Johnson, Rich, Podsakoff, & Mackenzie, 1995), the dynamic performance literature has rarely made this distinction.

Measurement error is a concern for both behavior- and results-based performance measures. While there is extensive history to understanding reliability of a given measure at a point in time (Nunnally & Bernstein, 1994) and the reliability (intra-rater and inter-rater) of job performance specifically (Bommer et al., 1995; Viswesvaran, Ones, & Schmidt, 1996), less attention has been paid to estimating the test–retest reliability of job performance ratings. Sturman et al. (2005) examined the consistency of job performance ratings (objective and subjective) by separating the variance due to (a lack of) test–retest reliability and performance (in)consistency. They supported their hypothesis that the test–retest reliability of subjective (behavioral) measures of job performance would be higher than the test–retest reliability of objective (results-based) measures. They argued that the greater unreliability of objective measures was due to environmental constraints beyond the control of employees (i.e., beyond the influence of their behaviors). This perspective is consistent with the findings of Stewart and Nandkeolyar (2006) who showed that a measure of environmental constraints affected employee performance trends. Specifically, they showed that the environmental factor of sales referrals explained 60% of variation in salesperson weekly performance.

These findings reveal that all measures of job performance are subject to error. "Objective" measures may be unaffected by a lack of intra- or inter-rater reliability, but they suffer from more test–retest unreliability than do "subjective" measures (Sturman et al., 2005). The result is that, regardless of the type of measure employed, measurement error is a methodological problem for all job performance research.

The findings from Sturman et al. (2005) highlight the importance of distinguishing between job performance$_{(behaviors)}$ and job performance$_{(results)}$. By measuring results instead of behaviors, such research is considering a related but fundamentally different phenomenon than the research on job performance generally considers to be the focal construct. Furthermore, as most jobs do not possess an "objective" measure of performance like jobs with sales data, it is not apparent if results based on objective measures explain the nature and trend of job performance$_{(behaviors)}$ in other contexts. The data availability of "objective" data may make them at first to appear preferable, but such measures do not directly speak to the construct of job performance$_{(behaviors)}$ that theory on job performance is looking to advance. While results-based measures may proxy job performance$_{(behaviors)}$, they capture (at least) the additional effects of environmental constraints and thus cannot contribute as well to theoretical development in this area.

I am not suggesting that research on job performance$_{(results)}$ has been for naught. Certainly, the results are useful for demonstrating how job performance$_{(behaviors)}$ and job performance$_{(results)}$ differ, illustrating how different methodologies can be used to study job performance over time, and providing a useful starting point for considering how we expect job performance$_{(behaviors)}$ to change with time. Studying job performance$_{(results)}$ also has advantages that it enables more within-person observations, and certainly job performance$_{(results)}$ is an outcome of interest to organizations. Nonetheless, to improve our understanding of job performance$_{(behaviors)}$

over time, the methodological conveniences of job performance$_{(results)}$ do not overcome the fundamental differences that exist between job performance$_{(behaviors)}$ and job performance$_{(results)}$. To advance our understanding of how the construct of job performance$_{(behaviors)}$ changes with time, dynamic performance research must place a greater emphasis on this criterion and forgo the conveniences associated with "objective" measures. Researchers will either need to deal with the difficulties associated with gathering subjective ratings of performance or accept and acknowledge the imprecision and unreliability of objective ratings of performance results.

Missing Data
In addition to measurement error, missing data is also a ubiquitous problem for research studying employee performance over time. While missing data issues are common for longitudinal research in general because of attrition in multiwave studies (Goodman & Blum, 1996; Newman, 2003), it is a particular problem in longitudinal studies of job performance because there are systematic relationships between job performance and attrition. First, extensive evidence reveals a relationship between job performance and voluntary turnover (e.g., Harrison et al., 1996; Sturman & Trevor, 2001; Trevor et al., 1997; Salamin & Hom, 2005; Williams & Livingstone, 1994). Second, companies use such mechanisms as probationary periods to fire low performers, creating a relationship between job performance and involuntary turnover (e.g., De Corte, 1994). Third, companies may promote high performers to other jobs, thereby creating another mechanism that can create a relationship between performance and the likelihood of missing data. The consequence of the systematic relationships between performance and attrition not only will cause data to be missing in longitudinal studies of job performance, but it will restrict the range in observed performance scores (Sturman & Trevor, 2001).

Research on missing data (e.g., Little & Rubin, 2002) has identified three types of missing data: missing completely at random (MCAR), missing at random (MAR), and not missing at random (NMAR). For data to be MCAR, it must both be "observed at random" (OAR) and "missing at random" (MAR). That is, (1) the pattern of missing data must not depend on the values of data that are observed (i.e., it is OAR), and (2) the likelihood that data is missing must not depend on the values of the data that are missing (i.e., it is MAR). If these conditions are met, then missing data will not likely bias population mean estimates (Little & Rubin, 2002). For predicting job performance (P_t), data is classified as MAR if the probability of missingness of P_t (i.e., the probability of not being able to observe job performance) depends on X (a predictor of job performance) but not after controlling for X. If this condition is not met (i.e., the probability that data is missing at time t depends on job performance at time t), then data is NMAR.

Because of the relationship between performance and turnover, MCAR is obviously not likely. Furthermore, if one were to observe a longitudinal sample of job performance where data was not missing, one would also have to question the generalizability of that data. Undoubtedly, one must consider whether data is MAR or NMAR. For data to be MAR, then the likelihood of missing data on P_t must only depend on characteristics from the prior time period(s) (X variables and/or $P_{(t-1)}$). For data to be NMAR, the likelihood of missing data on P_t depends on P_t. In many ways, by this definition, it seems that longitudinal performance data will be MAR. First, if someone is fired because of low performance, then data on P_t is missing because of the value of P_{t-1}. Similarly, if a high performer at P_{t-1} feels unrewarded and seeks new employment (i.e., leaves the company and is unobserved for P_t), then again missing data is MAR. On the other hand, the nature of performance measurement may cause data to be NMAR. For example, an employee may be performing badly during a given year (year t), and because of being self-aware of this performance, feedback from others, or being discharged, may leave the organization. Because supervisory ratings of job performance are measured annually, the measure for performance at time t would not occur. Nonetheless, the data is missing in this situation specifically because of performance in time t. In such a case, data would be NMAR.

To date, no research has specifically considered the issue of missing data with respect to longitudinal studies of job performance. It is not clear if missing data should be treated MAR or MCAR. What is clear, however, is that most research on dynamic performance has not directly addressed issues relevant to missing data. Specifically, most studies give the issue very little consideration, instead simply use list-wise deletion to address the missing data problem. That is, previous studies examining employee performance levels over time have most frequently eliminated from the sample those employees who leave the job before the full length of data collection (e.g., Henry & Hulin, 1987; Ployhart & Hakel, 1998; Rambo et al., 1983, 1987; Rothe, 1978). When interested in only predicting data in the final wave of a study (e.g., predicting performance in wave six of a six-wave study), then list-wise deletion does perform as well as other missing data techniques (Newman, 2003). However, when interested in predictors and information in earlier waves of the study (such as in trying to estimate coefficients explaining performance trends), then list-wise deletion generally performs worse than all other missing data techniques (Newman, 2003).

In his study of missing data techniques for longitudinal research, Newman (2003) concluded that list-wise deletion should be avoided, and instead one should employ maximum likelihood or multiple imputation approaches. Both of these approaches were shown to work best when generating parameter estimates; the full information maximum likelihood (a form of maximum likelihood estimation) and multiple imputation methods worked best for estimating standard errors. Based on this research, if one is studying longitudinal performance data and needs to employ a missing data technique, it appears that full information maximum likelihood or multiple imputation should be used. To date, this has not occurred for research on dynamic performance.

If one wants to employ LGCM, then missing data is a major concern because the technique requires the same number of observations per subject. Fortunately, programs like LISREL, AMOS, Mplus, and SAS provide routines for implementing FIML (e.g., in LISREL, one adds the command "mi = ." to the data step). On the other hand, one can avoid the missing data issue by using HLM, which does not require balanced data (although at least two points of data are needed to model a linear effect, three to model a quadratic effect, and so on, so missing data may still be an issue for analyses performed with HLM). This once again raises the debate as to whether one should use a LGCM or HLM approach. Currently, the issue cannot be resolved; each technique has advantages and disadvantages, and more methodological research is needed to specifically consider these sorts of issues for dynamic performance research. Given the importance of the contrast between HLM and LGCM approaches, research is needed on missing data techniques (or not using missing data techniques) for empirical work specifically on job performance over time. The field needs to know the consequences of choosing HLM over LGCM, and if job performance can be considered MAR or if it is NMAR.

In short, while advances in methodology present exciting opportunities for the analysis of longitudinal data, the nature of studying job performance over time creates specific problems that may influence the utility of these new techniques. Until the field has a better understanding of these specific issues, the interpretation of longitudinal results will always be open to some question.

THE FUTURE: NEW DIRECTIONS FOR DYNAMIC PERFORMANCE RESEARCH

The opportunities for future research to contribute to our understanding of job performance within the context of time are quite substantial. Yet, progress in this area will require both theoretical and methodological advances. Furthermore, it will be critical that the theoretical and methodological research have a reciprocal relationship, using findings in one area to guide the next steps of research in the other. In this section, I will identify a number of areas for future research and specific research questions that need to be addressed to better understand the dynamic performance phenomenon.

Further Specifying Longitudinal Models

The review of theory earlier in this article presented a number of different perspectives of dynamic performance: the changing-subjects and changing-tasks model; longitudinal extensions of static performance models; Ackerman's and Murphy's performance stage models; and Learning Curve Theory. These models, though, are surprisingly complementary, and taken together suggest that theory for modeling job performance over time is not as under developed as some have claimed.

The changing-subjects and changing-tasks models are more metaphorical than theoretical. They present two explanations as to why job performance changes with time, but otherwise do not provide the type of propositions requisite of a theory. However, when considering the longitudinal extension of static performance models, the changing-subjects and changing-tasks models facilitate the discussion of the types of effects that longitudinal models can detect, and they help present a structure for framing the discussion of any effects that are discovered.

The stage models provide clarification of the sort of variables that should affect performance change. Ackerman's and Murphy's works highlight that the effects associated with abilities should change with time. Previous research has already identified a number of factors that can be incorporated into these models (Steele-Johnson et al., 2000). Longitudinal applications of static performance models and approaches to modeling performance trends will reveal ways in which such effects should be observed and which additional variables should be considered. A stream of research, utilizing both cross-sectional and longitudinal designed, is therefore needed to answer this first set of research questions:

- What static variables have stable relationships with job performance?
- What static variables have changing relationships with job performance?
- What dynamic variables have stable relationships with job performance?
- What dynamic variables have changing relationships with job performance?

Searching for the predictors of performance and estimating the functional forms of their relationships with job performance require a variety of methodological approaches. Longitudinal analyses can examine within-person relationships to help answer the above questions. It is likely, though, that obtaining such data will be difficult, and any longitudinal analyses will suffer from methodological limitations (including missing data, multiple sources of error, and potentially low power). Therefore, I recommend that future research answering the questions above should be complemented with cross-sectional research. Research capturing a snap-shot of performance relationships will help identify the variables that relate to performance. Furthermore, any longitudinal model should include predictions as to what such a model implies for a point in time, and these hypotheses should be tested. Failure to support the point-in-time predictions from longitudinal models would falsify the model. Consequently, such tests are critical for theory development. Given the many difficulties associated with longitudinal studies of job performance, it would slow the potential progress of the field to ignore the value of appropriately designed cross-sectional research.

Further Refining Analytical Methods

Answering (at least to some degree) the questions above will clarify and specify the stage models of job performance. Nonetheless, confirmatory cross-sectional tests cannot conclusively prove any such longitudinal model, and longitudinal research is inevitably required to fully understand job performance within the context of time. The question remains as to how best to analyze these variables with a longitudinal design. HLM and LGCM are both potentially fruitful analytical techniques, but we still need guidance as to how these methods should be applied specifically to the issue of modeling job performance.

This is where Learning Theory can play an important role. A better understanding of the specific shape of the individual job performance learning curves will provide guidance into the structure of both LGCM and

HLM approaches for modeling performance trends. It is often espoused that theory should drive analytical models, and given the difficulty in justifying the form of highly parameterized polynomial models, it would be desirable to have a tested theoretical rationale upon which to base model design. In the operations literature, Learning Curve Theory has provided this sort of insight at an aggregated level of performance. The theory has the opportunity to provide similar guidance at the individual-level of analysis.

Learning Curve Theory should also be able to shed light on to the nature of how error terms are related over time. One of the key advantages of the LGCM approach is the flexibility of its form. This flexibility comes at the cost of additional parameters needing to be estimated (Rovine & Molenaar, 2001). Learning Curve Theory can shed light on more than just the nature of job performance trends, but also on the form of the model's error structure. By having a better understanding of the functional form of job performance over time, including of and between its coefficients and for its error terms, future research will be better able to employ the LGCM approach by fixing certain parameters based on appropriate theoretical estimates. This leads to a second set of research questions:

- How can Learning Curve Theory be applied to modeling job performance over time?
- How should longitudinal models of job performance represent performance curves (and what are the implications of failing to model these curves correctly)?
- What is the nature of the error structure for longitudinal models of job performance (and the implications of failing to consider this structure)?

Answering these questions will provide guidance to researchers as to how to design their models and allow research to move beyond questions of model structure (e.g., should performance be measured with a linear term, or up to cubic terms?) and instead focus on other practical and theoretical questions (e.g., what predicts or moderates the growth curves?).

Addressing Methodological Problems

Continuing the stream of research combining the performance and turnover literatures (e.g., Harrison et al., 1996; Sturman & Trevor, 2001) also seem to have useful theoretical and methodological implications. Turnover affects data attrition, which influences the existence of missing data. The need for balanced data is the most obvious difference between HLM and LGCM approaches, and although we have some insights about handling missing data in longitudinal studies, the nature of the missing data (MAR or NMAR) for longitudinal studies of job performance, the comparison of missing data techniques with LGCM versus HLM, and the implications of not employing missing data techniques with HLM, are unaddressed.

For the prediction of job performance over time, turnover is also a key outcome. One cannot really study performance over time without considering when performance no longer exists. While much of the discussion so far has focused on explaining or modeling existing data, understanding turnover and job performance is important for any sort of prediction problem. This leads to a third set of theoretical and methodological research questions:

- Is missing data in longitudinal studies of job performance MAR or NMAR?
- How should turnover and missing data be incorporated into models of job performance over time?
- What are the implications of the performance/turnover relationship for modeling job performance over time?

Refining Stage Models of Job Performance

Hopefully, progress can be made in understanding the structure of job performance over time and the processes involved in its modeling, but the field needs to understand the predictors and moderators of performance trends to better achieve the goal of understanding and affecting job performance over time. The Murphy and Ackerman models suggest that contextual factors can influence the nature of performance over time. In particular, both models mention job complexity, which other research has shown to be an important moderator of job performance predictors (e.g., Schmitt et al., 1984; Sturman, 2003; Sturman et al., 2005; Tubre & Collins, 2000). Unfortunately, the stage models are still relatively undeveloped in terms of their specific predictions. Addressing the research questions already articulated above will help identify the variables that should be included in revisions of the models. As more variables are included in these models, theoretical development of these models should follow so as to address how the newly specified variables relate to job performance over time.

It will also be important to clearly distinguish between the Ackerman and Murphy models, or perhaps further adapt them for the specific purpose of predicting job performance. A weakness of Ackerman's and Murphy's models is that they both have simplistic treatments of performance (task performance for Ackerman's model, and job performance in general for Murphy's model). Developments in the understanding of job performance have shown job performance to be multidimensional (Motowidlo et al., 1997; Rotundo & Sackett, 2002; Viswesvaran et al., 2005; Welbourne et al., 1998). When Murphy's paper was written, the literature on job performance had not yet made this distinction. In his work, Murphy defines his criterion, job performance, as "overall job performance", taking into account performance on specific tasks but also "variables such as success in maintaining good interpersonal relations, absenteeism and withdrawal behaviors, substance abuse, and other behaviors that increase hazards at the workplace" (p. 185). As such, his model's focus on overall job performance is comparable with Rotundo and Sackett's definition of overall job performance, and is similarly comprised on job task performance (e.g., "performance on specific tasks"), contextual performance (e.g., "maintaining good interpersonal relations" and "behaviors that contribute to...the achievement of goals associated with their jobs"), and counter-productive behaviors (e.g., "withdrawal behaviors, substance abuse, and other behaviors that increase hazards at the work place"). It is likely that there are different functional relationships for the predictors of the different dimensions of performance (Steele-Johnson et al., 2000). The current developments in understanding job performance as a multidimensional construct suggest that the stage models can be extended to consider the different dimensions of job performance. The need for future work developing and refining the performance stage models leads to this fourth set of research questions:

• How can the differences between the Ackerman and Murphy's models be resolved to yield a single dynamic model of job performance?
• How can such a resultant stage model of job performance be modified and updated to better understand job performance over time?
• How should models of job performance over time be adapted to incorporate the different dimensions of job performance?

Determining the Effects of Human Resource Interventions on Job Performance Over Time

So far, the research questions I have identified are aimed at improving the understanding and prediction of job performance; yet this knowledge has limited direct applied value. The desire to affect performance curves highlights the need to understand job performance and time when considering any sort of human resource intervention. While certainly prediction is valuable for selection decisions, the purpose of many human resource interventions is to affect employee performance. Research on job performance over time has the potential to benefit many varied fields of human resources.

It should be recalled that much of the early work on dynamic performance stemmed from a concern about the prediction of job performance. In particular, researchers considered the implications of dynamic performance for the validity of various selection devices. While the question of whether performance is dynamic has been resolved, the implications of this dynamism are still unknown. Research is needed into the validity of selection devices for predicting both initial performance levels and performance curves. The nature of this predictability should also be evaluated to improve decision-making. When performance was assumed to be static, decision-making with selection devices was simple: higher scores were better. However, there are likely to be tradeoffs when considering selection devices in a longitudinal context. How does one compare the utility of a device with high initial predictability but poor predictability in terms of performance trends, with a device with poor initial predictability but high validity for predicting performance trends?

Beyond selection, other functional areas of human resources would benefit from considering job performance over time. The purpose of many human resource interventions is to improve employee performance. For example, pay-for-performance is supposed to affect motivation to yield better performance; training programs are supposed to affect motivation or abilities to elicit higher performance. All of these interventions implicitly involve the passage of time to achieve the desired results. Given what we know about performance trends, simply looking at before/after change scores is incomplete with regard to understanding job performance over time. Longitudinal designs are needed to control for current performance trends to determine if a human resource intervention truly has the intended effect. This leads to a fifth set of research questions that would behoove future research on job performance over time to address.

- What are the temporal validities of common selection devices (e.g., unstructured interview, structured interview, cognitive ability tests, personality tests, assessment centers, integrity tests)?
- How do compensation systems (e.g., pay policy, pay hierarchy, bonuses, raises, pay-for-performance linkages, group-based incentives) influence job performance trends?

- How does training (e.g., training types, training delivery methods, trainee characteristics, trainer characteristics) influence job performance trends?
- What other human resource interventions affect the modeling of employee performance trends?

Introducing the Need to Predict Employee Performance Vectors

It is now clear that job performance is dynamic, multidimensional, and constrained by turnover. For these reasons, I argue that the performance prediction problem needs to evolve beyond predicting a single performance score to the prediction of what I will label *job performance vectors*. While such a data structure is not novel from a statistical point of view, the information that such a metric contains presents a new approach to human resource research and human resource decision-making.

I define a job performance vector as a $C \times N \times 3$ matrix of information on a given employee (or applicant). This matrix includes C dimensions of performance (e.g., task performance, citizenship behaviors, counterproductive behavior), projected for N time periods (e.g., annual performance for up to 10 year). The predicted performance level is one piece of information contained in the matrix (the first component of the third dimension), the estimated accuracy of this estimate (e.g., standard error) is the second component of the third dimension, and the third component provides the estimated probability of the performance being observed (i.e., the probability that the individual remains employed by the organization). Each individual's matrix can contain information on both past performance and the predicted levels of performance and turnover likelihood.

All human resource decisions that involve predicting performance (e.g., who to hire, who to promote, who to reward, who to train) can be based on the information contained in this matrix. Similarly, human resource interventions can be evaluated based on the their predicted effects on data contained in these matrices (e.g., what are the expected effects of implementing a new selection system, a new pay plan, a new training program, a new feedback system?).

Estimating performance vectors will require the combination of theory, empirical research, individual-specific information, and company-specific information. Existing theory and empirical evidence helps establish expected patterns. For example, Learning Curve Theory or past evidence from research predicting performance trends can provide a baseline of expected values. That is, with no other information, instead of assuming all performance has an expected value of the mean (0 if expressed in standardized scores), expected performance levels should follow some sort of learning curve. General company information can provide further information, such as the probability of turnover for any given position.

As new information is acquired, the vectors can be updated and refined, either based on company-specific investigations or from existing research. For example, once performance has been observed, subsequent expected performance levels and turnover probabilities can be updated. Information on job candidates, used in conjunction with the results of validation studies or existing research, can also refine this information. As more information is collected, both within the company and from research advances, the quality of information contained in the matrix can be improved. The methods used to derive the necessary information will also advance as companies perform their own research (e.g., validation studies) and as new studies emerge with relevant findings.

The idea of building, refining, and using performance vectors in human resource practice is new, and would certainly require new advances in methodology and decision making to implement successfully. First, tools would need to be developed that can combine information from a company's human resource information system with varied and complex research findings. Second, methods for empirically reviewing existing research findings would need to be applicable to studying many variables simultaneously rather than a single relationship in isolation. Third, theory would need to provide specific information on functional forms rather than just general information on whether an effect is positive or not. Fourth, all of this information would need to be able to be combined to yield specific point estimates (of performance levels, the accuracy of these estimates, and the likelihood of turnover) for job applicants and incumbents. Finally, the methods used to derive these estimates would have to be capable of "learning" and updating these values as new data is acquired and new research findings emerge. In short, this is no small task.

It is my belief that this task of *performance vectoring* presents a new but valuable approach to the applied prediction problem, and a new way to build a connection between research and practice. Fundamentally, the task is that of predicting performance over time; yet, the requirements of the task reveal how all realms of human resource research related to the prediction of job performance need to be combined to provide any hope of being able to make this task feasible. With *performance vectoring* being just introduced, any research trying to contribute to this area must begin by attempting to address the following three fundamental research questions:

- How can performance vectors be modeled?
- How can performance vectors be used to make human resource decisions?
- How can performance vectors be used to evaluate human resource programs?

CONCLUSION

The study of dynamic performance has a long history, but understanding the nature of job performance over time has had only limited development. I argue, based on what I see as clear and convincing evidence, that the answer to the question "is performance dynamic?" has been resolved. The answer is a resounding "yes"; job performance does change over time. The field has thus moved beyond this simple question to trying to understand the nature of job performance over time and its implications for human resource practice. Theoretical models are available that provide general information as to why performance changes or what performance trends may look like, but there has been no clear direction as to what variables to study, what questions to ask, what methods to employ, how to employ those methods, and how to interpret their results. Although greatly limited by the general difficulty of getting sufficiently large longitudinal datasets, the limitations of various methodological designs can be well understood and less-than-ideal datasets (including cross-sectional ones) can utilize complementary methods to make significant progress along this research path.

An employment *relationship*, by its very nature, connotes events, reactions, behaviors, and perceptions that occur over time. From an organization's point of view, a primary (if not *the* primary) outcome of this relationship is the employee's job performance. As such, what happens to performance over time is central to the employment relationship, but it is frequently ignored and far from well-understood. If simply the study of *the* criterion (i.e., job performance) has been cited as one of the most neglected elements in the applied prediction problem (Dunnette, 1963; Campbell, 1990; Motowidlo et al., 1997), performance within the context of time has received even less attention and is even less-well understood. And yet, between the available empirical examples, models and theories of learning, and methodological advances, there is genuine opportunity for our understanding of job performance over time to make significant strides in the future. Will future research perform these needed steps to make these contributions? Ironically, time will tell.

REFERENCES

Ackerman, P. L. (1987). Individual differences in skill learning: An integration of psychometrics and information processing perspectives. *Psychological Bulletin, 102*, 3–27.

Ackerman, P. L. (1988). Determinants of individual differences during skill acquisition: Cognitive abilities and information processing. *Journal of Experimental Psychology: General, 177*, 288–318.

Ackerman, P. L. (1989). Within-task intercorrelations of skilled performance: Implications for predicting individual differences? *Journal of Applied Psychology, 74*, 360–364.

Ackerman, P. L. (1992). Predicting individual differences in complex skill acquisition: Dynamics of ability determinants. *Journal of Applied Psychology, 77*, 598–614.

Adams, J. A. (1957). The relationship between certain measures of ability and the acquisition of a psychomotor response. *Journal of General Psychology, 56*, 121–134.

Adler, P. S., & Clark, K. B. (1991). Behind the learning curve: A sketch of the learning process. *Management Science, 37*, 267–281.

Alvares, K. M., & Hulin, C. L. (1972). Two explanations of temporal changes in ability-skill relationships: A literature review and theoretical analysis. *Human Factors, 14*, 295–308.

Alvares, K. M., & Hulin, C. L. (1973). An experimental evaluation of a temporal decay in the prediction of performance. *Organizational Behavior and Human Performance, 9*, 169–185.

Austin, J. T., Humphreys, L. G., & Hulin, C. L. (1989). Another view of dynamic criteria: A critical reanalysis of Barrett, Caldwell, and Alexander. *Personnel Psychology, 42*, 583–596.

Austin, J. T., & Villanova, P. (1992). The criterion problem: 1917–1992. *Journal of Applied Psychology, 77*, 836–874.

Barrett, G. V., & Alexander, R. A. (1989). Rejoinder to Austin, Humphreys, and Hulin: Critical reanalysis of Barrett, Caldwell, and Alexander. *Personnel Psychology, 42*, 597–612.

Barrett, G. V., Alexander, R. A., & Doverspike, D. (1992). The implications for personnel selection of apparent declines in predictive validities over time: A critique of Hulin, Henry, and Noon. *Personnel Psychology, 45*, 601–617.

Barrett, G. V., Caldwell, M. S., & Alexander, R. A. (1985). The concept of dynamic criteria: A critical reanalysis. *Personnel Psychology, 38*, 41–56.

Barrett, G. V., Caldwell, M. S., & Alexander, R. A. (1989). The predictive stability of ability requirements for task performance: A critical reanalysis. *Human Performance, 2*, 167–181.

Barrick, M. R., & Mount, M. K. (1991). The Big Five personality dimensions and job performance: A meta-analysis. *Personnel Psychology, 44*, 1–26.

Bass, B. M. (1962). Further evidence on the dynamic character of criteria. *Personnel Psychology, 15*, 93–97.

Bayley, N. (1949). Consistency and variability in the growth of intelligence from birth to eighteen years. *Journal of General Psychology, 75*, 165–196.

Bayley, N. (1955). On the growth of intelligence. *American Psychologist, 10*, 805–818.

Behling, O. (1998). Employee selection: Will intelligence and conscientiousness do the job? *Academy of Management Executive, 12*, 77–86.

Belkaoui, A. (1986). *The Learning Curve: A management accounting tool.* Westport, CT: Quarum Books.

Bemis, J. (1981). A model for examining cost implications of production rate. *Concepts: The Journal of Defense Systems Acquisition Management, 4,* 63–76.

Bommer, W. H., Johnson, J. L., Rich, G. A., Podsakoff, P. M., & Mackenzie, S. B. (1995). On the interchangeability of objective and subjective measures of employee performance: A meta-analysis. *Personnel Psychology, 48,* 587–605.

Borman, W. C. (1991). Job behavior, performance, and effectiveness. In: M. D. Dunnette & L.M. Hough (Eds), *Handbook of industrial and organizational psychology* (2nd ed., Vol. 2, pp. 271–326). Palo Alto, CA: Consulting Psychologists Press.

Boudreau, J. W. (1991). Utility analysis. In: M. D. Dunnette & L. M. Hough (Eds), *Handbook of industrial and organizational psychology* (Vol. 2). Palo Alto, CA: Consulting Psychologists Press.

Boudreau, J. W., & Berger, C. J. (1985). Decision-theoretic utility analysis applied to external employee movement. *Journal of Applied Psychology, 70,* 581–612.

Brogden, H. E., & Taylor, E. K. (1950). The dollar criterion: Applying the cost accounting concept to criterion construction. *Personnel Psychology, 3,* 133–167.

Campbell, J. P. (1990). Modeling the performance prediction problem in industrial and organizational psychology. In: M. D. Dunnette & L. M. Hough (Eds), *Handbook of industrial and organizational psychology* (Vol. 1). Palo Alto, CA: Consulting Psychologists Press.

Campbell, J. P., McCloy, R. A., Oppler, S. H., & Sager, C. E. (1993). A theory of performance. In: N. Schmitt & W. Borman (Eds), *Personnel selection in organizations* (pp. 35–70). San Francisco, CA: Jossey Bass.

Carlson, K. D., Connerley, M. L., & Mecham, R. L., III. (2002). Recruitment evaluation: The case for assessing the quality of applicants attracted. *Personnel Psychology, 55,* 461–490.

Carmines, E. G., & Zeller, R. A. (1979). *Reliability and validity assessment.* Newbury Park, CA: Sage.

Carr, G. W. (1946). Peacetime cost estimating requires new learning curves. *Aviation,* April, 76–77.

Chait, H. N., Carraher, S. M., & Buckley, M. R. (2000). Measuring service orientation with biodata. *Journal of Managerial Issues, 12,* 109–120.

Charles, D. C. (1953). Ability and accomplishment of persons earlier judged mentally deficient. *General Psychological Monographs, 47,* 3–71.

Costa, P. T., Jr., & McCrae, R. R. (1988). Personality in adulthood: A six-year longitudinal study of self-reports and spouse ratings on the NEO Personality Inventory. *Journal of Personality and Social Psychology, 54,* 853–863.

Costa, P. T., Jr., & McCrae, R. R. (1992). Four ways five factors are basic. *Personality and Individual Differences, 13,* 653–665.

Day, D. V., Sin, H., & Chen, T. T. (2004). Assessing the burdens of leadership: Effects of formal leadership roles on individual performance over time. *Personnel Psychology, 57,* 573–605.

Deadrick, D. L., Bennett, N., & Russell, C. J. (1997). Using hierarchical linear modeling to examine dynamic performance criteria over time. *Journal of Management, 23,* 745–757.

Deadrick, D. L., & Madigan, R. M. (1990). Dynamic criteria revisited: A longitudinal study of performance stability and predictive validity. *Personnel Psychology, 43,* 717–744.

De Corte, W. (1994). Utility analysis for the one-cohort selection-retention decision with a probationary period. *Journal of Applied Psychology, 79,* 402–411.

DeJong, J. R. (1957). The effects of increasing skill on cycle time and its consequences for time standards. *Ergonomics, 1*, 51–60.

Dennis, W. (1954). Predicting scientific productivity in later maturity from records of earlier decades. *Journal of Gerontology, 9*, 465–467.

Dennis, W. (1956). Age and productivity among scientists. *Science, 123*, 724–725.

Dudley, N. M., Orvis, K. A., Lebiecki, J. E., & Cortina, J. M. (2006). Meta-analytic investigation of conscientiousness in the prediction of job performance. Examining the intercorrelations and the incremental validity of narrow traits. *Journal of Applied Psychology, 91*, 40–57.

Duncan, T. E., Duncan, S. C., Strycker, L. A., Li, F., & Alpert, A. (1999). *An introduction to latent variable growth curve modeling: Concepts, issues, and applications.* Mahwah, NJ: Lawrence Erlbaum.

Dunham, R. (1974). Ability-skill relationships. An empirical explanation of change over time. *Organizational Behavior and Human Performance, 12*, 372–382.

Dunnette, M. D. (1963). A note on the criterion. *Journal of Applied Psychology, 47*, 251–254.

Edwards, J. R. (1994). The study of congruence in organizational behavior research: Critique and a proposed alternative. *Organizational Behavior and Human Decision Processes, 58*, 51–100.

Edwards, J. R. (2001). Ten difference score myths. *Organizational Research Methods, 4*, 265–287.

Farrell, J. N., & McDaniel, M. A. (2001). The stability of validity coefficients over time: Ackerman's (1988) model and the general aptitude battery. *Journal of Applied Psychology, 86*, 60–79.

Fleishman, E. A. (1953). A factor analysis of intra-task performance on two psychomotor tests. *Psychometrika, 18*, 45–55.

Fleishman, E. A. (1960). Abilities at different stages of practice in rotary pursuit performance. *Journal of Experimental Psychology, 60*, 162–171.

Fleishman, E. A., & Hempel, W. E., Jr. (1954). Changes in factor structure of a complex psychomotor test as a function of practice. *Psychometrika, 19*, 239–252.

Fleishman, E. A., & Rich, S. (1963). Role of kinesthetic and spatial-visual abilities in perceptual-motor learning. *Journal of Experimental Psychology, 66*, 6–11.

Gatewood, R. D., & Feild, H. S. (2001). *Human resource selection* (5th ed.). New York: Harcourt.

Ghiselli, E. E. (1956). Dimensional problems of criteria. *Journal of Applied Psychology, 40*, 1–4.

Ghiselli, E. E., & Haire, M. (1960). The validation of selection tests in the light of the dynamic character of criteria. *Personnel Psychology, 13*, 225–231.

Goodman, J. S., & Blum, T. C. (1996). Assessing the non-random sampling effects of subject attrition in longitudinal research. *Journal of Management, 22*, 627–652.

Guibert, P. (1945). *Le Plan de Fabrication Aeronautique.* Paris: Dunod. (English translation "*Mathematical Studies of Aircraft Construction*") available through Central Air Documents Office, Wright-Patterson AFB, Dayton, OH.

Guttman, L. (1955). A generalized simplex for factor analysis. *Psychometrika, 20*, 173–192.

Hackman, J. R., & Oldham, G. R. (1976). Motivation through the design of work: Test of a theory. *Organizational Behavior and Human Performance, 16*, 250–279.

Hanges, P. J., Schneider, B., & Niles, K. (1990). Stability of performance: An interactionist perspective. *Journal of Applied Psychology, 75*, 658–667.

Harrison, D. A., Virick, M., & William, S. (1996). Working without a net: Time, performance, and turnover under maximally contingent rewards. *Journal of Applied Psychology, 81*, 331–345.

Heise, D. R. (1969). Separating reliability and stability in test–retest correlation. *American Sociological Review, 34*, 93–101.

Heneman, H. G., Heneman, R. L., & Judge, T. A. (1997). *Staffing organizations.* Chicago, IL: Irwin.

Henry, R. A., & Hulin, C. L. (1987). Stability of skilled performance across time: Some generalizations and limitations on utilities. *Journal of Applied Psychology, 72*, 457–462.

Henry, R. A., & Hulin, C. L. (1989). Changing validities: Ability-performance relations and utilities. *Journal of Applied Psychology, 74*, 365–367.

Hertzog, C., Lindenberger, U., Ghisletta, P., & von Oertzen, T. (2006). On the power of multivariate latent growth curve models to detect correlated change. *Psychological Methods, 11*, 244–252.

Hertzog, C., & Schaie, K. W. (1986). Stability and change in adult intelligence: 1. Analysis of longitudinal means and covariance structures. *Psychology and Aging, 1*, 159–171.

Hertzog, C., & Schaie, K. W. (1988). Stability and change in adult intelligence: 2. Simultaneous analysis of longitudinal means and covariance structures. *Psychology and Aging, 3*, 122–130.

Hirschmann, W. B. (1964). Profit from the learning curve. *Harvard Business Review*, January–February, 128.

Hofmann, D. A. (1997). An overview of the logic and rationale of hierarchical linear models. *Journal of Management, 23*, 723–744.

Hofmann, D. A., & Gavin, M. B. (1998). Centering decisions in hierarchical linear models: Implications for research in organizations. *Journal of Management, 24*, 623–641.

Hofmann, D. A., Jacobs, R., & Baratta, J. E. (1993). Dynamic criteria and the measurement of change. *Journal of Applied Psychology, 78*, 194–204.

Hofmann, D. A., Jacobs, R., & Gerras, S. J. (1992). Mapping individual performance over time. *Journal of Applied Psychology, 77*, 185–195.

Hulin, C. L., Henry, R. A., & Noon, S. L. (1990). Adding a dimension: Time as a factor in the generalizability of predictive relationships. *Psychological Bulletin, 107*, 328–340.

Humphreys, L. G. (1960). Investigations of the simplex. *Psychometrika, 25*, 313–323.

Hunter, J. E. (1986). Cognitive ability, cognitive aptitudes, job knowledge, and job performance. *Journal of Vocational Behavior, 29*, 340–362.

Hunter, J. E., & Hunter, R. F. (1984). Validity and utility of alternate predictors of job performance. *Psychological Bulletin, 96*, 72–98.

Hurtz, G. M., & Donovan, J. J. (2000). Personality and job-performance: The Big Five revisited. *Journal of Applied Psychology, 85*, 869–879.

Jensen, A. R. (1980). *Bias in mental testing.* New York: Free Press.

Jöreskog, K. G. (1970). Estimation and testing of simplex models. *British Journal of Mathematical and Statistical Psychology, 23*, 121–145.

Kanfer, R. (1991). Motivation theory and industrial and organizational psychology. In: M. D. Dunnette & L. M. Hough (Eds), *Handbook of industrial and organizational psychology* (Vol. 1, pp. 75–170). Palo Alto, CA: Consulting Psychologists Press.

Kanfer, R. (1992). Work motivation: New directions in theory and research. In: C. L. Cooper & I. T. Robertson (Eds), *International review of industrial and organizational psychology* (Vol. 7, pp. 1–53). Chichester, England: Wiley.

Kanfer, R., & Ackerman, P. L. (1989). Motivation and cognitive abilities: An integrative/aptitude-treatment interaction approach to skill acquisition. *Journal of Applied Psychology, 74*, 657–690.

Keil, C. T., & Cortina, J. M. (2001). Degradation of validity over time: A test and extension of Ackerman's model. *Psychological Bulletin, 127*, 673–697.

Kjerstad, C. L. (1919). Form of the learning curves for memory. *Psychological Monographs, 26*, 1–89.

Klein, K. J., & Kozlowski, S. W. (2000). From micro to meso: Critical steps in conceptualizing and conducting multilevel research. *Organizational Research Methods, 3*, 211–236.

Kozlowski, S. W. J., & Klein, K. J. (2000). A multilevel approach to theory and research in organizations: Contextual, temporal and emergent processes. In: K. J. Klein & S. W. J. Kozlowski (Eds), *Multilevel theory, research and methods in organizations: Foundations, extensions, and new directions* (pp. 3–90). San Francisco, CA: Jossey-Bass.

Kunst, E. J. (1941). Variations in work performance under normal industrial conditions. *Psychological Bulletin, 38*, 530.

Laird, N. M., & Ware, J. H. (1982). Random effects models for longitudinal data. *Biometrics, 38*, 963–974.

Lawler, E. E. (1986). *High involvement management*. San Francisco, CA: Jossey-Bass.

Lawrence, B. S. (1988). New wrinkles in the theory of age: Demography, norms, and performance ratings. *Academy of Management Journal, 31*, 309–337.

Levy, F. K. (1965). Adaptation in the production process. *Management Science, 11*, B136–B154.

Little, R. J. A., & Rubin, D. B. (2002). *Statistical analysis with missing data* (2nd ed.). Hoboken, NJ: Wiley.

MacKinney, A. C. (1967). The assessment of performance change: An inductive example. *Organizational Behavior and Human Performance, 2*, 56–72.

McDaniel, M. A., Schmidt, F. L., & Hunter, J. E. (1988). Job experience correlates of job performance. *Journal of Applied Psychology, 73*, 327–330.

McEvoy, G. M., & Beatty, R. W. (1989). Assessment centers and subordinate appraisals of managers: A seven-year examination of predictive validity. *Personnel Psychology, 42*, 37–52.

Milkovich, G. T., & Newman, J. M. (2005). *Compensation*. New York: McGraw Hill.

Motowidlo, S. J., Borman, W. C., & Schmitt, M. J. (1997). A theory of individual differences in task and contextual performance. *Human Performance, 10*, 71–83.

Murphy, K. R. (1989). Is the relationship between cognitive ability and job performance stable over time? *Human Performance, 2*, 183–200.

Murphy, K. R., & Schiarella, A. H. (1997). Implications of the multidimensional nature of job performance for the validity of selection tests: Multivariate framework for studying test validity. *Personnel Psychology, 50*, 823–854.

Muth, J. F. (1986). Search theory and the manufacturing progress function. *Management Science, 32*, 948–962.

Newman, D. A. (2003). Longitudinal modeling with randomly and systematically missing data: A simulation of ad hoc, maximum likelihood, and multiple imputation techniques. *Organizational Research Methods, 6*, 328–362.

Noe, R. A. (2005). *Employee training and development* (3rd ed.). New York: McGraw-Hill.

Nunnally, J. C., & Bernstein, I. H. (1994). *Psychometric theory* (3rd ed.). New York: McGraw Hill.

Owens, W. A. (1953). Age and mental abilities: A longitudinal study. *General Psychological Monographs, 48*, 3–54.

Pegels, C. C. (1969). On startup of learning curves: An expanded view. *AIIR Transactions, 1*(3), 216–222.

Ployhart, R. E. (2004). Organizational staffing: A multilevel review, synthesis, and model. *Research in Personnel and Human Resources Management, 23*, 121–176.

Ployhart, R. E., & Hakel, M. D. (1998). The substantive nature of performance variability: Predicting interindividual differences in intraindividual performance. *Personnel Psychology, 51*, 859–901.

Ployhart, R. E., Holtz, B. C., & Bliese, P. D. (2002). Longitudinal data analysis: Applications of random coefficient modeling to leadership research. *Leadership Quarterly, 13*, 455–486.

Ployhart, R. E., Schneider, B., & Schmidt, N. (2006). *Staffing organizations: Contemporary practice and theory* (3rd ed.). Mahwah, NJ: Lawrence Erlbaum.

Prien, E. P. (1966). Dynamic character of criteria: Organizational change. *Journal of Applied Psychology, 50*, 501–504.

Rambo, W. W., Chomiak, A. M., & Price, J. M. (1983). Consistency of performance under stable conditions of work. *Journal of Applied Psychology, 68*, 78–87.

Rambo, W. W., Chomiak, A. M., & Rountree, R. J. (1987). Temporal interval and the estimation of the reliability of work performance data. *Perceptual and Motor Skills, 64*, 791–798.

Raudenbush, S. W. (2001). Toward a coherent framework for comparing trajectories of individual change. In: L. M. Collins & A. G. Sayer (Eds), *New methods for the analysis of change* (pp. 35–64). Washington, DC: American Psychological Association.

Raudenbush, S. W., & Bryk, A. S. (2002). *Hierarchical linear models* (2nd ed.). Thousand Oaks, CA: Sage.

Ree, M. J., & Earles, J. A. (1992). Intelligence is the best predictor of job performance. *Current Directions in Psychological Science, 1*, 86–89.

Rhodes, S. R. (1983). Age-related differences in work attitudes and behavior: A review ad conceptual analysis. *Psychological Bulletin, 93*, 328–367.

Rothe, H. F. (1946). Output rates among butter wrappers: I. Work curves and their stability. *Journal of Applied Psychology, 30*, 199–211.

Rothe, H. F. (1947). Output rates among machine operators: Distributions and their reliability. *Journal of Applied Psychology, 31*, 484–489.

Rothe, H. F. (1978). Output rates among industrial employees. *Journal of Applied Psychology, 63*, 40–46.

Rothe, H. F., & Nye, C. T. (1958). Output rates among coil winders. *Journal of Applied Psychology, 42*, 182–186.

Rothe, H. F., & Nye, C. T. (1959). Output rates among machine operators: II. Consistency related to methods of pay. *Journal of Applied Psychology, 43*, 417–420.

Rothe, H. F., & Nye, C. T. (1961). Output rates among machine operators: III. A nonincentive situation in two levels of business activity. *Journal of Applied Psychology, 45*, 50–54.

Rotundo, M., & Sackett, P. R. (2002). The relative importance of task, citizenship, and counterproductive performance to global ratings of job performance: A policy-capturing approach. *Journal of Applied Psychology, 87*, 66–80.

Rovine, M. J., & Molenaar, P. C. M. (2001). A structural equations modeling approach to the general linear mixed model. In: L. M. Collins & A. G. Sayer (Eds), *New methods for the analysis of change* (pp. 67–96). Washington, DC: American Psychological Association.

Ryan, A. M., McFarland, L., Baron, H., & Page, R. (1999). An international look at selection practices: Nation and culture as explanations for variability in practice. *Personnel Psychology, 52*, 359–391.

Ryan, A. M., & Tippings, N. T. (2004). Attracting and selecting: What psychological research tells us. *Human Resource Management, 43*, 305–318.

Salgado, J. F. (1997). The five factor model of personality and job performance in the European community. *Journal of Applied Psychology, 82,* 30–43.

Salamin, A., & Hom, P. W. (2005). In search of the elusive U-shaped performance-turnover relationship: Are high performing Swiss bankers more liable to quit? *Journal of Applied Psychology, 90,* 1204–1216.

Salthouse, T. (1979). Adult age and speed accuracy trade-off. *Ergonomics, 22,* 811–821.

Sayer, A. G., & Cumsille, P. W. (2001). Second-order latent growth models. In: L. M. Collins & A. G. Sayer (Eds), *New methods for the analysis of change* (pp. 179–200). Washington, DC: American Psychological Association.

Schaie, K. W. (1994). The course of adult intellectual development. *American Psychologist, 49,* 304–313.

Schmidt, F. L., & Hunter, J. E. (1998). The validity and utility of selection methods in personnel psychology: Practical and theoretical implications of 85 years of research findings. *Psychological Bulletin, 124,* 262–274.

Schmidt, F. L., Hunter, J. E., & Outerbridge, A. (1986). The impact of job experience and ability on job knowledge work sample performance, and supervisory rating of performance. *Journal of Applied Psychology, 71,* 432–439.

Schmidt, F. L., & Kaplan, L. B. (1971). Compositive vs. multiple criteria: A review and resolution of the controversy. *Personnel Psychology, 24,* 419–434.

Schmitt, N., Gooding, R. Z., Noe, R. A., & Kirsch, M. (1984). Meta-analyses of validity studies published between 1964 and 1982 and the investigation of study characteristics. *Personnel Psychology, 37,* 407–422.

Schneider, B. (1987). The people make the place. *Personnel Psychology, 40,* 437–453.

Smith, C. (1981). Effect of production rate on weapon system cost. *Concepts: The Journal of Defense Systems Acquisitions Management, 4,* 77–83.

Smith, P. C. (1976). Behaviors, results, and organizational effectiveness: The problems of criteria. In: M. D. Dunnette (Ed.), *Handbook of industrial and organizational psychology* (1st ed.). Chicago, IL: Rand McNally.

Stanford Research Institute. (1949). *Relationships for determining the optimum expansibility of the elements of a Peacetime Aircraft Procurement Program.* Palo Alto, CA: Stanford Research Institute.

Steele-Johnson, D., Osburn, H. G., & Pieper, K. F. (2000). A review and extension of current models of dynamic criteria. *International Journal of Selection and Assessment, 8,* 110–136.

Sterns, H. L., & Doverspike, D. (1989). Aging and the training and learning process. In: I. L. Goldstein (Ed.), *Training and development in organizations* (pp. 299–332). San Francisco, CA: Jossey-Bass.

Stevens, M. J., & Campion, M. A. (1999). Staffing work teams: Development and validation of a selection test for teamwork settings. *Journal of Management, 25,* 207–228.

Stewart, G. L., & Nandkeolyar, A. K. (2006). Adaptation and intraindividual variation in sales outcomes: Exploring the interactive effects of personality and environmental opportunity. *Personnel Psychology, 59,* 307–332.

Sturman, M. C. (2000). Implications of utility analysis adjustments for estimates of human resource intervention value. *Journal of Management, 26,* 281–299.

Sturman, M. C. (2003). Searching for the inverted U-shaped relationship between time and performance: Meta-analyses of the experience/performance, tenure/performance, and age/performance relationships. *Journal of Management, 29,* 609–640.

Sturman, M. C., Cheramie, R. A., & Cashen, L. H. (2005). The impact of job complexity and performance measurement on the temporal consistency, stability, and test-retest reliability of employee job performance ratings. *Journal of Applied Psychology*, *90*, 269–283.

Sturman, M. C., & Trevor, C. O. (2001). The implications of linking the dynamic performance and employee turnover literatures. *Journal of Applied Psychology*, *86*, 684–696.

Sturman, M. C., Trevor, C. O., Boudreau, J. W., & Gerhart, B. (2003). Is it worth it to win the talent war? Evaluating the utility of performance-based pay. *Personnel Psychology*, *56*, 997–1035.

Teplitz, C. J. (1991). *The Learning Curve Deskbook: A reference guide to theory, calculations, and applications*. New York: Quorum Books.

Tett, R. P., Jackson, D. N., & Rothstein, M. (1991). Personality measures as predictors of job performance: A meta-analytic review. *Personnel Psychology*, *44*, 703–742.

Thoresen, C. J., Bradley, J. C., Bliese, P. D., & Thoresen, J. D. (2004). The Big-Five personality traits and individual job performance growth trajectories in maintenance and transitional stages. *Journal of Applied Psychology*, *89*, 835–863.

Thorndike, R. L. (1940). Constancy of the I.Q. *Psychological Bulletin*, *37*, 167–186.

Thurstone, L. L. (1919). The learning curve equation. *Psychological Monographs*, *26*, 1–51.

Trevor, C. O., Gerhart, B., & Boudreau, J. W. (1997). Voluntary turnover and job performance: Curvilinearity and the moderating influences of salary growth and promotions. *Journal of Applied Psychology*, *82*, 44–61.

Tubre, T. C., & Collins, J. M. (2000). Jackson and Schuler (1985) revisited: A meta-analysis of the relationships between role ambiguity, role conflict, and job performance. *Journal of Management*, *26*, 155–169.

Tziner, A., Ronen, S., & Hacohen, D. (1993). A four-year validation study of an assessment center in a financial corporation. *Journal of Organizational Behavior*, *14*, 225–237.

Viswesvaran, C., Ones, D. S., & Schmidt, F. L. (2005). Is there a general factor in ratings of job performance? A meta-analytic framework for disentangling substantive and error influences. *Journal of Applied Psychology*, *90*, 108–131.

Viswesvaran, C., Schmidt, F. L., & Ones, D. S. (1996). Comparative analysis of the reliability of job performance ratings. *Journal of Applied Psychology*, *81*, 557–574.

Waldman, D. A., & Avolio, B. J. (1993). Aging and work performance in perspective: Contextual and developmental considerations. In: K. M. Rowland & G. R. Ferris (Eds), *Research in Personnel and Human Resources Management* (Vol. 11, pp. 133–162). Greenwich, CT: JAI Press.

Welbourne, T. M., Johnson, D. E., & Erez, A. (1998). The role-based performance scale: Validity analysis of a theory-based measure. *Academy of Management Journal*, *41*, 540–555.

Willett, J. B., & Sayer, A. G. (1994). Using covariance structure analysis to detect correlates and predictors of individual change over time. *Psychological Bulletin*, *116*, 363–381.

Williams, L. J., Edwards, J. R., & Vandenberg, R. J. (2003). Recent advances in causal modeling methods for organizational and management research. *Journal of Management*, *29*, 903–936.

Williams, C. R., & Livingstone, L. P. (1994). Another look at the relationship between performance and voluntary turnover. *Academy of Management Journal*, *37*, 269–298.

Wright, P. M., & Boswell, W. R. (2002). Desegregating HRM: A review and synthesis of micro and macro human resource management research. *Journal of Management*, *28*, 247–276.

Wright, T. P. (1936). Factors affecting the cost of airplanes. *Journal of Aeronautical Science, 3*, 122–128.

Yelle, L. (1979). The learning curve: Historical review and comprehensive survey. *Decisions Sciences, 10*, 302–324.

Zhang, D., & Willson, V. L. (2006). Comparing empirical power of multilevel structural equation models and hierarchical linear models: Understanding cross-level interactions. *Structural Equation Modeling, 13*, 615–630.

COGNITIVE, AFFECTIVE, AND CULTURAL INFLUENCES ON STIGMATIZATION: IMPACT ON HUMAN RESOURCE MANAGEMENT PROCESSES AND PRACTICES

Eugene F. Stone-Romero and Dianna L. Stone

ABSTRACT

Individuals are often stigmatized by virtue of their status on various dimensions and as a consequence, they typically evoke negative cognitions, affect, and emotions among observers. In addition, they are often the targets of both access and treatment discrimination in organizations. Thus, we present a model of the cognitive, affective, and cultural influences on stigmatization in organizations, detail how stigmatization affects human resource management processes and practices, and consider strategies that can be used to reduce the problems faced by stigmatized individuals in organizations.

Research in Personnel and Human Resources Management, Volume 26, 111–161
Copyright © 2007 by Elsevier Ltd.
All rights of reproduction in any form reserved
ISSN: 0742-7301/doi:10.1016/S0742-7301(07)26003-7

INTRODUCTION

I am the Negro bearing slavery's scars.

I am the Red man driven from the land.

I am the immigrant clutching the hope I seek,

and finding only the same old stupid plan

of dog eat dog, and mighty crush the weak. (Hughes, 1994)

This poem by Langston Hughes reflects some of the hardships faced by stigmatized individuals in the U.S. and suggests that their hopes and dreams are often thwarted by the highly competitive nature of the U.S. culture. Although the poem focuses on members of selected ethnic groups in the U.S., individuals in this and other countries are also often discredited by virtue of their status on such dimensions as disability (Colella, 2001; Colella & Stone, 2005; Stone & Colella, 1996), sexual orientation (Ragins & Cornwell, 2001; Ragins, Cornwell, & Miller, 2003), unattractiveness (Dipboye, Fromkin, & Wiback, 1975; Heilman & Stopeck, 1985; Hosoda, Stone-Romero, & Coats, 2003; Katz, 2003), age (Cleveland & Landy, 1981, 1983; Shore & Goldberg, 2005), mental health (Goffman, 1963; Stone-Romero, 2005), personality (Stone-Romero, 2005), biological sex (e.g., Broverman, Vogel, Broverman, Clarkson, & Rosenkrantz, 1994; Cleveland, Vescio, & Barnes-Farrell, 2005; Schein & Mueller, 1992), and religious affiliation (Korman, 1989). Moreover, stigmatization is not unique to people in the U.S. The same phenomenon spans the social systems of many nations. In this regard a religious scholar argued that such systems have divided people into groups for over 2,000 years, "the clean and unclean, the pure and defiled, sacred and profane" (Smith, 1994, p. 74) and these distinctions have hampered the development of compassionate and peaceful societies.

Research shows that not only are stigmatized (Goffman, 1963) or marked (Jones et al., 1984) individuals devalued in the U.S., but they are often excluded from organizations, preventing them from both (a) achieving their full potential and (b) experiencing a number of desirable social and economic outcomes (Cox, 1993; Dipboye & Colella, 2005; Stone & Colella, 1996; Stone, Stone, & Dipboye, 1992; Stone-Romero & Stone, 2005). In addition, unfair discrimination against stigmatized individuals precludes organizations from realizing the many contributions that they can make to the achievement of organizational goals.

In view of the pervasiveness of stigmas and the problems faced by stigmatized individuals, social scientists have attempted to understand the stigmatization process. One seeming goal of their efforts has been to eliminate the invidious distinctions that divide people into groups, and thereby reduce the problems faced by marked individuals (Allport, 1954; Brewer & Miller, 1984; Heatherton, Kleck, Hebl, & Hull, 2003; Goffman, 1963; Jones et al., 1984; Miller & Brewer, 1984; Stockdale & Crosby, 2004; Tajfel, 1974).

Focus of Previous Organizational Research on Stigmas

Most of the theory and research on stigmas in organizations has focused on such cognitive issues as categorization, stereotyping, and expectation effects (e.g., Stone & Colella, 1996; Stone et al., 1992). Interestingly, however, relatively little *organizational* research on stigmas has considered its emotional or affective correlates (Colella & Stone, 2005; Stone & Colella, 1996). However, affective and emotional reactions to marked individuals have been the focus of a number of works in social psychology (e.g., Bodenhausen, 1993; Mackie & Hamilton, 1993; Mackie, Hamilton, Susskind, & Rosselli, 1996). The relative neglect of the same factors in organizational research is unfortunate because many seminal works (Goffman, 1963; Jones et al., 1984) argue that stigmas often evoke strong, negative affective and/or emotional responses in others. Not surprisingly, the same responses may have profound effects on human resource management (HRM) processes and practices.

In addition, very little organizational research has considered cultural influences on the stigmatization process. In this regard, it is noteworthy that even though researchers have argued that often there is considerable agreement *within* a culture[1] about what constitutes a stigma, most stigma theories do not explain their consensual nature across cultures (Crocker, Major, & Steele, 1998). What's more, although research shows that stigmas vary *across* cultures, extant models of stigmatization have not considered the reasons for these differences. Given that there is often considerable agreement *within* cultures about what constitutes a stigma, we believe that cultural factors (e.g., values, norms) have important influences on the stigmatization process. For example, cultural norms specify how observers should respond to individuals with particular stigmas (Jones et al., 1984).

It is also noteworthy that although there is considerable interest in stigmas in the social sciences (especially social psychology), relatively little research has explicitly considered stigmas in the related fields of organizational behavior, HRM, and industrial and organizational psychology (notable exceptions include Bell, McLaughlin, & Sequeiro, 2003; Brief et al., 2000; Colella, 2001; Ragins & Cornwell, 2001; Stone et al., 1992; Stone & Colella, 1996). This is an important concern because the number of individuals with stigmas in the U.S. (e.g., older workers, people with disabilities, members of racial and ethnic groups) is growing, and these individuals will likely face a host of unfair discrimination-related problems in organizations. In addition, because of the way that stigmatized individuals are viewed and treated, their talents and skills will probably be unutilized or underutilized by organizations.

Purposes of this Article

In view of the above and the relative paucity of research on the antecedents and consequences of stigmatization in organizations (SIO), the primary purposes of this article are to (a) present a model of SIO that considers cognitive, affective, and cultural influences on stigmatization and HRM processes and practices, (b) describe the types of unfair discrimination faced by stigmatized individuals in organizations, (c) discuss the implications of this model for overcoming the unfair treatment of stigmatized persons in organizations, and (d) suggest directions for future research on SIO.

A MODEL OF STIGMATIZATION IN ORGANIZATIONS

The SIO model shown in Fig. 1 serves as the organizing framework for the analysis that follows. It focuses on the antecedents and consequences of SIO. A major and unique contribution of this model is its *joint consideration* of the cultural, cognitive, and affective factors associated with stigmatization and their impact on HRM processes and practices. In the sections that follow, we describe elements in the model and specify relations among them. Note that each of the relations in the model is shown with a numbered arrow. In the sections that follow, we make reference to the same arrows.

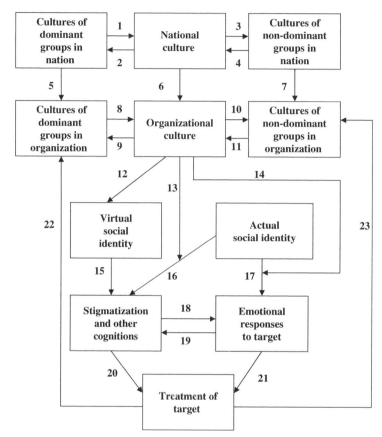

Fig. 1. A Model of Stigmatization in Organizations.

Human Resource Management Processes and Practices

A number of HRM processes and associated practices are central to the effectiveness of an organization's employees and, thus, to the effectiveness of the organization as a whole. Among these are human resource (HR) planning, recruiting and initially screening potential job applicants, selecting individuals for jobs, training and developing employees, managing the performance of workers, and dealing with layoffs, terminations, and retirement issues (Cascio & Aguinis, 2005; Gatewood & Field, 2001). As is explained below, the stigmatization of individuals (i.e., potential and actual job applicants, and job incumbents) can affect all of these processes and associated practices.

Multidisciplinary Perspective of the SIO Model

Our SIO model is based on theory and research in such disciplines as social psychology, anthropology, cross-cultural psychology, industrial and organizational psychology, HRM, organizational behavior, social psychiatry, and rehabilitation psychology. It extends extant models of stigmas in organizations (i.e., Stone et al., 1992; Stone & Colella, 1996) through the joint consideration of literature on such topics as stigmas (Goffman, 1963; Heatherton et al., 2003; Jones et al., 1984), social cognition (e.g., Brewer & Kramer, 1985; Macrae, Stangor, & Hewstone, 1996), culture (e.g., Triandis, 1994), social justice (Leventhal, 1976, 1980), and emotions and affect (e.g., Lazarus, Kanner, & Folkman, 1980; Mackie & Hamilton, 1993).

The description of our SIO model begins with a consideration of national culture and its effects on organizational culture. Following this we describe the concepts of stigmas and stigmatization. Then, we focus on factors that affect stigmatization. Next, we consider its consequences. Finally, we offer recommendations for practice and research.

Note that in the interest of brevity, most of the examples that are offered below have to do with stigma-related issues in U.S. organizations. This does not imply that stigmatization only occurs in such organizations. Quite to the contrary, some types of stigmas generate negative reactions across organizations in various nations. However, as explained below, several attributes of individuals have more stigmatizing consequences in some cultures than in others.

National Culture

In the paragraphs that follow, we assume that (a) in any given nation there are often one or dominant groups and one or more non-dominant groups, each of which has its own worldviews (including group-ideologies, values, norms, beliefs, and attitudes), (b) national culture is a reflection of the worldviews of both the dominant groups and the non-dominant groups, but (c) national culture is determined largely by the worldviews of the dominant groups. In the U.S., for example, national culture has been influenced greatly by the teachings of Christianity, especially Protestantism, and to a far lesser extent by the teachings of other religions (e.g., Buddhism, Islam, Judaism) or the beliefs of Native Americans (Deloria, 1994; Trice & Beyer, 1993). There are many signs of this, among them being (a) the phrase "In God We Trust" appears on U.S. dollar bills, (b) the saying "God Bless America" is commonly heard in the speeches of politicians, and (c) the ideologies of several Protestant sects (e.g., individualism, self-reliance, accumulation of wealth) have had a profound effect on the way that U.S. organizations are structured and managed (Stone-Romero & Stone, 1998; Trice & Beyer, 1993; Weber, 1958).

Cultural Homogeneity Issues
The homogeneity of the worldviews held by members of a society is a very important consideration, because in homogeneous cultures there is likely to be a relatively high degree of consensus on various cultural ideals. As a consequence, conflicts among dominant and non-dominant groups will be minimal. Moreover, individuals within the society will be unlikely to deviate from culture-based norms. In contrast, in non-homogeneous cultures there is likely to be ongoing conflict between the worldviews of the dominant and non-dominant groups (e.g., the present conflict between Islamic sects in Iraq). However, in order to promote the stability of system culture, members of dominant groups work toward the assimilation, margin-alization, or eradication of individuals in non-dominant groups (Berry, 1990, 1995; Kurzban & Leary, 2001; Stone-Romero, Stone, & Salas, 2003). The treatment of Native Americans by the Europeans who colonized the U.S. is a vivid illustration of this (Brown, 1970; Deloria, 1994).

In any social system (e.g., nation, organization), individuals may be representatives of a number of cultures or subcultures, each of which has its own worldviews. Thus, for instance, at a national level people in the U.S. subscribe much more strongly to the value of individualism than do people in such countries as Colombia, Venezuela, Peru, and China (Hofstede, 1980). However, this does not negate the fact that worldviews differ across various subcultures within any given nation. For example, within the U.S. the belief in individualism is stronger among (a) the economically advantaged than the disadvantaged, (b) Anglo-Americans than Native Americans, and (c) men than women (e.g., Triandis, 1994).

In spite of the existence of cultural heterogeneity within nations, there is strong evidence that the cultures of nations differ from one another in terms of a host of characteristics, including the extent to which there is support for such ideologies, values, and orientations as individualism, self-reliance, obedience to authority, masculinity, uncertainty avoidance, achievement, familism, power differences among individuals, and long-term perspectives in planning (Hofstede, 1980, 1991; Triandis, 1994; Trompenaars & Hampden-Turner, 1998). Thus, extant research provides a solid basis for arguing that there are important differences among national cultures in terms of these and other dimensions. However, it also shows that there are often non-trivial differences among the characteristics of subcultures within nations.

Even though any nation may have individuals who are representatives of various cultures or subcultures, the fact that there are national differences in cultures suggests that either (a) there is consensus among members of various cultures or subcultures about such matters as appropriate norms, values, and behaviors or (b) national cultures are determined largely by the views of people in dominant groups. For example, whereas the belief systems connected with Christianity and the Protestant ethic have had a major impact on U.S. culture, the belief systems associated with Islam have had a profound influence on the cultures of many middle Eastern nations (e.g., Iraq, Syria, Iran; Smith, 1994; Weber, 1958). In addition, the belief systems of Islam have had only a minor impact on U.S. culture, and the teachings of Christianity have had only a minor influence on the cultures of many Middle Eastern nations.

Ideologies and Cultures
There are often profound differences in the ideologies of nations and other social systems. *Ideologies* are sets of shared, interrelated beliefs about how things work, what is worth having or doing, and how people should behave (e.g., Trice & Beyer, 1993). Ideologies subsume *culture*, which can be defined as "a set of collective, shared, learned values which represent a broad tendency to prefer certain states of affairs over others" (Hofstede, 1980, p. 25). As noted above, there is clear evidence of national differences in values (e.g., Hofstede, 1980, 1991). Thus, the same evidence supports the view that ideologies differ across nations.

Effects of National Culture on Organizational Culture
Our SIO model posits that the culture of a nation influences the cultures of organizations within it (Arrow 2). This position is consistent with the views of Hofstede (1980, 1991) and others (Aycan et al., 2000; Erez & Earley, 1993; Trice & Beyer, 1993) who argue that national culture provides an ideological context for organizations, affecting such factors as (a) organizational values, (b) role expectations of job incumbents, and (c) standards used in judging the job performance of incumbents. For instance, as noted below, when the actual or stereotype-based attributes of

a job applicant or job incumbent are negatively discrepant from the normative standards of the organization the person will be stigmatized or discredited.

Consistent with the view that national culture influences organizational culture, results of research by Aycan et al. (2000) showed that dimensions of the cultures (e.g., paternalism, power distance) of employees in 10 nations were related to a number of variables descriptive of the internal work cultures of organizations (e.g., managerial assumptions concerning employee malleability, obligations toward others, and participation). In addition, the work culture variables were related to several HRM-related variables (e.g., job enrichment, empowering supervision).

Determinants of System Culture

Our SIO model posits that the culture of a social system (e.g., a society, an organization) is a function of the cultures of both the dominant groups (Arrow 1) and the non-dominant groups (Arrow 4). Note that in the interest of brevity, our discussion here deals with both societies and organizations. These groups derive their ideologies from their respective cultures. Note, however, the degree to which they influence system culture is a function of their relative levels of power (economic, political, military, etc.). Thus, for example, in most U.S. organizations, male, white Anglo-Saxon Protestants (MWASPs) have a considerably greater capacity to influence organizational cultures than do blacks, Latinos, Buddhists, American Indians, and females (Cox, 1993; Dipboye & Colella, 2005).

Conflict between Dominant and Non-Dominant Groups. In any given social system there is likely to be conflict between or among dominant and non-dominant groups (e.g., Tajfel, 1982a; Thomas & Chrobot-Mason, 2005). However, in most cases, the dominant groups will determine its outcome. Thus, for example, the culture of the U.S. has been influenced much more by the Europeans who colonized it than by the Native Americans who were indigenous to North America (Deloria, 1994).

Effects of Social System on the Culture of Dominant Groups[2]. Our SIO model postulates that the culture of a social system influences the cultures of its dominant groups (Arrow 2). Thus, to the degree that social system culture is an amalgam of the cultures of the dominant and non-dominant groups, the ideologies of the non-dominant groups will have some effect on the culture of the dominant groups (Arrows 2 and 4). As detailed below, one outcome of this in organizations is that views on the ideal characteristics of role incumbents may change over time. For instance, in contrast to the views that prevailed for many decades of the previous century, females are now regarded as suitable for service as pilots in the U.S. Air Force. Another outcome is that organizational policies may change to somewhat reflect the needs of members of non-dominant groups. For example, as greater numbers of females have entered the U.S. workforce, many organizations have shown an increased acceptance of HRM policies and practices that are "family-friendly" (e.g., flextime, maternity leaves).

Effects of Social System Culture on Non-Dominant Groups. As a result of not having as much power in social systems as members of dominant groups, members of non-dominant groups are typically placed in a position of having to either assimilate or be marginalized or eliminated (Berry, 1990, 1995; Brown, 1970; Deloria, 1994; Schneider, 1987; Stone-Romero et al., 2003). Not surprisingly, therefore, individuals in non-dominant groups often adopt some or all of the ideologies of the social system in which they are embedded (Arrows 1 and 3). Thus, for example, in order to be successful, business women often adopt the behaviors of their male counterparts. One dysfunctional consequence of this is that women who do so are disliked because they lack warmth (Fiske, Cuddy, Glick, & Xu, 2002) or are viewed as "bitches" (Heilman, 2001).

In work organizations, the just-noted arguments are buttressed by Schneider's (1987) ASA model-related prediction that individuals who enter organizations are typically subject to considerable assimilation pressures (see also Porter, Lawler, & Hackman, 1975; Stone-Romero et al., 2003). If they fail to assimilate, other organizational members work to promote their attrition.

Effects of Organizational Culture on Organizational Factors
Consistent with others (e.g., Hofstede, 1980, 1991; Katz & Kahn, 1978; Stone & Stone-Romero, 2004; Stone-Romero & Stone, 1998; Stone-Romero et al., 2003; Trice & Beyer, 1993), we argue that the cultures of organizations influence a number of organizational factors, including HRM processes and practices. Below we provide illustrations of this that relate to such processes and practices in U.S. organizations.

The Ideologies and Cultures of U.S. Organizations
A number of researchers have argued that U.S. organizations are dominated by Western European and Northern European ideologies and associated values (Cox, 1993; Stone & Stone-Romero, 2004; Stone-Romero & Stone,

1998; Stone-Romero et al., 2003; Trice & Beyer, 1993). This is an extremely important point because ideologies, serve a number of purposes, including providing views on (i.e., prototypes of) the nature of ideal job applicants and/or job incumbents. The same prototypes serve as the basis for the stigmatization of individuals whose characteristics are negatively discrepant from these ideals. We offer several examples of this below.

Rationality in Decision-Making and Other Processes. U.S. organizations often emphasize rationality and depersonalization in decision-making, including decisions about the hiring of workers (Cascio & Aguinis, 2005; Gatewood & Field, 2001; March & Simon, 1958; Trice & Beyer, 1993; Weber, 1958). As a result, they tend to have formal rules and procedures designed to (a) avoiding favoritism or partiality (e.g., considering personal needs of employees), and (b) separate the job or role from the job holder (Weber, 1958). For example, personnel selection decisions are often based on data derived from various types of standardized tests (e.g., cognitive ability, personality, work samples). Moreover, as a result of the norm to be rational, workers who appear to be "too emotional" are often viewed negatively in organizations. Thus, for instance, they are screened out during the selection process on the basis of their standing on measures of emotional stability (Stone-Romero, 2005).

Competitive Achievement. U.S. organizations tend to stress competitive achievement among workers and an intolerance of poor performance (Trice & Beyer, 1993). In addition, an emphasis is placed on hiring individuals with high levels of ability and motivation who will help the organization gain a competitive advantage in the marketplace. As a result, many individuals with race or ethnicity-related stigmas (e.g., blacks, Latinos, American Indians) are viewed as having lesser potential to meet role expectations than are most whites (Stone et al., 1992). As a result, many tests used in personnel selection result in considerable adverse impact against members of minority groups (Hough, Oswald, & Ployhart, 2001; Schmitt, Rogers, Chan, Sheppard, & Jennings, 1997).

Individualism and Self-Reliance. As a result of the value placed on individualism and self-reliance in the U.S. (Hofstede, 1980, 1991), workers are expected to be proactive and to do their work with little or no assistance from others (Stone-Romero & Stone, in press; Trice & Beyer, 1993). In this regard, Hsu (1961) argued that self-reliance is so highly valued in the U.S. that individuals who are viewed as bearing the stigma of not being self-reliant (e.g., individuals who are afforded affirmative action-based hiring preferences) are often viewed as "misfits" (Heilman & Haynes, 2005).

Equity. U.S. culture emphasizes the allocation of outcomes in organizations (e.g., pay, bonuses, promotions) on the basis of equity or proportionality. The norm is that people who make the greatest contributions should receive the greatest outcomes (e.g., Leventhal, 1976, 1980; Stone-Romero & Stone, 2005). Consistent with this norm, individuals who are viewed as contributing little (e.g., several ethnic minorities, women, the elderly) are thought to be less deserving of positively valent outcomes than individuals "who do their fair share." Regrettably, ingroup members generally establish performance standards and judge the degree to which individuals have met them (Leventhal, 1980; Stone-Romero & Stone, 2005).

Just World. Many people in the U.S. subscribe to the "just world" belief (Lerner, 1980). More specifically, they believe that good things happen to good people and bad things happen to bad people. In accordance with this view, suffering is typically viewed as a byproduct of an individual's own actions (Lerner, 1980). Thus, observers regard many stigmatized individuals (e.g., the disabled) as undeserving of the benefits accorded others in work organizations and other types of social systems (Colella & Stone, 2005; Stone & Colella, 1996).

Standardized Policies and Procedures. Consistent with beliefs in equity, and no doubt a consequence of the endorsement of bureaucracy theory-based views of organizations, a commonly held view in U.S. organizations is that individuals should be treated in accordance with standardized policies and procedures (Katz & Kahn, 1978; March & Simon, 1958; Stone & Stone-Romero, 2004; Weber, 1958). As a result, the norm is that people should not be afforded special treatment because it might give them an unwarranted competitive advantage over others (Colella, 2001; Colella & Stone, 2005; Stone & Colella, 1996). Consistent with this norm, individuals who are viewed as being parasitic (e.g., individuals with disabilities) are avoided or rejected by others (Kurzban & Leary, 2001).

Fitness. In the U.S., individuals who manifest such attributes as youth, attractiveness, physical fitness and endurance, heterosexuality, and mental health are more valued and have higher status than people who are viewed as being deficient in terms of the same attributes. In addition, the fit are viewed as more deserving of positive outcomes than the unfit (Kurzban &

Leary, 2001; Leventhal, 1976, 1980). Not surprisingly, therefore, a considerable stigma is associated with being unfit with respect to such criteria as physical abilities, personality, age, and attractiveness (Colella & Stone, 2005; Dipboye & Colella, 2005; Stone et al., 1992; Stone & Colella, 1996; Stone-Romero, 2005; Hosoda, Stone-Romero, & Coats, 2003).

Summary. In summary, the ideologies of cultures (including culture-specific values) influence views about the characteristics of ideal role incumbents in organizations. As a result, they affect both (a) the extent to which members of outgroups will be stigmatized in organizations, and (b) the treatment accorded them in organizations. And, as noted above, the same ideologies influence a number of HRM-related processes and practices.

Stigmas

In his seminal work on the management of spoiled identity, Goffman (1963) defined a *stigma* as a real or perceived deeply discrediting discrepancy between a person's virtual and actual social identities. A person's *virtual social identity* (VSI) represents what is expected of him or her in terms of such attributes as abilities, personality, physical appearance, values, attitudes, behavioral proclivities, and behaviors in a social system (e.g., an organization). It reflects what a person *should be* in a system, i.e., it represents the ideal. Thus, for example, in organizations, selection systems are designed to maximize the degree to which job applicants have attributes that are consistent with the given VSI. It typically varies as a function of the job for which an individual is recruited and selected. In addition, the VSI of an individual comes into play in such processes as performance management, worker compensation, and employee mentoring.

In contrast, to a VSI, an *actual social identity* (ASI) reflects the way the individual (i.e., target) is actually perceived (or is capable of being perceived) by an observer. As noted below, among the important consequences of an individual's ASI are the influences it has on observers' cognitions and emotions.

A person is said to be *stigmatized* (Goffman, 1963; Heatherton et al., 2003) or *marked* (Jones et al., 1984) when their ASI is negatively discrepant from their VSI. Stigmas or marks serve as the basis for targets (e.g., job applicants, job incumbents) being discredited by observers (e.g., organizational supervisors, peers, and subordinates).

Although there are many specific types of stigmas, Goffman (1963) viewed them as falling into one of three general categories, i.e., tribal stigmas (e.g., race, religion), abominations of the body (e.g., physical disabilities), and blemishes of character (e.g., mental illness). As is noted below, an observer's reactions to any given stigma are a function of such factors as its concealability, course, disruptiveness, aesthetic qualities, origin, and peril (Jones et al., 1984).

Motives for Stigmatizing Others
The literature on stigmas considers several motives (reasons, rationales, functions) for the stigmatization of targets by observers (e.g., Stephan, Ybarra, & Bachman, 1999) and the subsequent treatment of the targets by markers (i.e., those who stigmatize others) in social systems. In work organizations, the markers include recruiters, selection specialists, and members of an employee's role set (e.g., supervisors, peers, subordinates; Katz & Kahn, 1978).

It deserves noting that the literature on motives for stigmatizing others typically deals with issues that are not HRM-specific. However, it seems quite reasonable to assume that the same motives operate in work organizations. Thus, we believe that they are worthy of consideration here.

In the subsections that follow, we detail eight motives for stigmatizing targets. Note that even though they are described separately, in many instances the motives overlap. For instance, the political subordination of outgroup members often serves to enhance the esteem of ingroup members.

Enhancement of the Esteem of One's Own Group.   Social identity theory (e.g., Tajfel, 1974, 1978, 1981, 1982a, 1982b; Tajfel & Turner, 1979; Turner, 1982, 1987) and related perspectives (e.g., Crocker et al., 1998) posit that individuals stigmatize others in order to enhance the standing of their own group and, thereby, their self-esteem. For example, the esteem of ingroup members (e.g., MWASPs) can be enhanced to the extent that outgroup members (e.g., women, blacks, American Indians) are viewed as inferior and treated accordingly.

Limiting Ingroup Membership.   People strive to control membership in their ingroups. One mechanism for doing this is to exclude members of outgroups. This limits the number of individuals among whom valued resources must be divided, thus improving the welfare of those who have ingroup status. In work organizations, for example, women and racial minorities have often encountered the so called "glass ceiling." As a result, they seldom rise to top management positions (Broverman et al., 1994; Kanter, 1977; Schein & Mueller, 1992).

Dealing with Negative Interdependence. When groups are interdependent, it is possible for the actual or anticipated behavior of outgroup members to interfere with the attainment of goals of ingroup members (Thibaut & Kelley, 1959; Fiske & Ruscher, 1993). In such instances, the evoked threat will result in ingroup members experiencing negative affect and taking actions to reduce or eliminate the threat (Fiske & Ruscher, 1993). Thus, for example, in U.S. work organizations there has been considerable conflict between members of management (the ingroup) and unions (the outgroup). More generally, Schneider's (1987) ASA model suggests that ingroup members in organizations will take steps to promote the attrition of outgroup members.

Exploitation of Outgroup Members. In the interest of insuring the welfare of the ingroup, its members will strive to dominate (e.g., enslave, exploit) members of weaker outgroups (Kurzban & Leary, 2001). For example, in the southwestern part of the U.S., Mexican immigrants are often used as cheap sources of labor, who often perform dangerous or undesirable tasks. Moreover, in the U.S. there is a long history of the exploitation of Native Americans and blacks by whites (Deloria, 1994). These practices, no doubt, were a function of Europeans viewing "Africans as a low-status group that they safely domesticate and exploit because of their own superior technological power" (Fiske et al., 2002, p. 899).

Justification of Extant Structures. Stigmatization serves as a basis for the justification of extant of social, economic, or political structures, especially those that benefit ingroup members. For instance, such practices as slavery and the theft of land from indigenous people (e.g., American Indians) have often been justified by ingroup members viewing outgroup members (e.g., blacks, Asians) as subhuman or less worthy than ingroup members (Brown, 1970; Deloria, 1994; Fiske et al., 2002). In addition, stereotypes about women have diminished their opportunities in the world of work (Broverman et al., 1994; Kanter, 1977; Schein & Mueller, 1992).

Avoidance of Poor Social Exchange Partners. Stigmas are often a sign that a person will be a poor social exchange partner (Kurzban & Leary, 2001). This category includes people who (a) have unpredictable goals and behavior (e.g., the mentally ill), (b) possess low levels of intellectual, social, and economic capital (e.g., the poor, the infirm, the elderly), or (c) have a history of cheating others (e.g., criminals). Observers tend to distance themselves from such individuals and have negative emotional responses to them (e.g., Kurzban & Leary, 2001). In work organizations, selection systems screen out individuals who have such tendencies through the use of such procedures as integrity tests, personality tests (e.g., conscientiousness, emotional stability), and background checks.

Avoidance of Pathogens. As a result of adaptation, individuals are prone to avoid contact with people who are viewed as carriers of what are perceived to be communicable pathogens (Kurzban & Leary, 2001). For example, in the interest of insuring their own welfare, observers are likely to avoid contact with individuals who are thought to be carriers of such diseases as AIDS, leprosy, tuberculosis, syphilis, and cancer. The fact that some diseases are not actually communicable is often irrelevant to observers.

Avoidance of Threats to the Worldviews of Ingroup Members. Terror management theory posits that the anxiety of ingroup members is increased by contact with outgroup members who are viewed as having worldviews (including culture specific beliefs, values, and behavioral norms) that differ from those of the ingroup (Solomon, Greenberg, & Pyszczynski, 1991). The worldviews of the ingroup afford its members a sense of security and provide them with standards against which their behavior can be judged to be of value, assuring them some form of "immortality." As a result, threats to the same worldviews create anxiety because discrepant worldviews imply that those of the ingroup may be wrong, leading individuals to feel devalued and vulnerable, thus, decreasing their sense of worth (e.g., self-esteem), and heightening their sense of mortality. Therefore, in the interest of minimizing anxiety and other negative emotional states, ingroup members are likely to both denigrate and avoid contact with individuals who threaten their worldviews.

Note that the negative intergroup interdependence perspective of Fiske and Ruscher (1993) is highly consistent with terror management theory. In fact, Fiske and Ruscher (1993) argue that the *mere existence* of outgroup members who are perceived to differ from ingroup members on such dimensions as appearance, behavior, attitudes, and goals is sufficient to evoke threat among ingroup members. In addition, Schneider's (1987) ASA model is consistent with terror management theory.

It deserves adding that attitudes, beliefs, and behaviors that are regarded as very appropriate in one culture (i.e., worldview consistent) may be thought of as highly inappropriate in another. For example, Solomon et al. (1991) argue that in corporate America a highly competitive, rugged individualist is held in high regard. However, the same type of person would be ostracized in many Native American tribes and Asian nations. In addition, whereas it is becoming increasingly common for women to hold managerial positions in U.S. organizations, the norms of several nations (e.g., Afghanistan) dictate that women should neither be provided with a formal education nor allowed to work outside the home, especially in jobs in which they have power over males.

Representative Research Support.   In accordance with several of the above-noted points, research by Stephan et al. (1999) revealed that four psychological factors were related to the stigmatization of individuals (e.g., Mexicans, Cubans, Asians) who had immigrated to the U.S. More specifically, they were thought to (a) threaten the ingroup's power and well-being, (b) challenge the ingroup's worldview, (c) increase the anxiety resulting from contact with immigrants, and (d) elicit negative stereotypes of immigrants, providing a justification for their subordination.

Stigmatization
Stigmatization is the process through which an observer, operating in a specific context: (a) identifies a target's actual or inferred attributes (ASI), (b) compares these attributes with his or conception of the ideal individual (VSI), and (c) infers that there is a negative, discrediting discrepancy between the two identities. As noted below, stigmatization is based on both the observer's cognitions about the target and his or her emotional responses to the target. In addition, research shows that cognitions and emotions can affect one another. We consider this issue below.

At an intergroup level, stigmatization of outgroup members is a function of the ideologies (e.g., values, attitudes, preferences) of ingroup members. There is a *consensus* among ingroup members about the negative discrepancy between the VSIs and ASIs of outgroup members. As noted by Kurzban and Leary (2001, p. 199) "Not only do the members of a particular group mostly agree regarding who is and is not stigmatized, but they can typically articulate this shared belief." It merits adding that beliefs about stigmas are often a direct result of the socialization experiences of individuals in specific cultures (Kurzban & Leary, 2001). The reason for this is that socialization serves as the basis for VSIs.

Cultural Factors Affecting Stigmatization in Organizations
Our SIO model suggests that the cultures of both dominant and non-dominant groups influence the cultures of social systems. As noted above, the cultures of these groups influence the cultures of organizations (Arrows

8 and 11), affecting such properties of organizations as their norms, values, policies, and practices.[3] Through their effects on organizational culture, the cultures of the same groups influence views about the ideal role incumbent, i.e., VSI conceptions for role incumbents (Arrow 12). Thus, for example, in the U.S., the ideal manager is typically viewed as a young, attractive, tall, physically fit, heterosexual, male, white, Anglo-Saxon, Christian (e.g., Cox, 1993; Dipboye & Colella, 2005; Kanter, 1977; Korman, 1989; Stockdale & Crosby, 2004; Stone & Colella, 1996; Stone et al., 1992). Not only do organizational norms influence views about VSIs, but they also affect (a) the expectations that role senders develop about role incumbents and (b) the way in which role incumbents are treated by role senders (Katz & Kahn, 1978; Stone & Stone-Romero, 2004; Stone-Romero et al., 2003).

In the remainder of this article, we approach such issues as VSIs, stigmatization, and treatment of targets from the perspective of the observer being a member of a dominant group (e.g., a MWASP) and the target being a member of a non-dominant group (e.g., a minority group). One important reason for this is that members of dominant groups have the greatest capacity to influence views about VSIs and to control the outcomes that are allocated to such targets as job applicants and job incumbents (Stone-Romero & Stone, 2005).

Effects of Organizational Culture on Virtual Social Identity
Our SIO model specifies that organizational culture influences views about the VSIs of job applicants and/or incumbents (Arrow 12), including such factors as their race, ethnicity, gender, religion, expressed attitudes, scripts for performing role behaviors, and behavioral propensities (Cox, 1993; Katz & Kahn, 1978; Stockdale & Crosby, 2004; Stone & Stone-Romero, 2004; Stone-Romero et al., 2003). In this regard, literatures in such areas as interpersonal attraction (e.g., Byrne, 1971), social identity theory (e.g., Tajfel, 1974, 1978, 1981, 1982a, 1982b; Tajfel & Turner, 1979; Turner, 1982, 1987) and terror management theory (Solomon et al., 1991) all argue that individuals prefer dealing with similar others (i.e., those with similar worldviews). In addition, whereas people tend to have positive views about ingroup members, typically, their views about outgroup members are either less positive or negative (Tajfel, 1974, 1978, 1981, 1982a, 1982b; Tajfel & Turner, 1979; Turner, 1982, 1987). Thus, in organizations the prototypical incumbent for high status roles is generally one whose attributes mirror those of the dominant group (e.g., MWASP). However, outgroup members may be tolerated or even preferred for various low status roles (Kurzban & Leary, 2001). For example, the individuals who

colonized North and South America viewed blacks and the indigenous people of the Americas as quite appropriate for use as slave laborers (Deloria, 1994). And today, minority group members are over-represented in low status jobs.

Effects of Culture on Stereotypes and Other Cognitions
Our SIO model posits that culture (e.g., national, organizational) influences the cognitions that observers develop about targets (Arrow 13). That is, the impact of a target's ASI on the cognitive and emotional reactions of an observer will vary as a function of national and/or organizational culture. Stated somewhat differently, organizational culture moderates the relation between the ASI of targets and the observer's responses. The reason for this is that stereotypes about various groups are often culture-based (Triandis, 1994). Socialization experiences within cultures lead individuals to positively value certain attributes of individuals and devalue others. As a result, characteristics that are discrediting in one society may not always be viewed similarly in another (e.g., Al-Issa, 2003; Marin & Marin, 1991; Neutra, Levy, & Parker, 1977; Solomon et al., 1991). Examples of cultural differences in stereotypes and stigmas are offered below.

Cognitions about the Target
Views about the degree to which a target is stigmatized are only part of the set of cognitions that observers generate about a target. Research in social cognition (e.g., Mackie & Hamilton, 1993; Macrae et al., 1996) offers strong support for the view that observers categorize targets on the basis of information about a limited number of salient attributes (e.g., physical disability, race, appearance, age). A key reason for this is that categorization enables observers to simplify highly complex information about others (Allport, 1954; Mackie & Hamilton, 1993; Macrae et al., 1996). Thus, it may often play a role in various HRM processes and practices (e.g., recruitment, selection). For example, upon meeting potential job applicants, recruiters may categorize them on the basis of their race, age, and sex.

Stereotype-Based Inferences. Having categorized a target, the observer uses stereotypes about his or her category to infer the target's standing on such attributes as intelligence, task competence, interpersonal skills, emotional adjustment, and integrity. For example, research shows that African-Americans are often stereotyped as unintelligent, lazy, and lacking integrity (Dovidio, Gaertner, Niemann, & Snider, 2001), and people with disabilities are viewed as helpless, bitter, and incompetent (Stone & Colella, 1996). Not surprisingly, stereotype-based inferences can influence virtually all HRM processes (e.g., recruitment, selection, training, compensation, and mentoring).

Individuating Information. It deserves adding that cognitions about a target may not always be a sole function of stereotype-based inferences. *Individuating information* about the target may attenuate the impact of stereotypes on an observers' cognitions (e.g., Brewer, 1988; Fiske & Neuberg, 1990). Nevertheless, research shows that stereotypes typically play an important role in the inferences that observers generate about targets (Brewer & Miller, 1984; Macrae et al., 1996), especially when the observers (a) have little or no motivation or ability to attend to individuating information or (b) lack the cognitive resources needed to both attend to and process such information (e.g., Bodenhausen, 1993; Macrae et al., 1996). This can take place, for example, when recruiters are faced with the task of having to interview a large number of potential job applicants in a short time period.

Note, in addition, that the mere categorization of targets often serves to instigate cognitions and affective responses that are category-based and relatively automatic (e.g., Brewer & Miller, 1984; Dovidio & Gaertner, 1993; Fiske & Ruscher, 1993; Macrae et al., 1996). Moreover, the greater the observer's stereotypic beliefs, the greater his or her propensity to categorize targets (e.g., Zarate & Smith, 1990). Finally, because stereotypes are highly resistant to change, individuating information is unlikely to change stereotypes.

Expectations about the Target. Based on both stereotypes and affective responses to the target, the observer generates expectations about the behaviors that he or she is likely to exhibit (e.g., Rosenthal & Jacobson, 1968; Miller & Turnbull, 1986). Generally, these are based on beliefs about the typical member of the category to which the target has been assigned, and may be tied to views about his or her cognitive ability, interpersonal competence, motivation to work, and fit with the organization's culture. Thus, for example, prior to obtaining information about the actual work performance of an African-American job applicant, an interviewer may infer that he or she has neither the ability nor the motivation to exhibit acceptable job behavior.

Other Effects of Categorization. It deserves noting that one byproduct of categorization is viewing a target as either an ingroup or outgroup member. This leads to a number of important consequences, including viewing outgroup members (a) more negatively than ingroup members, (b) as more homogeneous than ingroup members, and (c) as different than the self and other ingroup members on various dimensions (e.g., Mackie & Hamilton, 1993; Macrae et al., 1996; Dovidio & Gaertner, 1993). Interestingly, however, negative cognitions about or feelings toward outgroup members do not always result in *self-reports* of beliefs or attitudes that are consistent with such cognitions or feelings. One reason for this is that egalitarian norms inhibit the public expression of attitudes or beliefs that suggest that an observer has biased or prejudicial views of others (e.g., Crosby, Bromley, & Saxe, 1980; Dovidio & Gaertner, 1993; Fiske & Ruscher, 1993).

Threat Evoked by the Target. Observers may use extant stereotypes as a basis for inferring the degree of threat that a target poses to the welfare of both the observer and the groups to which he or she belongs (Fiske & Ruscher, 1993; Lazarus, 1966, 1991; Lazarus & Folkman, 1984; Lazarus et al., 1980). For example, if a job applicant bears the mark of being "mentally ill," an interviewer (who also is responsible for making a hiring decision) may infer that he or she is unstable, overly emotional, and unpredictable, thus posing a threat to the welfare of both the interviewer and his or her organization. This mark may result from the applicant having a relatively low score on a measure of emotional stability, one of the dimensions of measures that are based on the Big Five conception of personality. Having knowledge of the same score, the observer then considers his or her ability to cope successfully with the threat posed by it (Lazarus, 1966, 1991; Lazarus & Folkman, 1984; Lazarus et al., 1980). For instance, the interviewer can cope with the threat by either (a) not hiring the applicant or (b) hiring the applicant, but assigning him or her to a job involving minimal contact with others, especially the interviewer. (Note that this cognitive appraisal perspective is explained below.)

Emotional Responses to the Target
A target's ASI serves as the basis for the observer's affective or emotional reactions (Arrows 17, and the path associated with Arrows 16 and 18), which are often tied to the target's social category (e.g., Bodenhausen & Macrae, 1996; Fiske et al., 2002; Kurzban & Leary, 2001; Heatherton et al., 2003). In order to avoid conceptual confusion, we next provide definitions of the overlapping concepts of affect and emotion.

Emotions. Cognition-arousal theory views emotions as the byproduct of physiological arousal and cognitions about its causes (Leventhal & Tomarken,

1986). In general agreement with this perspective, Stephan and Stephan (1993, p. 117) view emotions as "labeled changes in arousal that involve deviations from homeostatic activation levels." Note also that Vanman and Miller (1993, p. 214) view emotions as "differentiated states of positive and negative affect." There are a large number of emotions, including anger, disgust, fear, irritation, joy, fear, and sadness. However, regardless of the specific emotion, the extant literature supports the view that emotions are far more complex than affect.

Affect. Vanman and Miller (1993, p. 214) view affect "as an overall positive/negative subjective feeling." Similarly, Stephan and Stephan (1993, p. 117) note that affect "refers to feeling states that may range from strongly positive to strongly negative." In contrast to emotions, although affective states may influence cognitions, they are not typically the focus of a person's attention and do not interrupt ongoing streams of activity (Clark & Isen, 1982).

Conceptual Overlap. Even though the above-noted definitions seem to clearly differentiate between affect and emotions, the literature provides clear instances of the overlap of these concepts. For example, Bodenhausen (1993, p. 14) notes that intergroup situations often result in the evocation of integral affect, defined as "the emotion(s) elicited by social group itself and the usual conditions and contexts with which the group is associated." This definition blurs the distinction between affect and emotions. Thus, in order to avoid this problem, in the paragraphs that follow we use the terms (a) affect to refer to general positive versus negative feeling states, and (b) emotions to denote differentiated (labeled) affective states.

The Bases for Emotional Reactions to Stigmas. Stigmas often evoke both negative affective and emotional responses in others (Arrow 18), and some types of stigmas (e.g., abominations of the body, unsightly diseases) elicit more negative reactions than others (Goffman, 1963; Jones et al., 1984; Kurzban & Leary, 2001). In order to better explicate the bases for such reactions, we consider five general perspectives on emotions below. However, in advance of doing so, we note that there has been considerable controversy in psychology about whether emotional reactions to stimuli are automatic or are based upon cognitive appraisals of them (cf. Zajonc, 1980; Lazarus, 1966, 1991; Lazarus & Folkman, 1984; Lazarus et al., 1980). We recognize this controversy, but make no attempt to resolve it here.

(a) The biosocial perspective.

Some theorists have argued that many emotional reactions to stimuli (e.g., stigmatized individuals) are largely automatic or innate (Zajonc, 1980). As such, they require little or no cognitive mediation and are highly resistant to change. In support of the automatic perspective, experimental research by Vanman, Paul, Ito, and Miller (1997) showed that target race elicited emotional reactions that were not seemingly mediated by cognitions. In fact, whereas measures based on cognitions (e.g., self-reports of affect) showed that observers had more positive affective reactions to black as opposed to white targets, EMG-based measures showed the reverse pattern.

(b) The evolutionary perspective.

Kurzban and Leary (2001) argued that "from the standpoint of evolutionary psychology, emotions can be considered to be the differential activation of cognitive systems designed to guide the organism to adaptive behavior" (p. 200). That is, as a result of adaptive processes, observers are likely to exhibit specific emotional responses to targets with specific types of stigmas. First, the emotions of *anger, fear,* and *hate* are often evoked by stigmas (e.g., tribe, race, nationality) that have implications for the welfare of the observer and his or her ingroup members. For instance, *anger* stems from contact with targets who are viewed as having violated social norms or contracts (e.g., cheaters, drug addicts, pedophiles). In response to these emotions, the observer tries to punish the target. Emotional and behavioral responses to members of the Taliban or Al Qaeda provide clear illustrations of this.

Second, fear, hate, and anger result from contact with members of outgroups that are the considered fair game for exploitation (e.g., members of such minority groups as blacks, Mexicans, and American Indians). As a result of being outgroup members and evoking negative emotional reactions among observers, they frequently experience low levels of economic and social benefits (Kurzban & Leary, 2001).

Third, and finally, *disgust* is evoked by targets who are stigmatized by virtue of disease or disfigurement. This emotion is viewed as adaptive because it leads observers to avoid contact with targets who are viewed as carriers of pathogens (e.g., those associated with AIDS, leprosy, syphilis, smallpox).

(c) The cognitive appraisal perspective.

Lazarus and his colleagues (e.g., Lazarus, 1966, 1991; Lazarus & Folkman, 1984; Lazarus et al., 1980) contend that emotions are influenced by cognitive appraisals of stimuli in particular situations.

For example, Lazarus et al. (1980) argue that an observer's emotional reactions to a target are a function of primary and secondary appraisals. More specifically, *primary appraisal* concerns the question of "What are the implications of the stimulus (e.g., stigma) for my well-being?" For instance, a person may react more negatively to a person with leprosy than one who has rheumatoid arthritis because leprosy is contagious, whereas arthritis is not. *Secondary appraisal* has to do with the question of "Can I cope with the stimulus, and thus prevent harm to myself"? For instance, whereas an observer might cope with a person with AIDS by avoiding all interactions with him or her, coping with a target who suffers from disfiguring arthritis might involve avoiding eye contact with the person (Colella & Stone, 2005).

(d) The social structure model.

Fiske et al. (2002) proposed that emotions stem from stereotype-based information about outgroups. It affords as a basis for inferring a target's standing on the dimensions of warmth (e.g., nice, liked, tolerant, good natured, well-intentioned, sincere) and competence (e.g., confident, independent, competitive, intelligent, skillful). Their research revealed that members of groups were viewed as falling into four general categories: (a) *parasites* who had a low standing on both dimensions (e.g., the poor, welfare recipients, the homeless, poor blacks), (b) *successful competitors* who were low on warmth and high on competence (e.g., the rich, Jews, feminists, Asians), (c) *compliant subordinates* who were high on warmth and low on competence (e.g., housewives, individuals with mental retardation, people with disabilities, the elderly), and (d) *admired individuals* who were high on both dimensions (e.g., Christians, Whites, students, middle-class people).

The standing of an outgroup or its members on the just-noted dimensions is important because it provides cues as to the implications of the group's existence for the welfare of the observer and his or her ingroup. In addition, it affords a basis for inferring the types of emotions that will be elicited through contact with various types of outgroup members: First, outgroups that are thought to be warm, but not competent are not regarded as a threat because their low competence does not enable them to change the status quo. Thus, members of such groups are the targets of paternalistic prejudice, and the emotions evoked by them include pity, compassion, and sympathy (Colella & Stone, 2005). Second, outgroups that are regarded as low on warmth and high on competence are viewed as posing a considerable threat to the ingroup. Thus, they are the objects of envious prejudice, resulting in such emotions as envy and jealousy. Third, groups that are high in terms of both warmth and competence are admired and viewed as non-competitive. As a result, they evoke emotions of pride and admiration. Fourth, and finally, outgroups that are thought to be low on both warmth and competence are the targets of contemptuous prejudice. As a consequence, such outgroups arouse such emotions as contempt, disgust, anger, and resentment. Note that a set of four studies by Fiske et al. (2002) provided considerable support for their social structure-related predictions about the emotions elicited by members of various outgroups. Thus, the social structure framework is an appealing theory-based perspective on factors that influence emotional reactions to outgroup members.

(e) Negative interdependence perspective.

The above-described negative interdependence views of Fiske and Ruscher (1993) are generally consistent with the social structure perspective. Recall, they argued that negative emotions stem from the real or imagined threats that outgroup members pose to the welfare of ingroup members.

Convergence of Perspectives. A consideration of the just-noted perspectives on emotional reactions to stigmatized individuals reveals that they are generally quite compatible with one another. For example, both the evolutionary perspective and the social structure perspective suggest similar behavioral and emotional responses to "parasites." In addition, both the evolutionary and the cognitive appraisal perspectives indicate why negative emotions will be elicited by individuals who are viewed as carriers of pathogens. Moreover, the evolutionary and social structure views make similar predictions about the emotions evoked by outgroups that are low in both competence and warmth. More specifically, both suggest that they will be exploited by ingroup members and will arouse such emotions as disgust and contempt. These emotions make it easier for ingroup members (e.g., MWASPs) to dominate and exploit outgroup members (e.g., blacks, Mexican Americans, American Indians) in order to improve the welfare of the ingroup.

What the above suggests quite clearly is that the emotional reactions that are elicited by individuals (e.g., job applicants and job incumbents) can have a powerful effect on a number of HRM processes and practices. For example, to the degree that a white female manager feels threatened by a black male job applicant, he or she will not be likely to recommend that the applicant be hired.

Effect of Actual Social Identity on Emotional Reactions
Consistent with Arrow 17 in the SIO model, there is considerable evidence
that a target's ASI influences an observer's emotional reactions to him or
her (e.g., Fiske et al., 2002; Fiske & Ruscher, 1993; Goffman, 1963;
Heatherton et al., 2003; Jones et al., 1984; Kurzban & Leary, 2001;
Mackie & Hamilton, 1993). In addition, some marks (e.g., highly contagious
diseases) result in stigmatization in virtually in all cultures (Kurzban &
Leary, 2001). Interestingly, research reveals that even non-human animals
appear to stigmatize other creatures. More specifically, such animals (a)
create territories from which they exclude other animals, (b) form
hierarchies to dominate other animals, and (c) ostracize animals who have
diseases or pathogens. In addition, negative emotional reactions to various
types of stigmas have been found with both self-report measures and
physiological measures (e.g., Blascovich, Mendes, Hunter, Lickel, & Kowai-
Bell, 2001). This is very important because physiological measures
circumvent the possibility of observers' reports being distorted by
impression management and related motives.

As noted above, Goffman (1963) viewed stigmas as falling into one of
three general categories, i.e., abominations of the body, tribal, and
blemishes of character. However, the degree to which any given stigma
will evoke negative affective or emotional responses is a function of one or
more of the factors considered below (e.g., Jones et al., 1984).

Course or Stability.   Some stigmas remain constant over time (e.g., race)
and/or are relatively irreversible (e.g., amputations), whereas others change
(e.g., acne). Marks of the former variety typically lead to more negative
emotional reactions than those of the latter. In this regard, Weiner, Perry,
and Magnusson (1988) conducted two experiments to study the effects of
the stability (e.g., obesity vs. AIDS) and controllability of 10 stigmas on
reactions of pity, anger, and helping judgments. Results of Experiment 1
showed, for instance, that the greater the stability of the stigma, the lesser
the perceived efficacy of intervening to change it.

Disruptiveness.   Stigmas have differential capacities to disrupt social
interactions (e.g., communication) between a marked target and an
observer. For example, psychotic behavior is likely to be more disruptive
of interactions than is physical unattractiveness. In general, the greater the
disruptiveness of a mark, the more negative will be an observer's emotional
responses to it.

Aesthetic Qualities.   Appearance-related marks differ in terms of the degree to which they lead observers to regard a target as repulsive, ugly, or upsetting. As a result, some stigmas (e.g., severe physical deformities, severe facial scarring from burns) tend to evoke more negative emotional responses than do others (e.g., cleft palate, acne). For instance, Experiment 1 of Blascovich et al. (2001) showed that compared with a target without a facial birthmark, a target with such a mark evoked increased levels threat among subjects, as indexed by cardiovascular reactivity. In addition, the birthmark had effects on other measures (e.g., decreased performance on a word-finding task).

Origin or Controllability.   Stigmas differ in terms of the degree to which they can be attributed to the prior actions of the target (e.g., Dijker & Koomen, 2003; Dijker & Raeijmaekers, 1999; Jones et al., 1984; Weiner et al., 1988). For example, whereas race is considered not to be under the target's control, alcoholism and other forms of addiction are typically viewed as subject to his or her control. And research shows that the greater the degree to which a mark can be attributed to the actions of the target, the more negative the observer's emotional reactions to it. For example, research by Dijker and Raeijmaekers (1999) studied anticipated emotional responses (i.e., anxiety) to having simple contact with, giving a physical examination to, or giving an injection to hypothetical patients with diseases that varied in terms of being (a) non-serious (appendicitis, hepatitis) versus serious (kidney cancer, AIDS), and (b) non-contagious (appendicitis, kidney cancer) versus contagious (hepatitis, AIDS). The patients also varied in terms of sexual orientation (heterosexual vs. homosexual). Results showed, for example, that friendly feelings were lower toward homosexuals than heterosexuals with contagious diseases. One plausible explanation for this is that the homosexuals brought the diseases upon themselves.

   In three experiments, Dijker and Koomen (2003) studied the effects of personal responsibility for a stigma on emotional reactions to hypothetical interactions with stigmatized targets. Results of Experiment 1 revealed that as personal responsibility increased (a) pity and the desire to help the target decreased, and (b) anxiety and anger toward the target increased. In addition, Experiment 2 showed, for example, that (a) when a person was responsible for their illness, subjects had a tendency to avoid him and showed him less pity, and (b) as responsibility increased there were increases in both expected irritation in interacting with the target and the tendency to avoid the target. Finally, Experiment 3 showed, for instance, that as personal responsibility increased there were (a) increases in expected irritation, anger, and the tendency to avoid the target, and (b) decreases in pity, and the willingness to assist the target.

An experimental study by Rush (1998) examined subjects' affective reactions (e.g., likableness, pity, anger) to individuals with six types of stigmas, manipulating the controllability of each, for targets that varied in terms of race and sex. Among the findings were that reactions to individuals with non-controllable stigmas were more positive than reactions to people with controllable stigmas.

In addition, results of Experiment 1 of Weiner et al. (1988) showed, for example, that the less controllable the target's stigma (a) the greater the liking of the target and the willingness to assist the target, and (b) the lesser the anger toward the target. Their Experiment 2 produced highly similar results.

Peril. Some types of stigmas (e.g., leprosy, AIDS, psychopathic deviance) are likely to evoke greater levels of perceived threat among observers than others (e.g., baldness, paraplegia), and the greater the threat, the more negative will be the observer's emotional reactions. In support of this, Dijker and Raeijmaekers (1999) found that anxiety levels were greater for contact with patients who posed relatively high risk (i.e., injecting them) than for contact with those who posed low risk (i.e., examining them). In addition, contagiousness led to greater feelings of pity, powerlessness, and sadness. Moreover, Weiner et al. (1988) showed that compared with such non-threatening stigmas of a target as Alzheimer's disease, blindness, and cancer, the stigmas of AIDS and drug abuse resulted in (a) higher levels of blame and anger, and (b) lower degrees of liking, pity, and willingness to assist the target. Finally, Blascovich et al. (2001) found clear evidence of the effects of threatening stigmas on both physiologically and behaviorally indexed outcomes.

Seriousness. Emotional reactions to stigmas appear to vary with their seriousness. Dijker and Raeijmaekers (1999) found, for example, that in a simple contact condition, serious diseases evoked more anxiety among subjects than non-serious diseases. In addition, the greater the seriousness of the disease, the greater the levels of elicited pity, powerlessness, sadness, and the desire to provide help to a patient.

The study by Dijker and Koomen (2003) examined the effects of stigma seriousness on emotional reactions. Their Experiment 2 revealed, for example, that compared to a target with a non-serious illness, a target with a serious illness evoked greater levels of both (a) pity and (b) feelings of uneasiness and tension from interacting with the target.

Concealability.   Some marks (e.g., religious beliefs, aberrant sexual proclivities) are more concealable than others (e.g., obesity, disfigurement). In general, the greater the visibility of a mark, the more negative will be the observer's emotional reactions to it. The reason for this is obvious: to the degree that a stigma is hidden, it will not affect an observer's inferences about the ASI of a target.

Combined Factors.   Some types of stigmas have implications for multiple stigma dimensions. For example, prejudiced whites may view a black target as both unattractive and dangerous, even though his or her race is uncontrollable. Thus, research on multiple stigmas has implications for the effects of various dimensions on observers' affective or emotional reactions. In this regard, the results of a study by Vanman et al. (1997) are worthy of note. They examined emotional reactions to stigmas using both self-reports of affect and physiological measures (e.g., derived from a facial EMG). Results showed that whereas whites reacted more positively to blacks than whites on *self-report* measures, the EMG measures showed the *opposite* pattern. This is an extremely important finding because it casts doubt on the validity of self-reports of affect in obtrusive research on various types of stigmas (see also Crosby et al., 1980; Stone et al., 1992).

Changes in Emotional Reactions Induced by Increased Contact.   Interestingly, emotional reactions to some types of stigmas change as a function of increased levels of contact with a stigmatized target. For example, Blascovich et al. (2001) showed that whereas contact with a black (stigmatized) versus white (non-stigmatized) target led to a number of physiological and behavioral responses indicative of threat, increased contact tended to attenuate such responses. As noted below, this has implications for interventions aimed at reducing negative responses to stigmatized people (e.g., Fiske & Ruscher, 1993).

Moderating Effect of System Culture on Relation between Actual Social Identity and Cognitive Responses

The SIO model posits that system culture moderates the relation between a target's ASI and cognitive reactions to him or her (Arrow 13). In this regard, research supports the position that the cultural background of an observer moderates the relation between stereotypes of group members and the inferences made about them. For example, if the observer is a product of a collective culture, he or she is more likely to infer that a target's behavior results from situational factors than dispositional factors (Triandis, 1994). This prediction is consistent with the operation of a correspondence bias (Hamilton & Sherman, 1994) in individualistic cultures (Mackie et al., 1996). The same prediction has important implications for HRM processes and practices. For example, consider the attributions that are likely when people in the U.S. are presented with evidence that African-Americans are found largely in low-level jobs. Whereas people with individualistic views would be likely to infer that this resulted from a lack of motivation on the part of African-Americans, people with collective views (e.g., Colombians) would be prone to attribute the same evidence to such situational factors as unequal educational opportunities, biased hiring practices, and biases in job assignments.

Representative Research on Cognitive Reactions. Below we consider research on cross-cultural differences in stereotypes about several potentially stigmatizing attributes of individuals. In the interest of brevity we focus on a limited set of studies.

(a) Race.

Although race (i.e., being non-white) often serves as the basis for the stigmatization of targets in various nations, research shows evidence of cross-cultural differences in reactions to it. For example, in the U.S. stereotypes of blacks tend to be quite negative: relative to whites, they are viewed as being (a) less intelligent and achievement oriented, and (b) more lazy and aggressive (Stone-Romero, Stone, & Hartman, 2002). Even among African-Americans in the U.S., blacks with light skin are viewed more positively than those with dark skin. Interestingly, however, dark skin color does not always evoke equally negative stereotypes in other cultures. For example, skin color is not as stigmatizing in most Latin American and Caribbean nations (e.g., Cuba, Puerto Rico, Brazil) as it is in the U.S. (Marin & Marin, 1991). One reason for this is that people in Latin American and Caribbean nations often have mixed racial heritage, typically descending from three "racial" groups (i.e., Caucasian, black, and American Indian). In fact, in many Latin American countries (e.g., Peru, Ecuador, Mexico, Brazil) the vast majority of individuals are of mixed race or mestizo (i.e., having Caucasian and Indian ancestry).

(b) Age.

In the U.S. and many other Western nations, youth is a highly valued attribute, and compared with younger people, older individuals are viewed as being less competent, less able to compete in society, and less likely to adapt to environmental changes (e.g., Goldberg & Shore, 2003; Shore & Goldberg, 2005). In addition, consistent with these stereotype-based views, research shows that older workers in the U.S. typically receive lower job suitability ratings than younger workers (Cleveland & Landy, 1981, 1983). Interestingly, however, age is not a basis for stigmatization in many other cultures. One reason for this is that many Western religions emphasize that life is brief and finite, and this view leads individuals to fear the end of life and to view signs of age negatively. In contrast, many Eastern and Native American cultures view life as a cyclical, ongoing process that involves birth, death, and rebirth (Smith, 1994). As a result, people in many Asian and Native American cultures are taught to revere and respect their elders, regarding them as having great wisdom that can benefit their progeny.

(c) Illness.

Research reveals that there are cross-cultural differences in reactions to individuals with several types of illnesses (e.g., DeAngelo, 2000; Neutra et al., 1977; Saetermoe, Scattone, & Kim, 2001). For example, in the U.S. people with epilepsy are typically stigmatized by Anglo-Americans because their behavior is thought to be unpredictable (Stone et al., 1992). However, research by Neutra et al. (1977) found that among Navajos, hand trembling was regarded as a sign of shamanistic proclivity. As a result, it carried a positive connotation.

(d) Physical abilities and physical activity.

Physical disabilities are not as stigmatizing in some cultures as they are in others. For example, Asians are more likely to stigmatize people with physical disabilities than are African-Americans, Hispanic-Americans, and Anglo-Americans (Saetermoe et al., 2001).

(e) Mental illness.

Research shows that individuals from China are more likely to view dementia as a natural part of the aging process. Thus, they are less likely to stigmatize people with Alzheimer's disease than are Anglo-Americans (Hinton, Guo, Hillygus, & Levkoff, 2000). In addition, people in Islamic societies are more tolerant of mental illness than individuals in Western cultures, and are less likely to view "madness" as a stigma (Al-Issa, 2003). Moreover, traditional Mexican-Americans are more likely to view mental illness as a stigma than are Anglo-Americans (Castro, 1997). Finally, research by Kurumatani et al. (2004) compared the reactions of Japanese and Taiwanese teachers with a vignette describing the behavior of a child with schizophrenia. Results showed, for example, that relative to the Japanese teachers, teachers in Taiwan were more likely to attribute the behavior to schizophrenia, and to view it as having resulted from such causes as heredity, weakness of character, and stress. Interestingly, the Taiwanese teachers made greater internal and external attributions about the behavior of the child than did the Japanese teachers.

(f) Addictions.

Although people with addictions are viewed more negatively in the U.S. than individuals who are addiction free, there is a tendency to attribute some types of addictions (e.g., alcohol, tobacco) to biological causes (Stone et al., 1992). However, in many Islamic countries there are strong cultural taboos against using alcohol, and alcoholics are ostracized in society (Bush, White, Kai, Rankin, & Bhopal, 2003). In addition, smokers are often stigmatized in such countries as Pakistan and Bangladesh, and women who smoke in these countries are often considered outcasts by their families (Bush et al., 2003).

(g) Body image.

Research shows that there are cross-cultural differences in reactions to body size (Hebl & Heatherford, 1998; Matacin, 1995). For example, in the U.S., obese people are often stigmatized because they are viewed as having a weak character, and as incapable of exercising self-control (Bell et al., 2003). However, being overweight is less stigmatizing in Italy than it is in the U.S. One reason for this is the VSIs of women differ across these nations: Italian women are more likely to view larger body sizes as ideal than are American women (Matacin, 1995). Interestingly, however, ratings of ideal body size did not differ between Italian men and American men.

(h) Sexual orientation.

Research reveals cross-cultural differences in sexual orientation-based stigmas. In the U.S., people who are gay, lesbian, bisexual, or transgendered are often highly stigmatized (Ragins & Cornwell, 2001; Ragins et al., 2003). In addition, Hispanic-Americans are more likely to stigmatize gay men than are Anglo-Americans (Kurtz, 1999). In contrast, the Dine' (Navajo) are more tolerant of homosexuality than are Anglo-Americans (Witherspoon, 1977). One reason for this is that Dine' culture views all people as having both male and female identities, and is more permissive of letting individuals express these identities.

Interestingly, research by Schneider (2002) showed that people in the U.S. are more likely to stigmatize people with sexually erotic identities than are individuals in Germany. However, Germans are more likely to stigmatize those with non-sexually erotic identities than are people in the U.S.

(i) Religion.

Religion-based stigmas differ across (a) nations and (b) subcultures within nations. For instance, because the U.S. is a predominantly Christian nation (Smith, 1994), Jews are often stereotyped as being pushy, greedy, and lacking social skills (Fiske et al., 2002; Korman, 1989). As a consequence, Jewish-Americans are less likely to be hired for jobs requiring interpersonal competence and warmth than are Christians (Korman, 1989). Relatedly, research shows that Israeli immigrants to the U.S. often avoid contact with other Jews in the hopes of avoiding stigmatization (Shokeid, 1993).

The existence of cross-cultural differences in stereotypes about members of various religious groups is also clear from the ongoing religion-based wars in such nations as Bosnia, India, Iraq, Ireland, Israel, and Sudan. Members of the dominant religious groups in these nations often denigrate, aggress against, and attempt to annihilate those who do not share their religious beliefs. History provides far too many vivid and tragic illustrations of this.

(j) Affirmative action.

Research reveals sub-cultural differences in stereotypes about people who are hired under affirmative action programs (e.g., Evans, 2003; James, Brief, Dietz, & Cohen, 2001; Stanush, Arthur, & Doverspike, 1998). For instance, Anglo-Americans typically stereotype those who have been hired under such programs as less qualified for jobs than those who are not hired under the same programs (Evans, 2003; James et al., 2001). One explanation for this is that U.S. culture stresses that everyone should be treated equally in society, and no one should be given special treatment because it might provide them with a competitive advantage. Interestingly, however, research by Stanush et al. (1998) showed that relative to Anglo-Americans, Hispanic-Americans and African-Africans were less likely to negatively stereotype qualified candidates hired under affirmative action policies. This finding suggests that relative to members of groups that have not experienced unfair discrimination, members of groups that have are less likely to stigmatize affirmative action beneficiaries.

Changes in Stereotypes over Time.   It merits adding that both stereotypes and VSIs may change over time. Attributes that are viewed positively at one point in time may be viewed more negatively at a later point in time and vice-versa. For example, in the 19th century women with large body sizes were viewed as attractive in the U.S. However, by the 21st century women with large body sizes were regarded as lazy and/or lacking in self-control. The change in both VSIs and stereotypes may be due, in part, to differences in access to food between the 19th and 21st centuries. Consistent with the above-described evolutionary perspective of Kurzban and Leary (2001), in times of scarcity, women with large bodies might have been valued because of their potential to contribute to the survival of their families.

Moderating Effect of System Culture on Relation between Actual Social Identity and Emotional Responses
Consistent with Arrow 14 in the SIO model, research shows that cultural norms and values moderate the relation between the ASIs of targets and the emotional reactions of observers to targets (Jones et al., 1984). Prior to considering the same research, we detail several reasons for hypothesizing this moderating effect.

Bases for Hypothesizing Differential Emotional Responses. Given that cognitive appraisals of the ASIs of targets influence observers' emotional reactions, it seems reasonable to argue that the relation between these variables will vary as a function of cultural norms and values (Jones et al., 1984). The same norms and values may influence cognitive appraisals of stigmas by signaling the degree to which they threaten the observer. For instance, in cultures where people know that AIDS can not be communicated to others via casual contact, fear of individuals with AIDS should be lower than in cultures that lack this knowledge.

A second reason for positing that emotional reactions to ASIs are moderated by culture is that socialization experiences lead individuals to develop culture specific emotional reactions to individuals with stigmas (e.g., pity, anger, disgust, compassion, resentment). For example, the norm "to be kind" to people with specific types stigmas may lead observers to believe that it is more appropriate to display sympathy than disgust in encounters with individuals who have amputated limbs (Colella & Stone, 2005; Stone & Colella, 1996; Stone et al., 1992).

A third reason for positing cultural differences in emotional reactions to stigmas is that attributions about the causes of various conditions vary across cultures, and emotional reactions are typically most negative when targets are viewed as responsible for their stigma. For example, internal attributions are more likely in Western (individualistic) than in Eastern (collectivistic) cultures.

A fourth reason for arguing that emotional reactions to ASIs will differ across cultures is that norms about behaviors vary across cultures. For example, research reviewed above shows that stigmatization on the basis of some types of blemishes of character (e.g., obesity, drug addiction) differs across cultures and/or subcultures. In addition, tribal stigmas (e.g., based on membership in racial, ethnic, or religious groups) are a function of cultural norms and values.

Representative Research on Differential Emotional Reactions. A number of studies provide clear evidence of cultural differences in emotional reactions to stigmas. We consider representative research below in terms of several type of marks.

(a) Psychological problems.

Several studies have shown that culture influences individuals' reactions to mental illness and other psychological problems (e.g., Angermeyer, Buyantugs, Kenzine, & Matschinger, 2004; Crystal, Watanabe, & Chin, 1997; Dijker & Koomen, 2003; Papadopoulos, Leavey, & Vincent, 2002; Weiss, Jadhav, Raguram, Vounatsou, & Littlewood, 2001; Whaley, 1997). Angermeyer et al. (2004) showed, for example, that the relation between labeling a person with schizophrenia as mentally ill and the fear evoked by the person was stronger among individuals from Germany than people from Russia or Mongolia. Research by Crystal et al. (1997) was concerned with intolerance to targets who were viewed as different from the observers (i.e., students in the U.S., China, and Japan). The focus was on liking them as a friend or coworker on a class project. They found that Chinese students were more intolerant of (i.e., were repulsed by) having a child with signs of psychological withdrawal as a friend than were Japanese children. Moreover, research by Whaley (1997) showed that (a) relative to white respondents, both Hispanic and Asian respondents viewed mental patients as more dangerous, and (b) whereas among the white respondents, increased contact with such patients resulted in lower levels of perceived danger, the same was not true of black respondents.

(b) Behavioral problems.

Crystal et al. (1997) showed differential reactions to several types of behaviors across nations. Among these were that intolerance of (a) an aggressive friend was greater among Chinese students than U.S. students, and greater among U.S. students than Japanese students, (b) an aggressive coworker was greater among Chinese students than Japanese students, and (c) a mean friend was greater among Chinese students, than Japanese and U.S. students.

(c) Cognitive deficits.

Crystal et al. (1997) showed that as far as a friendship criterion was concerned, Chinese students were more intolerant of a child with a learning disability than students in the U.S. or Japan. However, with respect to having a learning disabled coworker, the U.S. students were more intolerant than students from either China or Japan.

(d) Physical activity or disability.

Crystal et al. (1997) reported that from either the perspective of a friend or a coworker, an unathletic child was less tolerated by students in (a) China than the U.S., and (b) the U.S. than in Japan. Related research by Crystal, Watanabe, and Chen (1999) considered students' emotional responses to (a) being a disabled person who would go swimming with a group of non-disabled people (disabled role), and (b) being a non-disabled person who would go swimming with a disabled person (interactant role). Among the findings were that relative to U.S. students, Japanese students (a) in the *disabled role* indicated that they would be more embarrassed, have generally bad feelings, and would feel like they were causing trouble for others, and (b) in the *interactant role* reported that they would feel greater empathy, but would prefer to do something else.

Jacques, Linkowski, and Sieka (1969) studied attitudes toward people with disabilities among subjects from the U.S., Greece, and Denmark. Results showed that the most positive attitudes were expressed by people in the U.S., followed by individuals in Denmark and Greece.

(e) Learning disabilities or cognitive deficits.

Crystal et al. (1997) showed that students in China were more likely to be intolerant of having a person with a learning disability as a friend than were students in the U.S. or Japan. However, the U.S. students were more intolerant of having a person with learning disabilities as a coworker than students in either China or Japan.

(f) Socioeconomic status.

Crystal et al. (1997) reported that U.S. and Japanese students were more intolerant of a poor child than were Chinese students. This was found in terms of both friend and coworker perspectives.

(g) Obesity.

Hebl and Heatherford (1998) found that race moderated the relation between body size and attractiveness. Black women viewed women with large body sizes as more attractive than did white women.

(h) Illness.

Not only does disease result in different degrees of stigmatization across cultures, but so do views about the contagiousness of various

conditions. For instance, African-Americans and Hispanic-Americans are more likely to fear contagion from germs than are Anglo-Americans (DeAngelo, 2000).
(i) Race.
   Porter and Beuf (1991) examined differences between the reactions of white and black patients to vitiligo (a disfiguring skin disease). Results showed that these groups did not differ in terms of the extent to which they were disturbed by the condition. However, blacks perceived the condition to be more stigmatizing than did whites.

Interplay between Cognitions and Emotions
In accordance with Arrows 18 and 19 in the SIO model, there is considerable support for the view that there is an interplay between cognitions about and emotional responses to a target (e.g., Dijker, 1989; Mackie & Hamilton, 1993; Vanman & Miller, 1993), including the perspective that emotions affect cognitions about targets. In this regard, Bodenhausen (1993) argued that strong emotions, whether negative (e.g., anger, anxiety) or positive (e.g., happiness) generally disrupt the capacity of observers to process information about targets. As a result, observers rely more on stereotype-based cognitions about targets than a careful consideration of their attributes. In addition, Stephan and Stephan (1993) argued that cognitions and affect are interconnected, parallel networks in which stereotypes about targets involve cognitions (e.g., about behaviors, traits) that are linked to emotions. As a result, the affect stemming from intergroup contact can elicit cognitions that are tied to the group.

There is also considerable support the view that cognitions about targets affect observers' emotional reactions to them (e.g., Blascovich et al., 2001; Stephan & Stephan, 1993; Weiner et al., 1988). Recall, for example, that Weiner et al. (1988) showed that emotional reactions to targets varied as a function of attributions about the controllability and stability of the stigmas of targets.

Taken together, the findings of these studies have important implications for HRM processes and practices. For example, to the degree that an interviewer has a negative emotional reaction to an interviewee, it will influence his or her cognitions about the interviewee. And, the greater the number and negativity of such cognitions, the more negative will be the interviewer's emotional reactions to the interviewee.

Treatment of the Target
Our SIO model postulates that the treatment accorded the target is largely a function of the observer's cognitive and emotional responses to him or her

(Arrows 20 and 21). Consistent with Stone-Romero and Stone (2005), we consider treatment-related issues in terms of three types of justice, i.e., distributive, procedural, and interactional.

Distributive Justice. Equity norms in the U.S. stress that a person's outcomes should be proportional to his or her inputs (Adams, 1963; Leventhal, 1976, 1980). In this regard, it merits noting that equity theory treats such characteristics as gender, race, disability, attractiveness, and social status as inputs that may serve as a basis for allocating differential levels of outcomes to targets (Adams, 1963; Leventhal, 1976, 1980). In addition, because of category-based expectancies, relative to non-stigmatized individuals, people who are marked are generally viewed as contributing fewer inputs. Thus, relative to people who are free of stigmas, marked individuals are viewed as less deserving of positive outcomes and more deserving of negative outcomes (Stone-Romero & Stone, 2005). As a result, for instance, when a non-disabled, MWASP allocator in the U.S. makes judgments about the relative inputs and deserved outcomes of various workgroup members: (a) whites will be regarded as more deserving of positive outcomes than blacks, and (b) people with disabilities will be seen as less deserving of positive outcomes than are people who are free of disabilities.

Regrettably, stigmas of various types and other factors that are not directly related to the target's actual job performance may be key determinants of their outcomes in organizations. In addition, in the absence of various types of constraints (e.g., legal restrictions, organizational policies against unfair discrimination) allocators are likely to allocate rewards and punishments to targets on the basis of their degree of stigmatization (Stone-Romero & Stone, 2005).

Interactional Justice. Our SIO model posits that stigmas influence the nature of interpersonal treatment accorded to targets. For example, because of the effects of similarity on interpersonal attraction observers will be more likely to form friendships with individuals who are similar to them on various dimensions (Byrne, 1971; Riordan, Schaffer, & Stewart, 2005). Note that both social identity theory (Tajfel, 1974, 1978, 1981, 1982a, 1982b; Tajfel & Turner, 1979; Turner, 1982, 1987) and terror management theory (Solomon et al., 1991) support the same prediction. In addition, Graen's work on leader–member exchange and role making processes (e.g., Graen, 1976; Graen & Scandura, 1987) suggests that the greater the similarity between a supervisor and a subordinate, the more harmonious will be their interpersonal relationship. Consistent with the foregoing, we predict that observers will treat individuals who are marked less favorably than people who are free of stigmas (Stone-Romero & Stone, 2005).

Examples of Cultural Differences in Fair Treatment. Although our SIO model does not show an explicit link between system culture and the way targets are treated, this relation deserves consideration. More specifically, we believe that system culture is an important determinant of the treatment accorded targets. One reason for this is that cultural values play a key role in determining allocation norms in both society and in organizational settings. For example, although norms in the U.S. dictate that outcomes should be allocated on the basis of equity or proportionality, allocation norms vary considerably across cultures. In this regard, Deutsch (1975) argued that fairness judgments may be based on such principles as equity, equality or need, depending on the society's relative emphases on the goals of production, social harmony, and humanitarianism. In accordance with this view, Wetherell (1982) showed that individuals from collective cultures were more likely to believe that outcomes should be allocated on the basis of equality than equity (proportionality). In addition, Rasinski (1987) found evidence of a relation between an individual's values and his or her preferences for outcome allocations based on equity, equality or need. Overall, what extant research shows is that whereas equity is the dominant allocation norm in Western cultures, equality or need norms tend to prevail in Eastern cultures. Thus, we believe that cultural norms will affect how outcomes are allocated to stigmatized persons in organizations.

Another reason for arguing that culture affects the allocation of outcomes is that cultural values determine beliefs about the deservedness of various targets. For example, as noted above, in Western cultures, the status rule dictates that those with higher status contribute greater inputs, and therefore, deserve greater outcomes (Leventhal, 1980). As a result, allocators in such cultures may believe that because stigmatized persons have lesser status, they make fewer contributions, and are less deserving of outcomes. However, the emphasis on equality or need-based allocations in Eastern cultures suggests that because of their neediness, stigmatized individuals deserve outcomes that are equivalent to those of non-stigmatized people. Interestingly, research supports this argument. More specifically, Crystal et al. (1999) showed that Japanese children were more likely to include children with disabilities (e.g., facial disfigurements) in their groups than were U.S. children. In addition, research by Wetherell (1982) showed that although both Polynesian children and European children demonstrated an ingroup bias in allocating outcomes, outgroup members were allocated greater levels of outcomes by the Polynesian children than by the European children. The behavior of the Asian children was no doubt based on cultural norms and values that stress collectivism, generosity, equality, and the maximization of the collective good (Kitayama, Markus, Matsumoto, & Norasakkunkit, 1997; Markus & Kitayama, 1991).

Effect of Treatment of the Target on the Cultures of Ingroups and Outgroups
Our SIO model assumes that the treatment of stigmatized targets leads to number of important consequences (e.g., Arrows 22 and 23). Among these are (a) enhancing the power and esteem of the ingroup, (b) decreasing the power and esteem of the outgroup, (c) reinforcing the negative stereotypes that ingroup members have of outgroup members, (d) reinforcing the outgroup's negative views of themselves, (e) justifying the way that outgroup members are treated in a social system, and (f) diminishing the motivation of outgroup members to remain in the social system. In view of this, it is important to consider strategies for reducing the problems caused by stigmas and stigmatization.

Interventions to Reduce Stigmatization and Associated Problems
We believe that an understanding of the cultural, cognitive, and emotional underpinnings of SIO should prove quite useful in identifying strategies for overcoming unfair discrimination against stigmatized people in organizations. Several strategies for doing this are briefly considered below.

Changing Societal Norms. The stigmatization of individuals and the treatment of them depends on social system norms about various factors (e.g., VSIs). Thus, one means of reducing stigma-related problems would be to have educational institutions work toward changing such norms (e.g., by socializing people to value the benefits of a pluralistic society). Another would involve having organizations work with the media to portray members of stigmatized groups in favorable ways. For example, *Fortune* magazine often showcases the accomplishments of their top managers who are black or female. Nevertheless, our advocacy of these practices should not be viewed as inconsistent with the need for legislation to reduce the unfair treatment experienced by members of stigmatized groups (e.g., Civil Rights Act, 1964; Americans With Disabilities Act, 1990).

Changing Organizational Cultures. The plight of stigmatized individuals might also be improved through several organizational changes that are related to HRM processes and practices. First, organizational norms, policies, and practices can be changed so as to reduce the likelihood of stigmatized individuals being treated unfairly (Stone-Romero & Stone, 2005). For example, selection procedures can be established that encourage the hiring of job applicants who have positive attitudes about diversity. Second, views about the VSIs of job incumbents (e.g., as communicated in employee handbooks and recruiting materials) can be changed so as to stress that the organization values diversity. Third, reward systems can be modified so as to (a) promote cooperative as opposed to competitive behavior among individuals in ingroups and outgroups, and (b) reduce the ability of ingroups to dominate outgroups. Fourth, organizations can increase the degree to which the actual performance of individuals (as opposed to their race, sex, etc.) serves as a basis for performance ratings and associated outcomes. Fifth, reward systems can be modified so as to take into account the values, needs, and preferences of individuals in both ingroups and outgroups (e.g., norms about fairness). To the degree that organizational cultures and related HRM policies and practices are modified so as to reinforce the value of diversity, emotional reactions to individuals in various stigmatized outgroups might become less negative.

Changing Observers' Cognitions. It may be possible to change cognitions about stigmatized individuals through strategies that enhance the ability and motivation of observers to attend to individuating information about targets. For example, situations can be created that facilitate the controlled processing of information about targets (e.g., Devine, 1989), thus reducing the degree to which cognitions about them are stereotype-based. However, it deserves stressing that even if cognitively-based strategies lead to positive changes in self-reports of stereotypes of outgroups, this may not change affective responses to outgroup members. The reason for this is that category-based responses to outgroup members have both cognitive and affective components (e.g., Dovidio & Gaertner, 1993). In addition, self-reports tend to be plagued with impression management biases (Crosby et al., 1980).

Recategorization of Outgroup Members. One strategy for overcoming categorization-related problems is to motivate observers to recategorize (as opposed to decategorizing) outgroup members (Dovidio & Gaertner, 1993). This may take the form of having observers focus on the commonality of the goals of ingroup and outgroup members (e.g., working toward the defeat of a common enemy). Cooperative goal structures are one means of reducing problems stemming from intergroup contact (Fiske & Ruscher, 1993; Vanman & Miller, 1993).

Increased Contact with Outgroup Members. Increased contact with outgroup members may lead to a reduction in the degree to which cognitions about them are stereotype-based. However, for increased contact to prove functional in changing observers' views, the contact must be positive (Brewer & Miller, 1988; Hewstone, 1996). In addition, it must result in the decategorization (more specifically, the personalization) of outgroup members.

Changing Observers' Emotional Reactions. As noted above, emotional reactions to members of many stigmatized outgroups are often automatic and appear to result from processes that have survival value in a society (Kurzban & Leary, 2001; Zajonc, 1980). As a result, they may be highly resistant to change. Nevertheless, some research suggests that negative affective reactions to outgroup members can be attenuated through increased contact (e.g., Bornstein, 1993). However, other research shows that increased contact results in more negative emotional responses (e.g., Vanman & Miller, 1993).

Some Research-Related Implications

Our SIO model posits that cognitive, affective, and cultural factors affect the stigmatization of individuals in organizational settings. As a consequence, the same factors influence HRM policies and practices. Thus, we encourage HRM-related research that considers these factors simultaneously. With respect to research, several issues deserve attention. First, most of the research on reactions to stigmas of various types has been conducted using student subjects and scenarios depicting hypothetical targets. Thus, research is sorely needed that deals with stigmatization in actual organizations and involves job applicants or incumbents as targets. Second, cross-cultural organizational research is needed that assesses observers' reactions to targets with different types of stigmas (Colella, 2001; Evans, 2003; Florey & Harrison, 2000; James et al., 2001). Such research should improve our understanding of the effects of culture on views about VSIs, ASIs, and a host of other factors associated with the stigmatization process. Third, research is needed to determine the relative effectiveness of various strategies for averting or overcoming the negative effects of SIO. Such research is extremely important because recent social psychological research suggests that stereotypes are over-determined; that is they are influenced by a confluence of factors (e.g., cognitive, affective, motivational, and cultural; Mackie et al., 1996). Unless we fully understand how these factors jointly affect stigmatization in organizational contexts, it will prove difficult to design and implement interventions aimed at reducing problems stemming from it.

CONCLUSIONS

Consistent with research in a number of disciplines, our SIO model considers the antecedents and consequences of stigmatization in organizational settings. An important contribution of the same model is its joint consideration of cultural, cognitive, and emotional factors associated with stigmatization. We hope that it serves to generate much needed research on stigmatization in organizational contexts, and motivate HRM-related changes that will reduce the many problems that stigmatized individuals face in such contexts.

NOTES

1. We use the term culture to refer to both cultures and subcultures. This avoids the need to repeatedly use the phrase "cultures and subcultures."
2. We recognize that in any social system there may be only a single dominant group. However, in order to simplify wording we use the term groups in place of the phrase "dominant group or groups."
3. Organizations have such properties as norms and values because there is a consensus (at least among the regnant organizational members) about various issues. In arguing that there is such a consensus we are not attempting to reify organizations.

REFERENCES

Adams, J. S. (1963). Toward an understanding of inequity. *Journal of Abnormal Social Psychology, 67*, 422–436.

Al-Issa, I. (2003). *Al-Junan: Mental illness in the Islamic world.* Madison, CT: International University Press.

Allport, G. W. (1954). *The nature of prejudice.* Cambridge, MA: Addison-Wesley.

Americans With Disabilities Act. (1990). Public Law No. 101-336, 104 Stat. 328 (1990). 42 U.S.C.A. § 12101 *et seq.*

Angermeyer, M. C., Buyantugs, L., Kenzine, D. V., & Matschinger, H. (2004). Effects of labeling on public attitudes towards people with schizophrenia: Are there cultural differences. *Acta Psychiatrica Scandanavica, 109*, 420–425.

Aycan, Z., Kanungo, R. N., Mendonca, M., Yu, K., Deller, J., Stahl, G., & Kurshid, A. (2000). Impact of culture on human resource management practices: A 10-country comparison. *Applied Psychology: An International Review, 49*, 192–221.

Bell, M. P., McLaughlin, M., & Sequeiro, J. M. (2003). Age, disability, and obesity: Similarities, differences, and common threads. In: M. Stockdale & F. Crosby (Eds), *The psychology and management of workplace diversity* (pp. 191–205). Malden, MA: Blackwell.

Berry, J. W. (1990). Psychology of acculturation. In: J. Berman (Ed.), *Cross-cultural perspectives: Nebraska symposium on motivation* (pp. 201–234). Lincoln, NB: University of Nebraska Press.

Berry, J. W. (1995). Psychology of acculturation. In: N. R. Goldberger & J. B. Veroff (Eds), *The culture and psychology reader* (pp. 457–488). New York: New York University Press.

Blascovich, J., Mendes, W. B., Hunter, S. B., Lickel, B., & Kowai-Bell, N. (2001). Perceiver threat in social interactions with stigmatized others. *Journal of Personality and Social Psychology, 80*, 253–267.

Bodenhausen, G. V. (1993). Emotions, arousal, and stereotypic judgments: A heuristic model of affect and stereotyping. In: D. M. Mackie & D. L. Hamilton (Eds), *Affect, cognition, and stereotyping: Interactive processes in group perception* (pp. 13–37). San Diego, CA: Academic Press.

Bodenhausen, G. V., & Macrae, C. N. (1996). The self-regulation of intergroup perception: Mechanisms and consequences of stereotype suppression. In: C. N. Macrae, C. Stangor & M. Hewstone (Eds), *Stereotypes and stereotyping* (pp. 227–253). New York: Guilford Press.

Bornstein, R. F. (1993). Mere exposure effects with outgroup stimuli. In: D. M. Mackie & D.L. Hamilton (Eds), *Affect, cognition, and stereotyping: Interactive processes in group perception* (pp. 195–238). San Diego, CA: Academic Press.

Brewer, M. B. (1988). A dual process model of impression formation. In: T. S. Srull & R. S. Wyer (Eds), *Advances in social cognition* (Vol. 1, pp. 1–36). Hillsdale, NJ: Erlbaum.

Brewer, M. B., & Kramer, R. M. (1985). The psychology of intergroup attitudes and behavior. *Annual Review of Psychology, 36*, 219–243.

Brewer, M. B., & Miller, N. (1984). Beyond the contact hypothesis: Theoretical perspectives on desegregation. In: N. Miller & M. B. Brewer (Eds), *Groups in contact: The psychology of desegregation* (pp. 281–302). Orlando, FL: Academic Press.

Brewer, M. B., & Miller, N. (1988). Contact and cooperation: When do they work? In: P. Katz & D. Taylor (Eds), *Eliminating racism: Means and consequences* (pp. 315–326). New York: Plenum Press.

Brief, A. P., Dietz, J., Cohen, R., Reizenstein, P., Douglas, S., & Vaslow, J. B. (2000). Just doing business: Modern racism and obedience to authority as explanations for employment discrimination. *Organizational Behavior and Human Decision Processes, 81*, 72–97.

Broverman, I. K., Vogel, S. R., Broverman, D. M., Clarkson, F. E., & Rosenkrantz, P. S. (1994). Sex-role stereotypes: A current appraisal. In: B. Puka (Ed.), *Caring voices and women's moral frames: Gilligan's view* (pp. 191–210). New York: Garland Publishing.

Brown, D. (1970). *Bury my heart at wounded knee: An Indian history of the American west.* New York: Henry Holt Books.

Bush, J., White, M., Kai, J., Rankin, J., & Bhopal, R. (2003). Understanding influences on smoking in Bangladeshi and Pakistani adults. *British Medical Journal, 326*, 962–967.

Byrne, D. (1971). *The attraction paradigm.* New York: Academic Press.

Cascio, W. F., & Aguinis, H. (2005). *Applied psychology in human resource management* (6th ed.). Upper Saddle River, NJ: Pearson Education.

Castro, A. (1997). Mexican-American values and their impact on mental health care. *Dissertation Abstracts International: Section B: The Sciences and Engineering, 57*(9-B), 5909.

Civil Rights Act. (1964). *The Equal Opportunity Act of 1972.* Public Law No. 92-261.

Clark, M. S., & Isen, A. M. (1982). Toward understanding the relationship between feeling states and social behavior. In: A. Hastorf & A. M. Isen (Eds), *Cognitive social psychology* (pp. 73–108). New York: Elsevier North Holland.

Cleveland, J. N., & Landy, F. J. (1981). The influence of rater and ratee age on two performance judgments. *Personnel Psychology, 34,* 19–29.

Cleveland, J. N., & Landy, F. J. (1983). The effects of person and job stereotypes on two personnel decisions. *Journal of Applied Psychology, 68,* 609–619.

Cleveland, J. N., Vescio, T. K., & Barnes-Farrell, J. L. (2005). Gender discrimination in organizations. In: R. Dipboye & A. Colella (Eds), *Discrimination at work: The psychological and organizational bases* (pp. 149–176). Mahwah, NJ: Erlbaum.

Colella, A. (2001). Coworker distributive fairness judgments of the workplace accommodation of employees with disabilities. *Academy of Management Journal, 26,* 100–116.

Colella, A., & Stone, D. L. (2005). Workplace discrimination toward persons with disabilities: A call for some new research directions. In: R. Dipboye & A. Colella (Eds), *The psychological and organizational bases of discrimination at work* (pp. 227–253). Mahwah, NJ: Lawrence Erlbaum.

Cox, T. (1993). *Cultural diversity in organizations: Theory, research, and practice.* San Francisco: Berrett-Koehler.

Crocker, J., Major, B., & Steele, C. (1998). Social stigma. In: D. T. Gilbert, S. T. Fiske & G. Lindsey (Eds), *The handbook of social psychology* (pp. 504–553). Boston, MA: McGraw-Hill.

Crosby, F., Bromley, S., & Saxe, L. (1980). Recent unobtrusive studies of black and white discrimination and prejudice: A literature review. *Psychological Bulletin, 87,* 546–563.

Crystal, D. S., Watanabe, H., & Chen, R. S. (1999). Children's reactions tom physical disability: A cross-national developmental study. *International Journal of Behavioral Development, 23,* 91–111.

Crystal, D. S., Watanabe, H., & Chin, W. (1997). Intolerance of human differences: A cross-cultural and developmental study of American, Japanese, and Chinese children. *Journal of Applied Developmental Psychology, 18,* 149–167.

DeAngelo, L. M. (2000). Stereotypes and stigmas: Biased attributions in matching older persons with drawings of viruses. *International Journal of Aging and Human Development, 51,* 143–154.

Deloria, V. (1994). *God is red.* Golden, CO: Fulcrum Publishing.

Deutsch, M. (1975). Equity, equality, and need: What determines which value will be used as the basis of distributive justice? *Journal of Social Issues, 31,* 137–150.

Devine, P. G. (1989). Stereotypes and prejudice: Their automatic and controlled components. *Journal of Personality and Social Psychology, 56,* 5–18.

Dijker, A. J. (1989). Ethnic attitudes and emotions. In: J. P. van Oudenhoven & T. M. Willemsen (Eds), *Ethnic minorities: Social psychological perspectives* (pp. 77–93). Amsterdam: Swets & Zeitlinger.

Dijker, A. J., & Koomen, W. (2003). Extending Weiner's attribution-emotion model of stigmatization of ill persons. *Basic and Applied Social Psychology, 25,* 51–68.

Dijker, A. J., & Raeijmaekers, F. (1999). The influence of seriousness and contagiousness of disease on emotional reactions to ill persons. *Psychology and Health, 14,* 131–141.

Dipboye, R., & Colella, A. (Eds). (2005). *Discrimination at work: The psychological and organizational bases: The psychological and organizational bases.* Mahwah, NJ: Erlbaum.

Dipboye, R. L., Fromkin, H. L., & Wiback, K. (1975). Relative importance of applicant sex, attractiveness, and scholastic standing in evaluation of job applicant resumes. *Journal of Applied Psychology, 60,* 39–43.

Dovidio, J. F., & Gaertner, S. L. (1993). Stereotypes and evaluative intergroup bias. In: D.M. Mackie & D. L. Hamilton (Eds), *Affect, cognition, and stereotyping: Interactive processes in group perception* (pp. 167–193). San Diego, CA: Academic Press.

Dovidio, J. F., Gaertner, S. L., Niemann, Y. F., & Snider, K. (2001). Racial, ethnic, and cultural differences in responding to distinctiveness and discrimination on campus: Stigma and common group identity. *Journal of Social Issues, 57,* 167–188.

Erez, M., & Earley, P. C. (1993). *Culture, self-identity, and work.* New York: Oxford University Press.

Evans, D. C. (2003). A comparison of the other-directed stigmatization produced by legal and illegal forms of affirmative action. *Journal of Applied Psychology, 88,* 121–130.

Fiske, S. T., Cuddy, A. J. C., Glick, P., & Xu, J. (2002). A model of (often mixed) stereotype content: Competence and warmth respectively follow from perceived status and competition. *Journal of Personality and Social Psychology, 82,* 878–902.

Fiske, S. T., & Neuberg, S. L. (1990). A continuum of impression formation, from category-based to individuating processes: Influences of information and motivation on attention and interpretation. In: M. Zanna (Ed.), *Advances in experimental social psychology* (Vol. 23, pp. 1–74). Orlando, FL: Academic Press.

Fiske, S. T., & Ruscher, J. B. (1993). Negative interdependence and prejudice: Whence the affect? In: D. M. Mackie & D. L. Hamilton (Eds), *Affect, cognition, and stereotyping: Interactive processes in group perception* (pp. 239–268). San Diego, CA: Academic Press.

Florey, A. T., & Harrison, D. (2000). Responses to informal accommodation requests from employees with disabilities. Multistudy evidence on willingness to comply. *Academy of Management Journal, 43,* 224–233.

Gatewood, R. D., & Field, H. S. (2001). *Human resource selection* (5th ed.). Mason, OH: South-Western.

Goffman, E. (1963). *Stigmas: Notes on the management of spoiled identity.* Englewood Cliffs, NJ: Prentice-Hall.

Goldberg, C. B., & Shore, L. M. (2003). The impact of age of applicants and of referent others on recruiters' assessments: A study of young and middle-aged job seekers. *Representative Research in Social Psychology, 27,* 11–22.

Graen, G. B. (1976). Role making processes within complex organizations. In: M. D. Dunnette (Ed.), *Handbook of industrial and organizational psychology* (pp. 1201–1245). Chicago, IL: Rand McNally.

Graen, G. B., & Scandura, T. (1987). Toward a psychology of dyadic organizing. In: L. L. Cummings & B. Staw (Eds), *Research in organizational behavior* (Vol. 9, pp. 175–208). Greenwich, CT: JAI Press.

Hamilton, D. L., & Sherman, J. W. (1994). Stereotypes. In: R. S. Wyer & T. K. Srull (Eds), *Handbook of social cognition* (2nd ed., Vol. 2, pp. 1–68). Hillsdale, NJ: Lawrence Erlbaum.

Heatherton, T. F., Kleck, R. E., Hebl, M. R., & Hull, J. G. (2003). *The social psychology of stigma.* New York: Guilford Press.

Hebl, M., & Heatherford, T. (1998). The stigma of obesity in women: The difference is black and white. *Personality and Social Psychological Bulletin, 24,* 417–426.

Heilman, M. E. (2001). Description and prescription: How gender stereotypes prevent women's ascent up the organizational ladder. *Journal of Social Issues, 57,* 657–674.

Heilman, M. E., & Haynes, H. (2005). Combating organizational discrimination: Some unintended consequences. In: R. Dipboye & A. Colella (Eds), *Discrimination at work: The psychological and organizational bases* (pp. 353–379). Mahwah, NJ: Erlbaum.

Hewstone, M. (1996). Contact and categorization: Social psychological interventions to change intergroup relations. In: C. N. Macrae, C. Stangor & M. Hewstone (Eds), *Stereotypes and stereotyping* (pp. 323–368). New York: Guilford Press.

Hinton, L., Guo, Z., Hillygus, J., & Levkoff, S. (2000). Working with culture: A qualitative analysis of barriers to the recruitment of Chinese-American family caregivers for dementia research. *Journal of Cross-Cultural Gerontology, 15,* 119–137.

Hofstede, G. (1980). *Culture's consequences: International differences in work-related values.* Beverly Hills, CA: Sage Publications.

Hofstede, G. (1991). *Cultures and organizations: Software of the mind.* London: McGraw-Hill.

Hosoda, M., Stone-Romero, E. F., & Coats, G. (2003). The effects of physical attractiveness on job-related outcomes: A meta-analysis of experimental studies. *Personnel Psychology, 56,* 431–462.

Hough, L. M., Oswald, F. L., & Ployhart, R. E. (2001). Determinants, detection, and amelioration of adverse impact in personnel selection procedures: Issues, evidence, and lessons learned. *International Journal of Selection and Assessment, 9,* 152–194.

Hsu, F. L. K. (1961). American core values and national character. In: F. L. K. Hsu (Ed.), *Psychological anthropology: Approaches to culture and personality* (pp. 209–233). Homewood, IL: Dorsey.

Hughes, L. (1994). *The collected poems of Langston Hughes.* New York: Knopf.

Jacques, M. E., Linkowski, D. C., & Sieka, F. L. (1969). Cultural attitudes toward disability: Denmark, Greece, and the United States. *International Journal of Social Psychology, 16,* 54–62.

James, E. H., Brief, A. P., Dietz, J., & Cohen, R. (2001). Prejudice matters: Understanding the reactions of Whites to affirmative action programs targeted to benefit Blacks. *Journal of Applied Psychology, 86,* 1120–1128.

Jones, E. E., Farina, A., Hastorf, A. H., Markus, H., Miller, D. T., & Scott, R. A. (1984). *Social stigma: The psychology of marked relationships.* New York: Freeman.

Kanter, R. M. (1977). *Men and women of the corporation.* New York: Basic Books.

Katz, D., & Kahn, R. (1978). *The social psychology of organizations* (2nd ed.). New York: Wiley.

Katz, S. (2003). Physical appearance: The importance of being beautiful. In: J. M. Henslin (Ed.), *Down to earth sociology: Introductory readings* (12th ed., pp. 313–320). New York: Free Press.

Kitayama, S., Markus, H. R., Matsumoto, H., & Norasakkunkit, V. (1997). Individual and collective processes in the construction of the self: Self-enhancement in the United States and self-criticism in Japan. *Journal of Personality and Social Psychology, 72,* 1245–1267.

Korman, A. K. (1989). The outsiders: On the relationship between Jewish Americans and corporate America in the problem of work and career. *Man and Work, 2*(1), 53–58.

Kurtz, S. P. (1999). Butterflies under cover: Cuban and Puerto-Rican gay masculinities in Miami. *Journal of Men's Studies, 7,* 371–390.

Kurumatani, T., Ukawa, K., Kawaguchi, Y., Miyata, S., Suzuki, M., Ide, H., Seki, W., Chikamori, E., Hwu, H., Liao, S., Edwards, G. D., Shinfuku, N., & Uemoto, M. (2004). Teachers' knowledge, beliefs and attitudes concerning schizophrenia: A cross-cultural approach in Japan and Taiwan. *Social Psychiatry and Psychiatric Epidemiology, 39,* 402–409.

Kurzban, R., & Leary, M. R. (2001). Evolutionary origins of stigmatization: The functions of social exclusion. *Psychological Bulletin, 127*, 187–208.

Lazarus, R. S. (1966). *Psychological stress and coping processes*. New York: McGraw-Hill.

Lazarus, R. S. (1991). *Emotion and adaptation*. New York: Oxford University Press.

Lazarus, R. S., & Folkman, S. (1984). *Stress, appraisal, and coping*. New York: Springer.

Lazarus, R. S., Kanner, A. D., & Folkman, S. (1980). Emotions: A cognitive phenomenologicial analysis. In: R. Plutchik & H. Kellerman (Eds), *Emotion: Theory, research, and experience* (pp. 189–217). New York: Academic Press.

Lerner, M. J. (1980). *The belief in a just world: A fundamental delusion*. New York: Plenum.

Leventhal, G. S. (1976). The distribution of rewards and resources in groups and organizations. In: L. Berkowitz & E. Walster (Eds), *Advances in experimental social psychology* (Vol. 9, pp. 91–131). New York: Academic Press.

Leventhal, G. S. (1980). What should be done with equity theory? New approaches to studying fairness in social relationships. In: K. J. Gergen, M. S. Greenberg & H. Willis (Eds), *Social exchange: Advances in theory and research* (pp. 27–55). New York: Plenum.

Mackie, D. M., & Hamilton, D. L. (Eds). (1993). *Affect, cognition, and stereotyping: Interactive processes in group perception*. San Diego, CA: Academic Press.

Mackie, D. M., Hamilton, D. L., Susskind, J., & Rosselli, F. (1996). Social psychology of stereotype formation. In: C. N. Macrae, C. Stangor & M. Hewstone (Eds), *Stereotypes and stereotyping* (pp. 41–78). New York: Guilford Press.

Macrae, C. N., Stangor, C., & Hewstone, M. (Eds). (1996). *Stereotypes and stereotyping*. New York: Guilford Press.

March, J. G., & Simon, H. A. (1958). *Organizations*. New York: Wiley.

Markus, H. R., & Kitayama, S. (1991). Culture and the self: Implications for cognition, emotion, and motivation. *Psychological Review, 98*, 224–253.

Marin, G., & Marin, B. V. (1991). *Research with Hispanic populations*. Newbury Park, CA: Sage.

Matacin, M. L. (1995). Body image, perceptions, and ideals in Italian men and women. *Dissertation Abstracts International Section B: The Sciences and Engineering, 55*(9-B), 4170.

Miller, N., & Brewer, M. B. (1984). *Groups in contact: The psychology of desegregation*. Orlando, FL: Academic Press.

Miller, D. T., & Turnbull, W. (1986). Expectancies and interpersonal processes. *Annual Review of Psychology, 37*, 233–256.

Neutra, R., Levy, J. E., & Parker, D. (1977). Cultural expectations versus reality in Navajo seizure patterns and sick roles. *Culture, Medicine and Psychiatry, 1*, 255–275.

Papadopoulos, C., Leavey, G., & Vincent, C. (2002). Factors influencing stigma: A comparison of Greek-Cypriot and English attitudes towards mental illness in north London. *Social Psychiatry and Psychiatric Epidemiology, 37*, 430–434.

Porter, J. R., & Beuf, A. H. (1991). Racial variation in reaction to physical stigma: A study of degree of disturbance by vitiligo among black and white patients. *Journal of Health and Social Behavior, 32*, 192–204.

Porter, L. W., Lawler, E. E., & Hackman, J. R. (1975). *Behavior in organizations*. New York: McGraw-Hill.

Ragins, B. R., & Cornwell, J. M. (2001). Pink triangles: Antecedents and consequences of perceived workplace discrimination against gay and lesbian employees. *Journal of Applied Psychology, 86*, 1244–1261.

Ragins, B. R., Cornwell, J. M., & Miller, J. S. (2003). Heterosexism in the workplace: Do race and gender matter? *Group and Organization Management, 28*, 45–74.

Rasinski, K. A. (1987). What's fair is fair, or is it? Value-differences underlying public views about social justice. *Journal of Personality and Social Psychology, 53*, 201–211.

Riordan, C. M., Schaffer, B. S., & Stewart, M. M. (2005). Relational demography within groups: Through the lens of discrimination. In: R. Dipboye & A. Colella (Eds), *Discrimination at work: The psychological and organizational bases* (pp. 37–61). Mahwah, NJ: Erlbaum.

Rosenthal, R., & Jacobson, L. (1968). *Pygmalion in the classroom.* New York: Holt, Rinehart, & Winston.

Rush, L. L. (1998). Affective reactions to multiple social stigmas. *The Journal of Social Psychology, 138*, 421–430.

Saetermoe, C. L., Scattone, D., & Kim, K. H. (2001). Ethnicity and the stigma of disabilities. African-American, Latin-American or European-American counterparts. *Psychology and Health, 16*, 699–714.

Schein, V. E., & Mueller, R. (1992). Sex role stereotyping and requisite management characteristics. *Journal of Organizational Behavior, 13*, 439–447.

Schmitt, N., Rogers, W., Chan, D., Sheppard, L., & Jennings, D. (1997). Adverse impact and predictive efficiency of various predictor combinations. *Journal of Applied Psychology, 82*, 719–730.

Schneider, A. (2002). A possible link between stigmatization of sexual-erotic identities and sexual violence. *Sexuality and Culture: An Interdisciplinary Quarterly, 6*(4), 23–43.

Schneider, B. (1987). The people make the place. *Personnel Psychology, 40*, 437–453.

Shokeid, M. (1993). One-night-stand ethnicity: The malaise of Israeli-Americans. *Social Science Research, 8*(2), 23–50.

Shore, L. M., & Goldberg, C. B. (2005). Age discrimination in the workplace. In: R. Dipboye & A. Colella (Eds), *Discrimination at work: The psychological and organizational bases* (pp. 203–225). Mahwah, NJ: Erlbaum.

Smith, H. (1994). *The illustrated world's religions: A Guide to our wisdom traditions.* San Francisco: Harper.

Solomon, S., Greenberg, J., & Pyszczynski, T. (1991). A terror management theory of social behavior: The psychological functions of self-esteem and cultural worldviews. In: M. P. Zanna (Ed.), *Advances in Experimental Social Psychology* (Vol. 24, pp. 93–159). San Francisco: Academic Press.

Stephan, W. G., & Stephan, C. W. (1993). Cognition and affect in stereotyping: Parallel interactive networks. In: D. M. Mackie & D. L. Hamilton (Eds), *Affect, cognition, and stereotyping: Interactive processes in group perception* (pp. 111–136). San Diego, CA: Academic Press.

Stephan, W. G., Ybarra, O., & Bachman, G. (1999). Prejudice toward immigrants. *Journal of Applied Social Psychology, 29*, 2221–2237.

Stockdale, M. S., & Crosby, F. J. (Eds). (2004). *The psychology and management of workplace diversity.* Malden, MA: Blackwell Publishers.

Stone, D. L., & Colella, A. (1996). A model of factors affecting the treatment of disabled individuals in organizations. *Academy of Management Review, 21*, 352–401.

Stone, D. L., & Stone-Romero, E. F. (2004). The influence of culture on role-taking in culturally diverse organizations. In: M. S. Stockdale & F. J. Crosby (Eds), *The psychology and management of workplace diversity* (pp. 78–99). Malden, MA: Blackwell Publishers.

Stone, E. F., Stone, D. L., & Dipboye, R. L. (1992). Stigmas in organizations: Race, handicaps, and physical unattractiveness. In: K. Kelley (Ed.), *Issues, theory and research in Industrial and Organizational Psychology* (pp. 385–457). Amsterdam: Elsevier.

Stone-Romero, E. F. (2005). Personality-based stigmas and unfair discrimination in work organizations. In: R. Dipboye & A. Colella (Eds), *Discrimination at work: The psychological and organizational bases* (pp. 255–279). Mahwah, NJ: Erlbaum.

Stone-Romero, E. F., & Stone, D. L. (1998). Religious and moral influences on work-related values and work quality. In: D. B. Fedor & S. Ghosh (Eds), *Advances in the management of organizational quality: An annual series of quality-related theory and research papers* (Vol. 3, pp. 185–285). U.S.: Elsevier Science/JAI Press.

Stone-Romero, E. F., & Stone, D. L. (2005). How can justice be used to explain discrimination and prejudice? In: J. Greenberg & J. A. Colquitt (Eds), *Handbook of organizational justice: Fundamental questions about fairness in the workplace* (pp. 439–467). Mahwah, NJ: Lawrence Erlbaum Associates.

Stone-Romero, E. F., & Stone, D. L. (in press). The dysfunctional consequences of individualism in organizations. In: M. Sutherland (Ed.), *Psychology and Caribbean development*. Jamaica, West Indies: Ian Randle Press.

Stone-Romero, E. F., Stone, D. L., & Hartman, M. (2002). Stereotypes of ethnic groups: Own views versus assumed views of others. Paper presented at the meeting of the Society for Industrial and Organizational Psychology. Toronto, Canada.

Stone-Romero, E. F., Stone, D. L., & Salas, E. (2003). The influence of culture on role conceptions and role behavior in organizations. *Applied Psychology: An International Review, 52*, 328–362.

Stanush, P., Arthur, W., Jr., & Doverspike, D. (1998). Hispanic and African American reactions to a simulated race-based affirmative action scenario. *Hispanic Journal of Behavioral Sciences, 20*, 3–16.

Tajfel, H. (1974). Social identity and intergroup behavior. *Social Science Information, 13*, 65–93.

Tajfel, H. (1978). *Differentiation between social groups: Studies in the social psychology of intergroup relations*. London: Academic Press.

Tajfel, H. (1981). *Human groups and social categories*. Cambridge: Cambridge University Press.

Tajfel, H. (Ed.), (1982a). *Social identity and intergroup relations*. Cambridge: Cambridge University Press.

Tajfel, H. (1982b). Social psychology of intergroup relations. *Annual Review of Psychology, 33*, 1–39.

Tajfel, H., & Turner, J. C. (1979). An integrative theory of intergroup conflict. In: W. Austin & S. Worchel (Eds), *The social psychology of intergroup relations* (pp. 33–47). Monterey, CA: Brooks/Cole.

Thibaut, J., & Kelley, H. H. (1959). *The social psychology of groups*. New York: Wiley.

Thomas, K. M., & Chrobot-Mason, D. (2005). Group-level explanations of workplace discrimination. In: R. Dipboye & A. Colella (Eds), *Discrimination at work: The psychological and organizational bases* (pp. 63–88). Mahwah, NJ: Erlbaum.

Triandis, H. C. (1994). Cross-cultural industrial and organizational psychology. In: H. C. Triandis, M. D. Dunnette & L. M. Hough (Eds), *Handbook of industrial and organizational psychology* (2nd ed., Vol. 4, pp. 103–172). Palo Alto, CA: Consulting Psychologists Press.

Trice, H., & Beyer, J. (1993). *The cultures of work organizations*. Englewood Cliffs, NJ: Prentice Hall.

Trompenaars, F., & Hampden-Turner, C. (1998). *Riding the waves of culture: Understanding cultural diversity in global business* (2nd ed.). New York: McGraw-Hill.

Turner, J. C. (1982). Towards a cognitive redefinition of the social group. In: H. Tajfel (Ed.), *Social identity and intergroup relations* (pp. 15–39). Cambridge, England: Cambridge University Press.

Turner, J. C. (1987). *Rediscovering the social group: A self-categorization theory.* Oxford, England: Basil Blackwell.

Vanman, E. J., & Miller, N. (1993). Applications of emotion theory and research to stereotyping and intergroup relations. In: D. M. Mackie & D. L. Hamilton (Eds), *Affect, cognition, and stereotyping: Interactive processes in group perception* (pp. 213–238). San Diego, CA: Academic Press.

Vanman, E. J., Paul, B. Y., Ito, T. A., & Miller, N. (1997). The modern face of prejudice and structural features that moderate the effect of cooperation on affect. *Journal of Personality and Social Psychology, 73,* 941–959.

Weber, M. (1958). In: T. Parsons (Trans.), *The Protestant ethic and the spirit of capitalism.* New York: Charles Scribner's Sons. Original work published 1904-05.

Weiner, B., Perry, R. P., & Magnusson, J. (1988). An attributional analysis of reactions to stigmas. *Journal of Personality and Social Psychology, 55,* 738–748.

Weiss, M. G., Jadhav, S., Raguram, R., Vounatsou, P., & Littlewood, R. (2001). Psychiatric stigma across cultures: Local validation in Bangalore and London. *Anthropology and Medicine, 8,* 71–87.

Wetherell, M. (1982). Cross-cultural studies of minimal groups: Implications for the social identity theory of intergroup relations. In: H. Tajfel (Ed.), *Social identity and intergroup relations* (pp. 207–239). Cambridge: Cambridge University Press.

Whaley, A. L. (1997). Ethnic and racial differences in perceptions of dangerousness of persons with mental illness. *Psychiatry Services, 48,* 1328–1330.

Witherspoon, G. (1977). *Language and art in the Navajo universe.* Ann Arbor, MI: University of Michigan Press.

Zarate, M. A., & Smith, E. E. (1990). Person categorization and stereotyping. *Social Cognition, 8,* 161–185.

Zajonc, R. B. (1980). Feeling and thinking: Preferences need no inferences. *American Psychologist, 35,* 151–175.

TOWARD A THEORY OF REPUTATION IN ORGANIZATIONS

Robert Zinko, Gerald R. Ferris, Fred R. Blass and Mary Dana Laird

ABSTRACT

In everyday life, as well as in work organizations, we engage in frequent and quite comfortable discourse about the nature of reputations, and we also see personal reputation used as a basis for important human resources decisions (e.g., promotions, terminations, etc.). Unfortunately, despite its recognized importance, there has been very little theory and research on personal reputation in organizations published in the organizational sciences. The present paper attempts to address this need by proposing a conceptualization of personal reputation in organizations. In this conceptualization, reputation is presented as an agreed upon, collective perception by others, and involves behavior calibration derived from social comparisons with referent others that results in a deviation from the behavioral norms in one's environment, as observed and evaluated by others. Implications of this conceptualization are discussed, as are directions for future research.

Research in Personnel and Human Resources Management, Volume 26, 163–204
ISSN: 0742-7301/doi:10.1016/S0742-7301(07)26004-9

INTRODUCTION

Reputation has been shown to be an important factor in assessing the worth of an organization (Gotsi & Wilson, 2001), or the value of a product (Feldwick, 1996), and it has been positioned as playing important roles in managerial behavior (Ferris, Fedor, & King, 1994) and leadership (Ammeter, Douglas, Gardner, Hochwarter, & Ferris, 2002; Blass & Ferris, 2007; Hall, Blass, Ferris, & Massengale, 2004). Nevertheless, very little theory and research on personal reputation has been reported, and the nature and dynamics of how a reputation is developed, and its impact on social interactions, has received limited attention in the organizational sciences literature (e.g., Ferris, Blass, Douglas, Kolodinsky, & Treadway, 2003).

There has been considerable research interest in recent years in corporate reputation (e.g., Rindova, Williamson, Petkova, & Sever, 2005; Fombrun, 1996), and new interest in subunit or department reputation (Ferris et al., in press-a). Unfortunately, after what appeared to be the beginning of a serious stream of research on personal reputation two decades ago (i.e., Gioia & Sims, 1983; Tedeschi & Melburg, 1984; Tsui, 1984), and a limited revival of interest in the mid-1990s (Bromley, 1993; Tsui, 1994), little work subsequently has been published in the organizational sciences literature in this area.

The purpose of the present paper is to address this need in the field by articulating the conceptual foundations and dynamics of this construct, and thereby move closer toward the formulation of a theory of personal reputation in organizations. We begin by establishing the construct domain and definition of personal reputation, followed by a review of the existing research on personal reputation in the organizational sciences. Then, we propose a model of personal reputation in organizations, including both antecedents and consequences, which incorporates multiple theoretical perspectives to address both the development (i.e., social comparison and self-regulation theories) and the transmission (i.e., signaling, social information processing and contagion, and communication theories) of reputation.

DEFINITION AND CONSTRUCT DOMAIN OF REPUTATION

Definition of Reputation

Although a single consensus definition of reputation has not been established in the organizational sciences, there does appear to be some common ground upon which to build one. Common throughout the published work on reputation in a number of disciplines is the notion that personal reputation refers to a generally agreed upon, collective perception of an individual by some referent others, influenced by the individual actors themselves, and which does not occur instantaneously, but emerges over some period of time (e.g., Ferris et al., 2003).

From their review, Ferris et al. (2003) distilled a definition of personal reputation that emphasized the perceptual character of the construct, its intentional nature, its focus on behaviors and characteristics of the individual actor, and its occurrence over time. Furthermore, they implicitly made reference to reputation as reflecting a collective perception by others, and possessing a predictive quality by increasing the likelihood of future behavior.

Thus, we employ the definition of personal reputation developed by Ferris et al. (2003), with the specific addition of the importance of collective perception and the reduced uncertainty of expected future behavior as follows: *Reputation is a perceptual identity formed from the collective perceptions of others, which is reflective of the complex combination of salient personal characteristics and accomplishments, demonstrated behavior, and intended images presented over some period of time as observed directly and/or reported from secondary sources, which reduces ambiguity about expected future behavior.*

Construct Domain Differentiation

Although we conceive of reputation as a separate and distinct construct in its own right, it is important to briefly discuss its construct domain delineation as compared with other constructs potentially construed as similar in nature. Rindova, Pollock, and Hayward (2006) distinguished among the constructs of reputation, legitimacy, status, and celebrity. Suggesting that reputation differs from the others in that it reflects a predictive measure, similar to what marketing scholars have proposed, Rindova et al. implied that both status and legitimacy are based more on networks and abidance with acceptable norms. They contended that both celebrity and reputation are based on others' perception of an individual (or group). Rindova et al. defined celebrity as those entities that "attract a high level of public attention and generate positive emotional responses from stakeholder audiences" (p. 51), and recent research has been conducted on both celebrity firms (Rindova et al., 2006) and celebrity Chief Executive Officers (CEOs) (Hayward, Rindova, & Pollock, 2004; Ranft, Zinko, Ferris, & Buckley, 2006; Wade, Porac, Pollock, & Graffin, 2006).

The model presented in this paper reflects the perspective set out by Rindova et al. (2006) by suggesting that reputation differs from fame and celebrity because it has a predictive nature. Moreover, Rindova et al. proposed that although other defining characteristics, such as status and legitimacy, may carry with them a predictive value, they are normally tied directly to a formal position in an organization; suggesting that status and legitimacy may be achieved by position alone because others will consider them more on station or network rather than on observable actions. Ironically, one can gain a reputation for being anything *but* legitimate when compared with expected norms (Haviland, 1977).

Ravlin and Thomas (2005, p. 968) characterized status as "differences in prestige and deference" that result in some sort of ranking, and de Botton (2004, p. vii) defined status as "one's value and importance in the eyes of the world". Roberts (2005) suggested that image is based on our own assessment of ourselves, rather than an audience's perception of us, which implies that individuals' reputations may be completely different from their images. Furthermore, individuals who are low in social astuteness may perceive their image as being the same as their reputation, rendering them completely erroneous in their assessment, as a function of their "flawed self-assessments," which can be due to an inability to understand other's perceptions of them (Dunning, Heath, & Suls, 2004).

Because it has been studied in so many different intellectual traditions and disciplinary perspectives, it is difficult to provide a single definition of identity. However, most would simply contend that identity refers to "... an internal cognition about the self," or perhaps a bit more specifically, "... a feature of the individual reflecting an internal process of self-definition" (Deaux, 2000, p. 225). Thus, although identity might appear to be similar in nature to reputation, important differences exist concerning the predominant inward looking construct of identity, and the external reflection of reputation. The explanation of reputation presented in this paper acknowledges not only the similarities of such constructs as image, fame, status, legitimacy, identity, and prestige, but also builds upon the revealed differences presented by past authors in order to present a more clearly delineated reputation construct.

RESEARCH ON PERSONAL REPUTATION IN ORGANIZATIONS

Research on the development and outcomes of personal reputation has been limited. However, in a review of the existing literature, Ferris et al. (2003)

suggested that individuals develop personal reputations through behaviors that range from passive conformity to others' expectations to active manipulation of the context. For example, Kilduff and Krackhardt (1994) found personal reputation to be as much a function of perceived associations with prominent others as it was a function of job performance. Furthermore, research has suggested that reputation is developed through accurate perceptions of advice networks (Krackhardt, 1990), and active engagement in political behaviors (Ammeter et al., 2002).

Building on early work on the reputational effectiveness of managers (Tsui, 1984), which is defined as constituents' judgments of the extent to which a manager is responsive to constituent expectations, Tsui (1994) developed a model of the antecedents, mediators, and outcomes of reputational effectiveness. According to this model, structural, social, and individual factors affect the homogeneity of contingency expectations, perceived dependence on and interdependence with other constituencies, and strength of social identification with these constituencies, which ultimately affect the manager's tendency toward responsiveness and attainment of reputational effectiveness. Ultimately, Tsui's (1994) model suggests that reputational effectiveness has positive outcomes for the unit, the manager, and the organization as a whole.

Although the development of personal reputation has been somewhat overlooked, a number of researchers have focused their attention on the outcomes of this construct. For example, in a series of experiments, Rosen, Cochran, and Musser (1990) found that an applicant's reputation was a more important predictor of interviewer evaluations of job suitability than the applicant's self presentation style.

Reputation also has been found to have implications for job incumbents. For example, when a novice negotiator knows his opponent has a negative reputation for distributive negotiation, the novice negotiator is more likely to use distributive tactics, thus hindering his or her opponent's performance (Tinsley, O'Connor, & Sullivan, 2002). Furthermore, Hall et al. (2004) suggested that leaders with positive reputations are afforded more trust, receive less monitoring, and are held to lower accountability standards. Finally, empirical research has found an interaction between reputation and helpful behaviors, such that helpful people with good reputations receive more rewards than helpful people with poor reputations (Johnson, Erez, Kiker, & Motowidlo, 2002).

Not only does an individual's reputation affect the way others approach him or her, but it also affects the behavior of the individual. For example, when individuals believe their reputation is threatened, they experience anxiety that spills over into their home life (Doby & Caplan, 1995). Furthermore, individuals' perceptions of their external reputation, which is communicated to other organizations through organizational events or cues that signal the organization's opinion of the individuals' job performance, affects their probability of searching for another job and leaving the organization (Kydd, Ogilvie, & Slade, 1990).

As can be seen in the previous discussion, most of the existing research on personal reputation has either focused on its antecedents or outcomes. However, with the exception of Tsui's (1994) work on reputational effectiveness, no research has provided a comprehensive explanation of the development *and* consequences of personal reputation. Therefore, the following sections will provide a theory of personal reputation that more precisely articulates the antecedents, consequences, moderators, and mediators of this important construct.

THEORETICAL FOUNDATIONS OF REPUTATION IN ORGANIZATIONS

The theoretical model presented in this paper not only supports the assumptions presented by Ferris et al. (2003), but also suggests several more. First, individuals will compare themselves with their peers (Festinger, 1954), and if that image does not match the impression they hold in their minds regarding their self worth or perceived worth by others (Baumeister, 1982a, 1982b), they may act in a reputation-building manner (Caste & Burke, 2002). Second, reputations are created by referent others who discuss observed or reported actions (Elmer, 1984; Carroll, Green, Houghton, & Wood, 2003).

Third, we contend that the formation of a reputation is contingent upon behavior deviating from the norm (Haviland, 1977; Levin & Arluke, 1987). Personal reputations are formed by standing out from the pack, by doing something different. Finally, we suggest that reputations are used to reduce uncertainty regarding an individual's future behavior (e.g., Kreps & Wilson, 1982; Milgrom & Roberts, 1982; Ferris et al., 2003).

Although the use of the term reputation is omnipresent in everyday work life, its scientific examination has been surprisingly neglected. With the exception of common anecdotal use, the fact of the matter is that we simply know very little about personal reputation, and how and why it is important. Consideration of the above assumptions begins to illuminate the factors that contribute to the formation of a reputation. Indeed, our model of how personal reputation forms seeks to incorporate these assumptions, along with relevant theory, in an effort to develop a systematic conceptualization of reputation in organizations that can help shed light on the process dynamics of this construct, and guide future research.

Theoretical Foundations of Reputation Development and Transmission

Social Comparison Theory
Social comparison theory was developed by Festinger (1954) to address how people evaluate their opinions and abilities when no objective standards are available, by comparing themselves with other people. Subsequently, Festinger's theory has been applied beyond "opinions and abilities" to include a number of personal attributes (e.g., Wood, 1989), which makes it relevant for the conceptualization of reputation in organizations. A considerable amount of research over the past several decades, since the articulation of social comparison theory, has dealt with the different types of referent comparisons people choose, the conditions under which each type is selected, and the effects of different choices on individuals' attitudes and behavior (e.g., Kulik & Ambrose, 1992; Wood, 2000).

Festinger (1954) initially suggested that individuals would compare themselves with people who were similar. However, in the subsequent half century, research has identified a number of different comparison bases or referents, including self-present, self-past, self-future, other (past, present, and future), and system (e.g., Goodman, 1974; Kulik & Ambrose, 1992). Furthermore, research has demonstrated that individuals do not necessarily compare themselves only with others who are similar, as Festinger originally argued. Instead, individuals have been found to also engage in downward comparisons (Wills, 1981), and upward comparisons (Collins, 1996).

Self-Regulation Theory
Self-regulation or self-control can be thought of as the effort people put forth in order to alter their own responses, which can include both attitudes and behaviors (e.g., Baumeister, Heatherton, & Tice, 1994). It entails starting, stopping, changing a process, or substituting one response or outcome for another in efforts to meet or achieve some standard. Much of the work on self-regulation originally stemmed from systems or control theory (Carver & Scheier, 1982).

The initial step refers to the input or perception of the current circumstances, and a comparison of these circumstances with some standard. A standard is a conception of how things should be, such as social norms, personal goals, and expectations of others (Baumeister et al., 1994). If there is a discrepancy between the current circumstances and the standard, then the person performs a behavior directed at achieving the standard. Once the person has performed the behavior, another test is performed in order to assess whether the standard was reached (i.e., the discrepancy has been reduced). If the standard was not met, the individual continues to try to achieve the standard by repeating the process, and monitoring progress until the standard is met. When the discrepancy has been reduced, the cycle ends (Baumeister et al., 1994; Carver & Scheier, 1982).

For purposes of the present conceptualization of reputation development in organizations, we suggest a modification of self-regulation theory in order to model the behavioral action involved in reputation building. That is, instead of adjusting one's behavior to meet some accepted standard, we argue that individuals building reputations monitor what behavioral norms or standards happen to be, but then demonstrate behavior that deviates from that standard in some particular way designed to convey certain impressions.

Then, it is this deviation from behavioral norms that becomes salient and attracts attention by an observing audience, which begins the cognitive processing that results in reputation development. In some ways, this perspective is not dissimilar from the adaptive self-regulation approach to managerial effectiveness proposed by Tsui and Ashford (1994). However, we would argue that the standard setting that managers would attempt to achieve in order to satisfy each of their constituencies would be gauged at a level that would be considered deviations (i.e., typically in a positive direction) from behavioral norms.

Therefore, we propose an integration of social comparison and self-regulation theories brought to bear on the systematic conceptualization of the reputation development process. Individuals formulate reputational aspirations and select referent comparisons that serve motivational, modeling, and social comparison evaluative objectives. Then, implementation of steps to accomplish and attain reputational objectives is conducted through self-regulation of work behavior.

Social Information Processing Theory
This theory is an extension of social learning theory. Social information processing theory suggests people must consider all of the mental processes that others use in relating to the social world around them in order to

comprehend how individuals perceive the actions of others (Salancik & Pfeffer, 1978). Individuals receive a set of cues that are based on social norms and expectations as input. The person's behavioral response to the cues occurs as a function of a mental processes that begins with encoding of those cues through sensation and perception. Most of the cues are inputted via selective attention, so the storage of cues in memory is not consistent with objective experience. This selective encoding is partially predictive of how the individual will respond to the observed situation.

The mental representation and interpretation of the cues (e.g., possibly involving attributions about cause) is dependent on the environment in which the cues were received. Once the stimulus cues are absorbed, the individual retrieves one or more possible behavioral responses from memory. The final step of processing is response evaluation and decision-making. This is where the individual evaluates the situation and decides how to respond (Dodge & Coie, 1987).

Salancik and Pfeffer (1978) used social information processing theory to explain job attitudes as they relate to job design. They suggested that when approaching a job, part of the attitude of the worker comes from experiences as well as how others portray the position. The emphasis on the social environment in explaining how individuals view jobs can be applied to how reputation is viewed. Ferris and Mitchell (1987) suggested that social information processing theory applies to self-monitoring in that it applies a set of conditions where individuals can alter their actions depending on the environment.

This suggests that individuals may behave in certain ways in attempts to build specific reputations (Bromley, 1993). It is based on the understanding that others will use social information processing to explain the actions of individuals attempting to build reputations. Those actions can be used to communicate a specific social message that will be interpreted in light of the contextual backdrop within which both the individual and the audience interact and operate (Elmer, 1984).

Social Contagion Theory

Social contagion theory is "the spontaneous spread of emotional and behavioral reactions among a group of people" (Yukl, 1998, p. 307). This theory suggests that organizational actors engage in a form of social 'talk' that allows them to arrive at a shared, socially constructed interpretation of their social environment. This social interaction not only works as a shared sense-making mechanism, but also helps collectively define the meaning of events (Degoey, 2000). This also explains the phenomenon that rumors are more often believed than are formal communications in organizations (Robbins, 2000).

Social contagion theory has been used to help explain such phenomena as feelings of job satisfaction (Krackhardt & Porter, 1985), levels of organizational commitment (Hartman & Johnson, 1989), and attributions regarding leadership (Meindl, 1990). In the case of personal reputation, social contagion helps explain not only the construct of reputation, but also the transference of reputation. Because reputation is a socially constructed concept (Ferris et al, 2003), which is transferred by informal conversations such as gossip (Elmer, 1984), agreement by others regarding its meaning is essential. Social contagion theory explains this agreement. Furthermore, because the audience that is agreeing upon the reputation of another may not actually be in direct contact with the reputation-building individual (Bromley, 1993), this shared, socially constructed interpretation of a reputation is essential.

Communication Theory
Basic communication theory is based on the sender-message-receiver communication model. Modern day adaptations take into account the various codes and subcodes that make up society, and allow for intermediaries or multiple source senders or receivers (Stern, 1994). In the case of personal reputation, the sender must consider not only the immediate audience, but also the context, environment, and possible intermediaries. In the field of management, attempts at communicating reputation most often have been referred to as signaling (e.g., Ferris et al., 2003; Tsui, 1984).

Signaling theory states that individuals coexist in markets of exchange, and that individuals signal others in these markets in attempts to transmit information or alter beliefs of others. In an effort to differentiate between potential and actual signals, Spence (1973, 1974) argued that potential signals represent observable, alterable characteristics, and actual signals are potential signals that influence others. Using this argument, reputation can be viewed as an actual signal because it represents observable and alterable characteristics that influence others.

It has been argued that reputation can be construed as an intentional effort at signaling (e.g., Ferris & Judge, 1991; Carroll et al., 2003). More specifically, reputation builders send as signals to others, and these signals tend to be more political than scientific in that they attempt to influence perceptions and meaning. Ferris, Hochwarter, Buckley, Harrell-Cook, and Frink (1999) suggested that reputations may be shaped or influenced by the individual to which the reputation is referent. They cited the influential role of reputation and its signaling capacity in an organizational setting by introducing tournament theory.

Proposed by Rosenbaum (1989), tournament theory suggests that those who are successful early in their careers are likely to experience greater success over the course of their careers. The theory suggests that this success is due to the perceptions that others form of them; and in the case of reputation, fast-track employees are promoted based on the reputation gained by early success. This idea is further supported by the theory that first impressions play an important part in building reputations because little is known about individuals when they first enter an organization, and a reputation is established in order to provide information in predicting future events (Baiman, 1991). In the case of tournament theory, reputation may be considered a signal to decision makers, whereby fast-track employees are identified and subsequently promoted based on their reputations of early success.

MODEL OF REPUTATION IN ORGANIZATIONS

Although the formation of a reputation can be unintentional, most often reputations are the result of volitional, conscious efforts (Bromley, 1993). Fig. 1 presents a conceptualization of the reputation development process, which moves from antecedents of reputational aspirations to social comparisons and self-regulation of work behavior, to observer assessed deviations from behavioral norms in the situation, to the search for causes and the reputation labeling process. Then, both the direct and secondary consequences

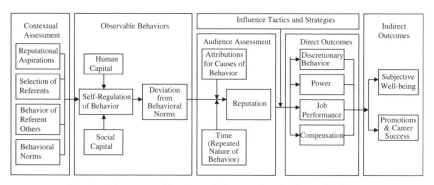

Fig. 1. Conceptualization of Reputation in Organizations.

of reputation are considered in the second phase of the model. In the following sections, we examine each of the linkages in the model in greater detail.

Antecedents of Reputation

Reputational Aspirations
Festinger (1954) hypothesized that individuals have an inherent desire to accurately evaluate their own opinions and abilities. When objective measures are not available (i.e., as is often the case in social settings), individuals often measure themselves against their colleagues. This evaluation of self will take into account not only individuals' self-esteem, but also how others view them. It is argued that individuals gain understanding of their own reputations through the behavior reflected back to them by others (Emler & Hopkins, 1990). Emler (1990) suggested that reputations reflect information that is shared and transmitted within a social context, and thus reputations are not developed, nor do they operate, in a vacuum. As stated previously, the main reasons for engaging in reputation-building behavior are to obtain rewards, or to fulfill an inner desire to convey to others around them a message concerning who individuals think they are (Baumeister, 1982a, 1982b).

Whether this drive is external (i.e., an attempt to gain external rewards) or internal (i.e., brought on by a desire to establish an identity in a group), the process of reputation building is the same. These aspirations are based on personal desires, and, as such, are subjective. That being said, individuals often will observe the treatment and rewards others receive, and wish the same for themselves. In doing so, they attempt to attribute what actions the individual (or group) is performing in order to receive these rewards, and then may try to emulate such actions in hopes of receiving the same treatment (Schunk, 1987).

Selection of Referents
Early research on social comparisons in organizational behavior suggested that individuals assess their situation using essentially the three referents of other, self, and system (Goodman, 1974), which may differentially affect the attitudes and behavior of those individuals. However, subsequent work in this area has identified a number of different referents used by individuals, including self-present, self-past, self-future, and other (i.e., past, present, and future). Indeed, Kulik and Ambrose (1992) identified twelve different potential referent categories.

According to Festinger (1954), a unidirectional drive upward is a desire by individuals to be slightly better then those with whom they compare themselves. This drive can "… be viewed as an indication of the desire to change one's position relative to others" (p. 127). In order to effectively fulfill the goal of changing one's position in an organization, an individual will assess the referent "self" as well as the "system." This assessment of self (Goodman, 1974) will consider the current standing the individual has in the company, compared with the reputational goals or aspirations of the focal individual. It will evaluate inputs and outputs of both positions, determining the discrepancies that need to be addressed.

The assessment of the "system" referent will help define the path reputation-building individuals must take in order to achieve their goals. The system referent refers to the structural aspects of the organization; for example, contractual agreements that the organization will provide for levels of power attained (March & Simon, 1958). Whereas these inputs and outcomes traditionally have been considered to be tied to formal positions and power, it can be assumed that in today's organizations, more informal power also could be tied to such positions. Based on the information gained by observing "system" as well as informal norms, individuals building reputations will attempt to deliver their message through actions that are intended to be received and interpreted by a specific audience (Elmer, 1984; Reicher & Elmer, 1988).

As mentioned earlier, time also has been suggested as an aspect of social comparison, whereby the past, present, and future may all cross, and create different combinations of, the referent categories. For example, anticipated self-future relates to reputation, where self-future is a comparison of the current self against the expected future self (Oldham, Kulik, Ambrose, Stepina, & Brand, 1986). This future self will reflect the goals toward which the present self is currently striving.

In order for individuals to achieve these goals (i.e., and become the future-self), they will find individuals (or groups) who have already achieved the goals, and model the aspects of their behavior after those of the referents they believe are responsible for the desired attributes (Schunk, 1987), within the context of the system. The individuals who are models or referents often are considered to be "standard setters" (Feldman & Ruble, 1981). That is, such "standard setters" help define the inputs and outputs for their level of achievement, and they often are individuals of extremely high ability. Therefore, to use them as a referent for upward social comparison is appropriate. Due to the complex nature of reputation, the referent selection process involves the self (i.e., comparing the present with future), other (i.e., comparing the self with a model or standard setter in an effort to define the behaviors that would grand the desired rewards), and the system that grants the rewards for specific behaviors.

Behavioral Norms
Norms for individual behavior largely are defined by an individual's role within a context of the network. As individuals interact with others, a network of roles and their attending behavioral expectations, known as a role-set, is established. These role-sets are laden with certain prescriptions for expected behavior (Merton, 1968; Katz & Kahn, 1978; Tsui, 1984).

Organizations can be characterized as collections of roles organized to meet some demand for goods or services, and to serve the needs of the individuals that make up the organizations (Friedkin, 1998; Katz & Kahn, 1978; Merton, 1968; Tsui, Egan, & O'Reilly, 1992). These roles are defined by the nature of the goods and services produced, as well as the organization level in which the roles reside. Tsui (1984) argued that the effectiveness of managers (i.e., as analyzed from their role set and the expectations of peers, superiors, and subordinates) is grounded in their self-interests, and their ability to satisfy their multiple (and often quite different) constituencies. As individuals deviate from these norms, others take notice (Elmer, 1984), and tend to reevaluate the individual based on the expected actions of the individual versus actual events (Weick, 1979).

Human Capital
Human capital theory argues that individuals generate increased worth or value for themselves by acquiring knowledge, skills, and credentials through educational and experiential attainments. Attainment of additional educational degrees contributes to the value of one's human capital, as does the prestige of the institutions from which the degrees were granted. Job knowledge and experience also build human capital, as do the skills one acquires through training. So, human capital is the knowledge and skill that an individual possesses, which are the direct result of their investments in education and training (Becker, 1993). Studies have indicated that factors such as age, race, and gender can affect the return on investments made in human capital.

As a component of reputation, human capital represents investments made by individuals to enhance their public image. In the form of credentials, human capital provides instant creditability and status for the holders, sending signals to others based on individual attributes they possess (Spence, 1973). Similarly, certain characteristics make individuals more marketable and mobile (Trevor, 2001).

Education, Experience, Expertise, and Demographic Characteristics. Because lifetimes are finite, age has to be considered in any discussion concerning the value of human capital. The timing of investments in human capital is a factor in the resulting value, with early investments in education and training being likely to yield greater life-long returns. The age of a college graduate reflects the potential stream of contributions, in that a younger person would be expected to have greater long-term potential. Also, age serves as a proxy for experience, whereby older individuals are believed to be more experienced.

Education and experience are both components of an individual's reputation that are affected by age, but the relationship is not always linear. As an example, consider Steve Jobs in his career at Apple computer. Early in his career, Jobs' reputation as a business visionary far exceeded any multiple of his age with either years of education or experience. In contrast, former IBM CEO John Akers had a reputation that developed over time as a more linear combination of age and experience.

Expertise. Most fields that study reputation would agree that individuals often are known for excelling in certain areas. In marketing, companies wish to be known for producing the "best" product (Scherer, 1980). In organization theory, companies wish to acquire a reputation for being considered at the top of their field (Barney, 1991). The study of inner city gangs has shown us that youths wish to gain a reputation for being tougher than those around them (Elmer, 1984). Most intentional, positive reputations are based on being known for excelling in a specific task. In fact, it can be argued that perceived expertise by one's peers is the first step toward gaining a reputation.

From the human capital perspective, gender and race have strong implications for reputation. Drawing from signaling theory, value is placed on various individual attributes in lieu of information on the person's actual capabilities (Spence, 1973). Demographic characteristics, such as gender, race, and age, are part of one's human capital, and thus one's reputational make-up. These characteristics might operate directly, as well as interactively with other attributes, to load into the composite personal reputation construct.

Reputation also is influenced by the set of personal characteristics individuals possess, and therefore, is reflective of one's intelligence, personality, and social effectiveness skills. Such characteristics serve as both foundational and facilitative bases of overt behavior, and they influence how people are perceived and evaluated in work settings, as well as affecting how individuals perform various aspects of their work roles. We identify and discuss representative constructs in this area, rather than conducting a comprehensive or exhaustive examination.

General Mental Ability.   One personal characteristic that we suggest has an influence on reputation, and has been actively researched for years, is intelligence, cognitive ability, or general mental ability (GMA). Schmidt and Hunter's (1998) review suggested that GMA tends to be the single most valid predictor of future job performance and learning. We would argue that GMA demonstrates its influence on reputation the extent to which it guides and facilitates work performance effectiveness.

Possessing GMA, and using it productively in the work environment, is important for reputation, but it is by no means the sole aspect of such personal capital. Indeed, the direct influence of GMA, as the primary predictor of individual performance, has been called into question when non-cognitive variables have been proposed to challenge its predictive effectiveness (McClelland, 1993; Sternberg & Wagner, 1993). Instead of posing arguments promoting a single personal characteristic, contemporary thinking seems to favor consideration of predictors that supplement the contribution of GMA, which might include personality measures and social effectiveness skills. We certainly see this is to be the case for the reputation construct.

Personality and Social Effectiveness.   Personality characteristics and social effectiveness reflect a second category of personal qualities that collectively we believe build personal capital and reputation. Patterns of behavior that individuals demonstrate at work, which are generated by personality traits, can expect to exert a strong influence on the reputations they earn. The program of research by Mount and Barrick (1995) has helped to establish the role of personality in the prediction of job performance (i.e., with particular reference to the Five-Factor Model). As a consequence of this research, personality generally is viewed by organizational scientists as possessing considerable potential to improve our understanding of people in organizations and their work behavior, including shedding important light on reputation.

Social effectiveness competencies contribute to personal reputation as well. The ability to effectively read, understand, and control social interactions in the workplace has been of interest to behavioral scientists for quite some time. In the organizational context, social effectiveness is reflected in the effective exercise of persuasion, explanation, and other influence mechanisms that reveal the ability to control others (Argyle, 1969). Political perspectives on organizations have suggested that in order to be effective in such environments, individuals must be socially astute and skilled interpersonally (e.g., Mintzberg, 1983; Pfeffer, 1981).

Perhaps the most critical type of social effectiveness needed in organizational settings is political skill, which is regarded as an interpersonal style construct that combines interpersonal perceptiveness or social astuteness with the capacity to adjust one's behavior to different contextual demands in ways that build trust, confidence, and genuineness, and effectively influence and control the responses of others (Ferris, Davidson, & Perrewé, 2005a; Ferris et al., 2005b). People high in political skill not only know precisely what to do in different social situations, but also exactly how to execute behavior with a sincere, engaging manner that disguises any ulterior motives, inspires believability, trust, and confidence, and renders influence attempts successful.

Recently, scholars have discussed the relationship between personality and social effectiveness. Hogan (1991) and Hogan and Shelton (1998) defined personality as including both an internal 'identity' component and an external 'reputation' component. According to Hogan, identity refers to how we think about ourselves and how we want others to think about us, and it serves to guide our behavior in social interactions. Reputation is viewed as the outside perspective on personality, and it refers to how others think about and evaluate our efforts to achieve our goals and be successful. In essence, identity is reflective of individuals' potential, and reputation is indicative of how successful they are at realizing their potential.

Hogan (1991) and Hogan and Shelton (1998) argued for an intricate relationship between personality and social effectiveness, suggesting that social effectiveness is what translates identity into successful goal accomplishment or reputation. Block and Kremen (1996) also addressed the relationship between social effectiveness and personality, suggesting that social effectiveness essentially maintains the personality system within tenable bounds, and allows for acceptable adaptation.

Mayer (2005) proposed a "systems framework" of personality, which focuses on the complete psychological functioning of the individual, and he organized personality into four major subsystems: Energy Lattice, Knowledge Works, Social Actor, and Conscious Executive. The Social Actor subsystem is most relevant for our purposes here, and Mayer (2005, p. 299) argued that it "represents the expression of personality in a socially adaptive fashion. It includes social skills, role knowledge, and emotionally preferred expressions."

Such views suggest the important connection between personality and social effectiveness, whereby personality brings to life, and external observation, the internal dynamics of one's personality characteristics. Ferris et al. (in press-b) proposed a conceptualization of the characteristic themes reflected by certain personality or dispositional constructs, and how they serve as antecedents or predictors of political skill.

Therefore, we envision personality as more distal constructs that shape and predict features of social effectiveness (e.g., political skill), which in turn are more proximal antecedents of reputation. Liu, Ferris, Zinko, Perrewé, Weitz, and Xu (in press) recently provided empirical support for these linkages. We suggest that political skill is a critical component in personal reputation development because it enables workers to more effectively navigate political environments and influence others in the work setting by conveying the proper image (Ferris et al., 2005a). As one's responsibilities increase, particularly in managing and leading others, political skill may be the one factor that best enables individuals to rise to lofty heights in their careers. To the degree that navigating organizational politics and influencing others are critical factors in managerial success, political skill will help individuals build reputations for savvy and leadership influence that is so valued in organizations today (Ferris et al., in press-b; Ferris et al., 2005b; Ferris et al., 2005a).

Self-Regulation of Behavior
As individuals assess their positions in organizations, they often feel a desire to alter their status. To do this, they must convince those around them of their new reputation. Once individuals find appropriate referents who are receiving the rewards or status to which they aspire, such individuals must identify and demonstrate those similar behaviors that should produce similar rewards. These behaviors must be considered in the context of the norms of the organization. The (other) referent chosen may be outside the organization (Oldham et al., 1986), so reputation-building individuals may need to adapt their behavior to the norms and referent system of the current environment.

The regulation of behaviors must be done with an awareness of the referent system, as well as consideration of the audience's response (Gotsi & Wilson, 2001). As the model suggests, we propose that human capital affects one's ability to self-regulate behaviors. It does this not only by supplying the necessary cognitive abilities to properly assess the surrounding norms, but also by providing the will power necessary to self regulate one's actions (Schmidt & Hunter, 1998).

Shearmur and Klein (1997) interpreted Adam Smith's *The Great Society* as viewing society as a "patchwork of reputational nexuses," and as such, it creates a framework within which impressions of others are formed. These authors argued that individuals' desire for approbation is socially learned, and is developed within the reputational patchwork. In line with our argument, they suggested that individuals can craft their own reputations, and more importantly, they suggested that individuals can alter the very framework that defines their reputations. This suggests that individuals who are self regulating, not only try to affect their behavior, but also may change the norms that are used to evaluate their behavior. That is, they might adapt their behavior to fit the situation, or they might maintain the existing behavioral repertoire, but exercise influence over and alter the contextual norms in acceptable ways, thus, effectively adapting the context to their behavior.

In order to discuss behavioral norms, it is necessary to define the context of the workplace. Jaques (1989) presented a useful perspective from which to view individuals in organizations, framing organizations as intricate webs of roles or positions that possess explicit and implicit expectations for behavior. These behavioral norms then become the baseline for judging behavior within the context of the organization.

Similarly, role theory proposes that each position in an organization has an inherent set of role expectations, which take the form of implicit contracts between individuals and their peers, subordinates, and supervisors (e.g., Katz & Kahn, 1978; Merton, 1968). Such sets of role expectations include cues on aspects of work-related behavior, such as, desired behaviors, organizational norms, values, attitudes, and justice. According to role theory, the behavior of individuals is judged against these behavioral norms in the eyes of their subordinates, peers, and supervisors, thus forming expectations that become cues for determining conformity (Tsui, 1984). To the extent that individuals deviate from the behavioral norms, their behavior becomes salient in the eyes of others. Therefore, at its most basic level, reputation formation is simply a measure of behavioral incongruence with specific role expectations.

The relationship between reputation and behavior in the workplace is significant because reputation inconspicuously affects not only the choice of work behaviors, but also the effectiveness of those behaviors. These behaviors simultaneously craft and reinforce the very reputation from which the actions and interpretations were derived. The ebb and flow of this reputational balance represents both the temporal and delicate nature of the context of social influence behavior in organizations. It is within this context that our personal reputation within the organization resides, and it is the inability to detach individual behavior from this context that makes the further evaluation of reputation necessary to extend our understanding of social influence within organizations.

Social Capital

Social capital is the ability to take advantage of opportunity through social networks (Burt, 1997). More specifically, social capital has been defined as "the actual and potential resources individuals obtain from knowing others, being part of a social network with them, or merely from being known to them and having a good reputation. In a sense, social capital provides individuals with an important type of credential – a favorable social identity that can be converted into significant, tangible benefits" (Baron & Markman, 2000, p. 107).

Within organizations, social capital at the individual level is the product of one's human capital and social networks. Burt (1997) has viewed human capital as individual ability and social capital as opportunity, where the organization provides opportunities through networks and individuals must possess the ability to take advantage of such opportunities. The mix of human capital and the ability to use social networks help define the personal reputations of organization members.

There are two opposing views on social capital development. Useem and Karabel (1986) suggested that social capital development results from "class-linked" personal contacts, whereas Coleman (1990) subscribed to the structural view, linking social capital to access to information and resources provided by structural networks. In either case, social capital helps to construct reputation because it conveys information concerning creditability that people will use to make judgments (Belliveau, O'Reilly, & Wade, 1996).

Several empirical studies have supported the value of social capital in providing useful outcomes that may contribute to one's reputation. For example, Siebert, Kraimer, and Liden (2001) found that social capital, through network development, had a positive impact on career success. Specifically, their study reported that access to information, resources, and mentoring were positively related to career success. To the extent that one can build a reputation for early success in one's career, the development of networks and use of the social capital in these networks can facilitate such success. Kilduff and Krackhardt (1994) found that the perception that individuals associated with prominent friends at work sent a signal of importance or distinction, and favorably influenced those individuals' performance reputations.

In a study of research scientists, Bouty (2000) discovered a positive relationship between social capital, measured by network affiliation, and resource acquisition. Interestingly, she found that access to resources was given based on personal contact and mutual trust. Thus, we might expect that trust would develop over time as part of one's reputation within the research networks.

In general, individuals attempt to influence others' perceptions of the social networks within which they are embedded (Cialdini & De Nicholas, 1989). They can be successful at this task because perceptions of the context in even relatively small organizational networks vary considerably from one person to the next (Krackhardt, 1990). Even when individuals are not trying to actively influence others, their actions may be interpreted by an audience as unusual (Haviland, 1977).

We believe that the various components of reputation combine in interesting, important, and quite complex ways. Indeed, similar in nature to how the resource-based view of the firm discusses this construct at the organization level, we envision a synergistic combination of qualities whereby the whole that is created is greater than the simple sum of the individual components (e.g., Barney, 1991). This creates a unique quality to personal reputation, and one that provides a source of personal sustained competitive advantage for the individual in social environments.

Deviation from Behavioral Norms
As shown in Fig. 1, reputation is based on observable actions, and these actions must stand out in such a way that observers will find them interesting enough to report to others (Haviland, 1977). When judging an incident, observers view the event with anticipations and assumptions about that event based on past information about the individual in question (Weick, 1979). These anticipations are based on the expected norms derived from roles that consist of those behaviors that are characteristic of the person and context being observed (Biddle & Thomas, 1966). The "surprise" (Weick, 1979, p. 4) is any deviation that varies too greatly from the norms for expected behavior in that context to be part of the role (Becker, 1963). When there is an inconsistency or surprise, the observer feels a need to explain it (Weick, 1979). Once the event is understood, the observer will attempt to attribute the cause of the event (Heider, 1958).

Also distinguishing the behavioral deviation in the eyes of observers is the way it is made salient and commands attentional focus. Social cognition scholars have defined salience as "the phenomenon that when one's attention is differentially directed to one portion of the environment rather than to others, the information contained in that portion will receive disproportionate weighting in subsequent judgments" (Taylor & Thompson,

1982, p. 175). Particularly in somewhat ambiguous situations, attention will be drawn to individuals who demonstrate behaviors that set them apart from others, leading to extreme evaluations (Taylor & Fiske, 1978). Thus, it is the salience of the deviant behavior that will attract observer attention, and begin the process of reputation building.

The possible deviations are anything that varies too widely from the average to be part of the role (Becker, 1963). Rindova et al. (2006) suggested that such deviance is what fuels celebrity status because the media reports on actions that represent deviations from the norm. Behaviors deviating from these roles force audiences to reevaluate the individual being observed (Biddle & Thomas, 1966). This reevaluation leads individuals to consider whether the focal individual is part of a group into which he/she was originally classified, or is regarded as an outsider (Becker, 1963). If an observer is able to reclassify an individual into a different group (i.e., dissolving the relationship between the norm and the individual), one where the repeated deviations are considered the norm, the future actions of the individual once again will be predictable, and make sense to the audience (Weick, 1979). Additionally, this new classification should reduce ambiguity regarding the individual in question.

Even if the deviations from the norm do not propel the reputation-building individual to a different normative status, it is still beneficial. Research has shown that when decision makers lack information about an employee, they rely on prevailing cognitions, such as stereotypes (Drazin & Auster, 1987). Furthermore, one manifestation of such prevailing cognitions can be reputation, and it could increase beneficial treatment in the workplace.

Attributions for the Causes of Behavior

Attribution theory is based on the assumption that individuals have an inherent need to explain the causes of events that surround them (Heider, 1958). So, this part of the model indicates that the relationship between the audience assessment of the behavioral deviation from norms and the conferring of reputation on the actor by the audience is moderated by the cause to which the behavior is attributed. Certainly, this relationship should be stronger the extent to which the audience makes a personal or dispositional (i.e., internal) attribution for the behavior, as opposed to a situational (i.e., external) one. The ascription of a dispositional attribution allocates causal responsibility for the behavior to the person, so that it cannot be explained away as a function of contextual forces, which would deprive the actor of such responsibility.

Markus and Zajonc (1985) suggested that individuals tend to draw attention from others the extent to which they possess features, or demonstrate behavior, that sets them apart from others. Furthermore, Taylor and Fiske (1978) concluded that when individuals distinguish themselves by attracting attention, they tend to be rated more extremely, are better remembered by others, and are more likely to have their focal behavior attributed dispositionally, so as to allocate causal responsibility to themselves.

Time (Repeated Nature of Behavior)
Although many scholars most likely would agree that a reputation may be lost or greatly diminished with one wrong move (e.g., Nixon and Watergate, Exxon and the Valdez, Firestone and the Ford Explorer), most have proposed that reputation must be proactively maintained over time (i.e., Ferris et al., 2003; Biddle & Thomas, 1966). Indeed, the very nature of reputation suggests that it is a time-dependent phenomenon, whereby it does not occur based on a single demonstration of a behavioral deviation from the norm. A single deviation from the norm, if radical enough, may launch an individual into celebrity status (e.g., Monika Lewinski), but by established definition, this does not create a reputation, because the deviation from the norms is not consistently repeated (Kreps & Wilson, 1982; Ferris et al., 2003).

Although an individual may become "known for an action," this would manifest itself in the form of fame or notoriety (Johnson, 2004), but because the information that is provided offers no predictive qualities (Scherer, 1980), it would not greatly aid in reputation building. We view reputation as becoming a solidified and stable shared perception by an audience only as the focal behavior is repeated over time, thus leading others to expect certain behaviors and actions from the focal individual.

In recent years, systematic attention has been drawn to the issue of time in the organizational sciences, suggesting that time be incorporated in meaningful ways to enrich theory and research (e.g., George & Jones, 2000). Phenomena like socialization and career progress, in addition to reputation, have a temporal component that is critical to an informed understanding of these constructs.

Reputation
Ferris et al. (2003) suggested a "capital as metaphor" perspective on reputation, which borrows from Fombrun's (1996) notion of "reputational capital" (i.e., as it applies to corporate reputations), and highlights the common notion that reputation has value. Ferris et al. argued that the

source of a reputation's value lies in how it allows others to use individuals' reputations to predict their future behavior. Tyler and Kramer (1996) suggested that the value of reputational effects stem from the degree of trust elicited in social interactions. From this social network perspective, indirect or third-party ties are a source of information that serves to enhance the trust one places in another.

This triangulation effect on an individual's reputation serves to increase the reputation's value among multiple constituents, and consequently, the reputational costs of non-cooperative behavior as well (Gulati & Westphal, 1999). Similarly, Tyler and Kramer (1996) noted this effect when they suggested that social institutions sanction those who violate trust, and that by making untrustworthy behavior costly, these social institutions assert both formal and informal control. This market conceptualization implies that the prediction of future behavior is a form of information that has value commensurate with its accuracy.

Klein (1997) argued that reputation is a proxy for trust, and he contended that social interactions take place under conditions of uncertainty. Furthermore, he argued that this uncertainty extends to the contextual details of the myriad of interactions in our daily lives, and in an effort to reduce uncertainty, individuals look for seals of approval on others, and covet those same seals for themselves. Complicating these interactions is the notion that an individual's reputation is constantly being redefined beyond the level of the dyadic exchange.

It has been proposed that personal reputation is a difficult to imitate asset that is acquired through social interaction. This is because personal reputation is developed in an environment of imperfect information, where individuals may use reputation to "signal" their intentions in a manner that suggests to the audience information that may or may not be known about the individual (Ferris & Judge, 1991; Spence, 1973, 1974). This "signaling" is based on the assessment individuals make of their environment, and it can be used to force an audience to reassess how an individual is viewed (Ravlin & Thomas, 2005).

The motivation to send these signals has been addressed in the sociological view of reputation, suggesting that reputation is used to link people to specific identities. These identities are employed to acknowledge an individual's attributes and status in the group (Elmer, 1984; Carroll et al., 2003). Individuals assess their status in an organization by comparing themselves with others around them (de Botton, 2004; Festinger, 1954). If this position is objectionable to them, they will attempt to change the image others have of them (Baumeister, 1982a) by sending out signals that are consistent with the group to which they aspire (Ravlin & Thomas, 2005).

Consequences of Reputation

As noted in the model in Fig. 1, reputation has both direct, or immediate, consequences, and indirect outcomes that work through the direct consequences. Because reputation is defined as a collective and shared perception by others, it is appropriate to consider consequences of reputation that operate on others, including performance ratings and compensation given by supervisors, and power and discretionary behavior granted to the focal person by both coworkers and superiors. However, it is also important to acknowledge that the reputation individuals develop also exert effects on themselves in the form of attitudes. Both are considered in this phase of the model.

Direct Outcomes

Discretionary Behavior.   As individuals establish their reputations, they are allotted more discretion regarding their actions (Diamond, 1989). Studies dealing with agency theory show organizations are willing to pay more for individuals with established reputations (Wernerfelt, 1988) because their reputations can act as socially mediated controls for self-interested behavior (Arrow, 1985). This ability to predict the actions of another suggests that a strong reputation can lead to trust in the individual regarding certain actions and behaviors (e.g., Tyler & Kramer, 1996). This reflects Whitmeyer's (2000) views of reputation, who suggested reputation is important "because it informs the formation of the subjective probability relevant to placing trust" (p. 190).

Both Greenberg (1990) and Knoke (1983) reflected similar views regarding reputation. Greenberg supported this argument using Hollander's (1958) notion of "idiosyncrasy credits" as a vehicle, by proposing that marginal latitude or "benefit of the doubt" was granted to those with particularly defined reputations. Knoke (1983) showed that greater freedom was given to organizations that have a high "influence reputation," defined as "an actor's reputation for influence" (p. 1068). These notions suggest that reputation has informational, predictive, and trust-enhancing value, and that those with strong, powerful reputations will be treated differently then those with lesser reputations.

Power.   Pfeffer (1992) suggested that as individuals gain reputation, they gain power, and that power gives individuals the ability to get things done easier, resulting in a stronger reputation, which brings more power. This idea that reputation brings power relates to Hollander's (1958) idiosyncrasy credit and referent power (as discussed above). Hollander suggested that individuals are able to store idiosyncrasy credits by being of value to a group. These credits then can be 'cashed in' to 'buy' increased discretion (within reason). Gioia and Sims (1983) showed reputation contributed significantly to subordinate perceptions of legitimate, referent, and expert power in the study of managers. Matthews (1988) supported the idea that reputation is purely a social construct, suggesting that reputation is power that is based less on reality than appearance.

French and Raven (1959) theorized five bases of power: reward power, coercive power, legitimate power, referent power, and expert power. Legitimate power is granted to individuals giving them power over other individuals. Because this basis is tied to a formal position (i.e., by the organization), reputation (i.e., being a social, not formal construct) may not have a direct effect upon it, but would likely have an indirect effect through autonomy and career success. Furthermore, because legitimate power is granted by organizations to individuals based on their positions, others holding that position may expect similar power. This again suggests that legitimate power is not based on reputation, since it is so easily passed on to whoever holds that particular position.

Both reward and coercive power depend on the ability of a subject to reward or punish an individual or group. It has been suggested that an increase in reputation results in an increase in power (Pfeffer, 1992). More powerful individuals have been shown to attract a larger allotment of resources than normally designated to their position (Keltner, Gruenfeld, & Anderson, 2003). This control of excess resources would allow a highly reputed individual the ability to grant rewards or punishments to others as consistent with their reputation (Stevens, 2002). Furthermore, as information and resources contribute to social power bases, personal reputations of individuals should increase as they can more readily access such information and resources (Kilduff & Krackhardt, 1994; Tsui, 1984), which should enhance their perceived influence and power (Brass, 1984; Brass & Burkhardt, 1993).

Referent power is the "ability to administer to another feelings of obligation or responsibility" (Hinkin & Schriesheim, 1989). When individuals have a strong, positive reputation, others around them will wish to be identified with such individuals. Current research regarding the phenomena of "basking in reflected glory" suggests such actions (see Snyder, Lassegard, & Ford, 1986 for a review of the "basking in reflected glory" literature). Expert power is based on the perception of an individual or group regarding a subject. Individuals compare their knowledge or proficiency regarding a topic against what they believe the subject's knowledge is regarding the same topic. If individuals or groups decide that the subject has advanced knowledge or skills, they will defer to the subject regarding that topic. Like referent power, expert power is not based on intimidation or external pressure, but a giving of the power by others.

As individuals gain reputation, they gain power (Pfeffer, 1992). However, because reputation is a social construct, the direct power gained will not be legitimate. Additionally, both reward and coercive power are based on the individual's ability to reward and punish others. This power may come from not only formal but also informal authority, and the authority to delegate tasks is an example of these powers. In order for a subject to act in such a manner, a certain level of autonomy first must be gained (e.g., if an individual is being closely monitored by a supervisor, this behavior may, or may not, be allowed). Therefore, it is proposed that although reputation can bring about coercive and reward power, it does so through autonomy (and career success), and therefore is not a direct outcome of reputation.

Job Performance.   We propose that reputation affects job performance, which is often measured by subjective ratings by a supervisor. Supervisor ratings have been known to be influenced by others, whereby influence tactics have been found to affect performance ratings, even when there are no actual differences in job performance. Furthermore, such ratings have been shown to be biased, distorted, and often not reflective of actual job performance (e.g., Ferris & Judge, 1991; Higgins, Judge, & Ferris, 2003). Because reputation is used to fill in where perfect information is not available, managers may use reputation to rate employees on related areas (see Thorndike, 1920 for an explanation of halo effect).

The idea that individuals may try to manage their reputations by getting others to evaluate them on the basis of process measures, such as effort, rather than outcomes, such as actual objective results, is not a new idea (e.g., March, 1984; Ferris et al., 1994). When individuals are hired based on reputation, they are paid more then their counterparts who lack such reputation (Wade et al., 2006). Because the reputation implies expertise in a specific area (Haviland, 1977), individuals with strong, positive reputations often may be given higher goals by their superiors as justification for the higher pay. Even if those reputable individuals do not accomplish the goals set forth, supervisors will still often rate high-reputation individuals higher than those with lesser goals, regardless of fulfilment of the goals set (Dossett & Greenberg, 1981). Furthermore, the more ambiguous the performance criteria, the more likely an enhanced reputation may affect evaluations (Eisenberg, 1984; Williams & Goss, 1975).

Compensation.   Compensation has been linked to reputation in a number of studies (i.e., Wade et al., 2006; Zajac & Westphal, 1995). There are several ways that compensation can be evaluated to include actual money paid as well as symbolic and status-enhancing indicators sent out about the individual in question. Managers have been shown to award higher pay raises to subordinates when the managers were dependent on the subordinates' expertise. This implies that a reputation for expertness is directly related to financial reward (Bartol & Martin, 1990). Furthermore, empirical research has shown that those with a stronger reputation receive more rewards than their counterparts (Wade et al., 2006).

Indirect Outcomes

Promotions and Career Success.   Promotions are considered some of the most political decisions made in organizations (e.g., Ferris & Judge, 1991). Early impressions by decision makers are said to affect this process greatly. Similarly, reputations can have considerable influence early on, due to lack of information that is available regarding the individual. The effects of these first impressions can be seen in the discussion of tournament mobility, and how people get positioned and can influence their ability to be successful in such competitions (e.g., Cooper, Graham, & Dyke, 1993; Rosenbaum, 1989).

Furthermore, as individuals are promoted at a rapid rate, they may gain a reputation as being "on the fast track." In such situations, these rising stars may enter into a loop of being promoted based on reputation, which gives the individual a more powerful reputation due to fast promotion, which leads to more promotions. Modeled after the idea that power brings more power (Pfeffer, 1981), those with strong, positive reputations may see not only faster promotions, but also other forms of career mobility.

Mobility suggests not only vertical movement though a single organization, but also passage through different positions, perhaps in a number of different organizations, over a reasonably extended period of time (e.g., over a person's entire career). The number of moves over a specified time period is not the focal issue, but the nature of the positions obtained as well as the quality of the organizations at which one accepts positions are indicators of reputation.

Subjective Well-Being.   Exploration into the subject of reputation suggests that almost all individuals strive for what they perceive to be a positive reputation. It has been suggested that this desire to be admired by ones peers is a basic drive to gain contentment (Caste & Burke, 2002). Subjective well-being can be explained as one specific measure of mental health, and it focuses on people's own evaluations not only of their lives as a whole, but also about specific domains of life, such as work, both in affective and cognitive terms (Warr, 1990). Diener (2000) defined subjective well-being as "people's evaluations of their lives – evaluations that are both affective and cognitive" (p. 34).

The various direct outcomes (i.e., discretionary behavior, power, job performance and compensation) of reputation discussed above are not totally independent of one another. Those individuals responsible for making decisions about performance ratings also may be in charge of assessing promotability and salary for a particular individual. Therefore, there is inevitably going to be cross-decision biases.

Because these outcomes may be granted to an individual in an overlapping manner, one can argue that they can be viewed as a form of resources to be gained by reputation. Because a strong, positive reputation may result in such reserves, reputation can be viewed as a manner of conserving such resources, because once a reputation is built, less energy may be spent maintaining it. The ability to replenish such resources has been shown to affect all aspects of well-being, such as burnout (Wright & Hobfoll, 2004), emotional exhaustion (Ito & Brotheridge, 2003), and stress (Hobfoll, 2001). Indeed, a powerful reputation not only helps replenish resources, but also provides opportunities to defend one's resources.

Moderators of the Reputation–Outcomes Relationships

In addition to the investigation of the direct effects of personal reputation on work outcomes, research should consider the potential moderating effects of reputation. Influence tactics and strategies that individuals employ should reflect their intended reputation. Both Donald Trump (i.e., *The Apprentice*) and Simon Cowell (i.e., *American Idol*) have established reputations as bullies. The influence tactics employed by both men are consistent with their reputations (i.e., harsh and direct), which all contribute to the desired "bully" image they worked at constructing, because it serves their purposes (Ferris, Zinko, Brouer, Buckley, & Harvey, in press-c).

In support, Tedeschi and Melburg (1984) argued that the selection and effectiveness of influence tactics by individuals will differ as a function of their reputations, and research has demonstrated initial support for such interactions when testing these notions in the laboratory, where reputation was manipulated (Rosen et al., 1990), and in the field, where positive reputation facilitated the favorable effects of political behavior on job performance and affective work outcomes (Hochwarter, Ferris, Zinko, Arnell, & James, 2007).

Implicit Model Assumptions
Although not included in Fig. 1, for purposes of clarity and ease of reading, the proposed conceptualization of reputation includes three feedback loops that have important meaning, which is consistent with the temporal nature of reputation noted above. One loop extends from Reputation back to Human Capital, and this suggests that as one cycles through this reputation-building process over time, "reputational capital" accrues, which is an indication of the relative value associated with a reputation (Fombrun, 1996). In essence, then, reputation (and the capital it accrues) becomes an important part of individuals' personal asset portfolio, and therefore, it becomes part of their human capital.

Another feedback loop extends back from Reputation to Deviation from Behavioral Norms, and this is included because as individuals build reputations, the very definition of what constitutes a deviation from conventional norms of behavior changes. Essentially, as reputations build, trust in the individual increases (e.g., Whitmeyer, 2000), there is less perceived need to monitor the individual's behavior (Wernerfelt, 1988), and such individuals are granted more "idiosyncrasy credits" (Hollander, 1958), and thus more latitude to deviate from norms for behavior, and incur greater discretion and autonomy (e.g., Ferris et al., 2003; Knoke, 1983).

Therefore, the very nature of what constitutes a deviation from behavioral norms becomes redefined for people with greater reputations. The third feedback loop extends from Reputation back to Social Capital, and indicates that as reputations grow, so do the alliances, coalitions, networks, and social capital one accrues. So, social capital both affects the development of reputations, and also is affected by reputation development over time.

DISCUSSION AND DIRECTIONS FOR FUTURE RESEARCH

Personal reputations at work play an important role in the selection of behaviors individuals choose to exhibit, as well as the audiences they choose to have view such behaviors. Although reputation is a construct we discuss actively in everyday life and in work settings, to date, there has been very little systematic work in the organizational sciences regarding the nature and process dynamics of personal reputation in organizations. The proposed conceptualization in this paper is an attempt to address that need, and to generate scholarly interest in this important area.

Although these initial results are encouraging, more research is needed to investigate how different influence tactics and strategies (i.e., particular combinations of tactics) interact with types of reputations to affect work outcomes of individuals. Thus, the notion of reputation as it applies to social influence may be one of the most promising, and yet challenging, areas of future inquiry, and builds on theoretical notions presented by Tedeschi and Melburg (1984). Reputation and influence behavior appear to be inextricably intertwined in everyday behavior, and it may be difficult to isolate on whether it is the reputation itself, or the influence behaviors strategically selected to create and/or reinforce the reputation, which explain the outcomes of reputation, such as interpersonal attraction and affect (Jones & Schrauger, 1970).

The active, intentional efforts individuals engage in to help form their own reputation is motivated by a desire to exercise control over the specific impressions that others form of them, and the images they convey (Bozeman & Kacmar, 1997). Therefore, individuals exhibit behaviors that are consistent with the reputation they desire (Baumeister & Jones, 1978; Tsui, 1984), and then are constrained in the future to demonstrate behaviors consistently that reinforce the reputation developed (Baumeister, 1982b).

Greenberg (1990) argued that "impression management strategies have the effect of reputation-building" (p. 138), and the consistent subsequent demonstration of such behaviors can contribute to reputation formation and solidification (Ferris et al., 2003). Also, Bromley (1993) argued that impression management behaviors can be used not only to sustain reputations, but also to deliberately manipulate them. Furthermore, adding to the complexity is that individuals are believed to possess multiple reputations (Schlenker, 1980; Tsui, 1984), and so they need to ensure that each is reinforced by the consistent display of reputation-appropriate behaviors. Recently, Roberts (2005) discussed similar issues of impression management behavior consistency and inconsistency in her conceptualization of professional image construction.

As we learn about how reputations are constructed, we may gain new insights into personal motivation. As individuals seek to establish or maintain their reputations within specific contexts, their behavior within those contexts should be predictable to the degree commensurate with their reputations' value. This argument posits that, as the costs of establishing and maintaining a reputation increase, so does its value within a given context. Furthermore, as the value of an individual's reputation to others increases, so then does the potential reward to the individual who possesses that reputation. Finally, as the reward potential of a reputation increases, the greater is the incentive for an individual to act in accordance with the expected behaviors suggested by the reputation.

This notion that reputation holds value is both implicitly understood, and has been explicitly addressed by Fombrun (1996) when discussing his idea of "reputational capital," and how firms accrue such benefits. He defined reputational capital as: "the amount by which the company's market value exceeds the liquidation value of its assets" (Fombrun, 1996, p. 92). Ferris et al. (2003) proposed a "capital as metaphor" perspective to suggest that personal reputations can be valuated in much the same way as Fombrun argued on behalf of corporate reputations.

This seems somewhat akin to the "human resource accounting" perspective that was introduced nearly half a century ago by Rensis Likert at the University of Michigan, working on a multidisciplinary team that included psychologists and behavioral accountants (e.g., Flamholtz, 1999). The perspective was simple in concept, but difficult in practice. Essentially, it argued that accounting principles could be used with human resources just as it is used with material resources, and investment, valuation, and return on investment calculations could be made. Although the actual practice of human resource accounting was shown to be impractical at the time, the contemporary notion of the valuation of personal reputation appears conceptually appealing. Indeed, Bok (1993) makes similar points implicitly (if not explicitly) about assigning value to reputations when he discussed the cost of talent today, with particular reference to corporate executives and other professionals.

Additionally, research is needed to explore the perceived dimensionality of the reputation construct. For example, it might be the case that reputations in organizations have a performance dimension that is distinct from a character (e.g., morals, values, integrity, etc.) dimension, or even an interpersonal dimension. Certainly, one of the many challenges facing researchers interested in reputation is the need to develop and validate a scale for measuring individual reputation. Until such a scale is developed, we will be unable to empirically explore the myriad of potential relationships between reputation and important work outcomes in organizations.

In exploring these dimensions, reputation should be considered in the context of groups. One may ask how the reputation of an individual affects that of the group. Although the construct of corporate reputations is well established, how a leader's reputation affects an organization is only just beginning (i.e., Hayward et al., 2004; Ferris et al., in press-c; Ranft et al., 2006; Wade et al., 2006). The interaction between an individual's reputation and his or her unit's reputation should be explored.

Furthermore, reputation should be explored as it relates to formal position. The power variable included in Fig. 1 only addresses one aspect, that being formal power. We suggest that there is an interaction between reputation and position, in that reputation may assist in the formation of prestige. Prestige, often defined as a reputation arising from success (Shenkar & Yuchtman-Yaar, 1997), is dependent on the position held by an individual. Indeed, for a time, position alone may grant an individual prestige (e.g., the President of the United States). By the same token, some positions, regardless of the reputation an individual may hold, will never be considered prestigious (e.g., sanitation worker). Because most positions fall somewhere in between, reputation may interact with the formal position to create prestige. Being "the best" in most fields can be considered prestigious.

Finally, research needs to explore the consequences of reputation, such as job performance, promotions and mobility, compensation, and career success. Theory and research has suggested that promotions and mobility decisions are made in tournament competitions, based on early signals of potential (e.g., Cooper et al., 1993). Perhaps future research will find that such signals of potential driving these decisions are reflective of the reputations developed early for these upwardly mobile individuals.

In discussing the career as tournament metaphor, Cooper et al. (1993) discussed the importance of the integration–differentiation balance in individuals' effectiveness in tournament competition. Integration involves conformity, fitting in, and so forth, and differentiation refers to standing out and being distinctive. How individuals develop reputations that allow them to stand out and be distinctive, as is the basis of our model, and at the same time still appear to fit with the norms can be a delicate balance to achieve, with potentially high stakes.

Future research in reputation should explore the effects of different reputations as they affect job and career outcomes in short, medium, and long-range time frames; thus, longitudinal research designs will be important. Also, in examination of long-term outcomes, we need to examine how people develop and maintain reputations through conscious and calculated strategies of influence that are designed or become emergent over a long period of time, and how the choice of reputation enhancement tactics/strategies might change at different points in the evolution of one's reputation.

The proposed conceptualization of personal reputation in organizations addresses the formation or development of reputation, which is an important part of the construct, but does not completely exhaust the full extent of the phenomenon. Indeed, once reputations are formed, they must be maintained, which involves some of the same processes that are discussed in this paper, particularly regarding the demonstration of consistent reputation-appropriate behavior over time. However, other processes may be involved in reputation maintenance. Additionally, the defense of a reputation involves more proactive and even aggressive attempts to polish up a perhaps tarnished image, which also goes beyond the scope of the present conceptualization. Ferris et al. (2003) have explicitly addressed issues regarding both reputation maintenance and defense in a preliminary manner. However, more specific theory and research is needed in the future.

CONCLUSION

Individual reputations represent a yet largely unexplored aspect of how people interact within organizations. The proposed conceptualization of personal reputation integrated a number of mutually reinforcing behavioral science theories in an effort to systematically articulate how reputations at work are formed or developed. Indeed, reputation may begin to address some of the inconsistent findings in research to date. Additionally, the potential implications of knowledge about personal reputation for what we know and think about managing human resources are significant, and may be of considerable interest to managers.

Certainly, reputations are likely an important consideration when making decisions to hire, retain, or promote individuals organizations. Finally, research on reputation offers promising insights into how and why certain individuals are valued more or less than others within specific contexts. Personal reputation may significantly contribute to our understanding of the interactions of individuals in organizations, and therefore, represents an important and exciting area for future research. We hope the present paper stimulates further work in this area.

ACKNOWLEDGMENTS

The authors wish to thank Paul Goodman for his comments on an earlier draft of this paper, and to Jerry Greenberg for his helpful comments, advice, and support concerning our program of research on personal reputation over the past several years.

REFERENCES

Ammeter, A. P., Douglas, C., Gardner, W. L., Hochwarter, W. A., & Ferris, G. R. (2002). Toward a political theory of leadership. *The Leadership Quarterly, 13*, 751–796.

Argyle, M. (1969). *Social interaction.* London: Methuen.

Arrow, K. J. (1985). The economics of agency. In: J. W. Pratt & R. J. Zeckhauser (Eds), *Principals and agents: The structure of business.* Boston, MA: Harvard Business School Press.

Baiman, S. (1991). Agency research in managerial accounting: A second look. *Accounting, Organizations and Society, 15*, 341–371.

Barney, J. (1991). Firm resources and sustained competitive advantage. *Journal of Management, 17*, 99–120.

Baron, R. A., & Markman, G. D. (2000). Beyond social capital: How social skills can enhance entrepreneurs' success. *Academy of Management Executive, 14*, 106–116.

Bartol, K. M., & Martin, D. C. (1990). When politics pays: Factors influencing managerial compensation decisions. *Personnel Psychology, 43*, 599–614.

Baumeister, R. F. (1982a). A self-presentational view of social phenomena. *Psychological Bulletin, 91*, 3–26.

Baumeister, R. F. (1982b). Self-esteem, self-presentation, and future interactions: A dilemma of reputation. *Journal of Personality, 50*, 29–45.

Baumeister, R. F., Heatherton, T. F., & Tice, D. M. (1994). *Losing control: How and why people fail at self-regulation.* New York: Academic Press.

Baumeister, R. F., & Jones, E. E. (1978). When self-presentation is constrained by the target's prior knowledge: Consistency and compensation. *Journal of Personality and Social Psychology, 36*, 608–618.

Becker, G. S. (1993). *Human capital: A theoretical and empirical analysis with special reference to education* (3rd ed.). Chicago, IL: University of Chicago Press.

Becker, H. (1963). *Outsiders: Studies in the sociology of deviance.* New York: The Free Press.

Belliveau, M., O'Reilly, C., & Wade, J. (1996). Social capital at the top: Effects of social similarity and status on CEO compensation. *Academy of Management Journal, 39*, 1568–1593.

Biddle, B., & Thomas, E. (1966). *Role theory: Concepts and research.* New York: Wiley.

Blass, F. R., & Ferris, G. R. (2007). Leader reputation: The roles of mentoring, political skill, contextual learning, and adaptation. *Human Resource Management, 46*, 5–19.

Block, J., & Kremen, A. (1996). IQ and ego-resiliency: Conceptual and empirical connections and separateness. *Journal of Personality and Social Psychology, 70*, 349–361.

Bok, D. C. (1993). *The cost of talent: How executives and professionals are paid and how it affects America.* New York: The Free Press.

de Botton, A. (2004). *Status anxiety.* New York: Vintage Books.

Bouty, I. (2000). Interpersonal and interaction influences on informal resource exchanges between R&D researches across organizational boundaries. *Academy of Management Journal, 43*, 50–66.

Bozeman, D. P., & Kacmar, K. M. (1997). A cybernetic model of impression management processes in organizations. *Organizational Behavior and Human Decision Processes, 69*, 9–30.

Brass, D. J. (1984). Being in the right place: a structural analysis of individual influence in an organization. *Administrative Science Quarterly, 29,* 518–539.

Brass, D. J., & Burkhardt, M. E. (1993). Potential power and power use: An investigation of structure and behavior. *Academy of Management Journal, 36,* 441–470.

Bromley, D. (1993). *Reputation, image, and impression management.* Chichester, UK: Wiley.

Burt, R. S. (1997). The contingent value of social capital. *Administrative Science Quarterly, 42,* 339–365.

Carroll, A., Green, S., Houghton, S., & Wood, R. (2003). Reputation enhancement and involvement in delinquency among high school students. *International Journal of Disability, Development and Education, 50,* 253–273.

Carver, C. S., & Scheier, M. F. (1982). Control theory: A useful conceptual framework for personality-social, clinical, and health psychology. *Psychological Bulletin, 92*(1), 111–135.

Caste, A. D., & Burke, P. J. (2002). A theory of self-esteem. *Social Forces, 80,* 1041–1068.

Cialdini, R. B., & De Nicholas, M. E. (1989). Self-presentation by association. *Journal of Personality and Social Psychology, 57,* 626–631.

Coleman, J. S. (1990). *Foundations of social theory.* Cambridge, MA: Belknap Press.

Collins, R. L. (1996). For better or worse: The impact of upward social comparison on self-evaluations. *Psychological Bulletin, 119,* 51–69.

Cooper, W. H., Graham, W. J., & Dyke, L. S. (1993). Tournament players. In: G. R. Ferris (Ed.), *Research in personnel and human resources management* (Vol. 11, pp. 83–132). Greenwich, CT: JAI Press.

Diener, E. (2000). Subjective well-being. The science of happiness and a proposal for a national index. *American Psychologist, 45,* 34–43.

Deaux, K. (2000). Identity. In: A. E. Kazdin (Ed.), *Encyclopedia of psychology* (Vol. 4, pp. 222–225). New York: Oxford University Press.

Degoey, P. (2000). Contagious justice: Exploring the social construction of justice in organizations. In: B. M. Staw & R. I. Sutton (Eds), *Research in organizational behavior* (Vol. 22, pp. 51–102). Oxford, UK: JAI Press/Elsevier Science.

Diamond, D. W. (1989). Reputation in debt markets. *The Journal of Political Economy, 97,* 828–862.

Doby, V. J., & Caplan, R. D. (1995). Organizational stress as threat to reputation: Effects on anxiety at work and at home. *Academy of Management Journal, 38,* 1105–1123.

Dodge, K. A., & Coie, J. D. (1987). Social information-processing factors in reactive and proactive aggression in children's peer groups. *Journal of Personality and Social Psychology, 53,* 1146–1158.

Dossett, D. L., & Greenberg, C. I. (1981). Goal setting and performance evaluation: An attributional analysis. *Academy of Management Journal, 24,* 767–779.

Drazin, R., & Auster, E. R. (1987). Wage differences between men and women: Performance appraisal ratings vs. salary allocation as the locus of bias. *Human Resource Management, 26,* 157–168.

Dunning, D., Heath, C., & Suls, J. M. (2004). Flawed self-assessment: Implications for health, education, and the workplace. *Psychological Science in the Public Interest, 5,* 69–106.

Eisenberg, E. M. (1984). Ambiguity as strategy in organizational communication. *Communications Monographs, 51,* 227–242.

Elmer, N. (1984). Differential involvement in delinquency: Toward an interpretation in terms of reputation management. *Progress in Experimental Personality Research, 13,* 173–239.

Emler, N. (1990). A social psychology of reputation. In: W. Stroebe & M. Hewstone (Eds), *European review of social psychology* (pp. 171–193). Chichester, UK: Wiley.

Emler, N., & Hopkins, N. (1990). Reputation, social identity, and the self. In: D. Abrams & M.A. Hogg (Eds), *Social identity theory: Constructive critical advances* (pp. 113–130). New York: Springer-Verlag.

Feldman, N. S., & Ruble, D. N. (1981). Social comparison strategies: Dimensions offered and options taken. *Personality and Social Psychology Bulletin, 7,* 11–16.

Feldwick, P. (1996). What is brand equity anyway, and how do you measure it? *Journal of the Marketing Research Society, 38,* 85–104.

Ferris, G. R., Blass, F. R., Douglas, C., Kolodinsky, R. W., & Treadway, D. C. (2003). Personal reputation in organizations. In: J. Greenburg (Ed.), *Organizational behavior: The state of the science* (2nd ed., pp. 211–246). Mahwah, NJ: Lawrence Erlbaum.

Ferris, G. R., Davidson, S. L., & Perrewé, P. L. (2005a). *Political skill at work: Impact on work effectiveness.* Mountain View, CA: Davies-Black Publishing.

Ferris, G. R., Fedor, D. B., & King, T. R. (1994). A political conceptualization of managerial behavior. *Human Resource Management Review, 4,* 1–34.

Ferris, G. R., Hochwarter, W. A., Buckley, M. R., Harrell-Cook, G., & Frink, D. D. (1999). Human resources management: Some new directions. *Journal of Management, 25,* 385–415.

Ferris, G. R., & Judge, T. A. (1991). Personnel/human resources management: A political influence prospective. *Journal of Management, 17,* 477–488.

Ferris, G. R., & Mitchell, T. R. (1987). The components of social influence and their importance for human resources research. In: K. M. Rowland & G. R. Ferris (Eds), *Research in personnel and human resources management* (Vol. 5, pp. 103–128). Greenwich, CT: JAI Press.

Ferris, G. R., Perrewé, P. L., Ranft, A. L., Zinko, R., Stoner, J. S., Brouer, R. L., & Laird, M. D. (in press-a). Human resources reputation and effectiveness. *Human Resource Management Review.*

Ferris, G. R., Treadway, D. C., Kolodinsky, R. W., Hochwarter, W. A., Kacmar, C. J., Douglas, C., & Frink, D. D. (2005b). Development and validation of the political skill inventory. *Journal of Management, 31,* 126–152.

Ferris, G. R., Treadway, D. C., Perrewé, P. L., Brouer, R. L., Douglas, C., & Lux, S. (in press-b). Political skill in organizations. *Journal of Management.*

Ferris, G. R., Zinko, R., Brouer, R. L., Buckley, M. R., & Harvey, M. G. (in press-c). Strategic bullying as a supplementary, balanced perspective on destructive leadership. *The Leadership Quarterly.*

Festinger, L. (1954). A theory of social comparison processes. *Human Relations, 7,* 117–140.

Flamholtz, E. G. (1999). *Human resource accounting: Advances in concepts, methods, and applications* (3rd ed.). Boston, MA: Kluwer Academic Publishers.

Fombrun, C. J. (1996). *Reputation: Realizing value from the corporate image.* Boston, MA: Harvard Business School Press.

French, J. R. P., Jr., & Raven, B. (1959). The bases of social power. In: D. Cartwright (Ed.), *Studies in social power* (pp. 150–168). Ann Arbor, MI: Institute for Social Research, University of Michigan.

Friedkin, N. E. (1998). *A structural theory of social influence.* New York: Cambridge University Press.

George, J., & Jones, G. (2000). The role of time in theory and theory building. *Journal of Management, 26,* 657–684.

Gioia, D. A., & Sims, H. P. (1983). Perceptions of managerial power as a consequence of managerial behavior and reputation. *Journal of Management, 25*, 63–81.

Goodman, P. (1974). An examination of referents used in the evaluation of pay. *Organizational Behavior and Human Performance, 12*, 170–195.

Gotsi, M., & Wilson, A. M. (2001). Corporate reputation: Seeking a definition. *Corporate Communications: An International Journal, 6*, 24–30.

Greenberg, J. (1990). Looking fair versus being fair: Managing impressions of organizational justice. In: B. M. Staw & L. L. Cummings (Eds), *Research in organizational behavior* (Vol. 12, pp. 111–157). Greenwich, CT: JAI Press.

Gulati, R., & Westphal, J. D. (1999). Cooperative or controlling? The effects of CEO-board relations and the content of interlocks on the formation of joint ventures. *Administrative Science Quarterly, 44*, 473–506.

Hall, A. T., Blass, F. R., Ferris, G. R., & Massengale, R. (2004). Leader reputation and accountability: Implications for dysfunctional leader behavior. *The Leadership Quarterly, 15*, 515–536.

Hartman, R. L., & Johnson, J. D. (1989). Social contagion and multiplexity: Communication networks as predictors of commitment and role ambiguity. *Human Communication Research, 15*, 523–548.

Haviland, J. (1977). *Gossip, reputation, and knowledge in Zinacantan.* Chicago, IL: University of Chicago Press.

Hayward, M. L. A., Rindova, V. P., & Pollock, T. G. (2004). Believing one's own press: The causes and consequences of CEO celebrity. *Strategic Management Journal, 25*, 637–655.

Heider, F. (1958). *The psychology of interpersonal relations.* New York: Wiley.

Higgins, C., Judge, T. A., & Ferris, G. R. (2003). Influence tactics and work outcomes: A meta-analysis. *Journal of Organizational Behavior, 24*, 89–106.

Hinkin, T. R., & Schriesheim, C. A. (1989). Development and application of new scales to measure the French and Raven bases of social power. *Journal of Applied Psychology, 74*, 561–567.

Hobfoll, S. E. (2001). The influence of culture, community, and the nested-self in the stress process: Advancing conservation of resources theory. *Applied Psychology: An International Review, 50*, 337–421.

Hochwarter, W. A., Ferris, G. R., Zinko, R., Arnell, B., & James, M. (2007). Reputation as a moderator of political behavior–work outcomes relationships: A two-study investigation with convergent results. *Journal of Applied Psychology, 92*, 567–576.

Hogan, R. J. (1991). Personality and personality measurement. In: M. D. Dunnette & L.M. Hough (Eds), *Handbook of industrial and organizational psychology* (2nd ed., Vol. 2, pp. 873–919). Palo Alto, CA: Consulting Psychologists Press.

Hogan, R., & Shelton, D. (1998). A socioanalytic perspective on job performance. *Human Performance, 11*, 129–144.

Hollander, E. (1958). Conformity, status, and idiosyncrasy credit. *Psychological Review, 65*, 117–127.

Ito, J. K., & Brotheridge, C. M. (2003). Resources, coping strategies, and emotional exhaustion: A conservation of resources perspective. *Journal of Vocational Behavior, 63*, 490–509.

Jaques, E. (1989). *Requisite organization.* Arlington, VA: Cason Hall & Co.

Johnson, D. E., Erez, A., Kiker, D. S., & Motowidlo, S. J. (2002). Liking and attribution of motives as mediators of the relationships between individuals' reputations, helpful behaviors, and raters' reward decisions. *Journal of Applied Psychology, 87*, 808–815.

Johnson, F. (2004). U2, mythology, and mass-mediated survival. *Popular Music and Society, 27,* 79–100.

Jones, S. C., & Schrauger, J. S. (1970). Reputation and self-evaluation as determinants of attractiveness. *Sociometry, 33,* 276–286.

Katz, D., & Kahn, R. L. (1978). *The social psychology of organizations* (2nd ed.). New York: Wiley.

Keltner, D., Gruenfeld, D. H., & Anderson, C. (2003). Power, approach, and inhibition. *Psychological Review, 110,* 265–284.

Kilduff, M., & Krackhardt, D. (1994). Bringing the individual back in: A structural analysis of the internal market for reputation in organizations. *Academy of Management Journal, 37,* 87–108.

Klein, D. B. (1997). Knowledge, reputation, and trust, by voluntary means. In: D. B. Klein (Ed.), *Reputation: Studies in the voluntary elicitation of good conduct* (pp. 1–14). Ann Arbor, MI: University of Michigan Press.

Knoke, D. (1983). Organization sponsorship and influence reputation of social influence associations. *Social Forces, 61,* 1065–1087.

Krackhardt, D. (1990). Assessing the political landscape: Structure, cognition and power in organizations. *Administrative Science Quarterly, 35,* 342–369.

Krackhardt, D., & Porter, L. W. (1985). When friends leave: A structural analysis of the relationship between turnover and stayers' attitudes. *Administrative Science Quarterly, 30,* 242–261.

Kreps, D. M., & Wilson, R. (1982). Reputation and imperfect information. *Journal of Economic Theory, 27,* 253–279.

Kulik, C. T., & Ambrose, M. L. (1992). Personal and situational determinants of referent choice. *Academy of Management Review, 17,* 212–237.

Kydd, C. T., Ogilvie, J. R., & Slade, L. A. (1990). I don't care what they say, as long as they spell my name right: Publicity, retention, and turnover. *Group and Organization Studies, 15,* 53–74.

Levin, J., & Arluke, A. (1987). *Gossip, the inside scoop.* New York: Plenum Press.

Liu, Y., Ferris, G. R., Zinko, R., Perrewé, P. L., Weitz, B., & Xu, J. (in press). Dispositional antecedents of political skill and reputation in organizations: A four-study investigation with convergence. *Journal of Vocational Behavior.*

March, J. G. (1984). Notes on ambiguity and executive compensation. *Journal of Management Studies,* (August), 53–64.

March, J. G., & Simon, H. A. (1958). *Organizations.* New York: Wiley.

Markus, H., & Zajonc, R. B. (1985). The cognitive perspective in social psychology. In: G. Lindzey & E. Aronson (Eds), *Handbook of social psychology* (3rd ed., Vol. 1, pp. 137–230). New York: Random House.

Matthews, C. (1988). *Hardball: How politics is played told by one who knows the game.* New York: Harper Perennial.

Mayer, J. D. (2005). A tale of two visions: Can a new view of personality help integrate psychology? *American Psychologist, 60,* 294–307.

McClelland, D. C. (1993). Intelligence is not the best predictor of job performance. *Current Directions in Psychological Science, 2,* 5–6.

Meindl, J. R. (1990). On leadership: An alternative to the conventional wisdom. *Research in Organizational Behavior, 12,* 159–203.

Merton, R. K. (1968). *Social theory and social structure (1968 enl. ed.).* New York: Free Press.

Milgrom, P., & Roberts, J. (1982). Predation, reputation, and entry deterrence. *Journal of Economic Theory*, *27*, 280–312.

Mintzberg, H. (1983). *Power in and around organizations*. Englewood Cliffs, NJ: Prentice-Hall.

Mount, M. K., & Barrick, M. R. (1995). The Big Five personality dimensions: Implications for research and practice in human resources management. In: G. R. Ferris (Ed.), *Research in personnel and human resources management* (Vol. 13, pp. 153–200). Greenwich, CT: JAI Press.

Oldham, G. R., Kulik, C. T., Ambrose, M. L., Stepina, L. P., & Brand, J. F. (1986). Relations between job facet comparisons and employee reactions. *Organizational Behavior and Human Decision Processes*, *38*, 28–47.

Pfeffer, J. (1981). *Power in organizations*. Boston, MA: Pitman.

Pfeffer, J. (1992). *Managing with power: Politics and influence in organizations*. Boston: Harvard Business School Press.

Ranft, A. L., Zinko, R., Ferris, G. R., & Buckley, M. R. (2006). Marketing the image of management: The costs and benefits of CEO reputation. *Organizational Dynamics*, *35*, 279–290.

Ravlin, E. C., & Thomas, D. C. (2005). Status and stratification processes in organizational life. *Journal of Management*, *31*, 966–987.

Reicher, S., & Elmer, N. (1988). Managing reputations in adolescents: The pursuit of delinquent and nondeliquent identities. In: H. Beloff (Ed.), *Getting into life* (pp. 13–42). London: Methuen.

Rindova, V. P., Pollock, T. G., & Hayward, M. L. A. (2006). Celebrity firms: The social construction of market popularity. *Academy of Management Review*, *31*, 50–71.

Rindova, V., Williamson, I. O., Petkova, A. P., & Sever, J. M. (2005). Being good or being known: An empirical examination of the dimensions, antecedents, and consequences of organizational reputation. *Academy of Management Journal*, *48*, 1033–1049.

Robbins, S. P. (2000). *Essentials of organizational behavior* (6th ed.). Upper Saddle River, NJ: Prentice Hall.

Roberts, L. M. (2005). Changing faces: Professional image construction in diverse organizational settings. *Academy of Management Review*, *30*, 685–711.

Rosen, S., Cochran, W., & Musser, L. M. (1990). Reactions to a match versus mis-match between an applicant's self-presentational style and work reputation. *Basic and Applied Social Psychology*, *11*, 117–129.

Rosenbaum, J. E. (1989). Organization career systems and employee misperceptions. In: M. B. Arthur, D. T. Hall & B. S. Lawrence (Eds), *Handbook of career theory* (pp. 329–353). New York: Cambridge University Press.

Salancik, G. R., & Pfeffer, J. (1978). A social information processing approach to job attitudes and job design. *Administrative Science Quarterly*, *23*, 224–254.

Scherer, F. (1980). *Industrial market structure and economic performance*. Chicago, IL: Rand McNally.

Schlenker, B. R. (1980). *Impression management: The self-concept, social identity, and interpersonal relations*. Belmont, CA: Brooks/Cole.

Schmidt, F. L., & Hunter, J. E. (1998). The validity and utility of selection methods in personnel psychology: Practical and theoretical implications of 85 years of research findings. *Psychological Bulletin*, *124*, 262–274.

Schunk, D. H. (1987). Peer models and children's behavioral change. *Review of Educational Research*, *57*, 149–174.

Shearmur, J., & Klein, D. B. (1997). Good conduct in the great society: Adam Smith and the role of reputation. In: D. B. Klein (Ed.), *Reputation: Studies in the voluntary elicitation of good conduct* (pp. 29–45). Ann Arbor, MI: University of Michigan Press.

Shenkar, O., & Yuchtman-Yaar, E. (1997). Reputation, image, prestige, and goodwill: An interdisciplinary approach to organizational standing. *Human Relations, 50,* 1361–1381.

Siebert, S. E., Kraimer, M. L., & Liden, R. C. (2001). A social capital theory of career success. *Academy of Management Journal, 44,* 219–237.

Snyder, C. R., Lassegard, M., & Ford, C. E. (1986). Distancing after group success and failure: Basking in reflected glory and cutting off reflected failure. *Journal of Personality and Social Psychology, 51,* 382–401.

Spence, A. M. (1973). Job market signaling. *Quarterly Journal of Economics, 87,* 845–856.

Spence, A. M. (1974). *Market signaling: Informational transfer in hiring and related screening processes.* Cambridge, MA: Harvard University Press.

Stern, B. B. (1994). A revised communication model for advertising: Multiple dimensions of the source, the message, and the recipient. *Journal of Advertising, 23,* 5–15.

Sternberg, R. J., & Wagner, R. K. (1993). The g-ocentric view of intelligence and job performance is wrong. *Current Directions in Psychological Science, 2,* 1–4.

Stevens, D. E. (2002). The effects of reputation and ethics on budgetary slack. *Journal of Management Accounting Research, 14,* 153–169.

Taylor, S. E., & Fiske, S. T. (1978). Salience, attention, and attribution: Top of the head phenomena. In: L. Berkowitz (Ed.), *Advances in experimental social psychology* (Vol. 11, pp. 249–288). New York: Academic Press.

Taylor, S. E., & Thompson, S. C. (1982). Stalking the elusive "vividness" effect. *Psychological Review, 89,* 155–181.

Tedeschi, J. T., & Melburg, V. (1984). Impression management and influence in the organization. In: S. B. Bacharach & E. J. Lawler (Eds), *Research in the sociology of organizations* (Vol. 3, pp. 31–58). Greenwich, CT: JAI Press.

Thorndike, E. L. (1920). A constant error in psychological ratings. *Journal of Applied Psychology, 4,* 25–29.

Tinsley, C. H., O'Connor, K. M., & Sullivan, B. A. (2002). Tough guys finish last: The perils of a distributive reputation. *Organizational Behavior and Human Decision Processes, 88,* 621–642.

Trevor, C. O. (2001). Interactions among actual ease-of-movement determinants and job satisfaction in the prediction of voluntary turnover. *Academy of Management Journal, 44,* 621–638.

Tsui, A. S. (1984). A role set analysis of managerial reputation. *Organizational Behavior and Human Performance, 34,* 64–96.

Tsui, A. S., & Ashford, S. J. (1994). Adaptive self-regulation: A process view of managerial effectiveness. *Journal of Management, 20,* 93–121.

Tsui, A. S. (1994). Reputational effectiveness: Toward a mutual responsiveness framework. In: B. M. Staw & L. L. Cummings (Eds), *Research in organizational behavior* (Vol. 16, pp. 257–307). Greenwich, CT: JAI Press.

Tsui, A. S., Egan, T. D., & O'Reilly, C. A. (1992). Being different: Relational demography and organizational attachment. *Administrative Science Quarterly, 37,* 549–579.

Tyler, T. R., & Kramer, R. M. (1996). Whither trust? In: R. M. Kramer & T. R. Tyler (Eds), *Trust in organizations: Frontiers of theory and research* (pp. 1–15). Thousand Oaks, CA: Sage Publications.

Useem, M., & Karabel, J. (1986). Pathways to top corporate management. *American Sociological Review, 44*, 184–200.

Wade, J. B., Porac, J. F., Pollock, T. G., & Graffin, S. D. (2006). The burden of celebrity: The impact of CEO certification contests on CEO pat and performance. *Academy of Management Journal, 49*, 643–660.

Warr, P. (1990). The measurement of well-being and other aspects of mental health. *Journal of Occupational Psychology, 63*, 193–210.

Weick, K. (1979). *The social psychology of organizing* (2nd ed.). Reading, MA: Addison-Wesley.

Wernerfelt, B. (1988). Reputation, monitoring, and effort. *Information Economics and Policy, 3*, 207–218.

Whitmeyer, J. M. (2000). Effects of positive reputation systems. *Social Science Research, 29*, 188–207.

Williams, M. L., & Goss, B. (1975). Equivocation: Character insurance. *Human Communication Research, 1*, 265–270.

Wills, T. A. (1981). Downward comparison principles in social psychology. *Psychological Bulletin, 90*, 245–271.

Wood, J. V. (1989). Theory and research concerning social comparisons of personal attributes. *Psychological Bulletin, 106*, 231–248.

Wood, J. V. (2000). Social comparison. In: A. E. Kazdin (Ed.), *Encyclopedia of psychology* (Vol. 7, pp. 332–333). Washington, D. C.: New York: American Psychological Association; Oxford University Press.

Wright, T. A., & Hobfoll, S. E. (2004). Commitment, psychological well-being and job performance: An examination of conservation of resources theory and job burnout. *Journal of Business and Management, 9*, 389–406.

Yukl, G. (1998). *Leadership in organizations*. Upper Saddle River, NJ: Prentice Hall.

Zajac, E. J., & Westphal, J. D. (1995). Accounting for explanations of CEO compensation: substance and symbolism. *Administrative Science Quarterly, 40*, 283–308.

THE CASE FOR DEVELOPING NEW RESEARCH ON HUMOR AND CULTURE IN ORGANIZATIONS: TOWARD A HIGHER GRADE OF MANURE

Christopher Robert and Wan Yan

ABSTRACT

The study of humor has a long tradition in philosophy, sociology, psychology, anthropology, and communications. Evidence from these fields suggests that humor can have effects on creativity, cohesiveness, and performance, but organizational scholars have paid it relatively little attention. We hope to "jump-start" such a research program. To do this, we first outline the theoretical rationale underlying the production and appreciation of humor, namely, its motivational, cognitive, and emotional mechanisms. Next, we review the literature linking humor to creativity, cohesiveness, and other performance-relevant outcomes. In particular, we note how this literature is theoretically well-grounded, but that the empirical findings are largely correlational and/or based on qualitative research designs. Finally, we go beyond the current humor literature by developing specific predictions about how culture might interact with humor in organizational contexts. Throughout the paper, we discuss

Research in Personnel and Human Resources Management, Volume 26, 205–267
Copyright © 2007 by Elsevier Ltd.
ISSN: 0742-7301/doi:10.1016/S0742-7301(07)26005-0

possible research directions and methodological issues relevant to the study of humor in organizations.

INTRODUCTION

"They say the seeds of what we will do are in all of us, but it always seemed to me that in those who make jokes in life the seeds are covered with better soil and with a higher grade of manure." (Ernest Hemingway)

This paper is about humor, though it is not intended to be humorous. However, "no one complains when a scientific analysis of sex fails to arouse its readers" (Davis, 1993, p. 4), so we make no apologies. Rather, we argue that humor is a universal human phenomenon that is underexplored as a valuable tool for understanding human behavior. Our sincerest wish is that by the time the reader finishes this paper, he or she will never laugh at humor again. But seriously folks … . We hope to convince you that although humor might appear to be inconsistent with the serious nature of work, it inserts itself in some form in most social contexts (Berger, 1987), and plays an important role in regulating social behavior in all societies (Caron, 2002). As such, we believe that humor can have significant implications for organizations and the management of their human resources.

We believe that part of the reason humor has remained relatively mysterious, particularly among organizational scholars, is that "humor has a hundred faces" (H.G. Mendelson). Indeed, humor is rife with complexity, duality, and incongruity. As soon as you think it is one thing, humor can appear to be its opposite. For example, humor can be obvious (e.g., slapstick, sarcasm), or subtle and sophisticated (e.g., satirical theatre). It can be crude and base (e.g., obscene humor), or used by revered holy men (e.g., Pope John Paul II and the Dalai Lama are both known for their sense of humor). It can be enduring and timeless (e.g., the works of Mark Twain, Shakespeare, Aristophanes), or pointedly contemporary (e.g., late-night television comedians). And humor can be pleasingly whimsical and silly (e.g., knock-knock jokes), deadly serious (e.g., gallows humor; Obrdlik, 1942), or even both simultaneously. On his deathbed in a Paris hotel, Oscar Wilde reportedly said "My wallpaper and I are fighting a dual to the death. One or the other of us has to go." Such complexity has caused many to treat humor as something unknowable or almost mystical.

Humor's obvious complexity notwithstanding, scholars from philosophy, sociology, psychology, communications, and anthropology have been interested in humor for hundreds or even thousands of years. Although their work has contributed substantially to the demystification of humor, and the development of theoretical and methodological approaches to the study of humor that are appropriate for their respective disciplines, relatively little of this work has filtered into the research of organizational scholars. Indeed, the first substantial signs of interest by organizational scholars in humor came with the publication of two papers on humor in the *Academy of Management Review* in the early 1980s. Malone's (1980) paper focused on the use of humor as a potential management tool, and noted the potential benefits and pitfalls of humor use by managers. Duncan (1982) went a step further by reviewing the limited literature on the topic, and put forth a number of specific research questions for exploring the use of humor in organizations.

However, a review of the organizational literature in the decades since the publication of those two papers reveals limited theoretical and empirical attention to the topic. One possible explanation for this apparent lack of interest is that theoretical approaches adopted by humor researchers from various disciplines constitute an odd patchwork of perspectives on humor. This is driven in part by the fact that much of the research on humor that is directly relevant to organizations has been published outside of the discipline or outside of the more popular and mainstream management journals. In addition, some humor research conducted *in* organizations has used organizations as a convenient context for the examination of humor, but does little to connect theory or findings to the broader organizational literature. Therefore, the first major goal of this paper is to provide a theoretical integration of the literature on humor and related phenomena that will serve to organize the disparate theoretical perspectives. Specifically, we argue that three primary mechanisms are important for understanding humor phenomena and their consequences in organizations: (a) a *motivational* mechanism that describes why individuals produce humor in interpersonal interactions, (b) a *cognitive* mechanism that describes how humor "works" and how humorous communications are distinguished from non-humorous communications by an audience, and (c) an *emotional* mechanism that serves to link the cognitive experience of humor with subsequent behavior. In the first major section of this article, we review the literature relevant to each of the three mechanisms, and highlight important relationships between mechanisms.

A second possible explanation for the limited coverage of humor in the organizational literature is that organizational researchers might not believe that humor is important or worthy of study. Indeed, Morreall (1991) notes that humor traditionally has been perceived as "frivolous and unproductive" (p. 359), and is incongruent with the perception that work is serious business (no pun intended). He jokes that children in school who show aptitude for music get sent to the music room, children with aptitude for art get sent to the art room, and children with an aptitude for humor get sent to the principal's office. Therefore, a second goal of this paper is to review the existing empirical literature on the effects of humor in organizational contexts to demonstrate why humor should be taken seriously. In the second section of this article, we will focus on three major categories of findings, including relationships between humor and creativity, humor and work performance or other performance relevant outcomes (e.g., job satisfaction), and humor and interpersonal cohesiveness. In describing these results, we will comment on the weight of evidence for causal links in each category.

The third and final goal of this article is to take a step beyond our current knowledge on humor in organizations by laying a conceptual foundation for future research on the interaction of humor and culture in organizations. This goal is motivated by the observation that organizations are becoming more and more culturally complex as a result of increasing cultural diversity within the workforces of many countries, and the ascendance of the multinational organization as an important organizational form. In addition, an influential body of cross-cultural research accumulated over the last few decades has documented the myriad ways in which culture helps to shape motivational, cognitive, and emotional processes (Triandis, 1994). Therefore, it stands to reason that culture might moderate the relationship between humor and organizational outcomes, insofar as it influences relevant motivational, cognitive, and emotional processes. In the third major section of this article, we develop predictions regarding how culture is expected to moderate the relationship between humor and important organizational phenomena.

WORKING DEFINITION OF HUMOR AND TERMINOLOGY

Before addressing our three major goals of integrating theory, describing empirical results, and developing hypotheses regarding culture, it is important that we define the scope and boundaries of the humor phenomena in which we are interested. Humor is extraordinarily complex, and elicits nearly as many definitions and conceptualizations as there have been books or articles on humor. For example, Martin (2001) notes that 'humor' can refer to a stimulus (e.g., a joke or witticism), a cognitive process, or some kind of emotional or behavioral response. In particular, a stimulus is often defined as humorous if it is followed by laughter or smiling behaviors, or positive affect. Some authors focus only on humor that is intentionally produced by individuals (e.g., Cooper, 2005), while others note that humorous stimuli can be non-social and unintentional (e.g., Wyer & Collins, 1992).

In this article, we follow Lynch's (2002) observation that "humor is fundamentally a communicative activity" (p. 423) and define humor as an intentional form of social communication delivered by a "producer" toward an "audience." While unintentional humor and humor created in non-social environments might be theoretically interesting in some contexts (e.g., why do we laugh when we notice that a cloud looks like a penis?), individuals within organizations must actively (intentionally) engage in social communication that directly or indirectly helps to accomplish tasks and the goals of the organization. Therefore, humor's role in shaping, facilitating, or undermining communication between individuals in organizational contexts is the primary focus of this paper.

Importantly, this definition of humor does not limit humor phenomena to verbal behavior, as humorous non-verbal behaviors (e.g., gestures) or stimuli (e.g., cartoons) can be produced that are intended to communicate some kind of message. In addition, we do not require that the humorous communication is found to be humorous by members of the audience (as indicated by behaviors such as laughter or smiling). One reason for this is that even if a member of the audience to a humorous communication experiences a cognitive reaction and subsequent positive affect in response (which we describe later), laughter and smiling are only two of a number of possible behavioral responses to humor (Hay, 2001). In addition, we are also interested in attempts at humor that fail to induce desired responses in the audience, because such attempts might still be informative about the producer's motivations, and might induce important responses in the audience to the failed humor. Indeed, a joke made at the expense of one group is not likely to be considered funny by members of that group, although it might be hilarious to others. Similarly, ingratiatory humor (Cooper, 2005) used as a form of persuasion might be perceived very negatively by an employee who is passed over for a promotion that is received by the ingratiator. Finally, as we note in the section below on motivational mechanisms, individuals might use communications that employ humorous forms for reasons other than to cause pleasant experiences of mirth in the audience. Therefore, we only require that the humor producer uses a communication style that includes elements of humor (e.g., incongruity – to be described in more detail later).

HUMOR MECHANISMS

The humor mechanisms described in this section follow a fairly logical progression. Starting with the humor producer, we assume that individuals engage in social communication because of underlying social motivations; i.e., people choose to communicate with others for some *reason*. Those reasons might be apparent to both the producer and the audience (e.g., to convey specific factual information), or might be more veiled (e.g., influencing social perceptions of the producer). We suggest that humor is commonly employed as a tool to make social communications more effective in particular circumstances, which we describe in more detail below. Once the communication is made, however, the focus must shift to the audience or recipients of the communication. In the section on cognitive mechanisms, we discuss the cognitive processes involved in interpreting social communications that involve humor. Finally, in the section on emotional mechanisms, we describe the emotional responses that are presumed to follow from the cognitive interpretation of humorous communications, and suggest that emotions might be the most proximal link to relevant behaviors or job attitudes.

Motivational Mechanisms

A fundamental question that the existing literature on humor use in organizational has tried to address is "why do people employ humor in organizational contexts?" This perspective on organizational humor focuses on the humor producer, and assumes that the producer is motivated, consciously or not (Martin, Puhlik-Doris, Larsen, Gray, & Weir, 2003), to achieve certain outcomes through social communication. Humor, then, can be viewed as a tool employed to help achieve those outcomes. Research in this vein is often framed in terms of the "type" of humor used. For example, Romero and Cruthirds (2006) suggest that the four humor styles developed by Martin et al. (2003) (i.e., affiliative, self-enhancing, aggressive, and self-defeating humor) reflect the humor producer's "intention" for using humor. That is, even though researchers might characterize a communication as including "affiliative humor," this designation reflects a presumption about why the producer employs humor in a particular context, or the end-state he or she is trying to achieve, rather than an analysis of the content or form of the humorous communication itself. As an example, the items employed by Avolio, Howell, and Sosik (1999) to measure leader's humor use included "[your leader] uses humor to take the edge off during stressful periods" and "[your leader] uses a funny story to turn an argument in his or her favor." This style of measurement essentially assesses the underlying social motives of the humor producer.

Although researchers have identified at least 24 different motives for using humor (Graham, Papa, & Brooks, 1992), at a broad level of generalization a fundamental distinction is often made between humorous communications that are intended to have positive effects on the audience, and those intended to have negative effects. Empirically, motivations for using humor in negative and positive contexts appear to be clearly distinguishable (e.g., Cooper, 2002; Graham et al., 1992; Sala, 2000), and perhaps higher order factors. In the two sections below, we describe some of the major positive and negative motivations for humor use discussed in the literature.

Before doing that, however, an important clarification must be made about the 'positive' and 'negative' humor distinction. Numerous authors have noted that humor has two sides (e.g., Davis & Kleiner, 1989). Malone (1980) referred to humor as being a "double-edged sword," alluding to the fact that while humor is typically seen as positive, it has the potential to be used for negative or destructive purposes. Similarly, Martineau (1972) observed that humor can have abrasive as well as lubricant properties in social interactions. These sentiments are undoubtedly consistent with most peoples' experience. However, it is important to distinguish between the *humor* that is employed and the underlying *intention* or motivation for employing it. Assigning the label "negative humor" to a communication that employs humor to convey a negative *message* is something like blaming the messenger. That is, the negativity is really a characteristic of the underlying *motivation* for the communication. We suggest that the term "negative humor" might best describe humor that is used as a tool or device to help send certain types of negative messages more effectively. Indeed, humor employed to send negative messages might soften the blow of an offensive or hostile message that might otherwise cause an aggressive response from the audience (Caron, 2002).

As an example, imagine that a manager is upset with his/her subordinate who shows up late for work for a third day in a row. In a tone dripping with sarcasm the manager tells the subordinate, "oh, you're a *model* employee." This statement has the *form* of humor because of the incongruity between the implicit and explicit messages (a point we return to later), and indeed, such a communication would likely be labeled by most as "negative humor." But using the term "negative humor" implies that the *humor* is the culprit, and that removing it will remove the negativity. However, humor is probably just one of a number of tools that the communicator can use to express his/her message, and without humor, some other communication or action channel might be chosen. Rather, an alternative to the (weakly) humorous jibe "you're a model employee," might be a more direct and upsetting statement like "you're an irresponsible and lazy person," or the more flatly offensive "you're an asshole." Given these options, is it right to criticize *humor* for its destructive capabilities, or should it be praised for taking the razor's edge off a very stern message? We hesitate to go so far as to suggest that all humor is positive. Humor might enable communicators to send negative messages that might never be sent otherwise. However, we believe that a more careful analysis of 'negative humor' might reveal that the negativity resides in the hearts of men rather than the comic tools they employ.

Positive Motivations and Humor Use
Of the two broad categories, positive motivations for employing humor in organizations have clearly received the most attention (Rodrigues & Collinson, 1995). One major theme of positive motivations for employing humor can be described as a motivation to build a sense of *cohesiveness* (or 'sense of community' or 'social integration') between producers and the audience to humor (Haig, 1988). A number of different explanations for how humor builds or maintains cohesiveness have been proposed. For example, Meyer (1997) suggested that humor builds cohesiveness by emphasizing shared values, and Coughlin (2002) suggested that "gallows humor" promotes cohesiveness by recognizing the mutual experience of traumatic or stressful events. Another way that humor might be employed to increase cohesiveness is through its ability to help communicators "mask" unpleasant content in their messages (Holmes, 2000). Specifically, the humor producer can take advantage of the ambiguity inherent in determining whether or not a seemingly humorous and playful message delivered face-to-face was actually intended to be playful (Ullian, 1976). Along these lines, Fine and De Soucey (2005) note that "joking constitutes an established frame that rescues interactions from friction" (p. 9). For example, the humor producer can reduce potential negative reactions associated with delivering criticism, reprimands, or disagreement by communicating such messages under a thin guise of humor. More specific to supervisor–subordinate relationships, Duncan (1984) suggests that humor can mask the authoritarian character of orders delivered to subordinates. In so doing, supervisors reduce perceived threats to their subordinates' sense of self-worth and autonomy.

Martineau's (1972) theory of the social functions of humor is relevant here, because it suggests that the relationships between the producer, audience, and target or "butt" of humor are central for understanding humor's effectiveness. He stresses that humor will have its most positive effects on cohesiveness when all parties to humor (i.e., the producer, audience, and butt) are members of an ingroup. This might even include humor with a disparaging tone, because it is acceptable for members of an ingroup to poke fun at their own faults and weaknesses. For example, Scogin and Pollio (1980) concluded that deprecating humor built cohesiveness in long standing groups, because teasing sends an implicit message that the target is included in the group. However, Martineau suggests that when parties to humor are not all part of the same ingroup, humor will emphasize intergroup distinctions, or be perceived as an attempt by the humor producer to control others' behavior, thus having great potential to destroy cohesiveness. Therefore, an important qualification to the notion that humor is motivated by a desire to build cohesiveness is that the impact of humorous social communications depends on the existing relationships between producer and audience.

Although developing and maintaining cohesiveness appears to be a major motivation for using humor, other positive motivations to use humor have also been noted in the literature. One such motivation might be to cope with anxiety or stress in a difficult situation. Motivations to use humor in this manner have been recognized for some time. For example, in a piece on morale and war, G. Stanely Hall noted that soldiers' use of humor on the front in World War I played an important role in maintaining morale and reducing mental strain in the face of death. He wrote "the instinct to turn the most solemn facts in the environment into a theme of laughter is partly an attempt of the individual to release his own thoughts from a present too excruciatingly agonizing to be long borne" (Hall, 1918, p. 380). More recent work has followed a similar theme, and has also focused on humor's role as a coping mechanism (Martin & Lefcourt, 1984). Although some evidence for a stress-buffering effect of humor has been obtained (e.g., Cann, Calhoun, & Nance, 2000; Nezu, Nezu, & Blissett, 1988), the weight of evidence supporting such a role for humor appears mixed, perhaps due to methodological weaknesses in studies exploring the effect (Lehman, Burke, Martin, Sultan, & Czech, 2001; Martin, 2001). Nevertheless, a universal presumption that humor helps individuals cope with life's difficulties (Abel, 2002) might still be manifest in conscious or unconscious *motivations* to use humor for this purpose.

Cooper (2005) has also suggested that humor production might be motivated by a desire to ingratiate oneself with one's superiors, subordinates, or coworkers. Specifically, she suggested that individuals intentionally use humor to create positive affect in their ingratiation target. Positive affect, in turn, increases the target's persuadability, and increases the likelihood that the target will confer benefits on the producer. One specific type of ingratiatory humor might be self-deprecating humor. Classic social psychological research found that a blunder or pratfall committed by an otherwise competent person tends to humanize that person and results in higher levels of attraction (Aronson, Willerman, & Floyd, 1966). A similar effect might be obtained when individuals make themselves the butt of their own jokes (e.g., Rodney Dangerfield's "I don't get no respect"). Martin et al. (2003) describe self-deprecating humor as a type of positive humor designed to put others at ease by showing that the producer does not take himself or herself too seriously. Although Coser (1960) found that high status individuals were unlikely to use self-deprecating humor, Duncan and Feisal (1989) suggest that judicious use of self-deprecating humor can smooth a manager's interactions with his or her subordinates by "letting the group know that he or she is a real person" (p. 28).

Negative Motivations and Humor Use

"The satirist shoots to kill while the humorist brings his prey back alive and eventually releases him again for another chance." (Peter De Vries)

Positive motivations for humor use notwithstanding, a growing body of recent research suggests that individuals might be motivated to use humor for negative purposes. One of the more discussed negative motivations involves aggression. Aggressive humor is a type of negative humor used to control others by putting them down or through ridicule (Martin et al., 2003; Meyer, 1990). Aggressive humor can serve as an important conservative force for maintaining the integrity of group norms. For example, humor can be used to identify what the group accepts to be "normal" and "abnormal" behavior (Fine & De Soucey, 2005), often by demonstrating the inferiority of outgroups or by derogating group members who violate norms (Meyer, 1997). In his review, Duncan (1982) noted that research suggests that high status people initiate most humor in organizations; a phenomenon termed the "high status humor monopoly" (p. 141). Indeed, a considerable body of early humor research supports Radcliffe-Brown's (1952) hypothesis that high status individuals in all societies have rights to joke and tease others without reprisal. For example, Bradney (1957) observed that when joking behavior occurs between people from different hierarchical levels, it was almost always directed from the top down. Importantly, both Coser (1960) and Lundberg (1969) found that humor in organizational contexts was directed in a status-maintaining downward direction, often in an aggressive form. More recent work by Holmes (2000) also found that supervisors' use of negative humor was often intended to maintain power differentials.

However, Malone (1980) noted that a dominant downward direction of humor, particularly aggressive humor, might start to change as organizations move toward less hierarchical structures. Indeed, a number of studies conducted since 1980 support his prediction. For example, Duncan (1984) found that substantial differences across organizations in downward and upward humor use could be partially accounted for by the degree of employees' acceptance of hierarchical differences. Vinton (1989) also found that although supervisors frequently used teasing humor instead of direct orders to help get things done, they did so to help maintain a collegial atmosphere that was also supported by the acceptance of lower level employees targeting managers as the butt of humor.

One way in which humor might be directed upward within organizational hierarchies is through the use of *subversive* humor. To some extent, subversive humor is the antithesis of a motivation to control that characterizes aggressive humor. Subversive humor is motivated by a desire to *destabilize* power structures and challenge dominant behavioral norms (Linstead, 1985). Unlike aggressive humor, subversive humor is more often veiled or indirect, and relies on the fact that humor can mask otherwise unacceptable challenges to the establishment (Holmes & Marra, 2002a). Indeed, Ullian (1976) notes that because humor is an indirect form of communication "the joker is protected from being charged with the responsibility for the serious content or the implications of the joke" (p. 129).

The use of humor by subordinates for the purpose of subverting and resisting the formal hierarchy are themes that have emerged from a number of empirical studies. For example, Collinson (1988) describes how shop-floor workers in a truck factory employed humor that served to resist that status system and organizational control. Similarly, Rodrigues and Collinson (1995) document an instance of subversive humor in the publication and dissemination of a humorous newspaper that was highly critical of the management in a Brazilian telecommunications firm. Taylor and Bain (2003) noted that 'pure clowning' was relatively rare in the two call centers they studied, whereas considerable mocking and ridicule directed at managers was common. They suggested that it was intentionally designed to undermine authority and subvert company culture. Finally, Holmes and Marra (2002a) found that subversive humor is much more common in work groups where hierarchical relationships are present than in friendship groups where maintenance of solidarity is stressed. In the work groups they studied, the person with the most status was often the target of both subtle humor (e.g., ironic comments), and direct humor (e.g., jocular abuse).

Summary of Motivations to Use Humor
A number of themes underlying positive and negative motivations to use humor in organizational contexts have been described in the humor literature. We summarized these themes under two broad categories, positive motivations (i.e., to develop cohesiveness, to mask negative message content, reduce stress or anxiety, and to ingratiate oneself with others), and negative motivations (i.e., the need to control and dominate others, the need to subvert authority and status). While we do not imply that this list of motivations to use humor in organizational contexts is necessarily comprehensive, we suggest that it represents a reasonable reflection of the current literature on humor that is relevant to organizations, and provides a good starting point for understanding the perspective of humor producers. And finally, we reiterate that the term 'negative humor' is potentially misleading, because it usually refers to the fact that humor is frequently used to help communicate negative messages, where the humor itself is not inherently negative.

Cognitive Mechanisms

"Analyzing humor is like dissecting a frog. Few people are interested and the frog dies of it."
(E. B. White)

The motivations of humor producers to use humor in their communications might be somewhat interesting in their own right. However, if one is truly interested in the *social* nature of humor in communication, it is essential that one understands how humor producers infuse humor in their communications, and subsequently, how those presumably humorous communications are interpreted or "appreciated" by the audience. The examination of this issue requires an understanding of the cognitive processes involved in distinguishing humorous communications from non-humorous communications; what makes something "funny"?

Incongruity Theory
The most influential and important theory that describes the cognitive basis of humor is incongruity theory (Bergson, 1956; Davis, 1993; Suls, 1972). Incongruity theory has roots in philosophy, and has been the most popular mechanism for explaining how humor works for many decades (e.g., Hazlitt, 1930). Davis (1993) integrates the literature on incongruity theory, and

demonstrates how other humor theories (e.g., superiority theory, relief theory) represent complementary, rather than conflicting accounts of how humor operates (see also Lynch, 2002; Suls, 1976). A foundational premise of incongruity theory is that people hold various beliefs and assumptions about how elements within the social and physical worlds are related to one another. When a specific social and/or physical domain is evoked by a communication, other domains and phenomena that are commonly associated with it are automatically primed and made more consciously accessible within a fairly coherent expectation system. Examples of expectation systems include "scripts" of social interactions (e.g., the conversation you have with a desk clerk when you check in to a hotel, or the conversation with a police officer when you are pulled over for speeding), or commonly held schemas (e.g., how bureaucratic government agencies have long lines, bad service, hassles). The humor producer essentially relies on his or her knowledge of the expectation systems held by the audience to create the experience of incongruity within the audience. This is done by systematically juxtaposing a primary expectation system with a secondary expectation system, which is elicited and unexpectedly connected with the primary system.

To illustrate, when a particular schema such as the waiter–customer interaction is elicited in a joke (e.g., "Waiter, there's a fly in my soup") an expectation about how the course of events should transpire is primed (e.g., "I'm sorry, let me take that away"). For something to be humorous there must be an unexpected deviation within the elicited expectation system. One experiences pleasure from the deviation because of the somewhat sudden violation of one system (e.g., "Don't worry sir, they don't eat much"), and its subsequent surprising resolution with another previously unrelated system. More specifically, the violation represented by an incongruity is brought into sharper focus when the incongruity links elements of the main expectation system (i.e., the waiter–customer script) with a second expectation system that one would not commonly associate with the first (i.e., the size and eating habits of flies). Importantly, the audience must understand how the two expectation systems are linked in order for them to be resolved. Without the resolution, the humor will fail. As another example, take the following joke:

> What's the difference between being in prison and being at work? In prison, you spend most of your time in an 8 × 10 cell, at work, you spend most of your time in a 6 × 8 cubicle.

Most people probably have an expectation system suggesting that incarceration is bad, and worse than freedom. It is easy to brainstorm elements of that system that are consistent with that expectation (e.g., physical threat, poor living conditions, lack of autonomy, etc.). However, in the sample joke, that expectation system is violated by the suggestion that being in prison might be *better* than being at work. It is then resolved by bridging the prison expectation system with another coherent but unexpectedly related expectation system: the concept that office workers are often corralled into confining, uncomfortable and depressing workspaces. The humorous part of the joke resides in the incongruity established by the juxtaposition and subsequent resolution of the 'prison' and 'workplace' expectation frames.

Incongruity is not only manifest in canned jokes such as those analyzed above, but can also be identified in other humor phenomena such as humorous comments, quips, or witticisms. For example, recall the Hemingway quote from the beginning of this paper "They say the seeds of what we will do are in all of us, but it always seemed to me that in those who make jokes in life the seeds are covered with better soil and with a higher grade of manure." In this multitiered witticism, Hemingway playfully contrasts the very serious topics of growth or success in life with the unserious topic of 'manure.' In this context, manure itself contains incongruity because while it is used to make things grow well, his use of the term manure rather than fertilizer in this context is clearly an allusion to the fact that people can sometimes be "full of shit." In addition, at a higher level of abstraction, Hemingway seems to be making a serious observation that in order to be successful in life, you can not take life too seriously.

Wyer and Collins' (1992) Theory of Humor Elicitation

The foundations of incongruity theory are used as a jumping-off point for Wyer and Collins' (1992) development of a number of additional theoretical principles for describing the cognitive mechanisms behind humor elicitation. Although a thorough description of their entire theory is beyond the scope of this paper, we describe five of their important principles. The first two are related, and are termed *non-replacement* and *diminishment*. The principle of non-replacement refers to the notion that the initial expectation system associated with the referent elicited by a humorous stimulus (e.g., a joke or cartoon) is not negated by the introduction of a second expectation system. For example, in the "fly in my soup" joke above, the customer's presumed disgust is not forgotten or "replaced" by the elicitation of the second expectation system (i.e., the motives of the fly to eat the soup and its limited digestive capacity). Rather, Wyer and Collins (1992) proffer a second principle, diminishment, which suggests that a humorous stimulus is funny when the features of a primary expectation system are diminished in importance when the incongruity established by the second expectation system is elicited. In the "fly in my soup" joke, the importance or reasonableness of the customer's complaint is diminished when the second expectation system regarding the limited digestive capacity of a fly is introduced. That is, the customer's complaint is initially perceived to be based on how disgusting it is to have a fly in one's soup. However, the shift in interpretation elicited by noting the fly's limited digestive capacity diminishes the importance of the customer's complaint, which can now be interpreted as the customer complaining because the fly might be eating his or her soup. The principles of non-replacement and diminishment are clearly relevant to ethnic or disparagement jokes (e.g., how many professors does it take to screw in a light bulb.... none, they get their graduate students to do that) where the punch lines tend to diminish the importance of some characteristic of the referent. For example, the initial expectation system for professors might include descriptors such as 'intelligent' and perhaps high in stature, whereas the punch line in the joke above diminishes the importance of those descriptors by eliciting another belief that professors appear lazy.

A third principle relates to the *comprehension difficulty* involved in interpreting a humor stimulus. Wyer and Collins (1992) suggest that humor stimuli elicit the most humor when comprehension difficulty is moderate. At low levels of comprehension difficulty, the link that must be made between a primary and secondary expectation system requires little effort, and involves a limited element of surprise or novelty. This explains why jokes that are funny to children are not funny to adults, who can easily anticipate the punch line. At moderate levels of comprehension difficulty, the audience "feels more challenged, and their success in comprehending the information is rewarding" (Wyer & Collins, 1992, p. 674). However, at high levels of comprehension difficulty, the audience might feel foolish, decreasing their enjoyment.

A fourth principle concerns the amount of elaboration involved in comprehending a joke after the two expectation systems are linked. Wyer and Collins (1992) suggest that humor stimuli are perceived to be funnier when the audience can elaborate extensively on various aspects of the humor's context. The "fly in my soup" joke could be elaborated by imagining the fly in the bowl actually eating the soup, or the angry look on the customer's face when the waiter tells them not to worry. The Hemingway quote above is also high on elaboration potential, as one can contemplate his various levels of meaning for some time. As another example, the first author recently ordered a birthday cake from a local bakery for his father-in-law, and asked that it read "Happy Birthday Bernie" on the top (quite original). However, when the cake was picked up, it read "Happy Burney Murney." This incident is so funny because it stimulates so many different elaborations: How could someone make such a bad mistake without catching it? What would the recipient's reaction be if presented with such a cake? Who the hell is Murney? etc. In contrast, simple jokes (e.g., knock-knock jokes) or puns are usually not very funny (especially a second or third time) because they have very little elaboration potential. This principle is very similar to Davis' (1993) observation that the degree to which humor is found to be funny tends to be proportional to the degree to which an incongruity clashes with a system's core characteristics. "Bad" jokes or silly humor targets the periphery of one's expectation systems, while humor that gets the biggest responses targets core values, beliefs, or institutions.

> "If you work on a lobster boat, sneaking up behind someone and pinching him is probably a joke that gets old real fast." (Jack Handey, Deep Thoughts)

A final principle concerns the motivations of the audience with respect to how they interpret a humorous stimulus, or their *information-processing goals*. A basic distinction can be made between information-processing goals or motivations to interpret the stimulus as humorous, and more specific information-processing goals. The latter might include a goal of simply understanding the content of the message, attempting to interpret unspoken meaning, or determining whether the humor producer is assaulting an important belief system. Davis (1993), for example, notes that when people are deeply committed to a belief system (e.g., regarding abortion), or when there are normative prohibitions against disparaging certain people or things (e.g., criticizing Chinese leader Mao during the 1960s), attempts at humor that create incongruities within those systems will be unsuccessful and/or met with anger. In contrast, when one has a goal of finding the humor in a stimulus, this might be similar to a play frame discussed by various authors (e.g., Caron, 2002). A play frame indicates one's receptiveness to humor, and might be induced by learned associations between particular contexts and laughter (e.g., going to a movie or comedy club, seeing a friend who is typically amusing), or by certain cultural signals for establishing play frames (e.g., setting up a joke with an introduction such as "Did you hear the one about...."). If an individual is not motivated to process information involved in a humorous stimulus in terms of a "play frame" in which incongruities and their humorous resolution are expected, the stimulus will result in less humor.

Neurological Basis for Humor

Because incongruity theory and the extensions proposed by Wyer and Collins (1992) are cognitive theories, they implicitly assume that brain activity parallels the processes described. Both theoretical models of brain activity and direct and indirect empirical studies of brain activity provide support for these cognitive mechanisms. For example, Berns, Cohen, and Mintun (1997) found that some parts of the brain function to predict events based on context information, while others serve to evaluate whether or not those predictions are true. The latter brain systems become activated when an unexpected or surprising stimuli appears (i.e., a punchline). These functions of these brain regions correspond closely with the process assumed by incongruity theory, in that incongruity theory suggests that there is an initial setting of expectations, followed by a violation of those expectations that occurs when a novel expectation system is linked with the first.

In another study of event-related potential (ERP) brainwaves, Derks, Gillikan, Bartolome-Rull, and Bogart (1997) found that a distinct P300 wave followed by a N400 wave were detected following joke punch lines when participants reported experiencing amusement in response to jokes. This corresponds with phases of humor cognition implied by incongruity theory, because the P300 wave is associated with information categorization, whereas the N400 wave is associated with recognition of an error or anomalous event, and indicates that initial categorization was unsuccessful. The authors also noted that when participants laughed in response to the humorous stimuli, this was associated with more total involvement of the cerebral cortex (which is involved with complex information processing). This finding is consistent with Wyer and Collins' (1992) principle that elaboration should be associated with amusement.

Finally, a study by Vaid, Hull, Heredia, Gerkens, and Martinez (2003) measured the mental accessibility of initial joke frames (expectations) and the unexpected or incongruous joke frame at points during the joke set up, during the establishment of incongruity, and at incongruity resolution. Results suggested that *both* initial and incongruity expectation systems were highly accessible during the introduction of the incongruity, whereas the initial joke frame became low in accessibility during joke resolution. This result is consistent with an incongruity theory view (e.g., Suls, 1972), as well as Katz' (1993) incongruity-based neural model of humor cognition, and Wyer and Collins' (1992) principle of diminishment.

Summary of Cognitive Mechanisms

A number of theories have been proposed to explain the cognitive mechanisms that underlie a person's experience of humor or amusement; i.e., what makes something funny? However, incongruity theory appears to have outlasted other theories. We believe that this is due to the ability of the theory to accommodate the predictions of other theories (Davis, 1993), as well as empirical evidence from cognitive and physiological studies such as those described above. Incongruity theory suggests that humor is elicited when two contrasting expectation systems are elicited within a given humor stimulus (e.g., a joke), but the incongruity between them is subsequently resolved. In addition, more recent development of the theory by Wyer and Collins (1992) (i.e., principles of non-replacement, diminishment, comprehension difficulty, cognitive elaboration, and information-processing motivations) helps to account for even more humor phenomena, and will be particularly useful when we describe the possible moderating impact of culture on the link between humor and important organizational phenomena. Finally, it is important to note that evidence from a number of empirical studies seems to indicate that the cognitive mechanisms underlying the perception of humor, incongruity in particular, are universal across cultures (Alden, Hoyer, & Lee, 1993; Shultz, 1976; Vuorela, 2005). This point becomes more relevant when we examine the influence of culture on the effects of humor.

Emotional Mechanisms

"Laughter is the sun that drives winter from the human face." (Victor Hugo)

"If we couldn't laugh we would all go insane." (Jimmy Buffet)

The cognitive explanations for humor interpretation are important in that they provide very useful guidance for understanding *why* people find some things to be 'funny' and other things not. However, although a cognitive explanation of humor might be a necessary component of the humor process, it seems to be insufficient for describing how we *experience* humor, and what it *does* to us. When we think about humor, we are more likely to think about the positive emotional or affective responses that we feel when we are amused, and the outward signs of emotion we see in others' smiles and laughter. This suggests that there is an important emotional mechanism underlying the process of humor appreciation.

Two types of research have confirmed that an emotional mechanism seems to be operating in the humor appreciation process. The first type of research has confirmed that individuals' subjective interpretations of their emotional states are influenced by humor. For example, Cann, Holt, and Calhoun (1999) found that participants who viewed a humorous videotape reported reduced anxiety and increased positive affect. Similarly, Abel and Maxwell (2002), in a study examining the combined effects of sense of humor and a humorous situation on stressful tasks, demonstrated that being exposed to a humorous stimulus alleviated anxiety and increased positive affect. Individuals' sense of humor, and presumably their ability to interpret life events through the lens of humor, also appears to moderate the influence of both positive and negative life events such that a sense of humor is more strongly associated with positive affect after *both* positive and negative life events (Martin, Kuiper, Olinger, & Dance, 1993).

Although the connection between humor and subjective interpretation of emotion is important, it does not necessarily confirm that the cognitive and emotional mechanisms of humor appreciation represent unique processes that are both important for humor appreciation. Such a demonstration is crucial, because incongruity by itself should not be sufficient to cause amusement or humor appreciation. For example, the joke "Why did the chicken cross the road? Because I like wearing sandals" involves incongruity, but is clearly not 'funny' (if you found that funny, we feel badly for you). While one's brain undoubtedly recognizes the incongruity in that "joke," an additional process must be activated that distinguishes simple incongruity identification (i.e., two incompatible things exist), and humorous incongruity interpretation that somehow links two presumably unrelated expectation systems and results in the unique subjective experience of mirth or amusement.

Research on brain activity and brain physiology associated with humor strongly suggests that humor appreciation includes related yet unique cognitive and affective (emotional) processes. Specifically, researchers have documented that brain activity that corresponds closely with an incongruity explanation of humor can be identified (for more technical details, see Derks et al., 1997; Fry, 2002; Vaid et al., 2003; Wild, Rodden, Grodd, & Ruch, 2003). However, additional brain activity associated with emotional responses to humor has also been identified. For example, in a study on humor and brain physiology, Shammi and Stuss (1999) found that individuals with damage in specific parts of the right frontal lobe emitted fewer behavioral and emotional responses to jokes (i.e., smiling and laughing), even when they reported that they were able to "get" the jokes and could distinguish the funny jokes from the non-funny ones. In other words, participants with deficiency in that specific area of the brain could only engage in half of the appreciation process (i.e., the cognitive part) but could not experience humor in the same way that people with undamaged brains do.

Recent neuroscientific research provides additional insight into the relationship between humor and brain activity, and is consistent with Edward DeBono's conclusion that "Humor is by far the most significant activity of the human brain." In an important brain imaging study, Goel and Dolan (2001) exposed participants to different types of humor, and observed their corresponding patterns of brain activity. Importantly, they found that different types of humor (i.e., semantic jokes and puns) were associated with brain activity in different parts of the brain, which, they hypothesized, corresponded to different types of processing. However, when the humor was perceived as amusing, different types of humor appeared to activate some common areas of the brain. Importantly, the common part of the brain that was activated in response to humor is thought to be a "reward center," and supports the argument that the cognitive and emotional mechanisms involved in the humor appreciation process might be integrated and related, yet unique. Similar results were also found in a recent study by Watson, Matthews, and Allman (2007), who found reward center-related activity in response to different types of humor (i.e., sight gags and language-based humor), as well as brain activity commonly associated with feelings of euphoria. Thus, the appreciation of humor might be intrinsically rewarding, and might result in tendencies for individuals to seek out humorous stimuli such as individuals who consistently make them laugh.

Although cognitive processes are important, and we argue below that the cognitive effects of humor on individuals might be important in and of themselves, we believe that the emotional responses to humor represent an important final step in the humor appreciation process. Humor's role in the activation of positive emotions, we believe, is a key aspect of the theoretical rationale for why humor in organizations is likely to be so important.

Finally, it is important to address the possibility that the use of humor in communications can be associated with negative affect as well. However, we repeat the same caution we raised above in relation to "negative humor." That is, although communications that include a humorous form might result in negative affect in the audience, it is inappropriate to blame humor. Rather, Wyer and Collins' (1992) principle of 'elaboration' suggests that if a humorous communication results in cognitive elaborations that are mostly associated with negative affect (e.g., self-doubt, uncertainty, dead puppies), then the "humor" will result in negative affect.

HUMOR AND ORGANIZATIONAL OUTCOMES

In this section, we review evidence regarding the potential effects of humor in organizational contexts. In so doing, we make an effort to evaluate the weight of empirical evidence supporting each category of humor effects in organizations. Given that many of humor's positive effects in organizations appear to be taken-for-granted in the practitioner-oriented literature, we hope this type of analysis will help focus researchers' efforts toward research questions that need the most attention. In addition, we attempt to highlight the theoretical mechanisms that are likely involved in the causal relationships between humor and these outcomes. Again, we hope this will provide researchers with guidance in the design of future research on humor in organizational contexts.

Humor and Performance Relevant Outcomes

In some cases, well-documented findings from considerable amounts of research on human resources topics are ignored by practitioners (Rynes, Brown, & Colbert, 2002). However, based on our reading of the current research literature on humor in organizations, in comparison with reports about humor appearing in the popular and practitioner literatures, the opposite might be true for humor. Specifically, empirical evidence for a link between humor and important performance-related outcomes is somewhat limited at this point, and seems to be far surpassed by the claims that are made about it, particularly in regard to claims made about performance.

One of the few exceptions is Susa's (2002) dissertation study, which found that positive humor used in the work environment (defined as "incongruity humor" and "relief humor") was related to higher job satisfaction, higher commitment levels, and higher performance ratings, whereas "negative humor" (defined as "superiority humor") was negatively correlated with those organizational outcomes. Other research linking humor and performance or performance relevant outcomes (e.g., job satisfaction) seems to fall in one of two categories: performance-related outcomes that result from humor's influence on positive affect, or performance-related outcomes caused by use of humor by leaders. In the sections below, we review the evidence for affect and leadership-related links between humor and performance.

Humor, Affect, and Performance

The relationship between humor and positive affect has received considerable supported in the literature (Cann et al., 1999; Kuiper, McKenzie, & Belanger, 1995; Martin et al., 1993). In fact, humor is frequently used as a positive mood induction in experimental studies (Carnevale & Isen, 1986; Kraiger, Billings, & Isen, 1989). Positive affect has been found to be directly or indirectly related to a number of important individual and organization-level performance variables. For example, Isen and Baron (1991) showed that even a small shift in positive affect can influence job satisfaction and task perceptions, and can have an effect on prosocial behaviors. In a more recent review, Brief and Weiss (2002) cited substantial evidence showing that affect is associated with various performance-relevant variables such as judgments, negotiation process, helping behaviors, and withdrawal behaviors. In addition, Seo, Barrett, and Bartunek (2004) argue that affect can influence performance through its impact on the direction, intensity, and persistence components of motivation.

Although humor might have a measurable impact on positive affect, it is implausible that the level of positive affect caused by isolated jokes or funny comments could have an enduring and meaningful impact on an audience. However, if the use of humor can have a *cumulative* effect, and if positive affect can persist or build within groups, such an influence might be possible. One way in which this might occur is through *emotional contagion*, a social process by which one's positive or negative affect is "caught" by others and spread throughout one's group (Hatfield, Cacioppo, & Rapson, 1994). Emotional contagion can occur through an intentional and conscious process called social sharing of emotions (Rimé, Mesquita, Philippot, & Boca, 1991) and/or through an automatic and unconscious mechanism called primitive emotional contagion (Hatfield et al., 1994). For example, Strazdins (2002) found that explicit discussion of individuals' emotions initiated emotional contagion processes whereby the moods of audience members converged toward those of the speaker. In addition, Bartel and Saavedra (2000) found that behavioral manifestations of emotion (e.g., facial expressions) were unconsciously mimicked by other group members, eventually resulting in mood convergence. Similarly, Barsade (2002) elicited mood convergence in several laboratory-based groups using a confederate trained to display emotion-laden behaviors. Barsade (2002) also found positive collective mood was associated with cooperation and higher task performance.

However, Seo et al. (2004) write "little is known about what causes core affective experiences at work and to what degree" (p. 435), and indeed, although these effects seem robust, little attention has been paid to underlying causes of the positive affect that subsequently becomes "contagious." We suggest that humor might represent a proverbial virus of emotional contagion in groups. Future research that specifically examines humor as a precipitating factor in initiating positive affect, and perpetuating it through emotional contagion processes, might help address an important unknown in the literature on positive affect. It might also be fruitful to explore how humor interacts with other contextual factors (e.g., leadership style, organizational culture) to impact emotions and performance-related outcomes.

Humor and Leadership

Leaders' use of humor is proposed as another channel through which humor exerts an influence on performance. Perhaps not surprisingly, books focusing on leadership advice often suggest that appropriate use of humor is one aspect of effective leadership. For example, in the 7th edition of *Successful Manager's Handbook* (Nelson-Neuhaus et al., 2004), the use of humor is suggested as an effective tool in many regards, such as establishing positive relationships with subordinates, demonstrating adaptability in a new environment, and motivating others. Although Duncan (1982) and Malone (1980) discussed the potential utility of humor as a tool for managers back in the early 80s, relatively little empirical research has been conducted to test this argument since then.

Among the limited number of studies on humor and leadership, an assumption that humor is associated with good leadership and favorable outcomes is generally supported. For example, Sala (2000) found that outstanding executives used more humor than average executives, and that humor use was positively correlated with bonuses and competency scores. Interestingly, he also found that use of humor was correlated with competencies associated with emotional intelligence (Goleman, 1994), supporting other research findings linking humor to social skills (Hampes, 1992). Cooper (2002) also found that leaders' use of positive humor increased the positive affect dimension of leader–member exchange, which in turn influenced organizational citizenship behaviors (positively), and turnover intentions (negatively). In addition, Decker (1987) found that employees who reported more use of humor by their supervisors reported higher job satisfaction. Similarly, Burford (1987) found that teachers' perception of principals' sense of humor was associated with satisfaction and loyalty. Instead of addressing the simple direct effect of leader's use of humor on employees' work behaviors, Vecchio, Justin, and Pearce (2006) explored the moderating role of leaders' use of humor. Their findings suggest that the impact of leader humor on intentions to quit and performance depends on the other attributes of the leader, including perceived degree of honesty and use of contingent rewards.

Two studies also examined the relationship between humor use and leadership quality. In a military context, Priest and Swain (2002) found that good leaders were rated higher in the use of humor. In a more extensive investigation of humor and leadership style, Avolio et al. (1999) found that transformational and contingent leadership styles were associated with greater humor use, but the laissez-faire style was negatively associated with humor use. In addition, Avolio et al. (1999) found that humor use as rated by subordinates was related to the manager's performance as rated by the manager's supervisor.

These studies seem to imply that a leader's use of humor might have both motivational and emotional components. On the motivational side, leaders might use humor to affiliate with their subordinates in order to increase group cohesiveness and build trust. Certainly, research exploring contextual or individual difference variables that influence motivations to use humor would help us understand how and why humor is initiated. On the emotional side, leaders' use of humor is associated with an affective influence on subordinates, which is associated with higher job satisfaction and other job attitudes (e.g., commitment) and attitude-related cognitions (e.g., turnover intentions). Judge and Ilies (2002) studied the affective component of job satisfaction, and showed that momentary moods (such as that which might be influenced by humor) are strong predictors of concurrent job satisfaction. In addition, a recent meta-analysis of 312 studies (Judge, Thoresen, Bono, & Patton, 2001) estimated that the true correlation between job satisfaction and performance is $\sim.30$, which is not inconsequential. So, even though the empirical evidence for the direct link between leader's use of humor and follower's performance has not been well established in research, it is plausible that leaders' use of humor might enhance subordinates' performance through higher job satisfaction.

Humor and Group Cohesiveness

"Good humor is one of the preservatives of our peace and tranquility." (Thomas Jefferson)

In an earlier section, we argued that an underlying desire to build cohesiveness is a likely motivation to use humor. Despite strong consensus regarding this function of humor, the evidence supporting a direct influence of humor on cohesiveness is somewhat weak by standards of evidence typically applied in the organizational literature. With the exception of a handful of studies which demonstrated that humor influences ratings of interpersonal attraction (e.g., Murstein & Brust, 1985; Cann, Calhoun, & Banks, 1997), most of the studies conducted over the last four decades that have concluded that humor is used to build cohesiveness in organizational contexts have relied upon some form of qualitative judgment on the part of the researchers to reach that conclusion.

For example, using a participant–observer methodology, Ullian (1976) coded joking interactions systematically along a number of dimensions (e.g., time, location, context, and target). After evaluating a small number of interactions, he concluded that joking was often used when a worker introduced potentially threatening new information to other workers. Similarly, Vinton (1989) and Consalvo (1989) also used a participant–observer methodology. Consalvo (1989), who described his study as "largely descriptive" (p. 286), evaluated taped interactions from 22 managerial meetings. He observed that the use of humor occurred in predictable phases that helped groups bond by helping them cope with initial disagreement and conflict. Vinton (1989) collected data with field notes, and used the "constant comparative method" to categorize types of humor. She concluded that humor is used for many specific purposes, but ultimately serves to "create bonds among the employees" (p. 165). Fine and De Soucey (2005) conducted ethnographic studies of mushroom collectors and meteorologists, and concluded that patterns of joking behavior, particularly those that were repeated over time, helped create cohesiveness by smoothing interaction, creating a shared collective identity, and distinguishing the group from others. Holmes and colleagues (e.g., Holmes, 2000; Holmes & Marra, 2002a, 2002b ; Holmes, Marra, & Burns, 2001) have conducted a number of studies using qualitative linguistic analysis of tape-recorded interactions with various groups, and have also concluded that one of the major functions of humor is to smooth social interactions and maintain cohesiveness and solidarity.

The fact that most of the studies that have shown a relationship between humor and cohesiveness are qualitative and required substantial researcher judgment by no means implies that their conclusions were wrong. Indeed, indirect evidence for an effect of humor on cohesiveness comes from a number of sources. One source of this evidence is research that has examined the role of humor on conflict behavior. For example, in a laboratory study on the use of humor in negotiation, O'Quin and Aronoff (1981) found that subjects who were presented with a demand that was accompanied by humor made greater concessions than subjects who received the demand only. In addition, although their results did not suggest that subjects in the humor condition liked their negotiation partner more, they did enjoy the task itself more. Carnevale and Isen (1986) focused more specifically on humor's ability to induce positive affect. They followed up on research showing that mediators use humor to decrease hostility in interactions (Carnevale & Pegnetter, 1985) and that humor can decrease aggressiveness (Baron, 1984) by inducing positive affect in a laboratory experiment. They found that participants in the humor-induced positive affect condition used fewer contentious tactics during negotiations, and were more likely to engage in problem solving.

"Laughter is the shortest distance between two people." (Victor Borge)

Another source of indirect evidence for a humor-cohesiveness relationship is research by Owren and Bachorowski (2003), which supports an evolutionary theory that links humor to cohesiveness through "hard-wired" human cognitive and emotional processes. Their empirical studies refute an older theory that laughter is meant to signal others that the *laugher* is in a positive mood. Rather, their research suggests that the evolved function of laughter is to trigger a positive mood state in *others*, which subsequently becomes associated with the individual doing the laughing. This finding dovetails nicely with Provine's (1993) finding that in natural settings, speakers laughed 46% more than their audience, indicating that the humor producers might influence their audience in part by punctuating their communication with laughter. It is also consistent with the literature on emotional contagion cited above. Importantly, Owren and Bachorowski (2003) note that laughter will not spontaneously elicit positive mood in an audience that is in a negative or neutral mood state. In fact, they suggest that laughter has its most potent effect when the audience has a learned association between the laugher and previously experienced positive mood. This implies that among group members that have had positive experiences with one another, humor and laughter serve to reinforce social bonds (Fine & De Soucey, 2005).

The research that has been conducted on the link between humor and cohesiveness, as well as the related research cited above, strongly suggests that people are motivated to use humor to create cohesiveness, and that the positive emotional responses frequently elicited by humor might provide the glue. In addition, it appears that humor and laughter might have evolved specifically to engender cohesiveness. However, much of the research that has explored this issue in organizational contexts has used qualitative methods that are susceptible to experimenter expectancy or confirmation bias effects. Therefore, a clear demonstration of a link between humor and group or organization-level cohesiveness, perhaps using well-established measures of cohesiveness (see Duncan, 1984, for an example of empirical research in which an ad hoc measure was used), has the potential to provide clear evidence for one of the foundational assumptions made about humor in organizations.

Other research questions regarding cohesiveness in organizations are also begging for attention. For example, it would be interesting to determine if humor use is different in high versus low cohesiveness groups, or in groups that have been together for a short versus long amount of time. Researchers could explore the possibility that the content of humor varies over time, or with the needs of the group at different points in time. For instance, while in the formation stage, group members might avoid using humor in communications that have a negative tone (e.g., sarcastic humor), to help ensure that group bonds have a chance to form. Alternatively, humor that helps convey negative emotions, concerns, aggression, or other phenomena associated with the forming stage of a group might be particularly frequent. However, in the later stages of a group, perhaps more humor might be employed that targets outgroup members, which might serve to reinforce the group's unique identity independent of outgroups and competitors.

Humor and Creativity

"I think the next best thing to solving a problem is finding some humor in it." (Frank A. Clark)

"The kind of humor I like is the thing that makes me laugh for five seconds and think for ten minutes." (William Davis)

A fairly common theme in the popular press and practitioner literature on humor is that humor *causes* (or "enhances," or "stimulates") creativity (e.g., Abramis, 1992; Caudron, 1992; Therrien, 2004). Barker (2002), for example, writes that exposure to humor seems to "widen pathways among the brain's lobes" (p. 168). A considerable body of empirical research supports the notion that humor and creativity are associated. Some of this research has examined the relationship between measures of individuals' *sense of humor* and measures of creativity, and has obtained significant correlations (e.g., Davis & Rimm, 1977; Humke & Schaefer, 1996; Kovac, 1999; Rouff, 1975; Wycoff & Pryor, 2003). Ziv (1980) distinguished between individual difference measures of humor production and humor appreciation, and found that although both were strongly correlated with a measure of creativity, humor production was more strongly correlated. Clearly, the weight of this evidence is suggestive of *some* kind of connection between individual humor characteristics and creativity, but the causal relationship is blurry because none of these studies examined actual expression of humor and subsequent creativity (see James, Brodersen, & Eisenberg, 2004, and Kaufmann, 2003, for a thorough discussion of the positive affect-creativity link). Other research *has* examined humor expression within groups, and evaluated those groups' creative performance. For example, Holmes (2000) found that humor use was common in creative contexts such as brainstorming, and was associated with creative performance in groups. Similarly, Firestien (1990) found that groups trained in creative problem solving were more creative than untrained groups, and exhibited more humor (i.e., more laughs and smiles). However, such research also suffers from some degree of causal ambiguity, because it is unclear whether humor is in an antecedent, consequent, or simultaneous relationship with creativity.

A limited number of experimental studies have been conducted that help establish the causal relationship between humor and creativity. For example, Smith and White (1965) found that humor was positively associated with creativity and effectiveness in small problem-solving groups. The most convincing experimental research, however, has been conducted by Ziv. In a series of experiments, Ziv (1976, 1983) found that students who listened to a humorous recording or watched a humorous video clip scored higher on a test of creativity than students who took the test only. In addition, students who were told to answer questions on the Torrence creativity test *humorously* scored higher on creativity than students in a control condition (Ziv, 1983). He suggested that such an instruction provided a cue for unconventional thinking.

Two theoretical explanations for why humor might result in creativity have been proposed. One potential mechanism works by humor's emotional mechanisms, and suggests that the positive mood brought about by humor results in decreased anxiety about searching for and voicing novel or original ideas (Ziv, 1988). Such an anxiety reduction function of humor through positive affect was also examined by Ford, Ferguson, Brooks, and Hagadone (2004), who found that women who used humor to cope with stress experienced less anxiety, which in turn increased their performance on a math test. This explanation is also consistent with the results of Smith and White (1965), who found that "defensiveness" was negatively associated with humor use in a small group. Generally, the influence of humor on positive affect and anxiety reduction is the basis for the belief that humor can be a stress reducer (Nezlek & Derks, 2001).

The cognitive mechanisms behind humor have also been implicated in the relationship between humor and creativity (Murdock & Ganim, 1993).

Ziv (1988), Koestler (1964), and others have hypothesized that the key cognitive aspect of humor, incongruity and its resolution, is very similar to the cognitive processes required for creativity. Specifically, both humor and creativity require that an individual momentarily connects two previously divergent or unrelated notions (or expectation systems) in a novel way. This might suggest that humor makes individuals more cognitively flexible and more accustomed to making associations between domains that are otherwise not seen as related. Enhanced cognitive flexibility might be similar to what Abramis (1992) and others have described in terms of "play" (Csikszentmihalyi, 1996; Murdock & Ganim, 1993). Physiologically, this might suggest that activation in the brain caused by humor primes or facilitates activation that is necessary for creative thinking (and possibly the reverse), although we are not aware of any research that has examined this hypothesis specifically. An interesting research study might examine whether humor that is topic specific is necessary for increasing humor, or if activation caused by humor more generally is all that is needed.

HUMOR AND CULTURE

"A difference of taste in jokes is a great strain on the affections." (George Eliot)

In Albert Brooks' recent film "Looking for Comedy in the Muslim World," there's a scene in which Brooks is standing in front of a large audience in a theater in India. He tells a joke that is greeted with absolute silence. After a moment, he says to the crowd "If you speak English, would you raise your hand?" Of course all 500 or so people raise their hands, to which Brooks says under his breath "Oh God." Certainly, the sense of utter embarrassment and extreme awkwardness arising from this failure to communicate is a feeling that most people who have interacted with people from different cultures have undoubtedly experienced in relation to humor, if on a smaller scale. Indeed, such experiences have led some people who consult about cross-cultural communication to conclude that humor is a topic that is best avoided when communicating with someone from a different culture. But, given humor's ability to enhance the effectiveness of communications, and its ubiquity across people and contexts, we believe a better strategy might be to understand humor and its relationship with culture better through systematic research. The preceding sections on humor theory and humor's effects in organizations provide the backdrop for the current section, in which our goal is to employ theory from cross-cultural research to examine how culture might influence humor processes.

To organize our discussion of this topic, we divide our analysis of cultural influences into the three categories represented by each of the humor process mechanisms discussed previously: socio-motivational, cognitive, and emotional. However, the conceptualization of "culture" for this purpose is not a simple matter, and it is important that we address this issue. Culture has been conceptualized in many different ways. For instance, Kluckhohn (1954) uses the analogy that culture is to society as memory is to the individual. Hofstede (1991) describes culture as a collective programming of the mind. At a somewhat more concrete level, Triandis (1994) describes culture as what "has worked" for a society, and what is worth passing on. Dawkins (1989) labels these specific elements of culture "memes," and suggests that like genes, memes replicate themselves through transmission from generation to generation within a society. Although specific conceptualizations of culture can vary substantially, they all highlight the notion that culture is shared by members of a society. In addition, they indicate that because culture is pervasive across people and time within a society, individuals are unlikely to be consciously aware of their own cultural values, beliefs, and assumptions. It is this unconscious influence on our behavior that makes the examination of culture so fundamentally interesting, and so practically important as the world shrinks and people from different cultures come into increasing contact.

Most of the cross-cultural literature on the influence of culture on human behavior, in organizational contexts and otherwise, has focused on dimensions of culture. Cultural dimensions are coherent sets of values, beliefs, or assumptions about the social or physical environment, which are meaningful to people around the world (i.e., people everywhere understand what you are talking about when you describe a dimension), but differ in strength of endorsement across societies. A great deal of the literature has focused on dimensions identified and/or developed by Hofstede (1980) in his seminal work at IBM (i.e., power distance, individualism–collectivism, masculinity–femininity, and uncertainty avoidance). Of these, the dimension of individualism–collectivism has clearly received the most empirical and theoretical attention, and appears to have important effects on cognition and behavior (see Triandis, 1995, for a comprehensive review). Power distance has also received considerable attention, and a number of authors have suggested that power distance might be particularly important in organizational contexts (e.g., Earley & Gibson, 1998). In our analysis, we focus substantially on individualism–collectivism and power distance to develop propositions about the influence of culture on humor processes.

Numerous other dimensions of culture have been proposed (see the Chinese Cultural Connection, 1987 and Schwartz, 1994), and are undoubtedly useful in various contexts. However, we evaluate only one additional dimension, known as cultural tightness (Pelto, 1968), which we believe might be particularly relevant to the examination of humor. In the sections below, we describe the three dimensions of individualism–collectivism, power distance, and tightness in more detail, and note why each dimension has particular relevance for understanding humor use in organizations.

Individualism versus Collectivism

Individualism–collectivism is the most frequently discussed dimension of societal culture isolated by cross-cultural researchers (e.g., Triandis, 1995). In their empirical examination of cultural values measures developed in different parts of the world, Smith, Dugan, and Trompenaars (1996) determined that individualism and collectivism are basic dimensions of human values across societies. At the center of the individualism–collectivism distinction is the notion of the group. For collectivists, the groups to which one belongs are a substantial source of identity, and important distinctions are made between members of one's ingroup and outgroup members. Because ingroups are so important to collectivists, the goals of the group take precedence over individual goals, and group norms tend to be more closely followed in collectivist than individualist societies. In contrast, in individualistic societies, people are loosely connected to groups, and tend to view relationships in terms of exchanges. Because individualism–collectivism is relevant to issues of relationships between people, and humor has been implicated as an important determinant of interpersonal cohesiveness, this cultural dimension might be particularly important for the examination of humor

Power Distance

Power distance is a cultural dimension identified and described at length by Hofstede (1980). It reflects the degree to which individuals perceive inequalities in status or power to be appropriate in a healthy society. In high power-distance societies, distinctions between those who are in formal positions of authority and those who are not are perceived as real and important. The phrase 'rank has its privileges' is acceptable in high power distance societies. Low power distance societies are more egalitarian. Institutions in low power distance societies are less likely to have many layers of bureaucracy, and distinctions made along power or status dimensions are attributed to a need for functionality rather than inherent differences in the worth of individuals. Because humor is used to both maintain power and authority and to subvert it, the notion of power distance might be particularly relevant with regard to explaining peoples' underlying motivations for using humor.

Tight versus Loose Cultures

Culture specifies what behaviors are desirable for members of the culture. Cultures differ not only in the number of imposed behavioral norms, but also in whether deviations from norms are to be punished severely. In tight cultures (e.g., Japan), where many behavioral norms exist, deviant behavior is not easily tolerated. Loose cultures (e.g., the U.S.), on the other hand, either have unclear norms or can tolerate deviance from norms (Pelto, 1968). Importantly, even tight societies include specific contexts that are loose (e.g., drinks after work in Japan). Because humor often disturbs the status quo (Davis, 1993), and can broach taboo subjects, the tightness/looseness distinction can be important for understanding differences in the use and function of humor across cultures.

Organizational Culture

It is also important to note that organizational cultures might vary along some of the same dimensions as societal cultures. One manifestation of that might be a correspondence between the cultures of organizations and the characteristics of the broader societal cultures in which they are embedded (Schneider, 1988). The logic behind this parallelism is that societal culture influences shared managerial assumptions and values (Kanungo & Jaeger, 1990), and managers, in turn, shape the organizational culture. Work by Aycan, Kanungo, and Sinha (1999) supports a correspondence between societal culture and human resource management practices, and empirical studies by Chatman, Polzer, Barsade, and Neale (1998) and Robert and Wasti (2002) both support the existence of individualism and collectivism dimensions of organizational culture. While we are aware of no empirical research the supports the existence of a dimension of organizational culture that parallels the societal dimension of power distance, Earley and Gibson (1998) suggest that an organizational culture dimension that distinguishes between high and low power distance organizations might be even more important than the individualism–collectivism distinction.

Culture and Motivational Mechanisms

Face and Humor

One of the more important drivers of communication norms in many cultures is the concept of 'face.' Face refers to "a claimed sense of favorable social self-worth that a person wants others to have of her or him" (Ting-Toomey & Kurogi, 1998, p.187). The importance of face is thought to be universal, as is the perception that face is a vulnerable resource because it can be easily enhanced or threatened in social interactions. Politeness theory (Brown & Levinson, 1987) contends that humor might be an important tool for saving the face of both speakers and listeners, because it can be used to camouflage otherwise face-threatening aggressive or insulting communication, to indicate solidarity, and to help avoid conflict by releasing repressed feelings (Holmes, 2000). In other words, individuals might be motivated to use humor that can "mask" communications, which, unvarnished, are likely to harm the face of the speaker or listener. Consider the following example:

> The boss turns to an employee who was absent from work the previous day: Tell me what happened yesterday, but don't forget that your grandmother has already died twice (Ziv, 1984, p. 34)

In this example, the boss is asking for the subordinate's explanation for absence, but in the interest of maintaining solidarity, the boss avoids being overtly challenging and conveys dissatisfaction by an indirect route. The humorous approach helps the subordinate save face and softens the situation with little loss of underlying message.

Although the use of humor as a face-saving technique is likely common and universal, the extent to which this function of humor is practiced might differ across cultures. Conversational constraints theory (Kim, 1993) contends that individualist and collectivist societies have different levels of preferences for face-saving behaviors. In collectivistic societies, individuals' sense of identity is defined substantially by their interdependent relations with others. Because interpersonal harmony and preference for affiliation are strongly emphasized, collectivists have a stronger preference for face-saving behaviors in conversation than do individualists. This is supported by

Kim (1994) who found that members of collectivistic cultures attribute higher importance to not hurting the hearer's feelings than members of individualistic cultures. Members of individualistic cultures, in contrast, put more emphasis on conversational clarity. All other things being equal, it follows that individuals in collectivist societies might engage in humor more frequently as a means of saving face.

Humor in Tight Cultures
Rules for the acceptable use of humor in tight societies or in tight organizational cultures are likely to be complex. Tightness implies that strong and clear norms for appropriate behavior are in place, perhaps manifest as rules or bureaucratic procedures. One common and effective way that individuals use humor and incongruity is by contrasting an established worldview (e.g., the acceptable way to do things) in a novel way with a different worldview (Davis, 1993). This style of humor can open peoples' eyes to alternative perspectives, thereby representing a subversive threat or challenge to the established order. Because this type of subversive humor attacks core assumptions, beliefs, and values, it is unlikely to be tolerated in tight environments. In work contexts embedded in tight cultures, where formal and unspoken rules for appropriate behavior are likely to be strong, humor might be considered inconsistent with a perception that work is "serious," (Morreall, 1991), and might be perceived as unproductive or distracting. This also suggests that tight environments might be similarly intolerant of distracting humor that employs weakly held belief systems, such "silly" humor (e.g., slapstick, vulgar humor).

On the other hand, Haig (1988) notes that humor often has a powerful 'conservative' influence. He notes that humor is often used to define ingroups and outgroups, reinforce the power structure, and communicate the accepted group norms and values. He cites examples of a number of societies in which humor is used in the form of ridicule and humiliation to punish and correct the behavior of those who violate rules. Thus, if humor is used in tight cultures, we expect it to be directed toward the maintenance of the social order and organizational discipline.

Humor, Cohesiveness, and Individualism–Collectivism
As discussed earlier, the role of humor in the development of interpersonal cohesiveness appears to be one of its major social functions. In examining this issue, Martineau (1972) suggested that understanding relationships between parties to humor (i.e., producer, audience, and target or 'butt') is essential for understanding the interpretations of humor, and ultimately, its effects within

a social system. Specifically, he proposed that humor will have its most positive effects on social integration and cohesiveness when the producer and audience perceive each other as members of an ingroup. This might even include humor with a disparaging tone delivered in an ingroup, because "criticism is considered a prerogative of group members" (pp. 119–120), and it is acceptable for members of an ingroup to poke fun at their own faults and weaknesses (as later demonstrated by Scogin & Pollio, 1980). Importantly, though, when the producer and audience are not perceived to be part of the same ingroup, humor that targets the ingroup will tend to emphasize intergroup distinctions, or be perceived as an attempt by the humor producer to control others' behavior. Thus, humor will harm cohesiveness. In contrast, consistent with social identity theory (Tajfel & Turner, 1986), when the butt of humor is seen as *outgroup*, the effect of humor is to increase the esteem of the ingroup.

The importance of the ingroup/outgroup status of the parties to a humorous communication suggests that individualism and collectivism might be useful constructs for understanding how humor might contribute to or detract from cohesiveness. Individualism is characterized by the relative ease with which individuals are accepted as part of the ingroup. In contrast, collectivists are slower to "warm up" to others and consider them ingroup, but once an individual is accepted as part of the ingroup, the bond is less transitory than bonds for individualists (Triandis, 1995). This suggests that if one attempts to use humor with a collectivist audience, particularly if the humor can be perceived as derogating the ingroup, it is particularly important that he or she is perceived as a member of the ingroup. However, if one is an *accepted* member of the ingroup, learned predispositions toward positive affect are likely present, and the use of humor might be particularly effective at creating cohesiveness, regardless of its tone.

Humor and Hierarchy
The idea that humor use is related to organizational culture and to motivations to retain power or control has been discussed by a number of authors (e.g., Dwyer, 1991; Kahn, 1989; Stephenson, 1951). In the section on motivational mechanisms, we noted that some literature supports a "high status humor monopoly" view of humor in organizations, which suggests that humor occurs mostly in a downward direction through the hierarchy (e.g., Bradney, 1957; Coser, 1960, Holmes, 2000; Lundberg, 1969). However, some research has shown that high status people in some contexts use light-hearted teasing humor, or even self-deprecating humor (Vinton, 1989). In addition, other research has described cases in which lighthearted

humor (e.g., Holmes & Marra, 2002a; Vinton, 1989) or even more aggressive humor (e.g., Rodrigues & Collinson, 1995) was directed upward through the hierarchy. Therefore, the literature is somewhat inconsistent in predicting *who* uses humor, and in what form, but it is clear that humor plays a role in either maintaining or subverting authority relationships.

The notion of power distance might be particularly useful for explaining these apparent inconsistencies. We consider power distance from two perspectives: (1) the perspective of the broader societal culture in which an organization is embedded, and (2) the perspective of a particular organization, and its cultural norms regarding the perceived legitimacy or prestige associated with rank and formal status. In societal cultures that are low in power distance, authority, rank, and status are not sacrosanct, and thus, can be challenged through the use of humor by individuals with lower status without violating societal norms. In societal cultures that are high in power distance, however, individuals will likely be hesitant to challenge authority through any means. In *organizations* that are high in power distance, where status and hierarchy are revered (rank has its privileges), individuals are sanctioned to maintain status and hierarchy relationships. Because maintenance of such relationships is mostly in the interests of the managers or supervisors who are in power, we might expect them to take active steps to retain power through the use of humor or otherwise. In contrast, in low power distance organizations, hierarchy is largely a matter of efficiency and functionality (*somebody* has to make the decisions), and/or expertise (people are supposedly promoted because of job specific knowledge or abilities). Therefore, titles and other indicators of formal status do not necessarily convey informal status. In such contexts, the use of aggressive or otherwise negative types of humor directed at subordinates would likely be counternormative.

Considered jointly, the classification of organizations and societies as high or low on power distance can provide the basis for some interesting and testable predictions. In *low* power distance organizations, embedded in *low* power distance societies, we suggest that humor might be especially common. Individuals with less formal status or power are "allowed" by both the society and the organizational culture to challenge the authority of managers or supervisors, and thus might do so out in the open with lighthearted or teasing humor intended to deflate formal status differences (Vinton, 1989). Supervisors or managers with more formal status are likely to be discouraged from using more aggressive forms of humor that serve to emphasize control and status distinctions. However, "teasing to get things done" (Vinton, 1989) might be used to help save face by masking the directness of orders, and self-deprecating humor might be used to reduce any sense of hierarchical differences brought on by formal titles and reporting relationships.

In high power distance organizations, located in low power distance societies, the sparks might fly. Specifically, low status individuals are sanctioned by the society to challenge authority, but the ability to use humor openly might be restricted by the threat of potential punishment by higher status individuals for violating organizational norms (e.g., low pay, no raises, termination, etc.). In such a case, individuals might respond with the use of subversive humor. Such humor is often difficult to trace to its origins, and can be particularly biting (see Linstead, 1985; Rodrigues & Collinson, 1995; Taylor & Bain, 2003). In contrast, managers are sanctioned to use humor by the organization, and might react negatively to the subversive humor used by subordinates by using their own aggressive humor (e.g., disparaging or ridiculing humor) to emphasize status differences and to "put employees in their place."

Humor use in organizations in *high* power distance societies might also show predictable patterns of humor use. Generally speaking, an ambient culture of respect for those in authority is created in high power distance societies. When organizational power distance is low, light hearted teasing humor (e.g., Scogin & Pollio, 1980) might be employed by lower status individuals, because such humor connotes acceptance by the group (Fine & De Soucey, 2005). In high power distance societies, low status individuals might also employ ingratiatory humor (Cooper, 2005) to butter up their managers and supervisors. Ingratiation has the biggest potential payoff when the ingratiation targets have power to give the humorist valued resources; this is most likely in high power distance organizations.

Besides ingratiation, however, the case of high power distance organizations located in high power distance societies might represent the proverbial "humor desert," with regard to humor directed up or down the hierarchy. In such contexts, because status and power are seen as legitimate in high power distance societies, both humor that is used to maintain collegiality (e.g., by making orders less direct), and humor used to maintain social distance and control, might be seen as unnecessary. This is because supervisors in high power distance societies are *expected* to issue orders and directives, so there is no need to "sugar-coat" or mask orders. Similarly, because subordinates accept the fact that leaders' power and status is legitimate, attempts to use humor as a form of subversion or resistance to maintain autonomy are unnecessary. In fact, a supervisor's attempt to maintain authority using aggressive humor (e.g., sarcasm, teasing employees) might even be seen as abusive, particularly given norms that would suppress retribution in kind. This might be particularly true given that leadership in high power distance societies often carries with it a flavor of paternalism, in which the leader is given power, but also has responsibility for looking after the welfare of his/her subordinates (Triandis, 1995).

In summary, our analysis of humor in the context of high and low power distance organizations and societies suggests that power distance might moderate motivations of both low and high status individuals to use both positive and negative forms of humor. Generally, we expect relatively little upward or downward focused humor when both the organizational and societal cultures are high in power distance (e.g., Chinese owned firms operating in China), and perhaps slightly more humor in the form of light-hearted (e.g., teasing, or bantering) humor that can be tolerated by societal norms when the societal culture is high in power distance, but the organizational culture is low in power distance (e.g., subsidiaries of companies headquartered in low power distance countries that are located in a high power distance country such as India). In contrast, we predict considerable use of upward and downward focused humor when both the organizational and societal cultures are low in power distance (e.g., firms that are known to downplay hierarchy such as Ben & Jerry's or Southwest Airlines, located in relatively low power distance countries). The most aggressive forms of humor are likely in high power distance organizations embedded within low power distance societies (e.g., subsidiaries of companies headquartered in high power distance societies, but located in low power distance societies). This is because the organizational culture supports hierarchical stratification, while simultaneously, the ambient societal culture supports efforts to challenge authority and control. This can lead to a veritable humor "arms race" in which the tone of humor can become more and more negative as employees who are both low and high in the formal hierarchy attempt to exercise autonomy or control, respectively.

Culture and Cognitive Mechanisms

As described above, the cognitive process of humor appreciation is complex and multifaceted (e.g., incongruity, comprehension difficulty, elaboration, etc.), indicating that there are multiple reasons why a humorous communication might fail to be perceived as humorous by an audience. However, we suggest that this failure is likely to be most true when a humor producer and his/her audience are from different cultures. Incongruity theory can help us understand why this might be the case. A basic tenet of incongruity theory is that in order for humor to be experienced as funny, the audience and humor producer must share the same expectation systems elicited by the joke's context. If they do not, then the joke's attempted incongruity will be meaningless. For example, while the 'prison' expectation system elicited in the joke reproduced above might be fairly universal (for all but the most primitive societies), the workplace expectation system that we take for granted in the U.S. (and is so cleverly leveraged in the "Dilbert" comics of Scott Adams) is probably only relevant in developed economies with substantial numbers of service sector workers in office environments. Without a schema for cubicle-based work, one can not resolve the incongruity established explicitly by saying that prison is better than work. Individuals in developing countries might understand all the words, but not really "get the joke." Similarly, if the humor being interpreted is very difficult to understand, or the audience has to "work too hard" to get the joke, it will not be perceived as very humorous. Wyer and Collins (1992) suggest that this is a function of the fact that if the audience to humor must spend all of their cognitive resources simply trying to understand the joke by resolving or linking its inherent incongruities (high comprehension difficulty), they will have no opportunity to engage in the cognitive elaboration associated with perceiving humor.

Cultural differences in information processing goals are also a potential problem for appreciating humor that is produced in a different culture than one's own. Differences in information processing goals occur not because of difficulty with humor content, but because cultures might differ considerably in their norms about which contexts are appropriate for the use of humor. That is, cultures prescribe which contexts are to be evaluated in terms of a "play frame" (Caron, 2002) which makes individuals sensitive to incongruities and their potential resolution. Many "play frames" might be similar across cultures. For example, comedic movies or plays are likely to put people from most cultures into a play frame where the information processing goal is to look for and attempt to resolve and elaborate on incongruities. Research by many authors over a number of decades (e.g., Bradney, 1957; Holmes & Marra, 2002b; Ullian, 1976) suggests that joking with equal status coworkers at work or outside work might be a common, if not universal, play context.

However, like Albert Brooks' character, people with experience interacting with individuals from different cultures will often tell tales of awkward, confusing, or frustrating interactions in which humor "missed its mark." The underlying cause of such humor blunders might often be traced to differences in information processing goals. As an example, the first author is American, and has a good friend from Singapore. One day on the golf course, the author tried to tell his Singaporean friend a joke that started "A duck walks into a bar....". The content of the joke is immaterial, because when the joke was finished, the friend asked "why would a duck walk into a bar?" This common joke introduction, which typically puts listeners in a play frame with a goal of processing information for its humor, was unfamiliar to the friend. Thus, the friend was never actually able to devote his attention to the content of the joke (which, incidentally, is very funny). The same friend also asked the first author why late night comedians like Jay Leno were "allowed" to make biting and sarcastic jokes about political leaders. He seemed deeply offended by the notion that people were allowed to make nasty or caustic remarks about leaders, and noted that leaders never receive the same public mistreatment in Singapore. Clearly, in listening to the personal political jokes of late-night comedians, the friend's ability to process the jokes using a play frame was substantially limited by his culturally determined experiences.

However, incongruity theory and its advancements (e.g., Wyer & Collins, 1992) provide valuable insights that make blanket recommendation against using humor in cross-cultural interactions somewhat premature, particularly given the potential benefits of using humor. First, the types of humor that are likely to "work" with diverse audiences are those that employ expectation systems that are relatively universal. Davis (1993) notes that humor might be appreciated by broad audiences if "at least some aspects of the expectation systems violated by incongruities and ambiguities are enduring and universal" (p. 27). Brown (1991) devotes an entire book to understanding universals, and notes that while much of an individual's knowledge is culture-bound, schemas surrounding many phenomena such as language, religious practices, family structures, war, government, and shelter are universal. Haig (1988) makes the observation that 'mother-in-law' jokes are likely to go over well in many societies. In the same vein, Hertzler (1970) notes that mass art, mass communication, and mass government (e.g., the European Union) might be associated with shared expectation systems, as might urban congestion, traffic, technological phenomena (e.g., the internet), and sports. Although this explanation for why humor often might not "go over well" in cross-cultural contexts might appear obvious, we believe that it might provide a core assumption for the study of humor and culture. Indeed, this implication of incongruity theory might be particularly useful for helping researchers define humor in field or laboratory studies, where systematic attempts to vary humor quality might be attempted.

An additional proposition relates to how the organization itself can provide a common context for humor. Schein (1985) suggests that organizational cultures consist of learned assumptions that develop when a firm deals with its problems of internal integration and external adaptation. Such shared assumptions might provide an important source of shared expectations. For example, humor within an organization might develop around common knowledge about the firm's industry, products, processes, history, or customers. Indeed, Vuorela (2005) suggests that members of the same organization or occupation are often able to use humor successfully among themselves, despite their differences in societal culture background. As an example, during the first author's visit to a factory in India, frequent electricity failures required time-consuming and annoying machine resets each time power was restored. During one of these episodes, an expatriate American manager approached some of the Indian employees on the shop floor and said "The city utility commissioner must be excellent. I hear he recently won an award for the most electricity restorations in India." While the first author did not immediately understand the joke, it received a great laugh from the Indian employees. It effectively utilized an expectation system that they shared with the American manager. Importantly, this joke likely served to cement bonds between the manager and line workers, by (a) expressing that the manager understood their situation, and did not blame them for the slow-down, and (b) increasing ingroup cohesiveness by identifying a common outgroup member (i.e., the utility commissioner). Indeed, in situations where individuals within an organizational enviro-ment have diverse societal culture backgrounds, we might expect that effective humor will have its roots in shared aspects of the organizational culture.

We put forth one final proposition regarding culture and incongruity theory. Berry's (1976) acculturation framework highlights a key indicator of how individuals might come to understand the expectation systems of another culture. Specifically, he suggests that individuals who value maintaining relationships with other groups are more likely to *assimilate* or *integrate* into a new culture, whereas those who do not will separate themselves or become marginalized. Therefore, active attempts to assimilate or integrate, as indicated by active behaviors such as interaction with natives, following local media, and familiarizing oneself with popular culture, should help expose individuals to expectation systems that might be elicited in humor. Importantly, though, even individuals who are motivated to experience a new culture might fail if they have low ability in the language associated with that culture (Berry, Kim, Minde, & Mok, 1987).

When an individual understands the cultural context, he or she is more likely to avoid producing jokes that are not be supported by the expectation system of the audience, or that will offend others by attacking deeply held assumptions, values, or beliefs. When an individual is very confident of his or her understanding of the culture and its expectation systems, successful humor production and the avoidance of cultural faux pas should be possible. Similarly, others' attempts at humor are more likely to be appreciated, potentially helping to cement the bonds between humor producer and audience that come from shared humor.

Again, although this principle is straightforward, we believe it might be fundamental to the study of humor and culture, and useful for exploring interesting phenomena. For example, it might be useful for the study of expatriate success. Developing a level of cultural understanding at which humor can be appreciated and produced might be an important indicator of success for expatriate managers, or those who work with a multicultural workforce. Indeed, successful navigation of humor within a novel culture might be an excellent indicator of acculturation and interaction adjustment (Black & Stephens, 1989). Furthermore, researchers have linked language ability to both acculturation (Berry et al., 1987), and to the appreciation of humor (Burke, 1995; Schmitz, 2002), but we are unaware of any research that has bridged this gap to explore links between acculturation and humor production and/or appreciation. Such a link might be a particularly fruitful avenue for a number of reasons. First, humor has been touted as an important tool for relieving stress (Feigelson, 1989), which is seen as an important negative outcome of the acculturation process. Furthermore, intergroup anxiety experienced by those who are attempting to acculturate is an important source of acculturative stress (Greenland & Brown, 2005), but humor might serve to reduce that anxiety by helping individuals cement interpersonal bonds through the shared common experience of laughter (e.g., Owren & Bachorowski, 2003). Therefore, an understanding of culturally based expectation systems might enhance humor production and appreciation, which has the potential to reduce acculturative stress, as well as some of the sources of that stress.

Humor, Creativity, and Power Distance

We noted previously that existing evidence supports a relationship between humor and creativity, based on humor's ability to increase mental flexibility and/or reduce anxiety. However, the societal culture dimension of power distance might suggest two important caveats to this fundamental relationship. First, as we noted above, high power distance might be associated with less use of humor, particularly between employees from different hierarchical levels. As such, the frequency of humor use in social communications might be decreased in high power distance environments, which would presumably reduce mental flexibility and increase anxiety relative to an environment in which humor flows freely.

Second, even if individuals at a given hierarchical level utilize humor considerably, and this facilitates cognitive processes consistent with the generation of creative or innovative ideas, high power distance might inhibit ideas from ever being put forth at the group level, or presented to superiors. This notion was supported by Van der Vegt, van de Vliert, and Huang (2005) who found that in high power distance societies, diversity in status-relevant characteristics (i.e., functional background and tenure) within a group were inversely related with a climate of innovation. They hypothesized that in high power distance societies, the presence of high status individuals tends to inhibit low status members from voicing creative ideas, or disagreeing with ideas posed by high status members. Conversely, in low power distance societies, diversity in terms of these characteristics was positively associated with innovative climate. In other words, although humor might be related to the generation of creative ideas at an individual level, social processes associated with power distance might keep those ideas from ever being offered.

Shane, Venkataraman, and MacMillan (1995) also found that it in high power distance societies people believe it is important that those who champion innovations should seek the support and acceptance of people in authority, rather than building broad consensus. If those in power are accepting of innovative ideas coming from subordinates, this would not be a problem. However, because power distance is associated with bureaucratic and hierarchical structures and highly centralized decision making, creative ideas and innovations might be less likely to be given a fair hearing and accepted by those in authority. This is consistent with Anderson, De Dreu, and Nijstad's (2004) contention that "innovation unavoidably involves challenging the status quo at some level of analysis and at some point in the process" (p. 160), and suggests that putting forward innovative or creative ideas might be a risky endeavor. As a consequence, perhaps through learned helplessness, even if they might otherwise be stimulated creatively by humor, employees might never develop habits of brainstorming creative ideas, or "thinking outside the box" because of the difficulty in getting one's ideas heard. Indeed, taking the initiative to develop and champion innovative ideas might be seen as closely related to empowerment, whereby individuals are encouraged to make and implement independent decisions. Yet some research has suggested that empowerment might be inconsistent with the values of high power distance societies (Robert, Probst, Martocchio, Drasgow, & Lawler, 2000).

Culture and Emotional Mechanisms

Earlier we argued that one of the reasons humor is an important phenomenon in organizations is that it can provide an initial stimulus for positive affect, which in turn can be spread through a process of emotional contagion. However, both the tendency to display one's emotions, and the tendency to respond to others with positive affect, might be influenced by culture. Indeed, in order for one's affective state to be caught and spread by others, interactants must be willing and able to express their emotions (Hatfield et al., 1994). Similarly, in order for humor to function as a facilitator of mood convergence, group members must be willing to use it and respond to it. While these assumptions are fully satisfied in existing group mood studies (e.g., Barsade, 2002; Bartel & Saavedra 2000; George 1990; Totterdell, 2000; Totterdell, Kellet, Teuchmann, & Briner, 1998), which relied exclusively on American samples, studies on emotion and culture challenge the generalizability of these assumptions. Most notably, researchers have identified cultural display rules, defined as "learned, culturally determined rules that govern the display of emotion depending on social circumstances" (Matsumoto 1990, p.196), that might influence emotional contagion processes. For example, Bond (1993) argued that emotional expressions of Chinese people are characterized by lower frequency, less intensity, and shorter duration. More generally, Andersen (1988) suggested that collectivists suppress emotional displays that are incongruent with the group mood. These findings suggest that culture might moderate the relationship between humor and performance, such that emotional contagion of positive emotions aroused by humor will be less likely in collectivist cultures.

However, the moderating effect might be even more complex. The theoretical framework proposed by Triandis (1995) regarding the importance of ingroups in collectivistic cultures is again relevant. According to Triandis (1995), collective cultures foster a great degree of cohesion or harmony in their limited ingroups, so group members are more inclined to present positive feelings toward ingroup members. Furthermore, in order to maintain the harmony required in their ingroups, collectivists tend to make a greater distinction between self-ingroup and self-outgroup relationships. This can be achieved by displaying negative emotions to outgroups and pleasant emotions to ingroups. Indeed, Matsumoto (1990) found that collectivists rated negative feelings as more appropriate in the presence of outgroup than ingroup members.

This suggests that members of individualistic cultures, who usually belong to a number of ingroups and who feel comfortable with relatively superficial relationships, do not differentiate between ingroups and outgroups as readily as do members of collective cultures. Therefore, they are unlikely to present different emotions based on the self-group relationship, and are more likely to display emotions according to their internal feelings. Under such conditions, positive emotions resulting from humor are most likely to be displayed and transmitted to others. Similarly, in collectivistic cultures, when the individuals within one's social sphere are members of one's ingroup, people are more readily affected by the positive mood invoked by humor, are likely to display their positive affect behaviorally (e.g., smiles and laughter), and perhaps initiate more humor because positive affect is appropriate. This creates conditions that are likely to result in positive emotional contagion. In contrast, when a collectivist group is composed of individuals who consider each other to be outgroup, they will be less inclined to appreciate humor, to react to it behaviorally, or to initiate humor. As a result, positive affect from humor is not likely to spread and build through emotional contagion.

DISCUSSION

Despite the fact that many people view the workplace as a realm of seriousness, popular management books and legions of consultants extol the virtues of humor as a management tool for businesses (Fry, 2004). Indeed, organizations spend considerable resources in an attempt to leverage humor to increase productivity, creativity, and cohesiveness (Caudron, 1992). Fortunately, the basis for these efforts seems fairly strong. The motivational mechanisms underlying humor production, and the cognitive and emotional mechanisms underlying humor appreciation, are well-justified theoretically, and are useful from a research perspective. However, empirical findings are far from definitive as there have been relatively few studies that have examined humor within broader networks of organizational phenomena and organizational theories. In addition, as noted above, there appear to be many synergies between culture theory and humor theory that suggest interesting research angles for the motivated researcher. This extension of humor research into the cross-cultural realm will have the effect of forcing humor researchers to describe their theories more carefully, and will also make research findings more applicable in organizations that are operating in an increasingly complex multicultural landscape. Indeed, we believe that researchers who are interested in humor have fertile ground in which to work.

In the remainder of this final section, we focus a little bit more on practical research questions and research issues. In particular, we highlight what we feel are two potentially rich research areas in the domain of human resource management: humor and training, humor and recruitment/ selection. We then touch on some important methodological and theoretical issues that those who are interested in pursuing research on humor in organizations might consider.

Humor and Training

"Once you get people laughing, they're listening and you can tell them almost anything." (Herbert Gardner)

In the 1970s, the well-known British comedian and member of Monty Python, John Cleese, created a company that produced and distributed training videos for organizations. As one might expect, Cleese's videos are infused with considerable humor, and he maintains that "humor in training increases retention and decreases anxiety," (Lundberg, 2006). Indeed, a quick scan of the internet reveals that many trainers, speakers, and other practitioners insist that humor has enormous potential for improving communication with the audience, audience participation and receptivity to new ideas, learning, and information retention. Certainly, if such claims are valid, an important role for researchers would be to explicate the specific mechanisms by which humor can have such effects, so that guidance about the use of humor could be given to trainers and other practitioners (see Kaupins, 1991, for an initial venture into this topic).

Unfortunately (or fortunately if you are a researcher in search of a topic in relatively uncharted territory), we are aware of very few empirical studies that address the role of humor in the training process. Nevertheless, corroborating evidence for humor's important role comes from other domains. For example, therapists and researchers studying therapeutic effects have recognized for decades that humor has great potential to enhance the therapeutic process (e.g., Fry & Salameh, 1993). It is believed to facilitate communication and rapport, and it can help both client and therapist raise subjects that might be difficult to broach directly (Dziegielewski, Jacinto, Laudadio, & Legg-Rodriguez, 2003). Open and clear channels of communication between trainer and trainee are often critical for training success, and the ability of humor to facilitate discussion of difficult topics (e.g., sexual harassment, diversity, sensitivity) might prove to be one of its most important functions. In education, humor has also been recognized for its potential to enhance the effectiveness of learning through its effects on attention and memory (Hill, 1988; Vance, 1987), and in the reduction of anxiety (Garner, 2005). Again, given the importance of learning and retention in the training process, such effects are clearly relevant to training in organizational contexts.

Research on the link between humor and training could focus on any of the three mechanisms described throughout this paper. Starting with the motivational mechanisms, humor could be explored with respect to humor producers' intentions to use humor. For example, trainers that use humor might be attempting to build cohesiveness, decrease status differences between themselves and trainees, increase the persuasiveness of their message by inducing positive affect in the audience, or increasing source credibility (Lyttle, 2001). Trainees that use humor might also be trying to build cohesiveness or rapport with the trainer or fellow trainees. However, trainees might also use humor as a form of communication about other issues. For example, Grugulis (2002) found that humor might be used to communicate criticism or challenge of the trainer by the trainee in a more masked or subtle way. A trainee might also use humor to mask direct criticism of the trainer's knowledge or techniques, or criticism of the validity of training more generally. In addition, humor might be used as an indirect way of communicating information about the trainee himself or herself, such as whether the material is easy or difficult to understand, or whether the message that is being delivered is accepted by the trainee.

Cognitive effects of humor might also be a topic for fresh research on humor and training. Specifically, given that the appreciation of humor is characterized by enhanced brain activity (e.g., Goel & Dolan, 2001; Watson et al., 2007), that such brain activity is associated with the individual's ability to connect disparate pieces of information (Fry, 2002), and with creativity, it seems logical to hypothesize that individuals in a learning context such as training might benefit from increased humor-induced neural activation and an enhanced ability to connect disparate pieces of knowledge or information.

Such an effect of humor has been proposed by others (e.g., Tamblyn, 2003), but remains largely untested in training contexts. Basic research could explore the possibility that humor enhances neural activation that aids in the process of information encoding, or in subsequent retrieval. Research with a more applied focus could use humor as an independent variable, and explore its effects on training effectiveness by examining various criteria such as attention during training, skill or knowledge demonstration immediately after training, and other long term learning or performance criteria (Konradt, Filip, & Hoffmann, 2003). Certainly the proposed positive effects of humor on training effectiveness must involve a number of subtleties that could be explored by research. For instance, is there some threshold of activation that must be surpassed to get humor effects on information processing? Can there be too much humor-induced activation, such that it actually interferes with the encoding process? Differences in cultural norms regarding the appropriate contexts for humor use moderate the impact of humor and thus the degree to which humor can enhance learning (see Zhang, 2005, for an examination of humor, power distance, and communication apprehension in Chinese college classrooms).

Finally, researchers might explore humor's impact on training by exploring humor's emotional mechanisms. Specifically, given the relationship between humor and positive affect, a likely scenario is that humor might influence training success as a result of its influence on positive affect. For example, effects of positive affect on information processing might be similar to the cognitive effects of humor. Isen's (1999) review of the literature suggests that even mild positive affect has a positive effect on learning, memory, problem solving, and flexibility in thinking. Humor also appears to decrease state anxiety (Ford et al., 2004), which might result in greater receptivity to new ideas or information. And finally, humor might enhance training effectiveness through its impact on positive affect, because positive affect makes people more persuadable (Cooper, 2005).

Again, although the fundamental mechanisms by which humor might impact training through its impact on emotions appear to be fairly well-supported, a number of important issues of scope and boundaries might be resolved through systematic research. For example, how much positive affect is too much? Is it possible to be "too happy" for training, and might that depend on the type of training involved? For example, positive affect might increase persuadability because it increases peripheral processing. In some cases, this might be desirable (e.g., sexual harassment training), but in training contexts where deeper processing is desirable (e.g., processing of complex technical information), a more central processing route and deeper processing will likely lead to more effective learning.

Humor and Selection/Recruiting

Humor's presumed effects on performance-related outcomes, creativity, and cohesiveness beg the question: "how can we harness those effects in organizations?" One route is to *do* things to increase the amount of humor in the organization. Humor consultants suggest things like putting up humor bulletin boards, having humor breaks during meetings, and sponsoring joke contests (Therrien, 2004). Organizations that are successful at creating a culture of humor do things like create humor rooms (Kodak), put together "joy gangs" (Ben & Jerry's), or have their CEO ride into an employee meeting on a motorcycle (Southwest Airlines) (Caudron, 1992). These types of specific ideas might be effective. However, an additional and perhaps complementary strategy might be to recruit and select employees for their sense of humor. Indeed, a consideration of humor's effects is not very meaningful if an organization does not include individuals who will produce humor and individuals who will appreciate humor.

A recruitment/selection perspective on humor in organizations is rife with interesting questions for researchers. One important issue is determining how important it is for *leaders* (e.g., managers, supervisors) to have a good sense of humor. We speculate that a good sense of humor might be particularly important for leaders for two reasons. First, leaders set the tone regarding the acceptability of humor expression in the workplace. If leaders are intolerant of playful behavior (e.g., telling jokes, making funny comments), or other expressions of humor (e.g., the posting of cartoons), this will stifle potential humor production among their subordinates. Second, important aspects of leaders' roles include communicating sensitive information (e.g., performance feedback) and maintaining cohesiveness and collegiality among subordinates. As we argued earlier, both of these roles can be supported by effective use of humor, and therefore, leaders with a sense of humor have additional tools for doing their jobs.

A second research question involves the issue of identifying the relative importance of humor production or appreciation as components of sense of humor. Although humor production and appreciation seem to be correlated (Ziv, 1988), any given individual might score higher on one than the other. Clearly, humor has to come from somewhere, so having some individuals who are high in humor production seems necessary for the initiation of any humor effects. However, the cognitive and emotional mechanisms of humor are thought to be stimulated primarily on the humor *appreciation* side, so we must have individuals who appreciate humor if we are to obtain the cognitive and emotional outcomes resulting from humor. One perspective on this issue might be that some degree of balance is necessary. In an interesting study on mens' and womens' preferences for sense of humor in the opposite sex, Bressler, Martin, and Balshine (2006) found that men tended to prefer people who appreciated their humor, whereas women had a stronger preference for people who produced humor. Similarly, Ziv and Gadish (1989) found that complementarity between spouses perceptions of one another's humor was associated with marital satisfaction. Although these results might suggest that workplaces with a balance between men and women might be particularly conducive to the generation and appreciation of humor, a more general prediction about having a mix of producers and appreciators who would complement one another's humor styles might represent a fruitful research avenue, particularly in smaller group settings.

"No mind is thoroughly well organized that is deficient in a sense of humor." (Samuel Taylor Coleridge)

To be useful in a selection context, measures of humor production and/or appreciation or some other means of evaluating them (e.g., interviews) must be explored. A key research issue in this vein is determining whether measures of humor are related to other important characteristics used in selection. As the Coleridge quote above implies, one such characteristic might be intelligence. For decades, researchers have documented that intelligence and giftedness and sense of humor are often correlated (e.g., Holt & Willard-Holt, 1995; Lehman & Witty, 1928). This relationship suggests that an examination of incremental validity of humor over and above general cognitive ability would be important. Alternatively, if measures of sense of humor are correlated with general cognitive ability, it would be interesting to determine whether humor could be used as a serviceable substitute for general cognitive ability, particularly if it would not result in adverse impact. Similarly, sense of humor might be related to other individual differences variables that could be used in a selection context such as personality, and there is some limited evidence that humor might be related to empathic concern, which is a component of emotional intelligence (Hampes, 2001). On the criterion side, measures of in-role task performance might be influenced by humor, particularly for jobs that require a considerable creative component. However, criteria such as job attitudes or extra-role behaviors would be more proximal to the emotional or affective impact of humor, and therefore, would be the best candidates for demonstrating the validity of sense of humor in a selection context. Perhaps Dostoyevsky was right when he wrote "If you wish to glimpse inside a human soul and get to know a man, don't bother analyzing his ways of being silent, of talking, of weeping, of seeing how much he is moved by noble ideas; you will get better results if you just watch him laugh. If he laughs well, he's a good man."

Methodological Issues

One practical issue faced by researchers is whether the basic tools and methodologies are in place for researchers who want to enter this area without having to "re-invent the wheel." The fact that humor has been of interest to researchers across disciplines has resulted in the application of diverse methodologies to its study. For example, participant observation (e.g., Linstead, 1985; Sykes, 1966), discourse analysis (e.g., Hatch, 1997), and quantitative content analysis (e.g., Holmes et al., 2001) have all been successfully employed. Social network analysis also represents a promising methodological approach to the study of humor in organizations. For example, one might examine whether individuals who use humor are likely to be highly central within workplace networks, to have larger networks, and to fill structural holes (e.g., Burt, Joanotta, & Mahoney, 1998; Klein, Lim, Saltz, & Mayer, 2004).

In addition, there is a growing body of research that employs survey measures of humor [e.g., the Multidimensional Sense of Humor Scale (Thorson & Powell, 1993), the Humor Styles Questionnaire (Martin et al., 2003), the Sense of Humor Questionnaire (Svebak, 1996), and the Situational Humor Response Questionnaire (Martin & Lefcourt, 1984)]. Although these measures, as well as survey measures of cultural values (e.g., Schwartz, 1994; Singelis, Triandis, Bhawuk, & Gelfand, 1995) or organizational outcomes might be useful, researchers must not be overreliant on such measures. Specifically, research using single informant, cross-sectional data collection is fraught with potential for ambiguous causality and misleading correlations (Köhler & Ruch, 1996). In particular, single-source of data biases are highly problematic if empirical relationships between humor and other socially desirable phenomena are to be examined. For example, as Avolio et al. (1999) note, when leader effectiveness and leader humor are rated by the same individual, ratings on one dimension are likely to influence ratings on the other dimension, resulting in inflated correlations. Multi-informant designs in which different individuals are asked to provide ratings for predictor and criterion variables will help address this problem, and longitudinal designs will help clarify problems with ambiguous causality. Importantly, both problems can be addressed by well-designed laboratory research, which is underutilized in the humor literature (see Martin, 2001, and Ziv, 1988 for exceptions).

An examination of humor and culture in organizations also raises a number of applied issues that could bear on the utility of humor use in organizations. Some of these were raised by Malone (1980) and Duncan (1982), and have gone largely unanswered in the last two decades. For example, Malone questioned whether humor can be used effectively as a managerial tool, and if so, can it be used by just anybody? That is, can an ability to produce humor in socially appropriate contexts be learned, or is it dependent on humor-related traits? Similarly, one might ask how important humor appreciation is as a component of humor's ability to influence organizationally relevant outcomes.

Theoretical Issues

As important as the practical and methodological issues is the need for researchers to build theoretically sound models that place humor appropriately within a causal network. Humor is both an elusive and flexible construct. It adapts well to placement as an antecedent to many outcomes, but equally plausible arguments can often be developed that describe it as a consequence of particular conditions, or as one of many consequences of some phenomenon. For example, with respect to leadership, humor can be conceptualized as a manifestation of the social skills necessary for good leadership (Sala, 2000), or it can be seen as a tool for individuals to influence one another (e.g., Cooper, 2005). For creativity, humor can be seen as an event that primes an individual to think creatively, or perhaps both creativity and humor are caused by some third dispositional variable. To further complicate matters, humor might stand in a reciprocal relationship with other phenomena. Owren and Bachorowski's (2003) work suggests such a relationship, wherein humor and laughter might be antecedents that promote positive affect, which in turn promotes more humor use, and so on.

Finally, we note that the study of humor and culture in organizations requires that researchers consider the notion of "levels." With respect to hierarchical levels, anthropological and sociological studies have paid particular attention to the direction of humor (e.g., who is allowed to produce humor) as well as the interpersonal contexts in which humor is used. As we have alluded throughout this paper, the issue of humor use across hierarchical levels is particularly relevant for the analysis of culture differences, given the substantial variability across societies and organizations in the degree to which hierarchical differences are accepted and maintained.

In addition, humor theorists must pay careful attention to levels of analysis and levels of theory (Klein, Dansereau, & Hall, 1994). The theoretical construct of humor is amenable to examination at multiple levels. For example, at the individual level, one might examine individual difference variables such as humor production, humor appreciation, or individual behaviors driven by humor. At the group level, humor can be treated as a climate variable, if, for instance, there is considerable within-group agreement about the receptiveness of a group to humor. At a more macro level, humor can be viewed as a cultural or societal level phenomenon. If, for example, one hypothesizes that societal norms influence individuals' predispositions toward humor production, differences between societies might be meaningful.

Culture also has the potential for treatment at different levels of analysis. Culture is usually conceptualized as a societal or organizational level construct. However, there is considerable evidence suggesting that cultural values such as individualism and collectivism can be examined meaningfully at the individual level of analysis (e.g., Robert & Wasti, 2002; Triandis, Leung, Villareal, & Clack, 1985), and that cultural values vary across geographic areas (Vandello & Cohen, 1999) and across some ethnic groups within the U.S. (Oyserman, Coon, & Kemmelmeier, 2002). Given the potential for variability within both societies and organizations, research that examines the relationship between humor and culture might fruitfully explore cultural values at the individual level of analysis.

Summary and Conclusions

The goals of this paper were threefold. The first and most important goal was to stimulate interest in the phenomenon of humor as a topic that is worthy of study by organizational researchers. Because humor is often seen as something frivolous, silly, or inconsequential, and certainly inconsistent with the serious nature of work, it has run mostly below the radar of organizational scholars. Indeed, we argued that one of the main reasons that humor is so pervasive in human communication is because it helps producers convey important messages by wrapping them in a cloak of play, such that the audience might barely register that something serious just happened. Indeed, Dwyer (1991) goes so far as to say "most of us just go on joking and laughing unaware of the historical, cultural, or power significations of what we do" (p. 18).

The second goal of the paper was to provide those who *are* interested in conducting research on humor in organizations with some useful guidance, and with a "higher grade of manure" in which to plant research ideas. To do this, we reviewed humor literature from psychology (including neuroscience), sociology, communications, and anthropology, as well as selected research that bears on humor processes less directly. The first part of our review focused on the descriptions of the theoretical basis underlying humor's effects in social interactions. Specifically, we explored the motivational basis behind *why* people use humor, as well as the cognitive and emotional mechanisms that underlie *how* people appreciate humor. Importantly, our review suggests that we know quite a lot about these mechanisms, particularly on the appreciation side where physiological evidence has confirmed the basic principles underlying incongruity theory and a link between humor appreciation and positive emotions. This fundamental understanding of the humor process is crucial as a launching point for serious research on humor in organizational contexts.

The second part of the review focused on describing the weight of current evidence for humor's effects on organizationally relevant outcomes. This review was designed to impose some organization on findings from a range of disciplines, and to provide researchers with a sense of which roads have been well-traveled, and which are still left unexplored. We concluded that the empirical evidence for relationships between humor and creativity, cohesiveness, and other performance-related outcomes is moderate at best, particularly with regard to any inference of causality. However, given that the theoretical basis for these relationships appears fairly sound, this conclusion should be viewed as a terrific opportunity for researchers, rather than a disappointment.

The final goal of this paper was to take a step into very new territory, by examining the potential influence of culture on humor use and outcomes in organizations. To do this, we drew on theory and research from the literature on cross-cultural psychology to develop specific and testable hypotheses. We hope the ideas outlined in the section on culture and humor stimulate interest in what we believe to be the most promising research opportunities addressed in this paper. Certainly, if one is interested in the role of humor in organizational contexts, it seems that the inclusion of culture as an important contextual variable would make the research more interesting, and more relevant to today's geographically dispersed and locally diverse organizations.

Oscar Firkins, the renowned writer and literary critic once said "Humor is not a postscript or an incidental afterthought; it is a serious and weighty part of the world's economy. One feels increasingly the height of the faculty in which it arises, the nobility of things associated with it, and the greatness of services it renders." This perspective comports with what we have been attempting to communicate in this paper. We believe that despite its apparent lightness and insignificance, humor is indeed a "weighty" issue that is deserving of substantial attention by researchers. Then again, our examination of humor teaches us that there's value in being humorous and playful, and not taking ourselves too seriously, so we leave you with the following:

> "Sometimes life seems like a dream, especially when I look down and see that I forgot to put on my pants." (Jack Handey, Deep Thoughts)

REFERENCES

Abel, M. H. (2002). Humor, stress, and coping strategies. *Humor*, *15*, 365–381.

Abel, M. H., & Maxwell, D. (2002). Humor and effective consequences of a stressful task. *Journal of Social and Clinical Psychology*, *21*, 165–198.

Abramis, D. (1992). Humor in healthy organizations. *HR Magazine*, *37*, 72–74.

Alden, D. L., Hoyer, W. D., & Lee, C. (1993). Identifying global and culture specific dimensions of humor in advertising: A multinational analysis. *Journal of Marketing*, *57*, 64–75.

Andersen, P. A. (1988). Explaining intercultural differences in nonverbal communication. In: L.A. Samovar & R. E. Porter (Eds), *Intercultural communication: A reader* (pp. 272–281). Belmont, CA: Wadsworth.

Anderson, N., De Dreu, C., & Nijstad, B. A. (2004). The routinization of innovation research: A constructively critical review of the state-of-the-science. *Journal of Organizational Behavior*, *25*, 147–173.

Aronson, E., Willerman, B., & Floyd, J. (1966). The effect of a pratfall on increasing interpersonal attractiveness. *Psychonomic Science*, *4*, 227–228.

Avolio, B. J., Howell, J. M., & Sosik, J. J. (1999). A funny thing happened on the way to the bottom line: Humor as a moderator of leadership style effects. *Academy of Management Journal*, *42*, 219–227.

Aycan, Z., Kanungo, R. N., & Sinha, J. B. P. (1999). Organizational culture and human resource management practices: The model of culture fit. *Journal of Cross-Cultural Psychology*, *30*, 501–526.

Barker, R. (2002, August 26). The art of brainstorming hiring diverse, even eccentric people, mixing them up in unexpected ways, and asking them to do something unusual can prompt surprising ideas. *Business Week*, *3796*, 168.

Baron, R. A. (1984). Reducing organizational conflict: An incompatible response approach. *Journal of Applied Psychology, 69,* 272–279.

Barsade, S. G. (2002). The ripple effects: Emotional contagion and its influence on group behavior. *Administrative Science Quarterly, 47,* 644–675.

Bartel, C. A., & Saavedra, R. (2000). The collective construction of work group moods. *Administrative Science Quarterly, 45,* 197–231.

Berger, A. A. (1987). Humor. *The American Behavioral Scientist, 30,* 6–15.

Bergson, H. (1956). Laughter. In: W. Sypher (Ed.), *Comedy* (pp. 61–191). Garden City, NY: Doubleday Anchor.

Berns, G., Cohen, J., & Mintun, M. (1997). Brain regions responsive to novelty in the absence of awareness. *Science, 276,* 1272–1275.

Berry, J. W. (1976). *Human ecology and cognitive style: Comparative studies in cultural and psychological adaptation.* New York: Sage/Halsted.

Berry, J. W., Kim, U., Minde, T., & Mok, D. (1987). Comparative studies of acculturative stress. *International Migration Review, 21,* 491–511.

Black, J. S., & Stephens, G. K. (1989). The influence of the spouse on American expatriate adjustment and intent to stay in Pacific Rim overseas assignments. *Journal of Management, 15,* 529–544.

Bond, M. H. (1993). Emotions and their expression in Chinese culture. *Journal of Nonverbal Behavior, 14,* 245–262.

Bradney, P. (1957). The joking relationship in industry. *Human Relations, 10,* 179–189.

Bressler, E. R., Martin, R. A., & Balshine, S. (2006). Production and appreciation of humor as sexually selected traits. *Evolution and Human Behavior, 27,* 121–130.

Brief, A. P., & Weiss, H. M. (2002). Organizational behavior: Affect in the workplace. *Annual Review of Psychology, 53,* 279–307.

Brown, D. E. (1991). *Human universals.* Philadelphia, PA: Temple University Press.

Brown, P., & Levinson, S. (1987). *Politeness: Some universals in language usage.* Cambridge: Cambridge University Press.

Burford, C. (1987). Humor of principals and its impact on teachers and the school. *Journal of Educational Administration, 25,* 29–54.

Burke, K. (1995). *Irony in context.* Amsterdam: John Benjamins Publishing Company.

Burt, R. S., Joanotta, J. E., & Mahoney, J. T. (1998). Personality correlates of structural holes. *Social Networks, 20,* 63–87.

Cann, A., Calhoun, L. G., & Banks, J. S. (1997). On the role of humor appreciation in interpersonal attraction, it is not laughing matter. *Humor, 10,* 77–89.

Cann, A., Calhoun, L. G., & Nance, J. T. (2000). Exposure to humor before and after an unpleasant stimulus: Humor as a preventative or a cure. *Humor, 13,* 177–191.

Cann, A., Holt, K., & Calhoun, L. G. (1999). The roles of humor and sense of humor in responses to stressors. *Humor, 12,* 177–193.

Carnevale, P. J., & Isen, A. M. (1986). The influence of positive affect and visual access on the discovery of integrative solutions in bilateral negotiation. *Organizational Behavior and Human Decision Processes, 37,* 1–13.

Carnevale, P. J., & Pegnetter, R. (1985). The selection of mediation tactics in public-sector disputes: A contingency analysis. *Journal of Social Issues, 41,* 65–81.

Caron, J. E. (2002). From ethology to aesthetics: Evolution as a theoretical paradigm for research on laughter, humor, and other comic phenomena. *Humor, 15,* 245–281.

Caudron, S. (1992). Humor is healthy in the workplace. *Personnel Journal, 71,* 1–4.

Chatman, J. A., Polzer, J. T., Barsade, S. G., & Neale, M. A. (1988). Being different yet feeling similar: The influence of demographic composition and organizational culture on work processes and outcomes. *Administrative Science Quarterly, 43,* 749–780.

Chinese Cultural Connection. (1987). Chinese values and the search for culture-free dimensions of culture. *Journal of Cross-Cultural Psychology, 18,* 143–164.

Collinson, D. L. (1988). 'Engineering humour': Masculinity, joking and conflict in shop-floor relations. *Organization Studies, 9,* 181–199.

Consalvo, C. M. (1989). Humor in management: No laughing matter. *Humor, 2,* 285–297.

Cooper, C. D. (2002). *No laughing matter: The impact of supervisor humor on leader-member exchange (LMX) quality.* Unpublished doctoral dissertation, University of Southern California.

Cooper, C. D. (2005). Just joking around? Employee humor expression as an ingratiatory behavior. *Academy of Management Review, 30,* 765–776.

Coser, R. L. (1960). Laughter among colleagues. *Psychiatry, 23,* 81–95.

Coughlin, J. J., III. (2002). *Gallows humor and its use among police officers.* Unpublished doctoral dissertation. James Madison University, Harrisonburg, VA.

Csikszentmihalyi, M. (1996). *Creativity: Flow and the psychology of discovery and invention.* New York: HarperCollins.

Davis, A., & Kleiner, B. H. (1989). The value of humour in effective leadership. *Leadership and Organizational Development Journal, 10,* i–iii.

Davis, G. A., & Rimm, S. (1977). Characteristics of creatively gifted children. *Gifted Child Quarterly, 21,* 546–551.

Davis, M. S. (1993). *What's so funny? The comic conception of culture and society.* Chicago, IL: University of Chicago Press.

Dawkins, R. (1989). *The selfish gene* (2nd ed.). Oxford: Oxford University Press.

Decker, W. H. (1987). Managerial humor and subordinate satisfaction. *Social Behavior and Personality, 15,* 225–232.

Derks, P., Gillikan, L. S., Bartolome-Rull, D. S., & Bogart, E. H. (1997). Laughter and electroencephalographic activity. *Humor, 10,* 285–300.

Duncan, W. J. (1982). Humor in management: Prospects for administrative practice and research. *Academy of Management Review, 7,* 136 142.

Duncan, W. J. (1984). Perceived humor and social network patterns in a sample of task-oriented groups: A reexamination of prior research. *Human Relations, 37,* 895–907.

Duncan, W. J., & Feisal, J. P. (1989). No laughing matter: Patterns of humor in the workplace. *Organizational Dynamics, 17,* 18–30.

Dwyer, T. (1991). Humor, power, and change in organizations. *Human Relations, 44,* 1–19.

Dziegielewski, S. F., Jacinto, G. A., Laudadio, A., & Legg-Rodriguez, L. (2003). Humor: An essential communication tool in therapy. *International Journal of Mental Health, 32,* 74–90.

Earley, P. C., & Gibson, C. B. (1998). Taking stock in our progress on individualism and collectivism: 100 years of solidarity and community. *Journal of Management, 24,* 265–304.

Feigelson, S. (1989). Mixing mirth and management. *Supervision, 50,* 6–8.

Fine, G. A., & DeSoucey, M. (2005). Joking cultures: Humor themes as social regulation in group life. *Humor, 18,* 1–24.

Firestien, R. L. (1990). Effects of creative problem solving training on communication behaviors in small groups. *Small Group Research, 21,* 507–521.

Ford, T. E., Ferguson, M. A., Brooks, J. L., & Hagadone, K. M. (2004). Coping sense of humor reduces effects of stereotype threat on women's math performance. *Personality and Social Psychology Bulletin, 30*, 643–653.

Fry, A. (2004). *Laughing matters*. Austin, TX: The Better Way Press.

Fry, W. F. (2002). Humor and the brain: A selective review. *Humor, 15*, 305–333.

Fry, W. F., & Salameh, W. (Eds). (1993). *Advances in humor and psychotherapy*. Sarasota, FL: Professional Resource Press.

Garner, R. (2005). Humor, analogy, and metaphor: H.A.M. it up in teaching. *Radical Pedagogy, 6*(2).

George, J. M. (1990). Personality, affect and behavior in groups. *Journal of Applied Psychology, 75*, 107–116.

Goel, V., & Dolan, R. J. (2001). The functional anatomy of humor: Segregating cognitive and affective components. *Nature Neuroscience, 4*, 237–238.

Goleman, D. (1994). *Emotional intelligence*. New York: Bantam Books.

Graham, E. E., Papa, M. J., & Brooks, G. P. (1992). Functions of humor in conversation: Conceptualization and measurement. *Western Journal of Communication, 56*, 161–183.

Greenland, K., & Brown, R. (2005). Acculturation and contact in Japanese students studying in Great Britain. *Journal of Social Psychology, 145*, 373–389.

Grugulis, I. (2002). Nothing serious? Candidates' use of humor in management training. *Human Relations, 55*, 387–406.

Haig, R. A. (1988). *The anatomy of humor: Biopsychosocial and therapeutic perspectives*. Springfield, IL: Thomas.

Hall, G. S. (1918). Morale in war and after. *Psychological Bulletin, 15*, 361–426.

Hampes, W. P. (1992). Relation between intimacy and humor. *Psychological Reports, 71*, 127–130.

Hampes, W. P. (2001). Relation between humor and empathic concern. *Psychological Reports, 88*, 241–244.

Hatch, M. J. (1997). Irony and the social construction of contradiction in the humor of a management team. *Organization Science, 8*, 275–288.

Hatfield, E., Cacioppo, J. T., & Rapson, R. L. (1994). *Emotional contagion*. New York: Cambridge University Press.

Hay, J. (2001). The pragmatics of humor support. *Humor, 14*, 55–82.

Hazlitt, W. (1930). Lectures on the comic writers, etc. of Great Britain. In: P. P. Howe (Ed.), *The complete works of William Hazlitt* (Vol. 6). London: J. M. Dent & Sons.

Hertzler, J. (1970). *Laughter: A socio-scientific analysis*. New York: Exposition Press.

Hill, D. (1988). *Humor in the classroom: A handbook for teachers (and other entertainers)*. Springfield, IL: Charles C. Thomas.

Hofstede, G. (1980). *Culture's consequences*. Beverly Hills, CA: Sage.

Hofstede, G. (1991). *Cultures and organizations: Software of the mind*. London: McGraw-Hill.

Holmes, J. (2000). Politeness, power, and provocation: How humor functions in the workplace. *Discourse Studies, 2*, 159–185.

Holmes, J., & Marra, M. (2002a). Over the edge? Subversive humor between colleagues and friends. *Humor, 15*, 65–87.

Holmes, J., & Marra, M. (2002b). Having a laugh at work: How humour contributes to workplace culture. *Journal of Pragmatics, 34*, 1683–1710.

Holmes, J., Marra, M., & Burns, L. (2001). Women's humor in the workplace: A quantitative analysis. *Australian Journal of Communication, 28*, 83–108.

Holt, D. G., & Willard-Holt, C. (1995). An exploration of the relationship between humor and giftedness in students. *Humor, 8*, 257–271.

Humke, C., & Schaefer, C. E. (1996). Sense of humor and creativity. *Perceptual and Motor Skills, 82*, 544–546.

Isen, A. M. (1999). Positive affect. In: T. Dalgliesh & M. J. Power (Eds), *Handbook of cognition and emotion* (pp. 521–539). Chichester, England: Wiley.

Isen, A. M., & Baron, R. A. (1991). Positive affect as a factor in organizational behavior. *Research in Organizational Behavior, 13*, 1–53.

James, K., Brodersen, M., & Eisenberg, J. (2004). Workplace affect and workplace creativity: A review and preliminary model. *Human Performance, 17*, 169–194.

Judge, T. A., & Ilies, R. (2002). Relationship of personality to performance motivation: A meta-analytic review. *Journal of Applied Psychology, 87*, 797–807.

Judge, T. A., Thoresen, C. J., Bono, J. E., & Patton, G. K. (2001). The job satisfaction-job performance relationship: A qualitative and quantitative review. *Psychological Bulletin, 127*, 376–407.

Kahn, W. A. (1989). Toward a sense of organizational humor: Implications for organizational diagnosis and change. *Journal of Applied Behavioral Science, 25*, 45–63.

Kanungo, R. N., & Jaeger, A. M. (1990). Introduction: The need for indigenous management in developing countries. In: A. M. Jaeger & R. N. Kanungo (Eds), *Management in developing countries* (pp. 1–23). London: Routledge.

Katz, B. F. (1993). A neural resolution of the incongruity-resolution and incongruity theories of humour. *Connection Science, 5*, 59–75.

Kaufmann, G. (2003). Expanding the mood-creativity equation. *Creativity Research Journal, 15*, 131–135.

Kaupins, G. E. (1991). Humour in university and corporate training: A comparison of trainer perceptions. *Journal of Management Development, 10*, 33–41.

Kim, M. S. (1993). Culture-based interactive constraints in explaining intercultural strategic competence. In: R. L. Wiseman & J. Koester (Eds), *Intercultural communication competence* (Vol. 19, pp. 132–150). Newbury Park, CA: Sage.

Kim, M. S. (1994). Cross-cultural comparisons of the perceived importance of conversational constraints. *Human Communication Research, 21*, 128–151.

Klein, K. J., Dansereau, F., & Hall, R. J. (1994). Levels issues in theory development, data collection, and analysis. *Academy of Management Review, 19*, 195–229.

Klein, K. J., Lim, B., Saltz, J. L., & Mayer, D. M. (2004). How do they get there? An examination of the antecedents of centrality in team networks. *Academy of Management Journal, 47*, 952–963.

Kluckhohn, F. (1954). Culture and behavior. In: G. Lindzey (Ed.), *Handbook of Social Psychology* (Vol. 2, pp. 921–976). Cambridge, MA: Addison-Wesley.

Köhler, G., & Ruch, W. (1996). Sources of variance in current sense of humor inventories: How much substance, how much method variance? *Humor, 9*, 363–397.

Koestler, A. (1964). *The act of creation*. New York: Macmillan Publishers.

Konradt, U., Filip, R., & Hoffmann, S. (2003). Flow experience and positive affect during hypermedia learning. *British Journal of Educational Technology, 34*, 311–330.

Kovac, T. (1999). Creativity and humor. *Psychologia a Patopsychologia Dietata, 34*, 346–350.

Kraiger, K., Billings, R. S., & Isen, A. M. (1989). The influence of positive affective states on task perceptions and satisfaction. *Organizational Behavior and Human Decision Processes, 44*, 12–25.

Kuiper, N. A., McKenzie, S. D., & Belanger, K. A. (1995). Cognitive appraisals and individual differences in sense of humor: Motivational and affective implications. *Personality and Individual Differences, 19*, 359–372.

Lehman, H. C., & Witty, P. A. (1928). A study of play in relation to intelligence. *Journal of Applied Psychology, 12*, 369–397.

Lehman, K. M., Burke, K. L., Martin, R., Sultan, J., & Czech, D. R. (2001). A reformulation of the moderating effects of productive humor. *Humor, 14*, 131–161.

Linstead, S. (1985). Joker's wild: The importance of humor in the maintenance of organizational culture. *The Sociological Review, 33*, 741–765.

Lundberg, A. (May 15, 2006). What's so funny? CIO. Retrieved June 30, 2006, from http://www.cio.com/archive/051506/edit.html

Lundberg, C. C. (1969). Person-focused joking: Pattern and function. *Human Organization, 36*, 22–28.

Lynch, O. (2002). Humorous communications: Finding a place for humor in communication research. *Communication Theory, 12*, 423–445.

Lyttle, J. (2001). The effectiveness of humor in persuasion: The case of business ethics training. *Journal of General Psychology, 128*, 206–216.

Malone, P. B., III. (1980). Humor: A double-edged tool for today's managers? *Academy of Management Review, 5*, 357–360.

Martin, R. A. (2001). Humor, laughter, and physical health: Methodological issues and research findings. *Psychological Bulletin, 127*, 504–519.

Martin, R. A., Kuiper, N. A., Olinger, L., & Dance, K. A. (1993). Humor, coping with stress, self-concept, and psychological well-being. *Humor, 6*, 89–104.

Martin, R. A., & Lefcourt, H. M. (1984). The situational humor response questionnaire: Quantitative measure of sense of humor. *Journal of Personality and Social Psychology, 47*, 145–155.

Martin, R. A., Puhlik-Doris, P., Larsen, G., Gray, J., & Weir, K. (2003). Individual differences in uses of humor and their relation to psychological well-being: Development of the humor style questionnaire. *Journal of Research in Personality, 37*, 48–75.

Martineau, W. H. (1972). A model of the social functions of humor. In: J. H. Goldstein & P.E. McGhee (Eds), *The psychology of humor* (pp. 101–128). New York: Academic Press.

Matsumoto, D. (1990). Cultural similarities and differences in display rules. *Motivation and Emotion, 14*, 195–214.

Meyer, J. C. (1990). Ronald Reagan and humor: A politician's velvet weapon. *Communication Studies, 41*, 76–88.

Meyer, J. C. (1997). Humor in member narratives: Uniting and dividing at work. *Western Journal of Communication, 61*, 188–208.

Morreall, J. (1991). Humor and work. *Humor, 4*, 359–373.

Murdock, M. C., & Ganim, R. M. (1993). Creativity and humor: Integration and incongruity. *Journal of Creative Humor, 27*, 57–70.

Murstein, B. L., & Brust, R. G. (1985). Humor and interpersonal attraction. *Journal of Personality Assessment, 49*, 637–640.

Nelson-Neuhaus, K. J., Skube, C. J., Lee, D. G., Stevens, L. A., Hellervik, L. W., Davis, B. L., & Gebelein, S. H. (Eds). (2004). *Successful manager's handbook: Develop yourself, coach others* (7th ed.). Minneapolis, MN: ePredix.

Nezlek, J. B., & Derks, P. (2001). Use of humor as a coping mechanism, psychological adjustment, and social interaction. *Humor, 14*, 395–413.

Nezu, A., Nezu, C., & Blissett, S. (1988). Sense of humor as a moderator of the relations between stressful events and psychological distress: A prospective analysis. *Journal of Personality and Social Psychology, 54*, 520–525.

Obrdlik, A. J. (1942). 'Gallows humor': A sociological phenomenon. *American Journal of Sociology, 47*, 709–716.

O'Quin, K., & Aronoff, J. (1981). Humor as a technique of social influence. *Social Psychology Quarterly, 44*, 349–357.

Owren, M. J., & Bachorowski, J. A. (2003). Reconsidering the evolution of nonlinguistic communication: The case of laughter. *Journal of Nonverbal Behavior, 27*, 183–200.

Oyserman, D., Coon, H. M., & Kemmelmeier, M. (2002). Rethinking individualism and collectivism: Evaluation of theoretical assumptions and meta-analyses. *Psychological Bulletin, 128*, 3–72.

Pelto, P. J. (1968). The difference between "tight" and "loose" societies. *Transaction, 5*, 37–40.

Priest, R. F., & Swain, J. E. (2002). Humor and its implications for leadership effectiveness. *Humor, 15*, 169–189.

Provine, R. R. (1993). Laughter punctuates speech: Linguistic, social and gender contexts of laughter. *Ethology, 95*, 291–298.

Radcliffe-Brown, A. R. (1952). *Structure and function in primitive society: Essays and addresses.* London: Cohen and West.

Rimé, B., Mesquita, B., Philippot, P., & Boca, S. (1991). Beyond the emotional event: Six studies on the social sharing of emotions. *Cognition and Emotion, 5*, 435–465.

Robert, C., Probst, T. M., Martocchio, J. J., Drasgow, F., & Lawler, J. L. (2000). Empowerment and continuous improvement in the United States, Mexico, Poland, and India: Predicting fit on the basis of the dimensions of power distance and individualism. *Journal of Applied Psychology, 85*, 643–658.

Robert, C., & Wasti, S. A. (2002). Organizational individualism and collectivism: Theoretical development and an empirical test of a measure. *Journal of Management, 28*, 544–566.

Rodrigues, S. B., & Collinson, D. L. (1995). 'Having fun"?: Humor as resistance in Brazil. *Organization Studies, 16*, 739–768.

Romero, E. J., & Cruthirds, W. (2006). The use of humor in the workplace. *The Academy of Management Perspectives, 20*, 58–69.

Rouff, L. L. (1975). Openness, creativity, and complexity. *Psychological Reports, 37*, 1009–1010.

Rynes, S. L., Brown, K. G., & Colbert, A. E. (2002). Seven common misconceptions about human resource practices: Research findings vs. practitioner beliefs. *Academy of Management Executive, 16*, 92–103.

Sala, F. (2000). *Relationship between executives' spontaneous use of humor and effective leadership.* Unpublished doctoral dissertation, Boston University.

Schein, E. H. (1985). *Organizational culture and leadership.* San Francisco, CA: Jossey-Bass.

Schmitz, J. R. (2002). Humor as a pedagogical tool in foreign language and translation courses. *Humor, 15*, 89–113.

Schneider, S. C. (1988). National vs. corporate culture: Implications for human resource management. *Human Resource Management, 27*, 231–246.

Schwartz, S. H. (1994). Beyond individualism and collectivism: New cultural dimensions of values. In: U. Kim, H. C. Triandis, C. Kagitcibasi, S.-C. Choi & G. Yoon (Eds), *Individualism and collectivism: Theory, method, and applications* (pp. 85–122). Newbury Park, CA: Sage.

Scogin, F. R., & Pollio, H. R. (1980). Targeting and the humorous episode in group process. *Human Relations, 33*, 831–852.

Seo, M., Barrett, L. F., & Bartunek, J. M. (2004). The role of affective experience in work motivation. *Academy of Management, 29*, 423–439.

Shammi, P., & Stuss, D. T. (1999). Humor appreciation: A role of the right frontal lobe. *Brain, 122*, 657–666.

Shane, S., Venkataraman, S., & MacMillan, I. (1995). Cultural differences in innovation championing strategies. *Journal of Management, 21*, 931–952.

Shultz, T. R. (1976). A cross-cultural study of the structure of humor. In: A. J. Chapman & H.C. Foot (Eds), *It's a funny thing, humor* (pp. 175–179). New York: Pergamon Press.

Singelis, T. M., Triandis, H. C., Bhawuk, D., & Gelfand, M. J. (1995). Horizontal and vertical dimensions of individualism and collectivism: A theoretical and measurement refinement. *Cross-Cultural Research: The Journal of Comparative Social Science, 29*, 240–275.

Smith, P. B., Dugan, S., & Trompenaars, F. (1996). National culture and the values of organizational employees: A dimensional analysis across 43 nations. *Journal of Cross-Cultural Psychology, 27*, 231–264.

Smith, E. E., & White, H. L. (1965). Wit, creativity, and sarcasm. *Journal of Applied Psychology, 49*, 131–134.

Stephenson, R. M. (1951). Conflict and control functions of humor. *American Journal of Sociology, 56*, 569–574.

Strazdins, L. (2002). Emotional work and emotional contagion. In: N. M. Ashkanasy, W. J. Zerbe & C. E. J. Härtel (Eds), *Managing emotions in the workplace* (pp. 232–249). New York: M. E. Sharpe Inc.

Suls, J. M. (1972). A two-stage model for the appreciation of jokes and cartoons: An information-processing analysis. In: J. H. Goldstein & P. E. McGhee (Eds), *The psychology of humor* (pp. 81–100). New York: Academic Press.

Suls, J. M. (1976). Cognitive and disparagement theories of humor: A theoretical and empirical synthesis. In: A. J. Chapman & H. C. Foot (Eds), *It's a funny thing, humor* (pp. 41–45). New York: Pergamon Press.

Susa, A. M. (2002). *Humor type, organizational climate, and outcomes: The shortest distance between an organization's environment and the bottom line is laughter.* Unpublished doctoral dissertation, University of Nebraska, Lincoln, NB.

Svebak, S. (1996). The development of the sense of humor questionnaire: From SHQ to SHQ-6. *Humor, 9*, 341–362.

Sykes, A. J. M. (1966). Joking relationships in an industrial setting. *American Anthropologist, 68*, 188–193.

Tajfel, H., & Turner, J. C. (1986). The social identity theory of intergroup behavior. In: S. Worchel & W. G. Austin (Eds), *Psychology of intergroup relations*. Chicago, IL: Nelson-Hall.

Tamblyn, D. (2003). *Laugh and learn: 95 ways to use humor for more effective teaching and training*. New York: AMACOM.

Taylor, P., & Bain, P. (2003). 'Subterranean worksick blues': Humour as subversion in two call centers. *Organization Studies, 24*, 1487–1509.

Therrien, D. (2004). Humour at work. *CMA Management, 78*, 12–14.

Thorson, J. A., & Powell, F. C. (1993). Development and validation of a multidimensional sense of humor scale. *Journal of Clinical Psychology, 49*, 13–23.

Ting-Toomey, S., & Kurogi, A. (1998). Facework competence in intercultural conflict: An updated face-negotiation theory. *International Journal of Intercultural Relations, 22*, 187–225.

Totterdell, P. (2000). Catching moods and hitting runs: Mood linkage and subjective performance in professional sport teams. *Journal of Applied Psychology, 85,* 848–859.

Totterdell, P., Kellet, S., Teuchmann, K., & Briner, R. B. (1998). Evidence of mood linkage in work groups. *Journal of Personality and Social Psychology, 74,* 1504–1515.

Triandis, H. C. (1994). *Culture and social behavior.* New York: McGraw-Hill.

Triandis, H. C. (1995). *Individualism and Collectivism.* Boulder, CO: Westview Press.

Triandis, H. C., Leung, K., Villareal, M., & Clack, F. L. (1985). Allocentric vs. idiocentric tendencies: Convergent and discriminant validation. *Journal of Research in Personality, 19,* 395–415.

Ullian, J. A. (1976). Laughing matter: Joking at work. *Journal of Communication, 26,* 129–133.

Vaid, J., Hull, M. R., Heredia, R., Gerkens, D., & Martinez, F. (2003). Getting a joke: The time course of meaning activation in verbal humor. *Journal of Pragmatics, 35,* 1431–1449.

Van der Vegt, G., van de Vliert, E., & Huang, X. (2005). Location-level links between diversity and innovative climate depend on national power distance. *Academy of Management Journal, 48,* 1171–1182.

Vance, C. (1987). A comparative study on the use of humor in the design of instruction. *Instructional Science, 16,* 79–100.

Vandello, J. A., & Cohen, D. (1999). Patterns of individualism and collectivism across the United States. *Journal of Personality and Social Psychology, 77,* 279–292.

Vecchio, R., Justin, J. E., & Pearce, C. L. (2006, August). All joking aside: The moderating effect of humor on relationships between leadership style and follower outcomes. Paper presented at the annual meeting of the Academy of Management, Atlanta, GA.

Vinton, K. L. (1989). Humor in the workplace: It is more than telling jokes. *Small Group Behavior, 20,* 151–166.

Vuorela, T. (2005). Laughing matters: A case study of humor in multicultural business negotiations. *Negotiation Journal, 21,* 105–129.

Watson, K. K., Matthews, B. J., & Allman, J. M. (2007). Brain activation during sight gags and language-dependent humor. *Cerebral Cortex, 17,* 314–324.

Wild, B., Rodden, F. A., Grodd, W., & Ruch, W. (2003). Neural correlates of laughter and humor. *Brain, 126,* 2121–2138.

Wycoff, E. B., & Pryor, B. (2003). Cognitive processing, creativity, apprehension, and the humorous personality. *North American Journal of Psychology, 5,* 31–44.

Wyer, R. S., & Collins, J. E. (1992). A theory of humour elicitation. *Psychological Review, 99,* 663–688.

Zhang, Q. (2005). Immediacy, humor, power distance, and classroom communication apprehension in Chinese college classrooms. *Communication Quarterly, 53,* 109–124.

Ziv, A. (1976). The effects of humor on creativity. *Journal of Educational Psychology, 3,* 318–322.

Ziv, A. (1980). Humor and creativity. *The Creative Child and Adult Quarterly, 5,* 159–170.

Ziv, A. (1983). The influence of humorous atmosphere on divergent thinking. *Contemporary Educational Psychology, 8,* 413–421.

Ziv, A. (1984). *Personality and sense of humor.* New York: Springer Publishing Company.

Ziv, A. (1988). Using humor to develop creative thinking. *Journal of Children in Contemporary Society, 20,* 99–116.

Ziv, A., & Gadish, O. (1989). Humor and marital satisfaction. *Journal of Social Pyschology, 129,* 759–768.

THE HAPPY/PRODUCTIVE
WORKER THESIS REVISITED

Thomas A. Wright and Russell Cropanzano

ABSTRACT

*For decades, since at least the famous Hawthorne studies, the happy/
productive worker thesis has forcefully captured the imagination of
management scholars and human resource professionals alike. According
to this "Holy Grail" of management research, workers who are happy on
the job will have higher job performance, and possibly higher job
retention, than those who are less happy. But what is happiness? Most
typically, happiness has been measured in the management sciences as
job satisfaction. This viewpoint is unnecessarily limiting. Building upon
a little remembered body of research from the 1920s, we suggest a
twofold, expanded view of this thesis. First, we suggest the consideration
of worker happiness as psychological well-being (PWB). Second,
incorporating Fredrickson's (1998, 2001) broaden-and-build model
of positive emotions as the theoretical base, we suggest that the job
satisfaction to job performance and job satisfaction to employee retention relationships may be better explained by controlling for the
moderating effect of PWB. Future research directions for human resource
professionals are introduced.*

Research in Personnel and Human Resources Management, Volume 26, 269–307
ISSN: 0742-7301/doi:10.1016/S0742-7301(07)26006-2
269

INTRODUCTION

Other things being equal, the American worker will be efficient and happy in proportion
as the general life for him, his parents, his wife, and his children is desirable.
(Edward L. Thorndike, *The Psychology of Labor*, 1922, p. 805).

As the quote from Thorndike, one of the applied psychology's preeminent leading early lights clearly suggests, issues surrounding the happy/productive worker thesis have long been questions of extreme interest and importance for organizational scholars and practitioners alike (cf., Hersey, 1932a, 1932b; Houser, 1927; Kornhauser & Sharp, 1932; Pennock, 1930). According to this "Holy Grail" of management research (Landy, 1985), all things being equal, workers who are "happy" with their work should have higher job performance and be less likely to turnover, while those who are less happy are assumed to be less productive and more likely to turnover. However, in sharp contrast to Thorndike's lofty expectations, for the past several decades, efforts to test the happy/productive worker thesis have often met with much skepticism (see Cropanzano & Wright, 2001; Davis-Blake & Pfeffer, 1989; Ledford, 1999; Organ, 1988a, for reviews).

There appear to be two primary explanations for this doubt. The first involves the undeniable emphasis in the social and management sciences on the negative aspects of human endeavor, often to the neglect of the positive aspects of human nature. For example, Luthans (2002b), in a recent computer search of contemporary literature in psychology, found approximately 375,000 articles on "negatives" (e.g., mental illness, burnout, depression, fear, and anger), but only about 1,000 articles on positive-based concepts and capabilities of people (e.g., hope, flourishing, enthusiasm). Amazingly, this constitutes a negative/positive publication ratio of 375/1! Obviously, a ratio this extreme in favor of negative-based articles is not solely the product of some chance event. This ratio is even more intriguing when one considers that over 50 years ago, Abraham Maslow (1954) entitled the last chapter of his seminal book, *Motivation and Personality*, "Toward a positive psychology." In this last chapter, Maslow very carefully proposed a research agenda for future scholars designed to investigate such positive-based concepts as growth, optimism, spontaneity, kindness, and the actualization of potential.

The second reason for the lack of success of many efforts designed to test the happy/productive worker thesis involves the fact that happiness has been typically operationalized as job satisfaction (Wright, 2005). Building upon a highly significant, but little remembered, body of 1920s research on employee well-being (Anderson, 1929; Culpin & Smith, 1927; Fisher & Hanna, 1931;

Hersey, 1929, 1930, 1932a, 1932b), we propose psychological well-being (PWB) as providing a greater measure of support for better understanding and explaining this "Holy Grail" management thesis.

This resurgence of research on PWB, the focus of the present review, confronts contemporary scholars and human resource professionals with an interesting challenge: The possibility that there are at least two happy/ productive worker *theses* – with job satisfaction and PWB each serving as operationalizations of employee happiness. In the pages that follow, we will explore these ideas in greater detail, and propose to the reader the possibility that these two operationalizations of happiness work together to maximize job effectiveness. First, we provide a definition of happiness. Second, the theoretical basis for *why* happiness (however, defined) is related to job performance and job retention decisions is introduced. Third, we provide a brief overview of research purporting job satisfaction–job performance and job satisfaction–job retention/withdrawal relationships. Then, we discuss the literature on PWB. Fifth, and based upon Fredrickson's (1998, 2001) broaden-and-build framework, we provide the theoretical framework for integrating the job satisfaction and PWB approaches to worker "happiness" by proposing that PWB may well act as a moderator to job satisfaction when considering *either* job performance and employee retention. Finally, both theoretical and practical implications of this possibility for human resource professionals are introduced.

Before commencing, however, we want to note that our "accentuate the positive" approach is not intended to "negate the negative." Certainly, we acknowledge the existence of scholarly research demonstrating that negative emotions and mood states can lead to enhanced productivity on some tasks, under certain situations. For example, Schwarz and Clore's (1993) feelings-as-information approach proposes that unpleasant moods can enhance systematic information processing that, in turn, can be relevant to performance in such monitoring-related tasks as computer programming. In addition, Forgas' (1995) affect infusion model (AIM) and Martin, Ward, Achee, and Wyer's (1993) mood-as-input model also propose the basis by which unpleasant moods may enhance performance. As a final example, there is evidence that negative moods can enhance creativity (George & Zhou, 2002). Relatedly, we are not proposing that the benefits of a positive perspective are without limits or constraints. In fact, research indicates that there may well be an upper limit to the possible benefits of adopting a positive approach (Fredrickson & Losada, 2005). That stated, our primary purpose is to call attention to the oft-neglected notion that "happiness" (as opposed to "unhappiness") can be beneficial in the workplace for not only the employee, but the organization as well.

HAPPINESS DEFINED

The mysteries surrounding the age-old pursuit of happiness have long fascinated members of the human race. Aristotle expounded upon this subject at length in the 4th century B.C. in the *Nichomachean Ethics*. For Aristotle, happiness or *eudaimonia*, was not a fleeting feeling or mood, but the product of a life well-lived and constituted the summation of a complete, flourishing existence (McMahon, 2004; Taylor, 1998). Over the centuries, theologians, philosophers, and lay people alike, have wrestled with this seemingly universal, Aristotelian pursuit of happiness. Taking their cue, theologians have labored to extend this present worldly quest to include the transcendental life hereafter (McMahon, 2004).

From a more pragmatic view, Diener (1984) noted that virtually every scientific approach to happiness converges around three distinct, defining phenomena. First, happiness is considered to be a subjective experience (Diener, 1994; Diener, Sandvik, Sedlitz, & Diener, 1993). This means that people are considered to be happy to the extent that they believe/perceive themselves to be happy. As a consequence, happiness involves some type of judgment as to the positives and negatives of one's life (Parducci, 1995; Wright, 2005). Second, happiness includes both the relative presence of positive emotions and the relative absence of negative emotions (Argyle, 1987; Diener & Larsen, 1993; Michalos, 1985; Warr, 1990). Finally, happiness is a global judgment. By this we mean that it refers to one's life as a whole. In addition, happiness exhibits some measure of stability over time (Diener, 1994; Diener, Suh, Lucas, & Smith, 1999; Myers, 1993), though it is not so stable that it can't be influenced by environmental events (Pavot, Diener, Colvin, & Sandvik, 1991; Sandvik, Diener, & Seidlitz, 1993) and responsive to therapeutic interventions (Lykken, 1999; Seligman, 1994, 1995, 2002). Taken together, one can conclude that happiness refers to a subjective and global judgment that one is experiencing a good deal of positive and relatively little negative emotion (Cropanzano & Wright, 2001; Wright, 2005).

However defined, the pursuit of happiness, coupled with an avoidance of unhappiness, has long been considered as fundamental to human motivation (Lawler, 1973; Myers, 1993; Russell, 1930; Wright, 2005). In the work domain, perhaps our opening quote from Thorndike (1922) best expressed this motivational importance. Highly consistent with Thorndike, a belief elemental to many theories of motivation is that humans seek what is pleasurable and avoid what is painful (e.g., Sullivan, 1989). Historically, this viewpoint was well articulated by the principles of utilitarianism and its best-known proponent, John Stuart Mill, who formulated the greatest happiness principle. That is, and simply stated, always act so as to produce the greatest happiness for the greatest number of people (Velasquez, 2002).

Certainly happiness, as defined here, is considered by many to be highly valuable, but oftentimes it is scarce as well (Wright, 2005). Just how scarce is happiness? An increasing number of researchers have suggested many Americans are not truly happy (cf., Myers & Diener, 1997; Wright & Cropanzano, 2000). This concern gains a measure of credibility when one considers that while the adjusted value of after-tax income at least doubled between 1960 and 1990, the percentage of Americans who report themselves as "very happy" remained constant at only 30% (Myers, 1993, pp. 41–42). Certainly this inherent value placed on happiness, coupled with its relative scarcity, highlights the importance of conserving, maintaining, or, even better, enhancing one's happiness (Hobfoll, 1988, 1989, 1998).

WHY HAPPINESS IS RELATED TO JOB PERFORMANCE AND JOB RETENTION

Happiness and Job Performance

If, as we (and many others) have argued, happiness is a valuable but often lacking resource or commodity, one would expect unhappy people to be especially sensitive to negative cues that signal potential threats to their already limited supply of positive feelings (Cropanzano & Wright, 2001; Hobfoll, 1989; Lee & Ashforth, 1996). Alternatively, those individuals blessed with an abundance of positive feelings can afford to be less concerned with these negative threats (Wright, 2005). As a consequence, unhappy people can be presumed to be more sensitive to negative events, while happy people are more sensitive to positive events (Cropanzano & Wright, 2001; Staw, 2004; Staw & Cohen-Charash, 2005). A growing body of empirical research has undertaken to examine this important proposition in greater detail. Experimental research by Seidlitz and Diener (1993) and Seidlitz, Wyer, and Diener (1997) found that those who were low on well-being were more likely to encode an ambiguous event as threatening as compared with their happier counterparts. Likewise, Larsen and his colleagues (Larsen & Ketelaar, 1989, 1991; Rusting & Larsen, 1999; Zelenski & Larsen, 1999) found that unfavorable feedback was more hurtful to those who were predisposed to negative feelings, and less hurtful to those who were predisposed to positive feelings. In addition, Rusting and Larsen (1997) found that favorable feedback yielded larger benefits to those predisposed to positive feelings, while the benefits were less for those predisposed to more negative feelings.

Similar results were obtained in a field experiment conducted by Brief, Butcher, and Roberson (1995). Brief et al. found that not only were negatively toned people less sensitive to a positive event at work when compared with those more positively toned, but also that their mood was more difficult to rise [in a positive direction] after a positive experience. In addition, these effects appear to continue over time due to the manner in which happy and unhappy people recall events (Wright, 2005). Simply stated, happy people tend to remember favorable events, while unhappy people tend to recall unfavorable ones (Seidlitz & Diener, 1993; Seidlitz et al., 1997). As noted by Cropanzano and Wright (2001), this tendency to emphasize the negative aspects of work life is likely to have deleterious consequences for employee job performance. This is especially so in any of the wide array of job settings involving a substantial amount of human interaction (Wright, 2005).

Happy people also tend to be more outgoing and extroverted (Diener, Sandvik, Pavot, & Fujita, 1992; Headley & Wearing, 1992; Myers & Diener, 1995). Conversely, unhappy people tend to be more cautious and protective in social situations, such as demonstrating an inclination toward introversion and/or shyness (Argyle, 1987). At times, unhappy people can even become hostile (for a further discussion, see Cropanzano & Wright, 2001; Wright, 2005). This contention is well supported in a longitudinal study by Bolger and Schilling (1991). These authors found that people who were predisposed to negative emotion were more likely to use argumentative interpersonal tactics, thereby provoking the anger of co-workers. Thus, it is not inconsistent that unhappy people report less co-worker and supervisory support than do their more happy counterparts (Staw, Sutton, & Pelled, 1994). Consistent with these findings, Lyubomirsky and Ross (1997) found that unhappy people were more readily attuned to social comparison information. They found that the moods of unhappy individuals were significantly altered by whether they performed better or worse than a peer. In contrast, happy individuals seemed more likely to heed social comparisons when they could be used in a manner that was self-protective in nature. These findings further suggest the possibility that happy people are more likely to perform better on the wide range of jobs that require significant amounts of social interaction (Cropanzano & Wright, 2001).

This [over]emphasis on negative events, coupled with the apparent minimization of social contact, eventually takes its toll. Relative to their happier coworkers, unhappy people are likely to have lower self-esteem (Diener et al., 1999; Myers, 1993; Wright, 2005). Similarly, unhappy individuals perceive that they have less control over events in their lives and are less optimistic about the future (Cropanzano & Wright, 2001; Dember & Brooks, 1989; Seligman, 1998). This sense of demoralization may make unhappy people less proactive (Argyle, 1987), more prone to stress symptoms (Myers & Diener, 1995), more likely to blame themselves for failures, and to generalize from failure experiences (e.g., Peterson & Seligman, 1984; Staw, 2004; Staw & Cohen-Charash, 2005). Considered together, these characteristics of unhappy people are likely to not only adversely affect one's own performance, but may well negatively impact the performance of their coworkers. As with job performance, employee retention has long been a subject of much interest to organizational scholars.

Happiness and Employee Retention

As reported by Douglas (1918), W.A. Grieve of the Jeffrey Manufacturing Company conducted the first scientific empirical investigation of employee retention in December 1914. In his ground-breaking research, Grieves examined the personnel files of 20 mid-western metal plants and found a rather substantial annual turnover rate of 157%. A number of other early studies reported similarly low rates of retention, with Frost (1920, p. 20) reporting turnover rates ranging from 0 to 8,000%! With these rates of turnover, researchers early on recognized that the benefits of employee retention were quite consequential for both the individual and organization (Snow, 1923).

In an interesting historical twist, unlike the more recent fascination with the role of PWB on job performance (Wright, 2005), early, applied research was very interested in the possible role played by PWB on employee withdrawal decisions. Fisher and Hanna's (1931) influential work on the "dissatisfied worker" is indicative of this early recognition that employee PWB strongly influences the potential for subsequent employee withdrawal. As strong testament to this recognition, Fisher and Hanna devoted an entire chapter of their seminal book to the role of employee emotional adjustment or well-being on employee withdrawal. More specifically, they noted that employee well-being was "responsible to a much greater extent for labor turnover than is commonly realized"(1931, p. 233). Their interest in the role of employee psychological or emotional well-being in employee withdrawal decisions was similarly shared by a number of other early researchers, including Eberle (1919) and Snow (1923). In particular, Eberle (1919) wrote about the relevance of "general" employee satisfactions, while Snow (1923) emphasized the role of "mental alertness" in employee decisions to withdraw.

During the Second World War, when issues surrounding employee retention decisions gained added prominence because of the shortage of civilian workers, Bender (1944) went so far as to propose that 60% of all job dissatisfaction was directly attributable to issues of employee well-being. In other words, those employees experiencing low emotional well-being were seen as more likely to be dissatisfied. Apparently far ahead of their time, a number of early organizational scholars were interested in not only the psychological determinants of employee well-being, but also the possible physiological or genetic determinants of well-being as well (Hersey, 1929; 1932a; 1932b; Mayo, 1933).

Physiological Basis for Happiness

As this review clearly demonstrates, there is an ever-increasing body of evidence that happy individuals significantly differ from those less happy on a wide range of psychological-based dimensions. In addition, and consistent with a number of pioneering applied scholars, there is a burgeoning body of research over the last 10–15 years indicating that these differences between happy and unhappy people may also have a physiological basis (for a further review of this very interesting line of research, see Staw, 2004; Staw & Cohen-Charash, 2005). For instance, Fredrickson and her colleagues (Fredrickson & Levenson, 1998; Fredrickson et al., 2000; Gross, Fredrickson, & Levenson, 1994) found that the feelings of sadness (unhappiness), fear, and anxiety arouse people's autonomic nervous systems, producing pronounced increases in blood pressure, heart rate, and vasoconstriction. Alternatively, more positive, happier feelings may be beneficial in helping to quell potentially harmful surges in cardiovascular activity. Furthermore, positive feelings provide additional benefits. For example, they have been shown to produce faster returns to baseline levels of cardiovascular activation following negative emotional arousal (Fredrickson & Levenson, 1998; Fredrickson, Mancuso, Branigan, & Tugade, 2000; Fredrickson, Tugade, Waugh, & Larkin, 2003), lower levels of cortisol (Steptoe, Wardle, & Marmot, 2005), reductions in subsequent-day physical pain (Gil et al., 2004), and in stroke reduction (Ostir, Markides, Peek, & Goodwin, 2001).

A fascinating growing body of research has helped to further pinpoint the possible physiological basis for happiness (Davidson et al., 2003; Staw, 2004;

Wright & Cropanzano, 2004). Through the use of EEG measures of brain activity, positive affect has been shown to be associated with left prefrontal activity, while negative affect is associated with right prefrontal activation (Davidson & Tomarken, 1989; Staw, 2004). According to Staw (2004), this frontal cerebral asymmetry reflects not only an individual's current emotional state, but also one's predisposition to experience positive vs. negative emotional states. More specifically, according to Tomarken, Davidson, and Henriques (1990), individuals with enhanced left side activation (at rest) typically indicate that they experience more intense emotional reactions to positive stimuli. Conversely, individuals with enhanced right side activation (at rest) typically indicate that they experience a heightened level of emotional response to negative stimuli.

These findings may prove to be beneficial to not only the individual employee, but also the employing organization as well. To take but one example, consider the effect of depression. According to the National Institute of Mental Health, about 19 million American adults, approximately 1 in 10, will suffer some form of depression (Coltrera, 2001). Furthermore, 6 million American children, more than one tenth the school-age population, will be prescribed antidepressants and stimulants (Wright & Wright, 2002). As these children grow up and get jobs, the effects of this increasingly prescription-dependent youth population will undoubtedly be felt in the marketplace. In 1990 dollars, Greenberg, Stiglins, Finkelstein, and Berndt (1993) estimated that depression cost the United States economy about $33.7 billion annually. Likewise, Druss, Rosenheck, and Sledge (2000) found that depression cost organizations more than hypertension, and about as much as heart disease, diabetes, and back problems. Similar results regarding cost were reported by Conti and Burton (1994).

The research examined to date provides a solid framework for the belief that there is both a psychological and physiological basis for individual happiness. Using research on the happy/productive worker thesis as our guide, we now examine the two prevailing approaches to operationalizing happiness in organizational research: job satisfaction and PWB. To that end, a brief historical overview of research purporting job satisfaction–job performance and job satisfaction–employee retention relationships is introduced next.

HAPPINESS AS JOB SATISFACTION

Within the organization sciences, job satisfaction has been, by far, the most common operationalization of workplace "happiness" (Wright, 2005).

While job satisfaction has been operationalized in a number of ways, it is usually considered to be an attitude (Weiss & Cropanzano, 1996). According to Brief (1998, p. 86), job satisfaction can be best defined as "an internal state that is expressed by affectively and/or cognitively evaluating an experienced job with some degree of favor or disfavor." Paradoxically, the most widely used job satisfaction measures (i.e., the Minnesota Satisfaction Questionnaire, the Job Description Index, etc.) contain minimal, if any, affectively toned scale items (Brief & Roberson, 1989). Irrespective of how job satisfaction has been traditionally defined, over the years, a number of applied scholars have considered the role of employee satisfaction as a correlate of any number of workplace outcome variables (e.g., Locke, 1969; Locke, 1976; Spector, 1997; Brief, 1998; Weiss, 2002). In this vein, Edward L. Thorndike (1922, p. 801) went so far as to propose a global measure of satisfaction or what he termed "satisfyingness" as the primary, fundamental aspect of human nature.

Interestingly, job satisfaction did not appear to be the job attitude of choice in the early days of applied psychology and management research (Kornhauser, 1933; Wright, 2005, for an additional review of early job attitude research, see Weiss & Brief, 2001 and Wright, 2006). For instance, even at a basic definitional level, a number of prominent researchers appeared to confuse and confound the terms "employee morale" and "job satisfaction" (Brayfield & Crockett, 1951; Organ & Near, 1985; Roethlisberger, 1941). In fact, much to their surprise, Organ and Near (1985) noted that the term "job satisfaction" was completely absent from the index of Roethlisberger and Dickson's (1939), *Management and the Worker*. Instead of job satisfaction, this seminal work on the Hawthorne experiments used such attitudinal terms as "sentiments" and "tone." These are important distinctions because, as aptly noted by Organ and Near (1985, p. 242), terms like sentiments (and tone) indicated much more than just satisfaction with one's job, but "referred to emotions, to feelings, to affect, to hedonic states." However, a cursory examination of the classic writings in management and industrial psychology clearly demonstrates how surprisingly infrequently, up to about 1950, the term "job satisfaction" appeared in the literature (Organ & Near, 1985; Wright, 2006).

As a case in point, consider research published in the *Journal of Applied Psychology* (JAP). JAP commenced publication in 1917, during World War I. Over the first quarter century of publication, from 1917 to 1941 to be exact, *only* two articles were published in JAP with the words "job/work satisfaction" in the title. In fact, surprisingly, the first JAP article on job satisfaction was not published until 1937 by the pioneering researcher,

Robert Hoppock. In this landmark study, Hoppock reported job satisfaction levels for a sample of APA vocational and industrial psychologists. According to Hoppock (1937, p. 300), as regards to their level of job satisfaction, psychologists appeared "neither better or worse than the average man of comparable position in other fields of work." The second article, by Donald E. Super, examined the relationship between employee occupational level and job satisfaction (Super, 1939). It would be almost another 10 years, or more precisely, 1948, before job satisfaction focused articles appeared again in JAP (Wright, 2006). As two examples, Kerr (1948) reported on the validity and reliability of the *Job Satisfaction Tear Ballot* and Nahm (1949) undertook a study on nursing satisfaction. As we will discuss next, this relative neglect of job satisfaction early on drastically changed with the increased awareness of a possible job satisfaction with job performance association.

Job Satisfaction and Job Performance

Irrespective of this lack of widespread interest early on in JAP and such other prominent outlets for organizational research as the *Personnel Journal*, starting in the 1950s and beyond, research focusing on job satisfaction grew by leaps and bounds. In fact, by the early 1950s, a growing number of researchers were publishing their job satisfaction research in JAP, including Kates (1950), Brayfield and Rothe (1951), and Carey, Berg, and Van Dusen (1951). So much so in fact, that by the early 1990s, Cranny, Smith, and Stone (1992) could reliably report that more than 5,000 published articles and dissertations had examined job satisfaction. Coupled with this growing general interest in job satisfaction as a variable of interest, was a similar fascination with the possible role of job satisfaction in the prediction of job performance (Organ, 1988a). As one might expect, this fascination was based more on a practical, than a theoretical basis (e.g., Fisher, 2000; Staw, 1986). In fact, according to one of the preeminent early researchers in job satisfaction, Patricia Cain Smith, much of the early interest in job satisfaction evolved from work on the supposed relationship between employee monotony and boredom with job performance (Cain, 1942; Smith, 1953, 1992). That is, and consistent with the practical basis for the Hawthorne experiments (Mayo, 1933; Roethlisberger & Dickson, 1939), if employee satisfaction is related to employee boredom, and employee boredom is related to performance, perhaps employee job satisfaction is related to job performance (Wright, 2005). Obviously, this strong interest in a job satisfaction/performance relationship has continued to the present day (Judge, Thoresen, Bono, & Patton, 1998, 2001).

Several reviews have provided excellent summaries of the job satisfaction/ job performance relation. In probably the earliest review regarding a possible link between work-related attitudes and job performance, Houser (1927, p. 27) concluded "... very high employee morale was not accompanied by a correspondingly high quality of employee performance." Likewise, Kornhauser and Sharp (1932, p. 402) similarly concluded in their seminal article that "... efficiency ratings of employees showed no relationship to their attitudes." Roughly 20 years later, in reviewing the growing body of literature to date, Brayfield and Crockett (1955, p. 421) concluded that "satisfaction ... need not imply strong motivation to outstanding performance." Similar conclusions were determined in a later review by Vroom (1964), who reported that the median association between these two variables was a rather modest + .14. Roughly 20 years after Vroom, a highly influential meta-analytic review by Iaffaldano and Muchinsky (1985) obtained a mean corrected correlation of + .17. Together, these reviews generated concern regarding the robustness of the relation between job satisfaction and performance (e.g., Cherrington, Reitz, & Scott, 1971; Fisher, 1980; Locke, 1976; Podsakoff & Williams, 1986; Staw, 1986). More recently, other studies have called these modest conclusions into question.

According to Judge and his colleagues (1998, 2001), while Iaffaldano and Muchinsky's (1985) .17 statistic is widely cited, it is often misunderstood. Specifically, the reported .17 is not the average association of overall job satisfaction to performance. Rather, this coefficient represents the average of the correlations between the facet measures of job satisfaction (e.g., pay, co-worker, promotion, supervision, work itself, etc.) and job performance. When one confines the analysis to overall satisfaction, the corrected correlation is actually a respectable .29 (Judge et al., 2001). Likewise, Petty, McGee, and Cavender (1984) place the job satisfaction to job performance relation at + .31 for professional workers. Certainly correlations in the .30 range are large enough to have financial "competitive advantage" or significant *practical* consequences for work organizations (cf., Cascio, 1991; Judge, Hanisch, & Drankoski, 1995; Wright, 2005). Unfortunately, Organ (1988b, Chapter 4) cautioned that Petty et al.'s analysis might have included performance criteria that were contaminated by indexes of citizenship behavior. In an attempt to address these inconsistencies, the most comprehensive (and promising for job satisfaction proponents) qualitative and quantitative analysis of the relation to date was undertaken by Judge et al. (1998, 2001).

In their meta-analysis, Judge and his colleagues reported the job satisfaction–job performance association to be roughly + .30, though they observed some important moderators. For example, they determined that some job satisfaction measures were more closely correlated to performance than others, ranging from an aggregated correlation of + .06 for research measuring job satisfaction with the GM Faces Scale to an aggregated correlation of + .51 for research using the Hoppock Job Satisfaction Blank to measure job satisfaction. Judge et al. also reported considerable differences across occupations, with the job satisfaction/job performance correlation being more robust in high-complexity jobs. In conclusion, their meta-analytic results found that measures of overall global job satisfaction exhibit higher correlations than facet measures of job satisfaction.

The positive associations obtained by Judge et al. (2001) and Petty et al. (1984) do not address the issue of causality, however. As noted by Wright (2005), there are three primary causal relations between job satisfaction and job performance: (a) job satisfaction may cause job performance, (b) job performance may cause job satisfaction, and (c) both job performance and job satisfaction may be caused by a variety of third variables (Petty et al., 1984; Wright & Cropanzano, 2000). During the 1960s and 1970s, several studies investigated these various causal paths, and at least minimal evidence was found for each causal path (for reviews, see Lawler & Porter, 1967; Nord, 1976; Schwab & Cummings, 1970). Unfortunately, as Judge et al. (1998, 2001) observed, the general doubt regarding the job satisfaction/job performance relation led to a decline in research. As a result, the possibility of a causal connection between these two variables, if any, remains a highly worthwhile topic for future research efforts. We next examine research investigating the job satisfaction to retention relationship.

Job Satisfaction and Employee Retention

The topic of employee retention continues to attract much attention (Harrison, Virick, & Williams, 1996; Sheridan, 1992; Steel, 2002). Over the years, one approach, strongly influenced by March and Simon's (1958) seminal work on the perceived ease and desirability of movement, focuses on the cognitive and affective bases to employee withdrawal (Harrison et al., 1996; Hom, Caranikas-Walker, Prussia, & Griffeth, 1992). In particular, cognitive-based research models typically emphasize such ease of move-ment criteria as perceived alternatives and job search behavior, while affective-based models have primarily focused on the perceived desirability of movement as evidenced by measures of employee job satisfaction (Mobley, 1982).

Prevailing theory and research have long maintained the importance of job satisfaction to the retention process (e.g., Frost, 1920; Lee, Mitchell, Sablynski, Burton, & Holton, 2004; Mobley, 1982). Unfortunately, and similar to the rather modest findings to date regarding job satisfaction and performance, Hom and Griffeth (1995) and Griffeth, Hom, and Gaertner (2000) reported meta-analytic findings demonstrating that job satisfaction typically accounts for less than 5% of employee withdrawal variance. While job satisfaction certainly remains a worthwhile variable for researchers to consider as regards both job performance and employee retention, we suggest that the consideration of job [dis]satisfaction by itself does not tell the complete story for *why* employees perform poorly/well and remain/ withdraw from their job (e.g., Hom & Griffeth, 1991; Hom et al., 1992; Tett & Meyer, 1993; Wright & Staw, 1999). Recently, a number of scholars have suggested that the modest findings to date regarding the job satisfaction–job performance (Judge et al., 2001; Wright & Cropanzano, 2004) and job satisfaction–employee retention relationships (Judge, 1993) may be better understood through examination of possible third-party or moderator variables.

Over 10 years ago, Judge (1993) noted the surprising lack of research investigating potential moderators of the job satisfaction to employee retention relationship. In like fashion, Judge and his colleagues (2001) suggested a number of potential moderators of the job satisfaction–job performance relationship. Building upon Judge et al. (2001) and Fredrickson (1998, 2001), Wright and Cropanzano (2004) and Wright and Bonett (2005, 2007) proposed employee PWB as an especially viable moderator of both the job satisfaction with performance and employee retention relationships. This possibility has lead to a renewed optimism among scholars about the prospects of finding practically meaningful relations between job satisfaction and job performance and between job satisfaction and employee retention. To that end, we next examine happiness considered as PWB.

HAPPINESS AS PSYCHOLOGICAL WELL-BEING

PWB has typically been conceptualized in terms of the overall effectiveness of an individual's psychological functioning (Gechman & Wiener, 1975; Jamal & Mitchell, 1980; Martin, 1984; Sekaran, 1985; Wright & Cropanzano, 2000; Wright, 2005). Unlike job satisfaction, which has significant cognitive *and* affective components, PWB is primarily an affective or emotional experience. In particular, using the circumplex model of emotion as the theoretical framework, PWB measures the hedonic or pleasantness dimension of individual feelings (J.A. Russell, 1980). PWB is typically operationalized as capturing both positive and negative emotional states on a single axis (Bradburn & Caplovitz, 1965; Cropanzano, Weiss, Hale, & Reb, 2003; Wright & Staw, 1999). In other words, the high pole is anchored by such hedonic or pleasantness-based descriptors as "joyous" (Wright, 2005). Alternatively, the low pole is anchored by such descriptors as "sad" and "annoyed." Thus, to be high on well-being is to be simultaneously low on negative emotion and high on positive emotion. In fact, a number of prominent scholars have more or less equated well-being with happiness (e.g., Diener, 1984; Myers, 1993; Seligman, 2002). Based upon the circumplex model, PWB can be contrasted with other conceptualizations measuring the level of activation or "affect intensity" of emotional experience (Brief & Weiss, 2002; Larsen & Diener, 1992; Watson, 1988; for a further review of the circumplex model, see Wright, 2005).

The role of the hedonic or pleasantness dimension of well-being (i.e., happiness vs. sadness or depression) in the determination of various individual outcomes has long been recognized in the applied sciences (Wright, 2005). Over a period of several years, starting in the mid 1920s, Rexford B. Hersey, at the Wharton School of Finance and Commerce, the University of Pennsylvania (1929, 1930, 1932a, 1932b) undertook a very thorough investigation of the relationship between worker well-being and productivity. Conducting longitudinal field research, Hersey (1929, p. 459) often spent the entire workday, and much time off the job as well, "in almost constant contact with the workers studied." As a result, Hersey was able to meticulously gather a wide range of worker data on blood pressure, colloid content of blood, weight, hours of sleep, illness, feelings of fatigue, tardiness, level of cooperativeness, verbal outbursts, well-being and happiness, and productivity and efficiency in an attempt "to obtain a complete picture of their whole life" (Hersey, 1929, p. 459). Focusing on positive well-being, Hersey (1932b, p. 289) noted in his seminal work, *Workers' Emotions in Shop and Home*, that "it would seem impossible to escape the conclusion that in the long run at least, men are more productive in a positive emotional state than in a negative [one]."

Alternatively, a number of Hersey's contemporaries focused on the negative or unpleasantness end of the well-being continuum (Elkind, 1931; Fisher & Hanna, 1931; McMurry, 1932). Working with employees of the R.H. Macy Company in New York, Anderson (1929) concluded that more than 20% of the work population were "problem" employees, suffering from various forms of psychological distress. In like manner, investigating British Post Office employees, Culpin and Smith (1927) surmised that upwards of 30% suffered from some form of manifested psychological distress. Unfortunately, interest on worker well-being issues, in both the United States and Great Britain, literally ground to a halt with the advent of the Great Depression (Uhrbrock, 1934).

Interestingly, roughly 10 years later, or about the time of the Second World War, hedonic well-being resurfaced as one aspect of employee morale (Organ & Near, 1985). As a case in point, in a review of the term *morale*, Child (1941, p. 393) noted three different conceptualizations of the construct. One conceptualization is of particular relevance here, as it refers "to a condition of physical and emotional well-being in the individual that makes it possible for him to work and live hopefully and effectively ...."[1] However, as noted by Organ and Near (1985), as the 1940s evolved, morale fell more and more into disfavor, with job satisfaction and job attitudes becoming virtually synonymous with each other (Wright, 2006). One distinction between PWB and job satisfaction is of particular relevance to the current discussion. Unlike job satisfaction, which is completely centered about the work context, PWB is a broader construct. Most typically, PWB is considered as a primarily affective-based "context-free" or global construct. Unlike various measures of job satisfaction, PWB is not tied to any particular situation (Kornhauser, 1965; Wright & Cropanzano, 2000).

Like our clinical psychology and public health counterparts, organizational theorists have also long recognized the extensive costs, in both human and financial terms, attributable to dysfunctional employee PWB (Anderson, 1929; Culpin & Smith, 1927; Fisher & Hanna, 1931; Hersey, 1932b). For instance, depression, loss of self-esteem, hypertension, alcoholism, and drug consumption, have all been shown to be related to work-related dysfunctional PWB (Ivancevich & Matteson, 1980). Because these variables have, in turn, been related to declines in work outcomes (George, 1992; Quick, Quick, Nelson, & Hurrell, 1997; Wright, 2005), it is possible that PWB, job performance, and employee retention are related (Daniels & Harris, 2000; Wright & Bonett, 1992; Wright, Bonett, & Sweeney, 1993; Wright & Cropanzano, 2000). In the next section, we will review direct evidence for this possibility.

A growing body of empirical research has found significant associations between various measures of well-being and measures of job-related performance. In an quasi-experimental study, Staw and Barsade (1993) determined that students who were high on well-being were superior decision-makers, showed better interpersonal behaviors, and received higher overall performance ratings. Staw and Barsade's study is important for two reasons. First, it used objective, quantifiable indices of performance (e.g., an "in-basket" measure). This argues against the possibility that correlations between well-being and job performance are simply misperceptions (Cropanzano & Wright, 2001; Robbins & DeNisi, 1994). Second, Staw and Barsade's quasi-experimental data suggest the possibility of a causal relation, in particular, that performance increases when well-being is high.

Potential external validity concerns were addressed in a later field study by Staw et al. (1994). In their longitudinal study, Staw and his colleagues assessed well-being by forming an ad hoc scale out of items indicating the presence of negative emotion (e.g., depression) and the absence of positive emotion. Eighteen months later they measured various criterion variables. In particular, when compared with those who were low in well-being, workers high in well-being had superior performance evaluations and higher pay. The key finding of their research was that well-being predicted both a subjective and an objective indicator of performance.

The body of work by Staw and his colleagues is suggestive that well-being causes increases in job performance. Additional support for this directional relationship is found in a two-year longitudinal study conducted by Wright et al. (1993). Using the 8-item Index of PWB developed by Berkman (1971a, 1971b), Wright and his colleagues found that average well-being (Time 1 and Time 2 together) was positively related to supervisory performance ratings at Time 3. A five-year longitudinal study by Cropanzano and Wright (1999) found similar results. Using the same Index of PWB, Cropanzano and Wright determined that average well-being measured six months apart (Time 1 and Time 2) was positively related to job performance measures at Time 3 (Year 4). The possibility of a causal path from well-being to performance was addressed in research by Wright and Staw (1999). Wright and Staw's two longitudinal studies – incorporating multiple measures of both performance and well-being – demonstrated that Berkman's measure of PWB significantly predicted supervisory performance ratings beyond the variance accounted for by prior supervisory performance ratings. In the aggregate, these findings strongly support the possibility that well-being is a cause of job performance (Wright, 2005).

It is also beneficial to consider the effects of other potential confounding variables. This was undertaken in a longitudinal study conducted by Wright and Bonett (1997). In this study, the authors determined that well-being was a positive predictor of job performance. Furthermore, the well-being–job performance relation remained significant even after controlling for the simultaneous effect of emotional exhaustion. Other possible confounding third variables are job satisfaction, negative affectivity (NA), and positive affectivity (PA). Given the demonstrated intercorrelations among these variables (e.g., Diener et al., 1999; Judge & Locke, 1993; Wright, Cropanzano, Denney, & Moline, 2002a), it could be that PWB and job performance are only associated due to the spurious relations with these other variables. On the basis of the limited information to date, this does not seem to be the case. In a cross-sectional study, Wright, Larwood, and Denney (2002b) found that PWB was positively related to job performance over and above the effects of emotional exhaustion, NA, and PA. These findings were replicated and extended in a longitudinal follow-up. Wright et al. (2002a) found that PWB and job performance (at Time 2) were positively related even when the effects of job satisfaction, NA, PA, and prior performance (at Time 1) were all taken into account. Finally, Wright and Staw (1999, Study 2) found that well-being remained significantly related to performance even when controlling for employee age, gender, tenure, educational level, and prior performance.

The fact that several studies (e.g., Wright et al., 2002a; Wright & Staw, 1999) were able to control for prior performance in the prediction of subsequent performance is important and warrants further attention. After all, while interesting, one could suggest that the findings reported between PWB and performance were merely a function of the type of performance instrument used (Ledford, 1999). Customarily, this line of research has used supervisory ratings of employee performance. In reviewing these results, one could legitimately propose that these findings are due to halo effects in the performance variable. That is, employees who are more psychologically well may be more fun to be around and more likeable (Wright & Cropanzano, 1998). This is a highly relevant suggestion because people (i.e., supervisors) tend to be more tolerant of those they favor or like. In this case, if true, supervisors may provide more positive evaluations for those more psychologically well (Robbins & DeNisi, 1994). In other words, rather than being directly related to changes in performance, PWB may be nothing more than a systematic source of halo in performance evaluations (Wright, 2005).

Though one cannot totally rule out the halo alternative, we offer four basic arguments to the halo option. First, recall that a number of the studies had longitudinal designs. This is significant because the longitudinal design has afforded opportunities to measure the influence of PWB on incremental changes in rated performance over time (Wright et al., 2002a; Wright & Staw, 1999). Thus, a major strength of the multiple measures of performance over time design is the ability to capture any halo contained in the prior measures of performance (Wright & Staw, 1999). Second, if halo were driving the results, Staw and Barsade (1993), in their laboratory study, would not have found significant relations between their measure of well-being and objective measures of performance. Next, PWB has been related to job performance in a number of studies which have also examined a number of possible third variable explanations, including job satisfaction, PA, NA, and emotional exhaustion. If rating bias was accounting for the obtained relation between PWB and performance, then one must also reasonably expect significant relations between these other variables and performance. As noted in previous reviews, while PWB is predictive of job performance, these other variables have not typically been related to performance (Wright, Cropanzano, & Meyer, 2004; Wright & Staw, 1999). Fourth, and finally, let's consider the worse case scenario that halo does play a role in the relation between PWB and supervisory ratings of performance. Given that many organizations currently emphasize these non-task-specific performance dimensions in their appraisal process (Wright & Cropanzano, 1998), the relation is predictive of "success" from the employees' point of view (Staw et al., 1994; Wright & Staw, 1999; Wright, 2005). In other words, in a number of the samples reported in this review, the employee received raises and promotions based upon these supervisory performance measures. We now turn our attention to the PWB with employee retention/withdrawal relationship.

Wright and Bonett (1992) found a pattern of results consistent with a proposed relationship between PWB and employee retention/withdrawal decisions. Using a longitudinal design, Wright and Bonett found that employees low in both job satisfaction and PWB were much less likely to stay on the job. In addition, those lowest in job satisfaction and PWB were most likely to, not only change their current job, but also their occupation as well. Unfortunately, Wright and Bonett failed to consider the possibility that PWB may moderate the job satisfaction–employee retention relationship. Using Weitz's (1952) gripe index, Judge (1993) did test whether an employee's [dis]satisfaction level would be more meaningful when considered within the backdrop of their predisposition to be satisfied in general or psychologically well. According to Judge, employees dissatisfied with their jobs, but high on general life satisfaction, would be most likely to leave their current job. Judge found partial support for his contentions, with those employees exhibiting positive life satisfaction or well-being, but dissatisfied with their job, demonstrating the highest withdrawal, or lowest retention, rates. Unfortunately, outside of the work of Judge (1993) and Wright and Bonett (1992), empirical work is lacking which investigates the possible moderating role of employee well-being on the job satisfaction–employee retention relationship.

Considered together, the available data point to a common conclusion: When happiness is operationalized as well-being, it is positively related to various measures of job performance and employee retention. For example, regarding job performance, field research has consistently found significant bivariate correlations between PWB and job performance ratings in the .30–.50 range, surpassing the typical results obtained for NA, PA, emotional exhaustion, and even job satisfaction (Wright, 2005). While less prevalent, research investigating the PWB and employee retention relationship is equally promising. These significant findings have both theoretical and practical implications. As a practical case in point, taking a bivariate correlation of .30 between PWB and job performance/employee retention indicates that almost 10% of the variance in job performance/employee retention is associated with differences in PWB. Conversely, a correlation of .50 indicates that a substantial 25% of the variance in job performance/ employee retention is associated with differences in PWB. In addition, regarding job performance, this seems to be the case regardless of whether the criterion variables are objective indices or subjective ratings (Staw & Barsade, 1993; Staw et al., 1994).

The effect also holds in quasi-experimental, cross-sectional, and long-itudinal studies, even after controlling for the effects of possible confounding variables (e.g., Wright et al., 2002a, 2002b; Wright & Staw, 1999). Despite its value, this literature is in need of extension as, when all is said and done, the work to date has emphasized only the main effect relations among well-being, performance, and retention. In the next section, using theory (cf., Fredrickson, 1998, 2001) emanating from the various "positive" move-ments: positive psychology, positive organizational behavior (POB), and positive organizational scholarship (POS) (Cameron, Dutton, & Quinn, 2003; Diener, 2000; Luthans, 2002a, 2002b, 2003; Seligman & Csikszentmihalyi, 2000), we propose an innovative integration of the most promising (PWB) and widely used (job satisfaction) approaches to workplace happiness.

FREDRICKSON'S (2001, 2003) BROADEN-AND-BUILD THEORY

As we have documented earlier, PWB, and to a lesser degree, job satisfaction, have merit as operationalizations of worker happiness. Despite significant doubt over the years, both models have recently received some measure of research support (Cropanzano & Wright, 2001; Judge et al., 1998, 2001). Unfortunately, these two approaches to operationalizing worker happiness have seldom been considered concomitantly. Moreover, those infrequent investigations that simultaneously examine job satisfaction and PWB usually only consider main effects. As one example, consider the two field studies reported by Wright and Cropanzano (2000). While Wright and Cropanzano explored the effects of PWB beyond those of job satisfaction, they did not consider the interaction between the two variables. While main effect studies have their place, ignoring the moderating effect of PWB is limiting, since there are good conceptual reasons to think that an interaction might take place.

Drawing on the stimulus of the "positive psychology" movement (Diener, 2000; Seligman & Csikszentmihalyi, 2000), a growing number of organizational researchers have called for a more positive-based, proactive approach to organizational research. This approach has been termed POB (Luthans, 2002a, 2002b) and POS (Cameron et al., 2003; Pratt & Ashforth, 2003; Wrzesniewski, 2003). Luthans (2003, p. 179) defined POB as "the study and application of positively-oriented human resource strengths and psychological capacities that can be measured, developed, and effectively managed for performance improvement in today's workplace." In a like manner, Cameron et al. (2003, p. 4) defined POS as being "... concerned primarily with the study of especially positive outcomes, processes, and attributes of organizations and their members. POS does not represent a single theory, but it focuses on dynamics that are typically described by words such as *excellence, thriving, flourishing, abundance, resilience,* or *virtuousness.*" In particular, we suggest Fredrickson's (1998, 2001, 2003) broaden-and-build model of positive emotions as one approach especially well-suited to help better understand the possible moderating role of PWB in the job satisfaction/job performance/employee retention relations.

Before considering Fredrickson's model, it is useful to compare this growing work on positive emotions, typified by Fredrickson and others, with the more customary emphasis of prior work on negative emotions. Historically, the prevailing models of emotion attempted to illustrate the general form and function of emotions (Fredrickson, 2002). With that objective in mind, most models were devised around prototypic and negative emotions like anger and fear (Fredrickson, 2003). The underlying theme of these traditional approaches (cf., Frijda, 1986; Lazarus, 1991; Levenson, 1994) was that emotions, by definition, are associated with specific action tendencies. According to Fredrickson (2003, p. 166), a specific action tendency is best described "as the outcomes of a psychological process that narrows a person's momentary thought–action repertoire by calling to mind an urge to act in a particular way (e.g., escape, attack, expel)." In other words, a specific action tendency is what helps to get our attention (Wright & Cropanzano, 2004). For example, the negative emotion, fear, is associated with the urge to escape. The negative emotion, anger, is associated with the urge to attack, and so on (Fredrickson, 2003).

According to Fredrickson (2003, p. 165), the key to these traditional, negative-based, models "… is that specific action tendencies are what make emotions evolutionarily adaptive: these are among the actions that worked best in getting our ancestors out of life-or-death situations." In other words, negative emotions narrowed behavioral urges toward specific actions for our human ancestors (e.g., fight, flight) that literally were life saving in nature (Fredrickson & Losada, 2005). Alternatively, the specific action tendencies for positive-based emotions are, by contrast, vague and under-specified (Fredrickson & Levenson, 1998; Fredrickson, 2003). As one example, the positive feelings associated with contentment have been linked with inactivity (Frijda, 1986). Recognizing this incompatibility of positive emotions with the basic premise of traditional models, Fredrickson developed her broaden-and-build model to help better capture the unique attributes and potential contributions of positive emotion.

According to Fredrickson's (2001, 2003) broaden-and-build theory, a number of positive feeling states, traits or emotions, including the experience of PWB, all share the capacity to "broaden" an individual's momentary thought–action repertories through expanding the obtainable array of potential thoughts and actions that come to mind (Fredrickson & Branigan, 2001). In particular, using laboratory experiments, Fredrickson and her colleagues (Fredrickson & Branigan, 2005; Fredrickson & Losada, 2005) demonstrated that relative to neutral states, positive emotions broaden or expand upon people's momentary thought–action repertories, while negative emotions narrow these same mechanisms. For example, the positive emotion, interest, fosters the desire to explore, assimilate new experiences, encounter new information, and grow. Similarly, psychologically well individuals tend to be more outgoing and extroverted, remember favorable events better, and are less likely to encode an ambiguous event as threatening as compared with their less psychologically well counterparts (Wright, 2005).

In addition, these benefits of broadened thought–action repertories merge over time. According to Fredrickson and Losada (2005, p. 679), these "broadened mindsets carry indirect and long-term adaptive value because broadenings …" assist in "building" the individual's enduring personal resources, ranging from physical, psychological, intellectual, and social in nature (Wright, 2003, 2005). This capacity to experience the positive is proposed to be crucial to one's capacity to thrive, mentally flourish, and psychologically grow (Fredrickson, 2001, 2003). This sense of flourishing appears to make psychologically well or happy people more proactive (cf. Argyle, 1987) and less prone to stress symptoms (Myers & Diener, 1995).

In the organizational sciences, the broaden-and-build model may be especially beneficial in providing a better understanding of both the job satisfaction–job performance and job satisfaction–employee retention/ withdrawal relationships. According to the broaden-and-build framework, the positive evaluative sentiments associated with high levels of job-related satisfaction are further broadened and built upon when the employee is also psychologically well in general (both on *and* off the job). While this possibility of a moderating effect of various positive emotions, such as PWB, on the job satisfaction to job performance/employee retention relations has long been recognized in organizational research (e.g., Judge, 1993; Kornhauser & Sharp, 1932; Locke, 1976; Pennock, 1930), the actual theoretical basis for this type of interaction was always rather tentative and ambiguous (cf., Gerhart, 1987; Judge, 1993; Staw, 2004; Wright, 2005).

The broaden-and-build model provides the necessary theoretical frame-work for positing that PWB moderates both the job satisfaction–performance and job satisfaction–employee retention/withdrawal relationships. First, regarding the job satisfaction–job performance relationship, the broaden-and-build dimension of Fredrickson's (2001, 2003) theory suggests that the adaptive and moderating nature of PWB is potentially more robust for those employees who are *both* psychologically well *and* satisfied with their job, than for those less psychologically well and/or satisfied with their job. In other words, through the impetus provided by high levels of PWB (a positive circumstance), employees who are also currently satisfied with their job (another positive circumstance) are proposed to be more easily able to "broaden-and-build" themselves over time based upon their ample supply of these positive-based feelings. As a result, and as reviewed earlier, these individuals are likely to become even more creative, resilient, socially connected, and physically and mentally healthy (Fredrickson, 2001; Wright, 2003, 2005).

Building upon prior research establishing main effect associations among job satisfaction, PWB, and job performance (Wright & Cropanzano, 2000), the broaden-and-build model suggests that satisfied and psychologically well employees are more likely than those less satisfied and psychologically well to have the necessary resources to foster and facilitate increased levels of job performance. In particular, research has clearly demonstrated that positive feelings can help enhance one's ability to be a better problem solver, decision maker, and evaluator/processor of events (e.g., Erez & Isen, 2002; Isen, 2003). In turn, research has consistently shown that these skills and abilities are related to job performance (Wright, 2005). As an added bonus, these effects would appear to persist over time due, in part, to the differential manner in which happy and unhappy people recall events. In fact, as a general consequence, a continued focus on positive feelings expands (broadens) and builds on these positive urges, creating a potentially "upwards spiral" effect, which is proposed to further enhance individual character development (Fredrickson & Joiner, 2002; Hobfoll, 1998; Wright, 2005). In sum, this capacity to constructively experience positive feelings has been proposed to be a fundamental human strength (Fredrickson, 2001; Wright, 2005).

In a like fashion, incorporating the broaden-and-build framework, employee retention can be considered as a positive circumstance, in the sense that the decision to remain on a job suggests a positive response by the employee toward the employer. In other words, the employee considers their current job situation as a good option, possibly even their best option and, as a result, they make the decision to remain on the job. Assuredly, this is not to contradict the well-known fact that turnover can be functional for an organization (Abelson, 1987; Campion, 1991), as on those occasions when low performers depart (McEvoy & Cascio, 1987; Trevor, Gerhart, & Boudreau, 1997). It does, however, assume that voluntarily choosing to remain on a job signifies some measure of satisfaction, while choosing to leave signifies a measure of dissatisfaction.

Recent research provides empirical support that PWB does moderate the relationships between both job satisfaction and job performance *and* between job satisfaction and employee retention. Regarding the job satisfaction–job performance relationship, and highly consistent with Fredrickson's model, Wright and Cropanzano (2004) reported that job performance was highest when employees reported high scores on *both* PWB and job satisfaction. Interestingly, job satisfaction did predict performance, but only if the employee also had a high level of PWB. In other words, job satisfaction was not a good predictor of job performance among employees with low levels of PWB. In fact, this moderating effect of PWB may account for some of the inconsistent findings of previous research examining the job satisfaction–job performance relationship.

Once again incorporating Fredrickson's (1998, 2001) broaden-and-build framework, Wright and Bonett (2005, 2007) found that PWB and job satisfaction interacted to predict employee retention. As anticipated, the relation between job satisfaction and retention was typically found to be stronger for those employees with high levels of PWB, than for those employees with low levels of PWB. These findings suggest that the more positive the PWB of the employee, the higher the probability that this employee will remain on the job, irrespective of the level of job satisfaction. Considered together, this research supports the supposition that high or enhanced employee PWB may be a key player in better understanding such important organizational outcome variables as job performance and employee retention. In our concluding section, we pose the following pivotal research question for future research: What are organizations and human resource professionals to do with these findings?

IMPLICATIONS FOR FUTURE RESEARCH

A number of human resource-based intervention strategies have been offered to better select, place, and train employees based upon their PWB. Typically, work interventions can take three general forms: composition, training, and situational engineering (Ilgen, 1999; Wright & Cropanzano, 2004; Wright, 2005). Composition focuses on selecting and placing individuals into appropriate positions, while training emphasizes assisting employees so that they better "fit" their jobs. Finally, situational engineering focuses on changing the work environment to make it more closely fit the needs and abilities of one's employees.

Composition

It would appear that the PWB of job applicants is reasonably consistent with their later PWB, as research has consistently established the stability of PWB (in the .60–.70 range) over time (Wright & Staw, 1999). In fact, Cropanzano and Wright (1999) established significant test–retest correlations of up to five years in duration. These findings support the premise that employees who report being psychologically well at one point in time are likely to be psychologically well at another point in time. Considered in conjunction with the present findings demonstrating a significant PWB to performance relationship, employee PWB may provide potentially useful insights for human resource personnel interested in maximizing employee performance through the selection of psychologically well job applicants. However, as a word of caution, the use of PWB as a selection criterion raises some potentially serious ethical considerations. For instance, the failure to select potential job applicants based on their level of PWB could possibly depress these individuals further, which in turn, could make these job applicants even more unemployable in the future (Wright, 2005). In turn, this can engender significant human and societal costs, for both the individual and organization involved. Given these potentially serious ethical and human/societal cost considerations, we note that it is very important for business executives and human resource personnel to carefully consider these ethical issues if choosing to use PWB in the selection process.

Coupled with these ethical considerations is a more practically based issue to consider before deciding to incorporate PWB in one's staffing system. If faking one's PWB can be useful in obtaining a desired job position or promotional opportunity, then it is likely that some job candidates might be motivated to fake their PWB responses (Cropanzano & Wright, 1999; Rosse, Stecher, Miller, & Levin, 1998). While certainly beneficial to the job candidate in potentially securing a job, this type of faking is unlikely to benefit the organization in the long run. As one possible remedy to the problem of applicant faking, we suggest that prospective employers seek out applicants who are both psychologically well, and exhibit ethical character and vitality (Quick, Gavin, Cooper, & Quick, 2000).

Consistent with the practice at leading colleges and universities, similarly inclined organizations could actively seek to hire and promote job candidates with either a documented history of making ethically based choices or a high potential for consistently making sound, ethical decisions. One especially promising approach to assist in better selecting potentially ethical applicants may be found in the recent work of Peterson and his colleagues (Park & Peterson, 2003; Peterson & Seligman, 2004). These authors have identified 24 positive traits, organized around six core virtues (e.g., wisdom and knowledge, courage, love, justice, temperance, and transcendence) that have consistently emerged over time and across history in philosophical and religious discussions on human goodness and worth. According to Quick et al. (2000), the value-added contribution of having psychologically well and ethical employees is significant for not only the individual employee, but can also result in increased adaptability, flexibility, and performance for the employing organization. We next offer the second intervention option of employee training.

Training

While PWB exhibits significant test–retest consistency over time, these results also indicate that individuals have substantial opportunities to learn ways to enhance their PWB through any number of training-based interventions (for reviews, see Cooper, Dewe, & O'Driscoll, 2001). While a review of the mental health literature is beyond the scope of this paper, we emphasize a number of strategies exist that help individuals lead happier and more fulfilling lives (Quick et al., 1997). Particularly promising are strategies where employees are trained to proactively self-monitor or manage their personal perceptions to enhance positive, and discourage negative, displays of emotion. For example, constructive self-talk is a learned technique that replaces negative with more positive or reinforcing self-talk (Eliot, 1995).

These techniques can also generate economic benefits for employers. For example, Wells et al. (2000) found that introducing a program to treat depressed workers improved employee mental health and decreased turnover. Likewise, Kessler et al.(1999) reported that the lost productivity due to absenteeism among depressed workers cost a firm nearly as much as treatment. Notice, of course, that Kessler et al.'s estimate is conservative, as they did not consider the economic impact of lower job performance. However, as well evidenced in our earlier discussion, and complementing Kessler et al.'s findings, low employee well-being has been consistently related to decreased job performance (Wright, 2005). At the very least, the literature reviewed here suggests that firms should think carefully before cutting back on essential services. For example, when one large, self-insured corporation reduced spending on employee mental health, workers were absent more frequently and were forced to use other health services. In the end, the organization failed to save money and employees were worse off (Rosenheck, Druss, Stolar, Leslie, & Sledge, 1999).

Situational Engineering

Situational engineering involves changing the work environment to promote worker PWB. This approach would appear quite promising, as there is a growing body of evidence that conditions at work affect employee PWB (Wright & Cropanzano, 2000). For instance, research has shown that something as basic as providing tangible social support on the job can minimize the negative impact of a stressful work environment (Kohn & Schooler, 1982). In addition, such family-friendly policies as flextime and childcare have been proposed to enhance worker well-being (Quick et al., 1997). Finally, research has demonstrated that an organization can promote enhanced employee PWB through the use of equitable-based pay systems (Wright & Cropanzano, 2004). We suggest that future research make the investigation of approaches designed to foster PWB through situational engineering a priority.

CONCLUDING THOUGHTS

In this review, we have attempted to provide evidence strongly supporting the incorporation of employee PWB, along with job satisfaction, in future considerations of the happy/productive worker thesis. By definition, because job satisfaction is specific to one's job, it excludes aspects of one's life external to the job. This relatively narrow focus stands in marked contrast to research on PWB, which incorporates aspects of one's life both on and off the job (Diener, 1984). Additional research is now needed to more closely examine the form and function of PWB. For example, while various forms of PWB (e.g., fatigued vs. agitated) are similar constructs because they possess large amounts of unpleasantness, they also differ because they possess differing measures of activation (Larsen & Diener, 1992). Awareness of these types of distinctions could be very relevant in better predicting employee behavior across different job situations. As an example, while experienced levels of enthusiasm and excitement might be influential in predicting performance or success in sales positions, experienced levels of fatigue or exhaustion might be more predictive in various client contact intensive positions, such as those in human services and social welfare. As well evidenced by our opening quote by Thorndike, the pursuit of workplace happiness is beneficial, not only the employee, but also the employee's family, friends, co-workers, even society at large.

NOTE

1. According to Child (1941, p. 394), the second conceptualization of morale "refers to the condition of a group where there are clear and fixed group goals (purposes) that are felt to be important and integrated with individual goals ...." Also with a group orientation, the third conceptualization of morale "pertains to all factors in the individual's life that bring about a hopeful and energetic participation on his part so that his efforts enhance the effectiveness of the group in accomplishing the task at hand."

REFERENCES

Abelson, M. A. (1987). Examination of avoidable and unavoidable turnover. *Journal of Applied Psychology, 72*, 382–386.

Anderson, V. V. (1929). *Psychiatry in industry*. New York: Harpers.

Argyle, M. (1987). *The experience of happiness*. London: Methuen.

Bender, J. F. (1944). Emotional adjustment of workers. *Personnel Journal, 22*, 301–307.

Berkman, P. L. (1971a). Measurement of mental health in a general population survey. *Journal of Epidemiology, 94*, 105–111.

Berkman, P. L. (1971b). Life stress and psychological well-being: A replication of Langer's analysis in the midtown Manhattan study. *Journal of Health and Social Behavior, 12*, 35–45.

Bolger, N., & Schilling, E. A. (1991). Personality and problems of everyday life: The role of neuroticism in exposure and reactivity to daily stressors. *Journal of Personality, 59*, 255–286.

Bradburn, N. M., & Caplovitz, D. (1965). *Reports on happiness*. Chicago, IL: Aldine.

Brayfield, A. H., & Crockett, H. F. (1951). An index of job satisfaction. *Journal of Applied Psychology, 35*, 307–311.

Brayfield, A. H., & Crockett, W. H. (1955). Employee attitudes and employee performance. *Psychological Bulletin, 52*, 396–424.

Brayfield, A. H., & Rothe, A. H. (1951). An index of job satisfaction. *Journal of Applied Psychology, 35*, 307–311.

Brief, A. P. (1998). *Attitudes in and around organizations*. Thousand Oaks, CA: Sage.

Brief, A. P., Butcher, A. H., & Roberson, L. (1995). Cookies, dispositions, and job attitudes: The effects of positive mood-inducing events and negative affectivity on job satisfaction in a field experiment. *Organizational Behavior and Human Decision Processes, 62*, 55–62.

Brief, A. P., & Roberson, L. (1989). Job attitude organization: An exploratory study. *Journal of Applied Social Psychology, 19*, 717–727.

Brief, A. P., & Weiss, H. M. (2002). Organizational behavior: Affect in the workplace. In: S. T. Fiske, D. L. Schachter & C. Zahn-Waxler (Eds), *Annual Review of Psychology* (Vol. 53, pp. 279–307). Palo Alto, CA: Annual Reviews.

Cain, P. A. (1942). *Individual differences in susceptibility to monotony*. Unpublished doctoral dissertation. Ithaca, NY: Cornell University.

Cameron, K. S., Dutton, J. E., & Quinn, R. E. (2003). Foundations of positive organizational scholarship. In: K. S. Cameron, J. E. Dutton & R. E. Quinn (Eds), *Positive organizational scholarship: Foundations of a new discipline* (pp. 3–13). San Francisco, CA: Berrett-Koehler.

Campion, M. A. (1991). Meaning and measurement of turnover: Components of alternative measures and recommendations for research. *Journal of Applied Psychology, 76*, 199–212.

Carey, J. F., Jr., Berg, I. A., & Van Dusen, A. C. (1951). Reliability of ratings of employee satisfaction based upon written interview records. *Journal of Applied Psychology, 35*, 252–255.

Cascio, W. F. (1991). *Costing human resources: The financial impact of behavior in organizations* (3rd ed.). Boston, MA: PWS-Kent.

Cherrington, D. J., Reitz, H. J., & Scott, W. E. (1971). Effects of contingent and non-contingent reward on the relationship between satisfaction and task performance. *Journal of Applied Psychology, 55*, 531–536.

Child, I. L. (1941). Morale: A bibliographical review. *Psychological Bulletin, 38*, 393–420.

Coltrera, F. (2001). *Understanding depression.* Boston, MA: Harvard Health Publications.

Conti, D. J., & Burton, W. N. (1994). The economic impact of depression in a workplace. *Journal of Occupational Medicine, 36*, 983–988.

Cooper, C. L., Dewe, P. J., & O'Driscoll, M. P. (2001). *Organizational stress: A review and critique of theory, research, and applications.* Thousand Oaks, CA: Sage.

Cranny, C. J., Smith, P. C., & Stone, A. (Eds). (1992). *Job satisfaction: How people feel about their jobs and how it affects their performance.* New York: Lexington.

Cropanzano, R., Weiss, H. M., Hale, J. M. S., & Reb, J. (2003). The structure of affect: Reconsidering the relationship between negative and positive affectivity. *Journal of Management, 29*, 831–857.

Cropanzano, R., & Wright, T. A. (1999). A five-year study of change in the relationship between well-being and job performance. *Consulting Psychology Journal: Practice and Research, 51*, 252–265.

Cropanzano, R., & Wright, T. A. (2001). When a 'happy' worker is really a "productive" worker: A review and further refinement of the happy-productive worker thesis. *Consulting Psychology Journal: Practice and Research, 53*, 182–199.

Culpin, M., & Smith, M. (1927). *A study of telegraphists' cramp.* Industrial Health Research Board Report. Number 43. London, England.

Daniels, K., & Harris, C. (2000). Work, psychological well-being and performance. *Occupational Medicine, 50*, 304–309.

Davidson, R. J., Kabat-Zinn, J., Schumacher, J., Rosenkranz, M., Muller, D., Santorelli, S. F., et al. (2003). Alterations in brain and immune function produced by mindfulness meditation. *Psychosomatic Medicine, 65*, 564–570.

Davidson, R. J., & Tomarken, A. J. (1989). Laterality and emotion: An electrophysiological approach. In: F. Boller & J. Grafman (Eds), *Handbook of neuropsychology* (pp. 419–441). Amsterdam: Elsevier.

Davis-Blake, A., & Pfeffer, J. (1989). Just a mirage: The search for dispositional effects in organizational research. *Academy of Management Review, 14*, 385–400.

Dember, W. N., & Brooks, J. (1989). A new instrument for measuring optimism and pessimism: Test-retest reliability and relations with happiness and religious commitment. *Bulletin of the Psychonomic Society, 27*, 365–366.

Diener, E. (1984). Subjective well-being. *Psychological Bulletin, 95*, 542–575.

Diener, E. (1994). Assessing subjective well-being: Progress and opportunities. *Social Indicators Research, 31*, 103–157.

Diener, E. (2000). Subjective well-being: The science of happiness and a proposal for a national index. *American Psychologist, 55*, 34–43.

Diener, E., & Larsen, R. J. (1993). The experience of emotional well-being. In: M. Lewis & J.M. Haviland (Eds), *Handbook of emotions* (pp. 404–415). New York: Guilford Press.

Diener, E., Sandvik, E., Pavot, W., & Fujita, F. (1992). Extraversion and subjective well-being in a U.S. national probability sample. *Journal of Research in Personality, 26*, 205–215.

Diener, E., Sandvik, E., Seidlitz, L., & Diener, M. (1993). The relationship between income and subjective well-being: Relative or absolute? *Social Indicators Research, 28*, 195–223.

Diener, E., Suh, E. M., Lucas, R. E., & Smith, H. L. (1999). Subjective well-being: Three decades of progress. *Psychological Bulletin, 125*, 276–302.

Douglas, P. H. (1918). The problem of labor turnover. *The American Economic Review, 8*, 306–318.

Druss, B. G., Rosenheck, R. A., & Sledge, W. H. (2000). Heath and disability costs of depressive illness in a major U.S. corporation. *American Journal of Psychiatry, 157*, 1274–1278.

Eberle, G. J. (1919). Labor turnover. *The American Economic Review, 9*, 79–82.

Eliot, R. S. (1995). *From stress to strength: How to lighten your load and save your life.* New York: Bantam Books.

Elkind, H. B. (1931). *Preventive management.* New York: B.C. Forbes.

Erez, A., & Isen, A. M. (2002). The influence of positive affect on the components of expectancy motivation. *Journal of Applied Psychology, 87*, 1055–1067.

Fisher, C. D. (1980). On the dubious wisdom of expecting job satisfaction to correlate with performance. *Academy of Management Review, 5*, 607–612.

Fisher, C. D. (2000). Mood and emotion while working: Missing pieces of job satisfaction? *Journal of Organizational Behavior, 21*, 185–202.

Fisher, V. E., & Hanna, J. V. (1931). *The dissatisfied worker.* New York: Macmillan.

Forgas, J. P. (1995). Mood and judgment: The affect infusion model (AIM). *Psychological Bulletin, 117*, 39–66.

Fredrickson, B. L. (1998). What good are positive emotions? *Review of General Psychology, 2*, 300–319.

Fredrickson, B. L. (2001). The role of positive emotions in positive psychology: The broaden-and-build theory of positive emotions. *American Psychologist, 56*, 219–226.

Fredrickson, B. L. (2002). Positive emotions. In: C. R. Snyder & S. J. Lopez (Eds), *Handbook of positive psychology* (pp. 120–134). New York: Oxford University Press.

Fredrickson, B. L. (2003). Positive emotions and upward spirals in organizations. In: K.S. Cameron, J. E. Dutton & R. E. Quinn (Eds), *Positive organizational scholarship: Foundations of a new discipline* (pp. 163–175). San Francisco, CA: Berrett-Koehler.

Fredrickson, B. L., & Branigan, C. A. (2001). Positive emotions. In: T. J. Mayne & G.A. Bonnano (Eds), *Emotion: Current issues and future directions* (pp. 123–151). New York: Guilford Press.

Fredrickson, B. L., & Branigan, C. A. (2005). Positive emotions broaden the scope of attention and thought-action repertoires. *Cognition and Emotion, 19*, 313–332.

Fredrickson, B. L., & Joiner, T. (2002). Positive emotions trigger upward spirals toward emotional well-being. *Psychological Science, 13*, 172–175.

Fredrickson, B. L., & Levenson, R. W. (1998). Positive emotions speed recovery from the cardiovascular sequalae of negative emotions. *Cognition and Emotion, 12*, 191–220.

Fredrickson, B. L., & Losada, M. F. (2005). Positive affect and the complex dynamics of human flourishing. *American Psychologist, 60*, 678–686.

Fredrickson, B. L., Mancuso, R. A., Branigan, C., & Tugade, M. (2000). The undoing of positive emotions. *Motivation and Emotion, 24*, 237–258.

Fredrickson, B. L., Maynard, K. E., Helms, M. J., Haney, T. L., Seigler, I. C., & Barefoot, J. C. (2000). Hostility predicts magnitude and duration of blood pressure response to anger. *Journal of Behavioral Medicine, 23*, 229–243.

Fredrickson, B. L., Tugade, M. M., Waugh, C. E., & Larkin, G. R. (2003). What good are positive emotions in crises? A prospective study of resilience and emotions following the terrorist attacks on the United States on September 11th, 2001. *Journal of Personality and Social Psychology, 84*, 365–376.

Frijda, N. H. (1986). *The emotions.* Cambridge: Cambridge University Press.

Frost, E. (1920). What industry wants and does not want from the psychologist. *Journal of Applied Psychology, 4*, 18–24.

Gechman, A., & Wiener, Y. (1975). Job involvement and satisfaction as related to mental health and personal time devoted to work. *Journal of Applied Psychology*, *60*, 521–523.

George, J. M. (1992). The role of personality in organizational life: Issues and evidence. *Journal of Management*, *18*, 185–210.

George, J. M., & Zhou, J. (2002). Understanding when bad moods foster creativity and good ones don't: The role of context and clarity of feelings. *Journal of Applied Psychology*, *87*, 687–697.

Gerhart, B. (1987). How important are dispositional factors as determinants of job satisfaction? Implications for job design and other personnel programs. *Journal of Applied Psychology*, *72*, 366–373.

Gil, K. M., Carson, J. W., Porter, L. S., Scipio, C., Bediako, S. M., & Orringer, E. (2004). Daily mood and stress predict pain, health care use, and work activity in African American adults with sickle cell disease. *Health Psychology*, *23*, 267–274.

Greenberg, P. E., Stiglins, L. F., Finkelstein, S. N., & Berndt, E. R. (1993). The economic burden of depression in 1990. *Journal of Clinical Psychiatry*, *54*, 405–418.

Griffeth, R. W., Hom, P. W., & Gaertner, S. (2000). A meta-analysis of antecedents and correlates of employee turnover: Update, moderator tests, and research implications for the millennium. *Journal of Management*, *26*, 463–488.

Gross, J. J., Fredrickson, B. L., & Levenson, R. W. (1994). The psychophysiology of crying. *Psychophysiology*, *31*, 460–468.

Harrison, D. A., Virick, M., & Williams, S. (1996). Working without a net: Time, performance, and turnover under maximally contingent rewards. *Journal of Applied Psychology*, *81*, 331–345.

Headley, B., & Wearing, A. (1992). The sense of relative superiority – Central to well-being. *Social Indicators Research*, *20*, 497–516.

Hersey, R. B. (1929). Periodic emotional changes in male workers. *Personnel Journal*, *7*, 459–464.

Hersey, R. B. (1930). A monotonous job in an emotional crisis. *Personnel Journal*, *9*, 290–296.

Hersey, R. B. (1932a). Rate of production and emotional state. *Personnel Journal*, *10*, 355–364.

Hersey, R. B. (1932b). *Workers' emotions in shop and home: A study of industrial workers from the psychological and physiological standpoint*. Philadelphia, PA: University of Pennsylvania Press.

Hobfoll, S. E. (1988). *The ecology of stress*. New York: Hemisphere.

Hobfoll, S. E. (1989). Conservation of resources: A new attempt at conceptualizing stress. *American Psychologist*, *44*, 513–525.

Hobfoll, S. E. (1998). *Stress, culture, and community: The psychology and philosophy of stress*. New York: Plenum.

Hom, P. W., Caranikas-Walker, F., Prussia, G. E., & Griffeth, R. W. (1992). A meta-analytical structural equations analysis of a model of employee turnover. *Journal of Applied Psychology*, *77*, 890–909.

Hom, P. W., & Griffeth, R. W. (1991). Structural equations modeling test of a turnover theory: Cross-sectional and longitudinal analyses. *Journal of Applied Psychology*, *76*, 350–366.

Hom, P. W., & Griffeth, R. W. (1995). *Employee turnover*. Cincinnati, OH: South/Western.

Hoppock, R. (1937). Job satisfaction of psychologists. *Journal of Applied Psychology*, *21*, 300–303.

Houser, J. D. (1927). *What the employer thinks: Executives' attitudes toward employees*. Cambridge, MA: Harvard University Press.

Iaffaldano, M. T., & Muchinsky, P. M. (1985). Job satisfaction and job performance: A meta analysis. *Psychological Bulletin, 97,* 366–373.

Ilgen, D. R. (1999). Teams embedded in organizations: Some implications. *American Psychologist, 54,* 129–139.

Isen, A. M. (2003). Positive affect as a source of strength. In: L. G. Aspinwall & U.M. Staudinger (Eds), *A psychology of human strengths: Fundamental questions and future directions for a positive psychology* (pp. 179–195). Washington, DC: American Psychological association.

Ivancevich, J. W., & Matteson, M. T. (1980). *Stress at work: A managerial perspective.* Glenview, IL: Scott, Foresman.

Jamal, M., & Mitchell, V. F. (1980). Work, nonwork, and mental health: A model and a test. *Industrial Relations, 19,* 88–93.

Judge, T. A. (1993). Does affective disposition moderate the relationship between job satisfaction and voluntary turnover? *Journal of Applied Psychology, 78,* 395–401.

Judge, T. A., Hanisch, K. A., & Drankoski, R. D. (1995). Human resources management and employee attitudes. In: G. R. Ferris, S. D. Rosen & D. T. Barnum (Eds), *Handbook of human resources management* (pp. 574–596). Oxford, England: Blackwell publishers.

Judge, T. A., & Locke, E. A. (1993). Effects of dysfunctional thought processes on subjective well-being and job satisfaction. *Journal of Applied Psychology, 78,* 475–490.

Judge, T. A., Thoresen, C. J., Bono, J. E., & Patton, G. K. (1998, August). The job satisfaction-job performance relationship: 1939–1998. Paper presented at the annual meeting of the Academy of Management, San Diego, CA.

Judge, T. A., Thoresen, C. J., Bono, J. E., & Patton, G. K. (2001). The job satisfaction-job performance relationship: A qualitative and quantitative review. *Psychological Bulletin, 127,* 376–407.

Kates, S. L. (1950). Rorschach responses, Strong Blank Scales, and job satisfaction among policemen. *Journal of Applied Psychology, 34,* 249–254.

Kerr, W. A. (1948). On the validity and reliability of the Job Satisfaction Tear Ballot. *Journal of Applied Psychology, 32,* 275–281.

Kessler, R. C., Barber, C., Birnbaum, H. G., Frank, R. G., Greenberg, P. E., Rose, R. M., Simon, G. E., & Wang, P. (1999). Depression in the workplace: Effects on short-term disability. *Heath Affairs, 18,* 163–171.

Kohn, M. L., & Schooler, C. (1982). Job conditions and personality: A longitudinal assessment of their reciprocal effects. *American Journal of Sociology, 87,* 1257–1286.

Kornhauser, A. (1933). The technique of measuring employee attitudes. *Personnel Journal, 9,* 99–107.

Kornhauser, A. (1965). *Mental health and the industrial worker: A Detroit study.* New York: Wiley.

Kornhauser, A., & Sharp, A. (1932). Employee attitudes: Suggestions from a study in a factory. *Personnel Journal, 10,* 393–401.

Landy, F. W. (1985). *The psychology of work behavior* (3rd ed.). Homewood, IL: Dorsey Press.

Larsen, R. J., & Diener, E. (1992). Promises and problems with the circumplex model of emotion. *Review of Personality and Social Psychology, 13,* 25–59.

Larsen, R. J., & Ketelaar, T. (1989). Extraversion, neuroticism, and susceptibility to positive and negative mood induction procedures. *Personality and Individual Differences, 10,* 1221–1228.

Larsen, R. J., & Ketelaar, T. (1991). Personality and susceptibility to positive and negative emotional states. *Journal of Personality and Social Psychology, 61*, 132–140.

Lawler, E. E., III. (1973). *Motivation in work organizations.* Monterey, CA: Brooks/Cole Publishing Company.

Lawler, E. E., & Porter, L. W. (1967). The effects of performance on job satisfaction. *Industrial Relations, 7*, 20–28.

Lazarus, R. S. (1991). *Emotion and adaptation.* New York: Oxford University Press.

Ledford, G. E., Jr. (1999). Happiness and productivity revisited. *Journal of Organizational Behavior, 20*, 25–30.

Lee, R. T., & Ashforth, B. E. (1996). A meta-analytic examination of the correlates of the three dimensions of job burnout. *Journal of Applied Psychology, 81*, 123–133.

Lee, T. W., Mitchell, T. R., Sablynski, C. J., Burton, J. P., & Holton, B. C. (2004). The effects of job embeddedness on organizational citizenship, job performance, volitional absences, and voluntary turnover. *Academy of Management Journal, 47*, 711–722.

Levenson, R. W. (1994). Human emotions: A functional view. In: P. Ekman & R. Davidson (Eds), *The nature of emotion: Fundamental questions* (pp. 123–126). New York: Oxford University Press.

Locke, E. A. (1969). What is job satisfaction? *Organizational Behavior and Human Performance, 4*, 309–336.

Locke, E. A. (1976). The nature and causes of job satisfaction. In: M. D. Dunnette (Ed.), *Handbook of industrial and organizational psychology* (1st ed., pp. 1297–1349). Chicago, IL: Rand McNally.

Luthans, F. (2002a). Positive organizational behavior: Developing and managing psychological strengths. *Academy of Management Executive, 16*, 57–72.

Luthans, F. (2002b). The need for and meaning of positive organizational behavior. *Journal of Organizational Behavior, 23*, 695–706.

Luthans, F. (2003). Positive organizational behavior: Implications for leadership and HR development and motivation. In: L. W. Porter, G. A. Bigley & R. M. Steers (Eds), *Motivation and work behavior* (pp. 178–195). New York: McGraw-Hill/Irwin.

Lykken, D. (1999). *Happiness.* New York: Golden Books.

Lyubomirsky, S., & Ross, L. (1997). Hedonic consequences of social comparison: A contrast of happy and unhappy people. *Journal of Personality and Social Psychology, 73*, 1141–1157.

McEvoy, G. M., & Cascio, W. F. (1987). Do good or bad performers leave? A meta-analysis of the relationship between performance and turnover. *Academy of Management Journal, 30*, 744–762.

McMahon, D. M. (2004). From happiness of virtue to the virtue of happiness: 400B.C.–A.D. 1980. *Daedalus, 133*, 5–17.

McMurry, R. N. (1932). Efficiency, work satisfaction and neurotic tendency. *Personnel Journal, 11*, 201–210.

March, J. G., & Simon, H. A. (1958). *Organizations.* New York: Wiley.

Martin, L. L., Ward, D. W., Achee, J. W., & Wyer, R. S. (1993). Mood as input: People have to interpret the motivational implications of their moods. *Journal of Personality and Social Psychology, 64*, 317–326.

Martin, T. N. (1984). Role stress and inability to leave as predictors of mental health. *Human Relations, 37*, 969–983.

Maslow, A. H. (1954). *Motivation and personality.* New York: Harper.

Mayo, E. (1933). *The human problems of an industrial civilization.* New York: Viking.

Michalos, A. C. (1985). Multiple discrepancies theory (MDT). *Social Indicators Research, 16,* 347–413.

Mobley, W. H. (1982). *Employee turnover: Causes, consequences, and control.* Reading, MA: Addison-Wesley.

Myers, D. G. (1993). *The pursuit of happiness.* New York: Avon Books.

Myers, D. G., & Diener, E. (1995). Who is happy? *Psychological Science, 6,* 10–19.

Myers, D. G., & Diener, E. (1997). The new pursuit of happiness. *The Harvard Medical Health Letter, 14,* 4–7.

Nahm, H. (1949). Satisfaction with nursing. *Journal of Applied Psychology, 32,* 335–343.

Nord, W. R. (1976). Attitudes and performance. In: W. R. Nord (Ed.), *Concepts and controversies in organizational behavior* (pp. 518–525). Glenview, IL: Foresman.

Organ, D. W. (1988a). A restatement of the satisfaction-performance hypothesis. *Journal of Management, 14,* 547–557.

Organ, D. W. (1988b). *Organizational citizenship behavior: The good soldier syndrome.* Lexington, MA: Lexington Press.

Organ, D. W., & Near, J. P. (1985). Cognition vs. affect in measures of job satisfaction. *International Journal of Psychology, 20,* 241–253.

Ostir, G. V., Markides, K. S., Peek, K., & Goodwin, J. S. (2001). The associations between emotional well-being and the incidence of stroke in older adults. *Psychosomatic Medicine, 63,* 210–215.

Parducci, A. (1995). *Happiness, pleasure, and judgment: The contextual theory and its applications.* Hillsdale, NJ: Erlbaum.

Park, N., & Peterson, C. M. (2003). Virtues and organizations. In: K. S. Cameron, J. E. Dutton & R. E. Quinn (Eds), *Positive organizational scholarship: Foundations of a new discipline* (pp. 33–47). San Francisco, CA: Berrett-Koehler.

Pavot, W., Diener, E., Colvin, C. R., & Sandvik, E. (1991). Further validation of the Satisfaction with Life Scale: Evidence for cross-method convergence of well-being measures. *Journal of Personality Assessment, 57,* 149–161.

Pennock, G. A. (1930). Industrial research at Hawthorne: An experimental investigation of rest periods, working conditions and other conditions. *Personnel Journal, 8,* 296–313.

Peterson, C. M., & Seligman, M. E. P. (1984). Causal explanations as a risk factor for depression: Theory and evidence. *Psychological Review, 91,* 347–374.

Peterson, C., & Seligman, M. E. P. (2004). *Character strengths and virtues: A handbook and classification.* New York: Oxford University Press.

Petty, M. M., McGee, G. W., & Cavender, J. W. (1984). A meta-analysis of the relationship between individual job satisfaction and individual performance. *Academy of Management Review, 9,* 712–721.

Podsakoff, P. M., & Williams, L. J. (1986). The relationship between individual job satisfaction and individual performance. In: E. A. Locke (Ed.), *Generalizing from laboratory to field studies* (pp. 207–245). Lexington, MA: Lexington Books.

Pratt, M. G., & Ashforth, B. E. (2003). Fostering positive meaningfulness at work. In: K. S. Cameron, J. E. Dutton, & R. E. Quinn (Eds), *Positive organizational scholarship: Foundations of a new discipline* (pp. 309–327). San Francisco: Berret-Koehler.

Quick, J. C., Gavin, J. H., Cooper, C. L., & Quick, J. D. (2000). Executive health: Building strength, managing risks. *Academy of Management Executive, 14,* 34–44.

Quick, J. C., Quick, J. D., Nelson, D. L., & Hurrell, J. J., Jr. (1997). *Preventive stress management in organizations.* Washington, DC: American Psychological Association.

Robbins, T. L., & DeNisi, A. S. (1994). A closer look at interpersonal affect as a distinct influence on cognitive processing in performance evaluations. *Journal of Applied Psychology, 79*, 341–353.

Roethlisberger, F. J. (1941). *Management and morale.* Cambridge, MA: Harvard University Press.

Roethlisberger, F. J., & Dickson, W. J. (1939). *Management and the worker.* Cambridge, MA: Harvard University Press.

Rosenheck, R. A., Druss, B., Stolar, M., Leslie, D., & Sledge, W. (1999). Effect of declining mental health service use on employees of a large corporation. *Health Affairs,* (September/October), 193–203.

Rosse, J. G., Stecher, M. D., Miller, J. L., & Levin, R. A. (1998). The impact of response distortion on preemployment personality testing and hiring decisions. *Journal of Applied Psychology, 83*, 634–644.

Russell, B. (1930). *The conquest of happiness.* New York: Liveright.

Russell, J. A. (1980). A circumplex model of affect. *Journal of Personality and Social Psychology, 39*, 1161–1178.

Rusting, C. G., & Larsen, R. J. (1997). Extraversion, neuroticism, and susceptibility to positive and negative affect: A test of two theoretical models. *Personality and Individual Differences, 22*, 607–612.

Rusting, C. G., & Larsen, R. J. (1999). Clarifying Gray's theory of personality: A response to Pickering, Corr and Gray. *Personality and Individual Differences, 26*, 367–372.

Sandvik, E., Diener, E., & Seidlitz, L. (1993). Subjective well-being: The convergence and stability of self-report measures. *Journal of Personality, 61*, 317–342.

Schwab, D. P., & Cummings, L. L. (1970). Theories of performance and satisfaction: A review. *Industrial Relations, 9*, 408–430.

Schwarz, N. N., & Clore, G. L. (1993). The use of emotion as information. In: P. Ekman & R.J. Davidson (Eds), *The nature of emotion: Fundamental questions.* New York: Oxford Press.

Seidlitz, L., & Diener, E. (1993). Memory for positive versus negative events: Theories for the differences between happy and unhappy persons. *Journal of Personality and Social Psychology, 64*, 654–664.

Seidlitz, L., Wyer, R. S., & Diener, E. (1997). Cognitive correlates of subjective well-being: The processing of valanced life events by happy and unhappy persons. *Journal of Research in Personality, 31*, 240–256.

Sekaran, U. (1985). The paths to mental health: An exploratory study of husbands and wives in dual-career families. *Journal of Occupational Psychology, 58*, 129–137.

Seligman, M. E. P. (1994). *What you can change and what you can't.* New York: Knopf.

Seligman, M. E. P. (1995). The effectiveness of psychotherapy: The Consumer Report's study. *American Psychologist, 50*, 965–974.

Seligman, M. E. P. (1998). *Learned optimism: How to change your mind and your life.* New York: Pocket Books.

Seligman, M. E. P. (2002). *Authentic happiness.* New York: Free Press.

Seligman, M. E. P., & Csikszentmihalyi, M. (2000). Positive psychology: An introduction. *American Psychologist, 55*, 5–14.

Sheridan, J. E. (1992). Organizational culture and employee retention. *Academy of Management Journal, 35*, 1036–1056.

Smith, P. C. (1953). The curve of output as a criterion of boredom. *Journal of Applied Psychology, 37,* 69–74.

Smith, P. C. (1992). In pursuit of happiness: Why study general satisfaction? In: C. J. Cranny, P.C. Smith & E. F. Stone (Eds), *Job satisfaction: How people feel about their jobs and how it affects their performance* (pp. 5–19). New York: Lexington Books.

Snow, A. J. (1923). Labor turnover and mental alertness test scores. *Journal of Applied Psychology, 7,* 285–290.

Spector, P. E. (1997). *Job satisfaction: Application, assessment, causes, and consequences.* Thousand Oaks, CA: Sage.

Staw, B. M. (1986). Organizational psychology and the pursuit of the happy/productive worker. *California Management Review, XXVIII*(4), 40–53.

Staw, B. M. (2004). The dispositional approach to job attitudes: An empirical and conceptual review. In: B. Schneider & B. Smitt (Eds), *Personality in organization* (pp. 163–191). Mahweh, NJ: Erlbaum.

Staw, B. M., & Barsade, S. G. (1993). Affect and managerial performance: A test of the sadder-but-wiser vs. happier-and-smarter hypotheses. *Administrative Science Quarterly, 38,* 304–331.

Staw, B. M., & Cohen-Charash, Y. (2005). The dispositional approach to job satisfaction: More than a mirage: But not yet an oasis. *Journal of Organizational Behavior, 26,* 59–78.

Staw, B. M., Sutton, R. I., & Pelled, L. H. (1994). Employee positive emotion and favorable outcomes at the workplace. *Organization Science, 5,* 71–91.

Steel, R. P. (2002). Turnover theory at the empirical interface: Problems of fit and function. *Academy of Management Review, 27,* 346–360.

Steptoe, A., Wardle, J., & Marmot, M. (2005). Positive affect and health-related neuroendocrine, cardiovascular, and inflammatory responses. *Proceedings of the National Academy of Sciences of United States of America, 102,* 6508–6512.

Sullivan, J. J. (1989). Self theories and employee motivation. *Journal of Management, 15,* 345–363.

Super, D. E. (1939). Occupational level and job satisfaction. *Journal of Applied Psychology, 23,* 547–564.

Taylor, C. C. W. (1998). Eudaimonia. In: E. Craig (Ed.), *Routledge encyclopedia of philosophy* (Vol. 3, pp. 450–452). New York: Routledge.

Tett, R. P., & Meyer, J. P. (1993). Job satisfaction, organizational commitment, turnover intention, and turnover: Path analysis based on meta-analytic findings. *Personnel Psychology, 46,* 259–293.

Thorndike, E. L. (1922). The psychology of labor. *Harper's Monthly Magazine, 144,* 799–806.

Tomarken, A. J., Davidson, R. J., & Henriques, J. B. (1990). Resting frontal asymmetry predicts affective responses to films. *Journal of Personality and Social Psychology, 59,* 791–801.

Trevor, C. O., Gerhart, B., & Boudreau, J. W. (1997). Voluntary turnover and job performance: Curvilinear and moderating influences of salary growth and promotion. *Journal of Applied Psychology, 82,* 44–61.

Uhrbrock, R. S. (1934). Attitudes of 4430 employees. *Journal of Social Psychology, 5,* 365–377.

Velasquez, M. G. (2002). *Business ethics: Concepts and cases* (5th ed.). Upper Saddle River, NJ: Prentice-Hall.

Vroom, V. H. (1964). *Work and motivation.* New York: Wiley.

Warr, P. (1990). The measurement of well-being and other aspects of mental health. *Journal of Occupational Psychology, 63,* 193–210.

Watson, D. (1988). Intraindividual and interindividual analyses of positive and negative affect: Their relation to health complaints, perceived stress, and daily activities. *Journal of Personality and Social Psychology, 54*, 1020–1030.

Weiss, H. M. (2002). Deconstructing job satisfaction: Separating evaluations, beliefs and affective experiences. *Human Resource Management Review, 12*, 173–194.

Weiss, H. M., & Brief, A. P. (2001). Affect at work: An historical perspective. In: R. L. Payne & C. L. Cooper (Eds), *Emotions at work: Theory, research, and application* (pp. 133–171). UK: Wiley.

Weiss, H. M., & Cropanzano, R. (1996). An affective events approach to job satisfaction. In: B. M. Staw & L. L. Cummings (Eds), *Research in organizational behavior* (Vol. 18, pp. 1–74). Greenwich, CT: JAI Press.

Weitz, J. (1952). A neglected concept in the study of job satisfaction. *Personnel Psychology, 5*, 201–205.

Wells, K. B., Sherbourne, C., Schoenbaum, M., Duan, N., Meredith, L., Unützer, J., Miranda, J., Carney, M. F., & Rubenstein, L. V. (2000). *Journal of the American Medical Association, 283*, 212–220.

Wright, T. A. (2003). Positive organizational behavior: An idea whose time has truly come. *Journal of Organizational Behavior, 24*, 437–442.

Wright, T. A. (2005). The role of 'happiness' in organizational research: Past, present and future directions. In: P. L. Perrewe & D. C. Ganster (Eds), *Research in occupational stress and well-being* (Vol. 4, pp. 221–264). Amsterdam: JAI Press.

Wright, T. A. (2006). The emergence of job satisfaction in organizational research: A historical overview of the dawn of job attitude research. *Journal of Management History, 12*, 262–277.

Wright, T. A., & Bonett, D. G. (1992). The effect of turnover on work satisfaction and mental health: Support for a situational perspective. *Journal of Organizational Behavior, 13*, 603–615.

Wright, T. A., & Bonett, D. G. (1997). The role of pleasantness and activation-based well-being in performance prediction. *Journal of Occupational Health Psychology, 2*, 212–219.

Wright, T. A., & Bonett, D. G. (2005). Using a Positive Organizational Behavior (POB) framework to better understand the role of job satisfaction, psychological well-being and job performance on employee retention. Paper presented at the 2005 meeting of the Academy of Management, Honolulu, Hawaii.

Wright, T. A., & Bonett, D. G. (2007). Job satisfaction and psychological well-being as nonadditive predictors of workplace turnover. *Journal of Management, 33*, 141–160.

Wright, T. A., Bonett, D. G., & Sweeney, D. A. (1993). Mental health and work performance; Results of a longitudinal field study. *Journal of Occupational and Organizational Psychology, 66*, 277–284.

Wright, T. A., & Cropanzano, R. (1998). Emotional exhaustion as a predictor of job performance and voluntary turnover. *Journal of Applied Psychology, 83*, 486–493.

Wright, T. A., & Cropanzano, R. (2000). Psychological well-being and job satisfaction as predictors of job performance. *Journal of Occupational Health Psychology, 5*, 84–94.

Wright, T. A., & Cropanzano, R. (2004). The role of psychological well-being in job performance: A fresh look at an age-old quest. *Organizational Dynamics, 33*, 338–351.

Wright, T. A., Cropanzano, R., Denney, P. J., & Moline, G. L. (2002). When a happy worker is a productive worker: A preliminary examination of three models. *Canadian Journal of Behavioural Science, 34*, 146–150.

Wright, T. A., Cropanzano, R., & Meyer, D. G. (2004). State and trait correlates of job performance: A tale of two perspectives. *Journal of Business and Psychology, 18,* 365–383.

Wright, T. A., Larwood, L., & Denney, P. J. (2002). The different 'faces' of happiness-unhappiness in organizational research: Emotional exhaustion, positive affectivity, negative affectivity and psychological well-being as correlates of job performance. *Journal of Business and Management, 8,* 109–126.

Wright, T. A., & Staw, B. M. (1999). Affect and favorable work outcomes: Two longitudinal tests of the happy-productive worker thesis. *Journal of Organizational Behavior, 20,* 1–23.

Wright, T. A., & Wright, V. P. (2002). Organizational researcher values, ethical responsibility, and the committed-to-participant research perspective. *Journal of Management Inquiry, 11,* 173–185.

Wrzesniewski, A. (2003). Finding positive meaning in work. In: K. S. Cameron, J. E. Dutton & R. E. Quinn (Eds), *Positive organizational scholarship: Foundations of a new discipline* (pp. 296–308). San Francisco, CA: Berrett-Koehler.

Zelenski, J. M., & Larsen, R. J. (1999). Susceptibility to affect: A comparison of three personality taxonomies. *Journal of Personality, 67,* 761–791.

THIRD PARTY INTERVENTIONS ACROSS CULTURES: NO "ONE BEST CHOICE"

Donald E. Conlon, Christopher J. Meyer, Anne L. Lytle and Harold W. Willaby

ABSTRACT

In this article, we focus on alternative dispute resolution procedures, in particular third party procedures. We describe eight different procedures and provide examples of how these procedures are used in different cultural contexts. We then evaluate the procedures in terms of how they impact four key criteria that have been noted in the literature related to negotiation: process criteria, settlement criteria, issue-related criteria, and relationship criteria. We subsequently explore the potential impact of culture on evaluations of these criteria. We finish with a discussion of future directions for research and practice, emphasizing that procedural recommendations should be made carefully when the criteria for effectiveness and applicability are derived from US-centric research. In other words, there is not "one best choice" for third party procedures universal to the myriad cultures on our planet.

Research in Personnel and Human Resources Management, Volume 26, 309–349
Copyright © 2007 by Elsevier Ltd.
ISSN: 0742-7301/doi:10.1016/S0742-7301(07)26007-4

INTRODUCTION

In the last three decades, there has been a growing acceptance of the use of alternative dispute resolution (ADR) procedures in lieu of litigation for business and other types of disputes (Coltri, 2004), as well as intra-organizational disputes (Brown, 1983). With this acceptance have come a wide variety of third party ADR procedures: some of these are traditional and commonly used for business disputes and labor–management relations; others are novel and tend to be used for specific types of disputes (e.g., insurance claims disputes). In some contexts, case intake officials or the disputants themselves may have a variety of ADR procedural choices at their disposal to resolve a conflict (Edelman, 1984). As the field of ADR has evolved into a plethora of options for parties in dispute, the ability of researchers, policy makers, and consumers to distinguish between, evaluate, and ultimately choose between various third party procedures becomes not only increasingly important, but is also increasingly complex.

This variation in third party procedures becomes even more complex when one goes beyond the organizational setting of dispute resolution to consider the influence of culture and cultural context on ADR procedural preferences (Diamant, 2000; Sacks, Reichert, & Proffitt, 1999). The influence of culture in disputes is no longer an issue solely relevant to global business people who travel to and set up contracts in other countries. The business and organizational environments in which we find ourselves today are often cross-cultural or global in their nature, even for individuals who might not actually cross cultural boundaries physically. For example, an E-bay seller sitting at home in the USA might be drawn into a dispute by an E-bay buyer located in Europe, India, or Australia, with the initial choice of procedure and type of third party potentially impacting the speed and success of the resolution. Given that dispute resolution procedures are embedded within culture (Brett, 2001), the reality of our global world requires that we begin to systematically explore how ADR procedures and their associated criteria apply across cultures and cultural boundaries. We argue that the assumptions for procedural recommendations from culturally bound research about how disputes should be settled may not hold across cultural context.

Different cultures have characteristic profiles that are manifested in norms, values, assumptions, institutions, and systems (Lytle, Brett, Barsness, Tinsley, & Janssens, 1995). In this paper, we focus on selected cultural dimensions that have been commonly used in previous research, such as individualism vs. collectivism (Hofstede, 1980; Schwartz, 1994; Triandis, 1995) and power distance or egalitarianism vs. hierarchy (Hofstede, 1980;

Schwartz & Bilsky, 1990). Although there are undoubtedly other dimensions of culture that are important and relevant, we have limited most of our discussion to several dimensions that have been the subject of empirical research and we believe particularly salient to ADR procedural preferences.

In this paper, we first describe a range of widely used and cited third party procedures and present examples of where and how these procedures are implemented across different cultural contexts. We then suggest that procedural choice is built upon preferences across a number of key criteria from the literature, and explore the potential impact of culture on evaluations of these criteria. We argue that a given procedure may be viewed idiosyncratically through the lens of a given set of cultural norms. Thus criteria cannot be assumed consistent across cultures (Tinsley, 2004).[1] We finish with a discussion of future directions for research and practice, emphasizing that procedural recommendations should be made carefully when the criteria for effectiveness and applicability are derived from US-centric research. This paper serves to stimulate thinking and research about how culture changes the implementation of ADR practices, emphasizing that there is not "one best choice" for third party procedures universal to the myriad cultures on our planet.

Types of Third Party Procedures

As the popularity of ADR has grown, so has the number of possible procedural choices. Below, we briefly review contractual third party procedures that are in relatively common use in business or community disputes as alternatives to going to court. Many of these procedures are also widely used for public-sector labor management relations where avoiding labor strikes is a high priority. While other procedures exist (10 different species of ADR, 1993), many of those are only slight variations in the procedures described here.

Mediation
Mediation is a procedure where a third party assists disputants in achieving a voluntary settlement. While mediation was once thought of as a procedure most frequently used in industrial relations and international relations disputes, its use has grown dramatically in the last twenty years. Mediation is found in a host of environments, including business disputes, legal disputes, labor management negotiation, environmental disputes, family and divorce proceedings, community disputes, landlord–tenant disputes,

bioethics and medical disputes, and international relations (Moore, 2003; Slaikeu, 1996; Dubler & Liebman, 2004). In addition, mediation in its many variations has been a traditional part of some culture's communities and societies for centuries (i.e., Rudin, 2002; Chan, 1997; Chia, Partridge, & Cong, 2004). Examples of mediation have been described or studied in such countries as China (Diamant, 2000; Wall & Blum, 1991), Korea (Woo, 1999; Kim, Wall, Sohn, & Kim, 1993), Malaysia (Mansor, 1998; Wall, Blum, & Callister, 1999), Thailand (Roongrengsuke & Chansuthus, 1998), Japan (Callister & Wall, 1997), and in cultural groups such as the Navajo Nation (Meyer, 2002) and Aboriginal Canadians (Rudin, 2002).

Kressel and Pruitt (1985) suggest that mediation frequently follows several "stages" where mediators focus on different sets of activities. "Stage" models of mediation suggest that mediators typically (1) begin with actions designed to establish a relationship between the disputants and the mediator (e.g., Kolb, 1985), followed by (2) an effort to build trust and cooperation between the disputants (e.g., Moore, 2003), and then (3) move to consideration of the substantive issues under dispute (e.g., Carnevale, 1986). It is in this last stage that proposals for settlement might be proposed by the third party and some pressure in the form of positive or negative incentives might be applied to convince parties to make concessions (see Moore, 2003 or Kressel & Pruitt, 1985, for examples of stage models of mediation). There is wide variation in how much attention mediators pay to building relationships vs. finding settlements (Bush & Folger, 1994). In truth, mediators can influence dispute settlement in many ways, for a mediator is free to choose the inclusion and sequence of stages that he or she wants in an effort to help the parties reach a settlement.

It is worth noting here that the procedure we call mediation is implemented in different ways by the "mediator" outside of the US cultural context. For example, in the traditional "mediation" processes used in rural China, the third party is often a village elder or state authority who controls the process and imposes a solution onto the parties (Peerenboom & Scanlon, 2005). As well, in traditional mediation in the Singaporean Malay community, the third party is a community elder or high status individual known to the parties who starts with airing of the problem or issues in the first stage followed by an administering of punishment if there is an admission of wrong-doing (Chia et al., 2004). Such examples show that not only is there variety in the methods that mediators use to implement mediations *within* cultures, but also differences in the role itself and its scope *across* some cultures.

Of the different methods of third party interaction, mediation is generally the least costly and the outcome often produces considerable disputant satisfaction in the US (Brett, Barsness, & Goldberg, 1996). Mediation can remove barriers to finding a solution and enhance the outcome of a negotiation (Lewicki, Saunders, & Minton, 1999). Voluntary settlement rates between 60 and 80% are typical (Brett, 2001; Kressel & Pruitt, 1989) though there is sometimes high variance in settlement rates. A variety of factors can influence whether mediation will be successful. Wall, Stark, and Standifer (2001) highlight three factors that can influence mediation success. First, contextual features within which dispute resolution is embedded play a role. This factor includes variables such as culture, the status of the mediator and the parties, the time that the mediation takes place, and the interdependence of the disputants. For example, in some cultures research has shown that there are norms for seeking the assistance of third parties to resolve (or help resolve) conflicts, and so disputants may feel comfortable and motivated to initiate third party interventions (i.e., Brett, 2001; Chan, 1998; Mansor, 1998; Callister & Wall, 1997).

Second, characteristics of the mediator matter (Kolb, 1985; Bowling & Hoffman, 2003). This factor includes the formal training of the mediator, the mediator's expertise in substantive issues in dispute (Arnold & O'Connor, 1999; Arnold, 2000), level of bias or neutrality (Conlon & Ross, 1993), the particular "approach" that the mediator takes to resolving the dispute (Ross, Conlon, & Lind, 1990), and the disputants' acceptance of the rules and norms that govern the mediation procedure (McGrath, 1966). Especially in more hierarchical or traditional cultural settings, the preferred mediator is often a well-respected community member or someone with high status (Rudin, 2002; Chia et al., 2004, Meyer, 2002).

Finally, characteristics of the disputants play a role in mediation success. The relative power of the disputants, the emotional hostility of the parties, and the trust or mistrust they feel toward each other all affect the mediation process (Coltri, 2004; Carnevale, Lim, & McLaughlin, 1989). For example, mediation is usually more effective when the conflict is mild (Carnevale & Pruitt, 1992); as the level of conflict increases, the probability of settlement decreases (Depner, Canata, & Ricci, 1994).

Although mediation may be effective in many disputes, particularly when the level of hostility is not extreme, it does not always produce a settlement, at least in cultures that abide by the "formal' definition of mediation where disputants have outcome control. The implementation of mediation in some cultural contexts rarely leads to impasses, because either the "mediator" has a mandate from the collective to subordinate the individual interests to those of the group, or in hierarchical cultures, a higher authority is expected to make the decision and disputants would be expected to comply (Meyer, 2002;

Woo, 1999; Chia et al., 2004; Rudin, 2002). In modern-day Korea, for example, mediators have decision-making authority in civil mediations with the power to hand down a decision if the parties do not agree or the mediator thinks the decision to which they have agreed is judged unreasonable (Woo, 1999). In this sense, such processes do not allow disputants real outcome control, in which case, mediation in some cultures is not necessarily the same as mediation by the formal definition consistent with a US-centric conceptualization. In cultures where mediators have a high degree of decision-making authority, a US-centric view of this process would more closely approximate arbitration, which we discuss next.

Arbitration

Arbitration is one of the most widely known and used third party procedures (Lewicki et al., 1999). In arbitration a third party holds a hearing at which time the disputants state their positions on the issues, call witnesses, and offer supporting evidence for their respective positions. After evaluating the evidence and considering other relevant factors, the third party issues a binding settlement (Elkouri, Elkouri, Goggin, & Volz, 1997). *Grievance arbitration* settles a very narrow dispute, most commonly over either the interpretation or the application of a specific clause in an existing contract within an ongoing contractual relationship. *Interest arbitration* is a broader focused form of arbitration (Olson & Rau, 1997), that does not focus on contract language interpretation and is the focus in our analysis (hereafter we simply refer to interest arbitration as "arbitration"). Arbitration is used to resolve small claims business disputes, consumer complaint disputes such as in the securities industry, contested insurance claims, and disputes over automobile "lemons" (cf. Kressel & Pruitt, 1989; Lewicki et al., 1999; Podd, 1997), in addition to its history of use in the labor relations field.

Whereas there is considerable literature surrounding the behavior of mediators, there is much less surrounding the behavior of arbitrators. This is because arbitrators do not usually exert as much influence over the *process* of dispute settlement as do mediators. Generally speaking, arbitrators do not engage in the various tactics used by mediators described previously. Compared with a mediator, an arbitrator more closely resembles a judge hearing evidence and casting a ruling. An arbitrator's focus is on producing an outcome, which the procedure always does, either through a binding settlement imposed by the arbitrator, or by the disputants who may reach an agreement on their own prior to the arbitrator's ruling. While arbitration always produces a settlement, it is not without problems. In low power distance, individualist cultures in particular, disputants may not be as likely to comply with or implement an involuntary decision against their individual interests if it is not legally or otherwise enforceable. Alternatively, in hierarchical, collectivist cultures, disputants may feel pressured to comply with the decision of a high status third party for the collective interest regardless of other explicit forms of enforcement.

Binding Arbitration
The above description of arbitration is most applicable to a version of the procedure known as conventional, or binding arbitration. In binding arbitration, the third party is free to craft any outcome that he or she perceives to be fair. While the assumption is that the final positions advocated by each party in the arbitration hearing phase may determine the range within which the arbitrator will determine the outcome, this is only an assumption. In fact, binding arbitration allows the third party considerable flexibility to make any decision, inside or outside the range suggested by the parties' proposals.

Binding arbitration is widely used across many different cultural contexts; for example, recent practitioner articles on arbitration discuss the procedure in Brazil (Pucci, 2005), China (Chan, 1997), Germany and Switzerland (Montaqu-Smith, 1998), New Zealand (McAndrew, 2003), and Mexico (Buckley, 2005) in addition to the United States. However, the implementation of binding arbitration across cultures may differ depending on the legal philosophies and cultural environments in which it exists. For example, in European countries, where civil law is the basis for proceedings, the arbitrator's role is to *decide* based on legislation, policies, and general principles, while in common law countries like the United States, the arbitrator's role is to *settle* based on precedent of previous cases and the merits of each party's case (Montaqu-Smith, 1998). In addition, German arbitrators have a specific expectation that they have the responsibility to find conciliation if at all possible between the parties (Montaqu-Smith, 1998).

Final Offer Arbitration
Several other forms of arbitration have grown out of conventional or binding arbitration. The first of these is final offer arbitration (FOA), sometimes called "baseball arbitration" in the United States because it is used for salary adjustments in that sport. FOA has also been used to set prices in the water sector in Chile to reduce the chance of the parties (the regulator and the regulated firm) submitting widely divergent offers (Montero, 2005), and for police compensation disputes in New Zealand to encourage voluntary settlements where the costs of strikes are high (McAndrew, 2003). In FOA,

disputing parties negotiate and then submit their "last, best offers" (final offer) to the arbitrator (Lewicki, Weiss, & Lewin, 1992; Feuille, 1975). The arbitrator then must choose which of the two offers will be imposed on the parties.

FOA was developed with the goal of encouraging parties to make more "reasonable" final offers than they sometimes do in binding arbitration. In *binding* arbitration parties may have an incentive to cease making concessions in the expectation that the arbitrator's outcome will "split" the difference between the two last offers, thereby resulting in a more advantageous outcome to the disputant. While the evidence is mixed, some research suggests that *final offer* arbitration does encourage parties to make more reasonable final offers, reducing what the literature refers to as the "chilling effect" (Hebdon, 1996; Feuille, 1975; Stokes, 1999). This reduction in the "chilling effect" is expected because each side has heightened concern over the potential costs incurred if the arbitrator rules for the other side – the risk of "losing it all" looms large.

A second objective of FOA is to encourage parties to find their own voluntary settlements rather than becoming dependent on the arbitrator to resolve disputes. Rather than risk the uncertainty inherent in FOA, disputants would be highly motivated to reach their own agreements, thereby reducing what the literature refers to as the "narcotic effect" (Olson, 1988). This is the rationale behind using FOA to settle labor disputes in some public sector organizations in approximately 10 states in the US (Crawford, 1981; Serrin, 1983). However, from the perspective of the third party, FOA provides little discretion to the third party, as their ability to craft what they feel is truly a fair settlement is severely constrained. All they can do is choose from one of the two outcomes.

FOA is particularly popular in the US, where a common-law system results in proceedings that tend to have a more aggressive approach (Montaqu-Smith, 1998). Perhaps because of the associated individualistic values as well as a focus on individual positions coupled with low uncertainty avoidance, we find that US disputants are likely to want to "bet" everything that they will "win" in the process. Therefore, they would rather put their own offers on the table than have the arbitrator "split the solution down the middle" as often happens in binding arbitration (Brams & Merrill, 1986). On the other hand, we do not find this procedure to be popular in European countries with a civil-law tradition, or in Asian countries where there is more concern for relationship or principles than "who gets what" (Montaqu-Smith, 1998).

Double Final Offer Arbitration

Double FOA (Van de Kragt, Stark, Notz, & Boschman, 1989) is similar to FOA in that the third party must choose from submitted final offers and cannot craft a unique settlement as in binding arbitration. In double FOA, however, the disputant submits two final offers of roughly equivalent value to the arbitrator; the opposing side does the same. The arbitrator then determines which side's offers are to be imposed and then the losing party chooses the final outcome (e.g., the arbitrator chooses the union's two offers and management chooses which of the two are implemented) from the two submitted by the successful party (Van de Kragt et al., 1989). A recent study found that one benefit of double FOA compared with both binding and regular FOA is that there is less of a "narcotic" effect in repeated bargaining situations, and therefore a higher degree of voluntary settlement (Dickinson, 2004). Another benefit of double FOA is that decision acceptance by the "losing" party should be higher, as they at least get to choose the form of the unpleasant outcome that they will have to endure. Therefore, this procedure might be especially appropriate in contexts (cultural or otherwise) where the need for face saving and desire to push forward individual interests is high, as then the losing party is able to appear to gain face by having some control and choice over the implemented outcome.

Night Baseball Arbitration

A third variation on FOA is the use of "night baseball" arbitration (Ross, 2005; Coltri, 2004). Here, the disputants put their final offer(s) in sealed envelopes. They present arguments, evidence, and expert testimony to support their unarticulated positions on the issues. This is so that the arbitrator can decide the issues based on the evidence without being distracted by the formal positions taken by each side (10 different species of ADR, Nov./Dec. 1993, p. 19). The arbitrator then adjourns to create a non-binding opinion; because the opinion is not limited to any specific proposals, it is, in this sense, like binding arbitration. Next, the arbitrator opens the two envelopes containing the final offers and compares the offers with his or her own non-binding opinion. The final offer that is closest to the arbitrator's own opinion is selected and becomes the binding agreement. Although less widespread than FOA, this procedure has been used in insurance disputes (e.g., medical malpractice claims), personal injury disputes, and division of ownership of intellectual property disputes (Montaqu-Smith, 1998), often where only one – generally a distributive – issue is involved (e.g., how much money should be paid).

Final Offer Arbitration by Issue vs. Package

A final note of complexity to add to these forms of FOA is that one can also decide whether to use the final offers of the parties "by issue" vs. final offer "by package". In final offer by package (or double final offer by package or night baseball by package), the third party is constrained to picking one side's entire set of offers across all issues in dispute. In final offer by issue, the arbitrator can pick some offers made by each disputant, selecting, for example, management's final offer on salary adjustments but the union's final offer on health care co-payments. A "final offer by package" procedure can be difficult to implement, as parties can put in attractive solutions on a key issue or issues to lure the arbitrator to their solution, but then also include more extreme or "unfair" solutions to other issues (Zack, 2003). Therefore, some practitioners suggest that FOA and its derivatives are more fairly used across single issues than for packages (Zack, 2003).

Fact Finding

This procedure has historically been used in some states in the US (e.g., Iowa) for public-sector labor contract negotiations. Here, a third party or panel of third parties holds hearings to identify the issues and the positions of the parties, resulting in a non-binding but formal recommendation that may guide disputants as to what an arbitrated settlement might look like (Dickinson & Hunnicutt, 2005). The fact finders may employ mediation tactics, or they may function more like a board of inquiry. Typically, the fact finders will issue a report in which the members of the panel recommend a settlement for the dispute (Olson, 1988; Schneider, 1988). This report may go only to the parties themselves (providing a "prominent solution" for continuing bilateral negotiations), or it may also go to an external decision maker (e.g., a state legislature's budget committee for public-sector labor disputes). A recent study has shown that fact-finding as a process prior to binding arbitration increases the rate of voluntary negotiated settlements relative to the use of binding arbitration alone, as the non-binding recommendation serves as a focal point for the disputants on which they anchor (Dickinson & Hunnicutt, 2005). These authors suggest that the formalized suggestion or explicit recommendation as a preliminary step to any ADR procedure may be a key element to encouraging voluntary settlements.

Comparing this focal point element of fact finding with mediation procedures brings into consideration an interesting point. Mediators may also serve a similar function of establishing focal points by suggesting possible agreements. Recall that mediators have wide latitude in the stages they include and the sequence of those stages. Thus, we may view fact finding as an ADR method in a stand-alone fashion, or we may see it as a component of mediation.

Mediation-Arbitration

Mediation-arbitration (hereafter called "med-arb") consists of (1) mediation, followed by (2) arbitration if mediation fails to secure an agreement by a predetermined deadline (Ross & Conlon, 2000). The same third party serves as both mediator and arbitrator, and may use either binding or final-offer forms of arbitration (Kagel, 1976; Brewer & Mills, 1999). The procedure is incremental: only if mediation fails to produce an agreement does the arbitration phase occur, which culminates with the third party imposing a binding settlement on the parties. This temporal arrangement matches the suggestions of many scholars (e.g., Ury, Brett, & Goldberg, 1988) who argue that dispute resolution procedures should be arranged in a "low-to-high-cost sequence" for the users (pp. 62–63). Others have also suggested that mediation precede arbitration because it removes less control over the ultimate outcome from the disputants (e.g., Starke & Notz, 1981). Finally, a field experiment comparing med-arb with straight mediation found that med-arb led disputants to be less hostile and more problem-solving oriented in their behavior, though there was no difference in voluntary (mediated) settlement rates (McGillicuddy, Welton, & Pruitt, 1987). In the California Nurses Association collective bargaining in 1971, for example, med-arb was used to avert a strike by keeping communications on track and focusing parties on problem-solving (Polland, 1973).

There are examples of the med-arb procedure across a variety of cultural contexts. In civil law-oriented countries such as Germany and Switzerland, med-arb fits with the expectation that an arbitrator will first try to find conciliation, and then decide on the appropriate way to apply laws, rules, legislation, or principles (Montaqu-Smith, 1998). The China International and Economic Trade Arbitration Commission has chosen a single-third party med-arb procedure to deal with foreign related construction disputes, reflecting the Chinese preference to first try to resolve disputes through amicable mechanisms and increased understanding before the third party hands down a binding decision (Chan, 1997). In civil mediation procedures in Korea, the court appoints a mediator, who then has decision-making authority if he/she thinks the decision is not reasonable or the parties cannot come to agreement (Woo, 1999). The lines between mediation and arbitration blur in some cultural environments, as mediation sometimes looks like arbitration, and arbitration sometimes looks like mediation. That is, a high status third party may take a very directive and potentially controlling role in resolving disputes while simultaneously taking care to maintain harmony and minimize social disruption along the way to resolution.

Arbitration-Mediation

A second hybrid procedure, arbitration-mediation (hereafter called "arb-med"), consists of three phases. In phase one, the third party holds an arbitration hearing. At the end of this phase, the third party makes a decision, which is placed in a sealed envelope and is not revealed to the parties. The second phase consists of mediation. Only if mediation fails to produce a voluntary agreement by a specified deadline do the parties enter the third phase, called the ruling phase. Here, the third party removes the ruling from the envelope and reveals the binding ruling to the disputants (Cobbledick, 1992; Robertson, 1991). To assure that the envelope contains the original ruling and not a later ruling (e.g., a ruling created after the mediation phase), the third party may ask each side to sign the envelope across the seal at the beginning of mediation. The benefits of arb-med are around time and the maintenance of relationships. Arb-med is efficient with a rapid, binding arbitration phase at the beginning, and then sets a deadline for how long the mediation phase can last. Therefore, parties are not motivated to delay and posture, as any time they waste means that the arbitrator's decision will be used rather than their own. As well, it reduces the risk of soured relations that can sometimes happen in med-arb if the initial mediation phase becomes contentious and fails (Zack, 2003).

The arb-med procedure has been used in particularly difficult union–management disputes in the automotive and steel industries (in South Africa) and police and firefighter disputes (in the US), and is suggested as a possible solution to airline contract disputes in the US, where avoiding soured relations that can result from lengthy mediation processes is critical (Zack, 2003). A recent empirical study supports these examples, finding that arb-med was effective in resolving some of the most difficult disputes and led to more settlements in the mediation phase than did med-arb (Conlon, Moon, & Ng, 2002). Thus, if a critical goal is to create conditions that lead disputants to resolve their own disputes, arb-med may be an interesting advance, and may even be well suited to handling particularly difficult disputes.

CRITERIA FOR EVALUATING THIRD PARTY PROCEDURES

To compare third party procedures in their application and appropriateness for any given dispute, we need an understanding of them across a meaningful set of criteria to appreciate similarities and differences. There are also other practical reasons for clearly defined criteria; agencies are accountable to clients or funding agencies and individual third parties may be given a performance evaluation based on particular criteria. In addition, we must recognize that particular procedures are not defined the same way and might be implemented differently across cultures, making direct comparisons of procedures challenging. This paper builds on existing literature (e.g., Lissak & Sheppard, 1983; Meyer, Gemmell, & Irving, 1997; Sheppard, 1983, 1984; Thomas, Jamieson, & Moore, 1978; Thomas, 1992) to evaluate criteria arranged into four categories or sets: process criteria, settlement criteria, issue criteria, and relationship criteria. Table 1 categorizes the procedures detailed in the previous section according to these criteria. We then consider several specific dimensions of each category of criteria and discuss how these dimensions may be influenced by cultural factors.[2] We conclude each section with propositions.

Process Criteria

Our first criteria deals with the dispute-resolution *process*: the typical methods used by the third party to direct how the disputants, third party, and parties related to the dispute interact. Although there are many potential dimensions related to this criteria, we focus on three dimensions, outlined below.

Does the Third Party Exercise Process Control?
Building on the classic organizing framework of procedures articulated by Thibaut and Walker (1975), process control refers to control over the development, presentation, and voicing of information that potentially can influence the outcome of the dispute. Does the third party intervene in how the disputants present evidence and discuss the issues (e.g., separating the parties, employing role reversal, playing devil's advocate), or does the third party relinquish such process control to the parties themselves (Thibaut & Walker, 1975, 1978; Sheppard, 1983; Lewicki & Sheppard, 1985)? Previous research has suggested that process control is important because it influences

Table 1. Categorizing Third Party Procedures by Process, Settlement, Issue, and Relationship Criteria.

	Mediation	Arbitration	Final Offer	Double FOA	Night Baseball	Fact-Finding	Med-Arb	Arb-Med
Process criteria								
Does the third party use process control	Yes, expected	Limited	Limited	Limited	Limited	Yes, expected	Yes then limited	Limited then Yes
Suggest settlements	Sometimes (dealmakers)	Unusual	Unusual	Unusual	Unusual	Yes	Yes then no	No then yes
Transaction costs	Moderate	Low	Low	Moderate	Moderate	High	Moderate	High
Settlement criteria								
Must third party determine settlement?	No	Yes	Yes	Yes	Yes	No	Sometimes	Sometimes
Is voluntary settlement reached?	Yes	No	No	No	No	Yes	Sometimes	Sometimes
Settlement timing	N/A	Late	Late	Late	Late	N/A	Late	Early
Probability of integrative settlement	High	Low	Lowest	Low	Low	Moderate	High (med only)	High (med only)

Discretion over settlement character	N/A	High	Limited – choose from two offers	Very limited – choose winning side	Limited – choose from two offers	N/A	Depends on the form of arbitration	Depends on the form of arbitration
Can third party reject voluntary settlement	No	No	No	No	No	No	No	Yes, if agreement is incomplete
Speed of settlement	Slow	Fast	Fast	Moderate	Moderate	Slow	Variable	Slow
Subjective success measures	Very high	High	Moderate	Moderate	Moderate	Low	Very high	Moderate
Issue-related criteria								
Issue clarification	Yes	No	No	No	No	Yes	Some	Yes
Chilling effect	Yes	No	Yes	Yes	Yes	No	Yes	Yes
Narcotic effect	No	No	Yes	Yes	Yes	No	Yes	Yes
Relationship criteria								
Relationship enhanced?	Yes	No	No	No	No	No	No	No
Commitment to implement settlement	Yes	No	No	Yes	No	No	Yes	Yes

perceptions of procedural justice: when parties are allowed voice, when the disputants are treated with dignity and respect, and when processes are considered "fair", there is greater compliance with decisions (Folger, 1977; Lind, Lissak, & Conlon, 1983).

While mediators have the choice to exert little to no control over the process (an inaction strategy, Carnevale, 1986), they more often are described as having high process control and no decision control (ability to impose a settlement upon the disputants (Thibaut & Walker, 1975). Arbitrators (in all types of arbitration), on the other hand, exercise more limited process intervention but have considerable control over the outcome (Sheppard, 1984). In fact, arbitrators are typically reticent to exert much control over the process, instead allowing the participants to present their cases as they see fit. Among the hybrid procedures (med-arb and arb-med), the level of process control changes over time depending on the stage of the procedure being implemented. Thus, hybrid procedures include stages with different levels of process intervention from the third party.

Existing US research suggests that with other factors being equal, parties generally prefer to control the process themselves, especially when they cannot control the outcome. For example, litigants usually prefer adversarial adjudication procedures (where the disputants' exercise greater process control) over inquisitorial adjudication procedures (where the third party exercises greater process control) as more just (Walker, LaTour, Lind, & Thibaut, 1974; LaTour, 1978). However, disputant preferences for high levels of process control may not generalize across all cultural contexts. While there is some evidence at an abstract level that the concern for process control is pan-cultural (Lind, Erickson, Friedland, & Dickenberger, 1978; Leung, Au, Fernandez-Dols, & Iwawaki, 1992; Leung, 1987), cultural values or expectancies around behavioral strategies might inhibit the observed preferences for process control in real dispute environments (Lind & Early, 1992; Bond, Leung, & Schwartz, 1992; Morris & Leung, 2000).

For example, in individualist and egalitarian cultures, there may be expectations around the rights of every individual to "have their say" and assert their own set of individual interests, with numerous US-based studies finding a preference for procedures that allow disputants voice (e.g., Lind & Tyler, 1988). In collectivist cultures, however, a focus on individual interests in the first place may be counter to the preferences of each individual who sees him or herself as a member of a collective (Leung & Tong, 2004). Such disputants might not feel it is appropriate or preferable to put their own individual interests forward if there is the chance of conflicting with the collective interest. Even when representing a group within the collective, there still might be a hesitation to "having a say" because of potential conflicts with the broader set of community interests. In collectivist cultures, we suggest that there may be some preference for process control to rest with a respected third party who has the mandate to "do the right thing" with respect not only to the individuals concerned, but to the broader collective interests of the community or relevant stakeholders. Such a third party may not be close to the classic characterization of third party as a disinterested neutral. Interestingly, there is some evidence that in some collectivist cultures, there may be a preference for more power-based or directive dispute resolution procedures (i.e., that a high status or authoritative third party take control over the process or decision) for the purpose of avoiding direct discussion of sensitive issues and minimizing the social disruption of a drawn-out confrontational dispute process (Leung, 1997; Tinsley, 1997; Yang, 1993).

While we may see cultures with more egalitarian values encourage or allow a more open exchange of information and opinions to the third party within and across status lines (Tinsley, 2004), low status individuals in cultures with less egalitarian values may not feel comfortable with high levels of process control. In more hierarchical cultures, control over the process of dispute resolution may be viewed as the responsibility of those in a higher position, or those with more knowledge or information, therefore maintaining established hierarchies and power during the dispute resolution process (Leung & Stephan, 1998). In general, cultures high in power distance, where those of lower status accept unequal social conditions, are associated with greater tolerance of harsh treatment by authorities (James, 1993).

We might expect that desire for process control might also vary according to disputants' level of comfort with direct confrontation in their cultural context: to "speak up", or at least to "speak up" without negative consequences. For example, evidence for the relationship between having voice and judgments of procedural fairness have been found in the United States, West Germany, France, and Great Britain (Lind et al., 1978). As well, there are greater preferences for direct information sharing in low context culture disputes and negotiations, while those from high context cultures prefer indirect methods of influencing outcomes (Adair, Okumura, & Brett, 2001; Brett, 2001). Furthermore, those who fear negative consequences in their cultural contexts (whether societal, organizational, or familial) may have little desire to directly air their own opinions or present their own evidence. In such cultural environments that discourage open airing of dissenting opinions, disputants, even when feeling strongly about an issue, may not choose to openly share information about it.

Does the Third Party Offer Suggestions, such as Possible Settlements?
Suggesting settlements is a specific type of "content control" where "the intervening party attempts to determine *what* is to be discussed..." (Sheppard, 1983, p. 200). To the extent that the suggestions are acceptable to each disputant, this criterion has some similarity with what Sheppard (1984, p. 169) describes as "level of intervener process neutrality" in that the suggestions may be perceived on a continuum from being biased against a disputant, to even handed, to biased in favor of the disputant (Arad & Carnevale, 1994; Conlon & Ross, 1993). Kolb (1985) observes that some mediators, whether in the mediation process or the mediation stages of the med-arb or arb-med procedures, are "Dealmakers" who tend to make such suggestions, whereas others, whom she calls "Orchestrators", do not. She reports that Dealmakers tend to be found in public sector labor relations where strikes are usually illegal, whereas Orchestrators tend to be found in the private sector.

Fact finders more consistently recommend settlements as part of their role. These recommendations often carry substantial weight with the parties and with others who may be in a position to provide outcomes (e.g., a state legislature). However, fact finders do not have any decision control, and only serve to inform parties of the potential outcome of some future procedure if they choose to embark on it. Arbitrators in all forms of arbitration, on the other hand, do not generally provide any recommendations or offer suggestions, as their role is to allow disputants to present evidence as they wish; the third party then uses this information to make a decision.

Preferences for third party style in terms of content control may differ across cultures. In collectivist cultures, there may be expectations that the third party has a mandate to consider the wider set of community or organizational interests, and therefore, would be expected to consider a larger problem than that presented by each individual disputant (Brett, 2001). Therefore, there may be a higher preference for the third party in a collectivist culture to take on a more directive or active role in finding solutions than in a more individualistic culture. In more egalitarian cultures, we may find that while third party suggestions for settlement are an acceptable part of the dispute resolution procedure if the settlement suggestions are perceived as fair by both parties (Conlon & Ross, 1993, 1997), disputants would be comfortable to take an active part in the creation of ideas for settlement, and may be more committed to the solution if they felt they took part in creating it (Pruitt, 1981). In hierarchical cultures, however, we may find that lower status disputants would expect the third party as the "expert" or "authority figure" to take control of the situation and make suggestions for settlement or to actually dictate a resolution (Leung & Stephan, 1998). In fact, disputants in this situation might actually feel that the third party was "shirking" their responsibility if disputants were asked to come up with their own solutions. There is evidence that disputants in hierarchical cultures prefer the early involvement of a third party in dealing with conflicts rather than trying to resolve them on their own (e.g., Brett, 2001), where disputants may be more satisfied and committed to a solution if they themselves have had a major part in creating it (Pruitt, 1981).

Transaction Costs of the Procedure

Some procedures require more time and resources (e.g., money) for both disputants and the third party. Brett et al. (1996) report that participants believe that mediation is less expensive than adjudication or arbitration. While arbitration costs are typically low (certainly lower than adjudication), they may be somewhat higher for double FOA (where the third party must spend extra time in order to evaluate *four* proposals) and for night baseball arbitration (where the third party must take the time to write a non-binding decision and then take additional time to compare it with each side's offer and select a winner). Med-arb may be, on average, cheaper than arb-med because some (if not most) cases will settle in the mediation phase. However, with arb-med, the costs of an arbitration hearing must be borne even if the parties settle in mediation, because the arbitration hearing precedes mediation. Fact-finding can occur before any of the formalized procedures as a preliminary step to encourage parties to come up with a voluntary agreement. In this sense, if another procedure follows fact-finding, additional costs must be considered for the subsequent procedure. If, however, the fact-finding recommendation dissuades parties from engaging in a subsequent procedure and they find a voluntary settlement, the costs of the additional procedure are avoided.

If one takes the position that time is money (e.g., third parties often charge by the hour), third party procedures that lead to a speedy resolution of the dispute will be less costly, and preferred, to more costly procedures. But, the "time is money" view of the world is likely to be more of a Western value. In collectivist cultures, for example, third parties and disputants might feel that a significant investment in time is well worth the maintenance of harmony, and in some very delicate situations, third parties may have a preference to spend more time making sure that disputants are treated well, that the relationship between them is maintained or improved, or that the underlying drivers of the dispute are addressed and resolved.[3]

Even within the US, some disputes may benefit from a heightened sensitivity to relationship and the concomitant time demands. In instances where a transaction dispute is embedded within a valued, ongoing relationship, investment of time and resources in the short term can pay dividends over a longer term in the form of cooperative behavior and trust. Conversely, even in collectivist cultures, where the focus on relationships are heightened (compared with individualist cultures), some one-off transactions may benefit from a greater focus on time-cost savings at the expense of the relationship.

This discussion of dimensions related to process criteria and the cultural implications of these dimensions for third party procedures leads to the following testable propositions.

Proposition 1. Third parties in egalitarian and individualist cultures will impose less pressure on disputants and make fewer suggestions for settlement during mediation procedures, relative to third parties in hierarchical and collectivist cultures.

Proposition 2. Transaction costs (e.g., time, money) will be of greater importance to disputants from egalitarian and individualistic cultures, compared with disputants from hierarchical and collectivist cultures. However, within egalitarian and individualistic cultures, transaction cost importance will also be dependent on expectations of future interaction among disputants. Thus, we expect to see a higher degree of variance in the importance of transaction costs among egalitarian and individualistic cultures, as compared with hierarchical or collectivist cultures.

Proposition 3. Procedures that allow individuals to have voice and to take part in generating the solutions will be perceived more favorably in egalitarian and individualist cultures, as compared with hierarchical and collectivist cultures.

Settlement Criteria

Certainty of Settlement

In some dispute situations, an important criterion for procedural choice is whether or not a settlement is guaranteed. Fact-finding, for example, does not seek to generate a resolution or agreement but rather seeks an opinion on the likely outcome if there were to be a subsequent procedure. In fact, a major objective of the fact-finding process is to encourage parties to find their own voluntary agreement in order to avoid a potentially unattractive imposed outcome. Mediators, on the other hand, have the objective to facilitate parties to generate agreements, but since they do not have decision control, outcomes are voluntary and therefore not always certain. Mediators also have the discretion to end their involvement in a dispute at any time, regardless of whether a solution was forthcoming or not, if they feel the parties are not bargaining in good faith. Terminating their involvement may be one of the mediator's key sources of power that can put considerable pressure on one or both parties in a dispute. Arbitrators, regardless of the form of arbitration, are contractually engaged to resolve a dispute and cannot decide they no longer want to be involved. Certainty of an outcome therefore, is highest for the different forms of binding and FOA arbitration procedures.

Certainly within cultures, preferences around certainty for settlement would vary across different situations and disputes. Acknowledging this variance within culture, there still may be cultural differences on preference for guaranteed outcomes as opposed to less certain outcomes reflecting cultural values around propensity for risk or uncertainty avoidance.

Is a voluntary agreement reached? Some procedures (e.g., arbitration) specify that the third party is required to fashion and impose a settlement, whereas others (e.g., mediation and fact-finding) encourage voluntary agreement and allow participants to fashion that solution in whatever way they wish (Conlon, 1988). For some disputants, this dimension is crucial to determining procedural choice (Pierce, Pruitt, & Czaja, 1993). Yet, even with arbitration or the hybrid procedures, it is possible for *voluntary* agreements to be reached before a third party generated solution is imposed. Just as judges sometimes mediate in their chambers, some arbitrators will, upon rare occasion, mediate. Arbitrators sometimes allow the parties to have "one last chance" to negotiate privately prior to hearing the third party's decision. Thus, one relevant dimension that must be considered when comparing various third party procedures is whether a dispute is settled voluntarily vs. whether the decision is imposed by a third party (Carnevale et al., 1989).

With all other factors being equal, in some cultures (perhaps those with individualist and egalitarian values) it is generally assumed that procedures where the parties voluntarily resolve conflicts are better (or are at least perceived more favorably by disputants) than those where a decision is imposed by the third party (Kressel & Pruitt, 1989; Brett & Goldberg, 1983). We might find in hierarchical and collectivist cultures, however, there is less desire for voluntary resolution, as disputants might be comfortable agreeing to an imposed settlement because it is designed to meet the needs of the group – especially if a high status third party is responsible for making the decision. Furthermore, those "lower" in the hierarchy would actively avoid taking part in the creation of a settlement, with the assumption that those of higher position or status have the responsibility, knowledge, or skill to do so. In some cases, we might even imagine a great resistance to lower status individuals being forced to participate in solution generation. In one author's own consulting experiences in China, lower status workers were often highly resistant to resolving any problems they considered "manager's work" and did not want the responsibility for decisions (perhaps not to be blamed in the future if things went wrong). This makes the implementation of Western "empowerment" and "participation" initiatives difficult.

Probability of an Integrative Settlement

If a settlement is reached, whether by voluntary agreement or by third party decision, then the nature of that settlement must be considered. Simply securing a settlement for the sake of having a settlement may result in relatively poor outcomes for one or all of the disputants. Some procedures may lend themselves to high "quantity and quality of facts, ideas, or arguments elicited" (Sheppard, 1984, p. 169), which in turn leads to finding integrative ("win-win") agreements. Integrative agreements typically involve creative problem solving and/or combining several issues to fashion a "package deal". Mediation is often identified as a procedure that facilitates the production of integrative agreements that are "mutually beneficial", "lasting", and high in "overall success" (Carnevale et al., 1989; Carnevale & Henry, 1989; Carnevale & Pruitt, 1992). Similarly, med-arb and arb-med have been shown to promote integrative problem-solving in their respective mediation phases (Conlon et al., 2002; McGillicuddy et al., 1987). While fact-finding in itself does not facilitate agreements directly, it encourages subsequent discussions that can lead to voluntary integrative solutions via the "focal point" mechanism discussed earlier.

Integrative agreements often have objectively higher payoffs than compromises, where issues are frequently "split down the middle". Conventional arbitration is often criticized for producing such compromises. While binding arbitrators do have the power to impose integrative agreements on disputants, their decisions are usually limited by the positions, perspectives, and offers the disputants choose to present, and often result in the arbitrator simply choosing a middle ground (Feuille, 1975). In FOA, night baseball, and double FOA, disputants have the incentive to offer something just slightly more reasonable than the other side so that their position may "win" in the eyes of the arbitrator. Such motivation also does not promote integrative "win-win" agreements.

Culture complicates the desire for integrative outcomes as well, because in traditional negotiation and dispute resolution research, integration is judged solely by the individual interests of those directly involved in the dispute, and the maximization of individual interests is considered an important and valid pursuit (Brett, 2001). It is difficult if not impossible to judge the level of integration with broader community or organizational interests, which in some cases may not directly involve the individual level interests in any individual dispute. In collectivist cultures, the primary concern may be a less definable set of collective interests that is not easily "integrated" by the sharing of disputant's individual level interests, and measurement may be further complicated by the potential difference between short term maximization of interests and longer term welfare of a greater collective (Tinsley, 1997, 2001). Furthermore, there may be a desire to maintain social harmony and therefore not actually engage in a detailed, potentially confrontational process to elicit individual interests and then continue to search for integration. In this case, social harmony is the greater level interest that is maximized rather than the individual level interests.

One would expect that integration of individual level interests would be desirable in low power distance or egalitarian cultures, where there is an underlying assumption that individual level interests are all equally important and legitimate as a basis for resolution (Tinsley, 2004). But, in cultures where there are established hierarchies and the distribution of resources is not expected to be equal, there may be no overt objective to maximize the welfare of the lower status individual in the conflict. This is because a lower status individual's interests may be considered less important, and therefore not to be taken into consideration equally with interests of a higher status individual.

Discretion over Settlement Character
A third party in binding arbitration in principle has the power to fashion any decision as s/he sees fit. A third party in FOA or night baseball has that power curtailed by the rules of the procedure, because the third party must select between the disputants' proposals (Coltri, 2004). From the third party's perspective, a procedure is considered superior to the extent that a third party has the discretion to tailor the decision to fit what s/he thinks will best serve the parties' needs. It is possible, however, in highly rule-oriented cultures, that deference to a particular rule or standard is seen as the most

legitimate basis on which to decide the solution to a dispute. For example, Germanic cultures tend to value explicit contracting and egalitarianism (Tinsley, 2001), and resolution by a particular rule may be preferred to the third party having individual discretion to decide according to individual interests. For in such cultures, individual interests are not necessarily paramount, it is the abstract, generalized principles or the maintenance of an important principle that takes precedence (Montaqu-Smith, 1998).

Third Party Rejection of Voluntary Settlements

Some contractual third party procedures do not allow for the rejection of voluntary settlements between the two disputants; indeed, for many procedures such as mediation or fact-finding, voluntary agreements are the goal. In some procedures, however, we may find that the third party has the prerogative to reject an unacceptable or incomplete voluntary agreement. For example, in arb-med or med-arb, the third party can reject an incomplete settlement and impose an arbitrated decision. We anticipate that disputants in individualist, egalitarian cultures may feel frustrated and offended when their voluntary agreements are overruled by a third party, even if the third party's solution is objectively better (i.e., has higher payoffs to both sides; is more integrative).

In collectivist cultures, however, we may find as we argued for process control above, that voluntary agreements are not as sought after as in individualist cultures. A collectivist disputant might not be frustrated or offended if the third party imposes a solution that is designed to attend to the interests of a broader collective, because collectivists are more likely to allow the subjugation of their individual interests to that of the group (Brett, 2001). In fact, such a decision might be welcomed, with disputants knowing that the solution has attended to more interests than just their own.

Similarly, disputants from more hierarchical cultures may expect that the third party will take responsibility to make a decision, regardless of what the disputants suggest in terms of outcomes (if they suggest anything at all). There would be the perception that a higher status third party "knows best" or has more knowledge than lower status others. In some cultures, in fact, we might expect that the third party's primary purpose would be to come up with solutions as the disputants may not feel comfortable to suggest any themselves.

Furthermore, we might expect that in rule bound cultures, it could be offensive to go outside the bounds of accepted and legitimate rules or standards to pursue individual level interests (Tinsley, 2004). If the third party determines that the disputants' suggested outcome does not reflect the accepted principles, they may be willing to forsake their own personal short-term gain to make sure that the principle is upheld fairly and consistently within the collective.

Speed or Timing of the Determined Settlements
In some procedural contexts, the third party has the flexibility to allow a settlement to occur (or can dictate a settlement) at any time in the process; for others, the third party is constrained by rules or expectations as to when s/he must render a binding decision. While more lengthy procedures may have certain advantages (e.g., issues may be examined thoroughly, the parties make concessions, or negotiate their own settlement), generally when people are in conflict, existing research shows that they want efficiency – a speedy resolution to their dispute (Sheppard, 1984). In some contexts the third party has also been found to be under some pressure to reach a speedy settlement (Elangovan, 1995). While most ADR procedures are more efficient and faster than going to court, mediation and fact finding in general are comparatively slower than the different forms of arbitration.

Expectations and constraints around speed of settlement, however, are not always consistent within procedure, whether mediation, fact finding, or the different forms of arbitration. For example, there may be a med-arb procedure in one instance that does not limit the time spent during the mediation phase, and only moves into the arbitration phase if all attempts at voluntary agreement are exhausted. Alternatively, other implementations of the procedure may have specific expectations around how much time is allowed for the mediation phase and then disputants are forced into the arbitration phase whether or not they are ready. Perhaps one procedure that has more consistency is the arb-med procedure, where most of the second mediation phases have specific deadlines before the initial arbitrated decision is imposed.

The perception that "time is money" is particularly strong in the US, where efficiency of dispute processes (but allowing enough time for the parties to voice their individual level interests) is an important criteria for the selection of procedures. In collectivist cultures, a different factor may drive the desire for disputes to be settled quickly and quietly: the desire for there to be a minimum social disruption to harmony (Leung 1997; Tinsley, 1997). In individualist cultures where the satisfaction of individual interests is paramount, disputants will prefer to have third party decisions rendered late because that allows the parties the maximum opportunity to present evidence (and perhaps to engage in impression management tactics) to influence the outcome (Conlon & Fasolo, 1990). However, in collectivist cultures, it is possible that rendering a decision quickly may help to prevent or avoid social disruption and maintain harmony (Tinsley, 1997; Leung, 1997). Furthermore, in cultures where saving face is a critical issue, short, quick processes and settlements may be preferable as not to expose either of the parties to a public exposure of possible wrongdoings or mistakes that could compromise personal reputations.

In other cultural contexts, however; other values may take precedence, making a longer, more thoughtful dispute process preferred in certain situations. Cultures where disputants are particularly concerned about the potential loss of face that can occur when disputes are handled carelessly may prefer a more thoughtful and slow procedure – for if great care is taken in the resolution of a dispute, the chance of offending someone by making a careless mistake and causing the loss of face is decreased.

Subjective Measures of Success

This dimension is maximized if the disputants (and/or their constituents) are satisfied with the procedure and its outcomes and see both the procedure and outcomes as fair and successful (Thomas et al., 1978; Meyer et al., 1997).[4] While one can conceptually distinguish procedural satisfaction from procedural fairness (Sheppard, 1984), these two dimensions are often highly correlated and have similar consequences: people do not want to use procedures that they do not like or do not see as fair (Lind et al., 1978; Sheppard, 1985).

The literature taking a functionalist view of justice suggests that there is a universal concern for justice (Leung & Tong, 2004; Leung & Stephan, 1998) and that justice rules are pan-cultural (Morris & Leung, 2000). The importance or salience of different rules and the way in which they are implemented, however, has been suggested to vary significantly across cultures (Morris & Leung, 2000). While procedural fairness and satisfaction may be important across cultures, we may find different types of procedures or procedural criteria are perceived as fair or satisfactory within a cultural group.

All other things being equal, a procedure is considered superior if the disputants' believe that the procedure is fair and satisfactory (Carnevale et al., 1989), that is, according to whatever criteria drive perceptions of fairness and satisfaction. For example, in highly hierarchical cultures, perceptions of what is "fair" to a lower status individual might be very different from what is considered "fair" from the perspective of a higher status individual. Lower status individuals in such cultures have been found to be highly tolerant of harsh treatment by authorities (James, 1993), and may not have expectations for equal treatment. This is not to say, however, that disputants would prefer harsh treatment, but that they might not consider it "unfair".

The following propositions are suggested by our review of different dimensions of settlement criteria:

Proposition 4. Procedures that allow for outcome control and voluntary agreement by disputants will be seen as more favorable by disputants in egalitarian and individualist cultures, as compared with disputants in hierarchical and collectivist cultures.

Proposition 5. Procedures that give the third party latitude in considering collective interests, and broad, longer term impacts will be viewed as less favorable in egalitarian and individualist cultures, as compared with hierarchical and collectivist cultures.

Proposition 6. Third parties who reject or abrogate settlements achieved by disputants will be perceived more negatively by disputants in egalitarian and individualist cultures, as compared with disputants in hierarchical and collectivist cultures.

Proposition 7. Procedures which allow for greater certainty in terms of settlement (as opposed to impasse) will be seen as less favorable in egalitarian and individualist cultures, as compared with hierarchical and collectivist cultures.

Proposition 8. Procedures which allow for faster resolutions (settlements) will be seen as less favorable in egalitarian and individualist cultures, as compared with hierarchical and collectivist cultures.

Issue-Related Criteria

Clarification of the Issues

When there is no settlement, issue-related criteria may be relevant for assessing the success of a third party intervention. People in dispute often define issues (and positions on the issues) differently and fail to recognize such differences. Sometimes underlying issues heighten the conflict, yet these remain unspoken and unexplored (Sheppard, 1984). A third party can play a valuable role in clarifying the issues for the parties. Mediation and, to a lesser extent, fact finding offer a real possibility of clarifying the issues for the parties (and perhaps identifying underlying issues that might not be otherwise discussed). Similarly, both hybrid procedures (med-arb, arb-med) afford an opportunity to clarify the issues and explore underlying issues in the mediation phase. By contrast, arbitration (in all of its forms) tends to take the issues and positions at face value just as the parties present them.

Again, this dimension might be viewed through different lenses across cultures. While some disputants might prefer a procedure where they individually have greater understanding, input and control in the process or outcomes, disputants from other cultures may not value this. For example, if individuals in a collective culture do not want to disrupt social harmony, they may not spend that much time discussing the underlying reasons for the dispute or wish to get into detail to clarify the underlying issues. It is possible that in some cases, they may feel more comfort with simply being dictated a solution that is judged to be good for the collective and not want to be confronted with unpleasant and potentially disruptive discussions. Alternately, in high power distance cultures where disputants feel the responsibility of the third party is to craft a solution, they may feel perfectly comfortable to trust that the third party is knowledgeable and will do the right thing. They may not place a high priority on detailed understanding of the dispute, but simply want a solution to be dictated (Tinsley, 1998).

The Chilling Effect

A third party may also help the disputants make concessions on unresolved issues. If the disputants were unable to resolve all of their issues in dispute on their own, and the third party was able to help them do so, then the third party has played a valuable role. The "distance in positions is narrowed" (Carnevale et al., 1989, p. 227) and the parties are objectively closer to an agreement than they were before. Subjectively, such concessions may "build momentum" for later discussion and agreement. Indeed, research suggests that this "face-saving" capacity is one of the strengths of mediation, whether as a stand alone procedure or as a phase in one of the hybrid procedures (Pruitt & Johnson, 1970).

But as we noted earlier, third party involvement can sometimes lead to the so-called *chilling effect* (see Stevens, 1966; Feuille, 1975; Kochan, 1980). The chilling effect results in parties failing to make concessions that they otherwise could make and can reduce the probability of voluntary settlement. For some procedures, such as FOA, night baseball arbitration, or double FOA, the uncertainty of the third party's decision causes additional concession-making behavior toward their actual limits, because each side wishes to present a position to the arbitrator that is slightly more reasonable than that of the other side (Hebdon, 1996; Feuille, 1975; Stokes, 1999). Alternately, in the mediation phase of med-arb, the uncertainty of what sort of decision might follow in the arbitration phase may lead to greater concession making (Conlon et al., 2002).

Third party procedures that facilitate maximum concession making (reducing the chilling effect) on unresolved issues may be preferable in many cultures, especially those where individual positions are paramount and directly spoken and asserted by disputants. But this criterion is culturally bound, as it assumes the superiority of discovering and integrating individual level interests, and assumes that disputants will present their positions individually and competitively. As we have suggested before, there may not always be an objective to find the "best" or "most integrative" solution from an individual disputant perspective, as wider stakeholders interests might take priority. The chilling effect might not be relevant for certain disputes in collectivist cultures, as there may be a hesitation to put individual positions forward, especially if there is the possibility of causing confrontation or the loss of face if a disputant does not reach his or her spoken, public desired outcome. Additionally, there might be limited relevance in hierarchical cultures, for if the parties expect that the third party will ask the questions and make the decisions, perhaps parties do not always come in with a "position" per se nor might they actively choose to make concessions.

The Narcotic Effect

One of the best known concerns about arbitration is the "narcotic effect", where disputants may become overly reliant on an arbitrator and not attempt to resolve disputes on their own (cf., Lewicki et al., 1999). In research on this topic, FOA sometimes shows less of a narcotic effect than binding arbitration (see Olson, 1988 for a discussion) and double FOA comparatively less than either of the above (Dickinson, 2004). Generally, we see nothing in mediation or fact finding that reduces the likelihood of a narcotic effect – the parties are likely to become dependent on the use of these third parties unless the third parties take special steps to train the disputants to resolve their own conflicts.

In some cultures, especially those with individualistic and egalitarian values, we expect a preference for procedures that encourage parties to resolve disputes themselves. But, in other cultures, we would expect the third party to be an integral part of any dispute resolution process. For example, in hierarchical cultures, it may not be considered appropriate for disputants to take responsibility to solve their own disputes, and there may be strong norms preventing them from doing so. For especially in cultures where hierarchy is very strong, pushing decisions and control down the chain is not always desirable. It is considered the manager's job to take control and make the decision so that the disputants don't have to worry about this.

As well, in collectivist cultures, we might suggest that individuals are not encouraged to solve their own problems, as there may not be a desire for a focus on individual interests. It may be preferable for a respected, knowledgeable third party to ensure the "right" interests were taken into account in the situation (i.e., the broader collective). In fact, in some collectivist and hierarchical cultures (i.e., East Asian cultures), we often find that a preferred dispute resolution option is to seek out a higher status third party to assist in conflicts that may arise between subordinates (Brett, 2001; Tse, Francis, & Walls, 1994). Thus, the narcotic effect is likely to be even stronger in such cultural contexts.

Proposition 9. Disputes occurring in egalitarian and individualistic cultures will be more susceptible to a chilling effect, resulting in a greater proportion of disputes being appropriate for the use of FOA (and related procedures), as compared with disputes in hierarchical and collectivist cultures.

Proposition 10. Recurring negotiations that occur in egalitarian and individualistic cultures are less likely to exhibit the narcotic effect than are recurring negotiations that occur in hierarchical or collectivist cultures. Moreover, the presence of a narcotic effect will be perceived as less favorable among egalitarian and individualistic cultures than among hierarchical and collectivist cultures.

Relationship Criteria

Relationship Enhancement
Some procedures offer the potential for maintaining – or even enhancing – the relationship between the disputants (Bush & Folger, 1994; Elangovan, 1995; Thomas et al., 1978). As articulated by authors such as Bush and Folger (1994), mediation can focus on transforming relationships in addition to settling the immediate issues in dispute. Carnevale et al. (1989) report that "improving the relationship between the disputants" is an important criterion for evaluating the success of mediation. As described elsewhere within the context of mediation (Ross & Conlon, 2000), mediators may be evaluated based on how well they: (1) reestablish trust between the disputants, (2) deescalate the level of hostility between the parties, (3) help both disputants address power imbalances and other power-related issues within their relationship, and (4) help the parties have a more cooperative

motivational orientation. Kressel and Pruitt (1989), however, note that for many disputes mediation is unable to accomplish these goals because the intervention is too short and the relationship problems are too entrenched.

Relationship enhancement is not necessarily a primary goal of other reviewed procedures. Fact finders and arbitrators (of all "stripes") generally view improving relations among the disputants as beyond the scope of their authority. In the hybrid procedures of med-arb and arb-med, however, relationship enhancement (e.g., restoring broken trust; deescalating emotional conflict) is possible in the mediation phases, although ultimately ensuring a decision rather than improving the relationship is their primary mandate. Med-arb, for example, allows the possibility for parties to increase levels of understanding and cooperation, sometimes resulting in voluntary agreements before the implementation of the arbitration phase. Arb-med in a sense helps to preserve relationships by imposing structure and deadlines around the final mediation phase and discouraging uncooperative delaying and posturing behaviors.

Both individualist and collectivist cultures might be predicted to benefit from enhancing relationships, but for different reasons and perhaps to different degrees. For individualists, it encourages cooperation and potential integration of individual interests for a better solution and reduction of future conflict. For collectivists, it is important to maintain harmony and reduce potential animosity between individuals and the collective. In hierarchical cultures, however, we might find that this criteria is not as relevant, as low status individuals may be comfortable simply taking the advice of a third party to behave in a certain way toward the other party. In this case, they would follow the instruction, regardless of whether or not the procedure enhanced the relationship.

Commitment to Implement the Settlement

For many disputes, the parties must work together to implement the settlement, whether voluntary or imposed (Elangovan, 1995; Carnevale et al., 1989). When the disputants are committed to implementing the settlement, they are more likely to do so fully and enduringly; when one party is not so committed, s/he may simply fail to carry out the settlement and the other party may have to return to a third party forum to attempt to force compliance.

Procedural design may impact the commitment to implement a settlement. For example, McEwen and Maiman (1989) report that most disputants using mediation with small claims disputes are likely to implement the agreement whereas slightly less than half of those going to court implemented the judge's decision. Presumably, this is because people are more committed to implement voluntary than imposed settlements. These effects may also extend to hybrid procedures if an agreement is negotiated in the mediation phase.

We also see participation in the generation of an agreement impacting commitment to follow through with arbitration decisions. For example, Starke and Notz (1981) report that FOA "winners" (those whose proposed offer was accepted by the third party) are significantly more committed to implementing the imposed settlement than either FOA "losers" (those whose proposed offer was not accepted), or those who had a third party generated decision imposed on them in binding arbitration. One of the alleged advantages of double FOA over other forms of arbitration is that because the losing side can select between the winner's two offers, the loser is more committed to fully implementing the arbitrated outcome. However, little empirical research has confirmed this advantage for the double FOA procedure.

Generally, in egalitarian and individualistic cultures when the parties have voice and play a role in the determination of the outcome, they tend to feel that the agreement is more fair and are more committed to the outcome (Carnevale et al., 1989). In some cultures, however, it may be that commitment is driven not by voice, but by punishments for not complying, or lack of acceptance or other negative consequences from the collective. Furthermore, we may find that commitment may stem from other factors not currently explored in Western research. For example, we might find in hierarchical cultures, the commitment of low-status disputants to implement an outcome would be stronger under direction from a higher status third party than under their own voluntary agreement. Whatever the drivers, we suggest that in general, disputant commitment to the implementation of a settlement is desirable.

Proposition 11. Procedures that maximize relationship enhancement (maintain harmony, avoid social disruption, and save face) will be seen as more favorable than procedures that do not. This preference will be exacerbated in hierarchical and collectivist cultures, relative to egalitarian and individualist cultures.

Proposition 12. Disputant compliance with third party-imposed outcomes will be weaker in egalitarian and individualist cultures, as compared with hierarchical and collectivist cultures. In addition, the motivation to comply with imposed outcomes will be driven by legal concerns in egalitarian and individualistic cultures, whereas it will be driven by deference to authority and concern for face in hierarchical and collectivist cultures.

SUMMARY AND CONCLUSION

In our discussion, we have discussed a number of third party ADR procedures and have applied four categories of criteria drawn from the literature that are useful for comparing third party procedures: process-related, settlement-related, issue-related, and relationship-related criteria (e.g., Lissak & Sheppard, 1983; Sheppard, 1983, 1984). We have offered ideas about how these criteria might be perceived differentially across cultures, emphasizing that Western research findings about procedural preferences do not necessarily generalize to other cultural contexts.

Many different dispute resolution procedures exist within each culture and are used for different situations (Brett, 2001; Tinsley, 1998, 2001), procedures that "fit" a particular culture's set of values, norms, systems, and beliefs are likely to be preferable to those that do not. While we realize that there are many unique combinations of cultural dimensions that drive potential differences in procedural choice, we have sought to identify only two major groups of cultures (egalitarian/individualistic cultures with direct communication and hierarchical/collectivist cultures with indirect communication) and explore how procedural choices might differ and make suggestions for future research. We have limited our discussion for a number of reasons. Firstly, these two major groups because we consider these to provide the greatest contrast for ADR procedures among cultural dimensions that are currently understood from a theoretical perspective as well as from an empirical base. Secondly, from a global population perspective, these two cultural groups encompass, generally speaking, a large proportion of the world's citizens. Lastly, in the spirit of disclosure, these are the two cultural groups with which we are most familiar. By no means should this discussion be considered to be exhaustive of the world's great variety of cultures. Likewise, this discussion should not be viewed as a comprehensive treatment of third party procedures, evaluation criteria, and the moderating effect of culture. In the interest of parsimony, we have economized where we thought appropriate while retaining sufficiently rich detail to provide the reader with an appreciation of the complexity inherent to the domain we have delimited.

In this article we have reviewed and summarized a suite of ADR procedures. We have examined various criteria for evaluating those procedures. One important contribution we have made is to discuss the moderating role of culture in the application and enactment of ADR procedures as well as the criteria for evaluating the effectiveness of their use. We caution the reader to view culture in both a broad and narrow sense. In a broad sense, national or ethnic culture can render manifestations of individual and societal values, beliefs, norms, and behavior which differ significantly across large collectives of individuals who share a common origin or background. In the narrow sense, within a collective of individuals with a common national or ethnic background, there is wide scope for local variation – values, beliefs, norms, and behavior may significantly differ across regions, language or dialect groups, firms, communities, families, and individuals. Even within the same local group, these factors can change – a collective or individual can experience variation over time and context in the salience of particular dimensions of cultural values. For example, in times of prosperity and harmony, some dimensions of the culture may be more prominent than others for a community, whereas in times hardship and discord other dimensions are rendered more meaningful.

The meta-themes from this article should be evident to the reader by now: research which is culturally bounded is inherently ethnocentric, and potentially disregards important local factors leading to false assumptions; naïve transferal of ADR procedures across cultures can result in misapplication, and misappraisal of effectiveness of a given third party procedure; criteria for characterizing or evaluating third party procedures should be carefully and skillfully utilized with a cogent understanding of the implication of cultural values.

In short, the assumption that there exists a universal formula for selecting and evaluating third party ADR procedures can at best lead to wasted efforts in a futile search, and at worst can lead to misguided attempts to address conflict among disputants resulting in deleterious outcomes. This is not to say that we should be paralyzed in our attempts to disseminate third party procedures. Rather we encourage practitioners and researchers alike to test the assumptions underlying their conceptual and theoretical models of ADR procedures as they foray into cultures with which they are unfamiliar. In this way we will learn (often through trial and error), some universals, some non-universals, and some general heuristics for incorporating moderating effects. Let us keep in mind that, at least at this stage in our understanding of third party procedures, there still exists no "one best choice".

NOTES

1. While there is within culture diversity of conflict resolution strategies (Brett, 2001; Tinsley, 1998, 2001), certain strategies may be more preferred and used more often.

2. We do not assume here that these are the only criteria important across cultures. We expect future research may discover new criteria, and that relevance and importance of criteria will vary across cultures.

3. There is an obvious competing prediction here for collectivists. It is possible that preferences for face saving and animosity reduction might result in a desire to have quick resolutions to disputes as opposed to taking time to carefully tend to disputants for the same ultimate purpose. We await an empirical test of these competing predictions.

4. It is important to note that subjective and objective measures of success are not identical; sometimes parties prefer compromises to integrative tradeoffs even though the resulting outcome quality is objectively lower (Conlon & Ross, 1997).

REFERENCES

10 different species of ADR. (1993, Nov./Dec.). *Across the Board, 30*(9), 18–19.

Adair, W., Okumura, T., & Brett, J. M. (2001). Negotiation behavior when cultures collide: The U.S. and Japan. *Journal of Applied Psychology, 86*(3), 371–385.

Arad, S., & Carnevale, P. J. D. (1994). Partisanship effects in judgments of fairness and trust in third parties in the Palestinian-Israeli conflict. *Journal of Conflict Resolution, 38*, 423–451.

Arnold, J. A. (2000). Mediator insight: Disputants' perceptions of third parties' knowledge and its effect on mediated negotiation. *International Journal of Conflict Management, 11*, 318–336.

Arnold, J. A., & O'Connor, K. M. (1999). Ombudspersons or peers? The effect of third-party expertise and recommendations on negotiation. *Journal of Applied Psychology, 84*, 776–785.

Bond, M. H., Leung, K., & Schwartz, S. (1992). Explaining choices in procedural and distributive justice across cultures. *International Journal of Psychology, 27*(2), 211–225.

Bowling, D., & Hoffman, D. A. (2003). *Bringing peace into the room: How the personal qualities of the mediator impact the process of conflict resolution.* San Francisco, CA: Jossey-Bass.

Brams, S. J., & Merrill, S. (1986). Binding versus final offer arbitration: A combination is best. *Management Science, 32*(10), 1346–1355.

Brett, J. M. (2001). *Negotiating globally: How to negotiate deals, resolve disputes and make decisions across cultural boundaries.* San Francisco, CA: Jossey Bass.

Brett, J. M., Barsness, Z., & Goldberg, S. (1996). The effectiveness of mediation: An independent analysis of cases handled by four major service providers. *Negotiation Journal, 12*, 259–269.

Brett, J. M., & Goldberg, S. B. (1983). Mediator-advisors: A new third-party role. In: M.H. Bazerman & R. J. Lewicki (Eds), *Negotiating in organizations* (pp. 165–176). Beverly Hills, CA: Sage.

Brewer, T. J., & Mills, L. R. (1999, November). Combining mediation and arbitration. *Dispute Resolution Journal, 54*(4), 32–40.

Brown, L. D. (1983). *Managing conflict at organizational interfaces.* Reading, MA: Addison-Wesley.

Buckley, T. (2005). Working it out. *Business Mexico, 15*(7), 46–47.

Bush, R. A. B., & Folger, J. P. (1994). *The promise of mediation: Responding to conflict through empowerment and recognition.* San Francisco, CA: Jossey-Bass.

Callister, R. R., & Wall, J. A. (1997). Japanese community and organizational mediation. *Journal of Conflict Resolution, 41*(2), 311–328.

Carnevale, P. J. D. (1986). Strategic choice in negotiation. *Negotiation Journal, 2*, 41–56.

Carnevale, P. J. D., & Henry, R. (1989). Determinants of mediator behavior: A test of the strategic choice model. *Journal of Applied Social Psychology, 19*, 481–498.

Carnevale, P.J.D., Lim, R. G., & McLaughlin, M. E. (1989). Contingent mediator behavior and its effectiveness. In: K. Kressel & D. G. Pruitt (Eds), *Mediation research* (pp. 213–240). San Francisco: Jossey-Bass.

Carnevale, P. J. D., & Pruitt, D. G. (1992). Negotiation and mediation. In: M. Rosenberg & L. Porter (Eds), *Annual Review of Psychology* (Vol. 43, pp. 531–582). Palo Alto, CA: Annual Reviews, Inc.

Chan, A. C. F. (1998). Business negotiation with the Chinese: Evidence from China, Taiwan, and Hong Kong. In: K. Leung & D. Tjosvold (Eds), *Conflict management in the Asian Pacific* (pp. 147–166). New York: Wiley.

Chan, E. H. W. (1997). Amicable dispute resolution in the People's Republic of China and its implications for foreign-related construction disputes. *Construction Management and Economics, 15*, 539–548.

Chia, H. B., Partridge, J. E. L., & Cong, C. L. (2004). Traditional mediation practices: Are we throwing the baby out with the bath water? *Conflict Resolution Quarterly, 21*(4), 451–462.

Cobbledick, G. (1992). *Arb-med: An alternative approach to expediting settlement.* Working paper, Harvard Program on Negotiation, Harvard University, Boston, MA.

Coltri, L. S. (2004). *Conflict diagnosis and alternative dispute resolution.* Upper Saddle River, NJ: Pearson/Prentice Hall.

Conlon, D. (1988). The mediation-intravention discussion: Toward an integrative perspective. *Negotiation Journal, 4*, 143–148.

Conlon, D. E., & Fasolo, P. M. (1990). Influence of speed of third party intervention and outcome on negotiator and constituent fairness judgments. *Academy of Management Journal, 33*, 833–846.

Conlon, D. E., Moon, H., & Ng, K. Y. (2002). Putting the cart before the horse: The unexpected benefits of arbitrating before mediating. *Journal of Applied Psychology, 87*, 978–984.

Conlon, D. E., & Ross, W. H. (1993). The effects of partisan third parties on negotiator behavior and outcome perceptions. *Journal of Applied Psychology, 78*, 280–290.

Conlon, D. E., & Ross, W. H. (1997). Appearances do count: The effects of outcomes and explanations on disputant fairness judgments and supervisory evaluations. *The International Journal of Conflict Management, 8*, 5–31.

Crawford, V. P. (1981). Arbitration and conflict resolution in labor–management bargaining. *American Economic Association Papers and Proceedings, 71*(2), 205–210.

Depner, C. E., Canata, K., & Ricci, I. (1994). Client evaluations of mediation services: The impact of case characteristics and mediation service models. *Family and Conciliation Courts Review, 32*, 306–325.

Diamant, N. J. (2000). Conflict and conflict resolution in China: Beyond mediation-centered approaches. *The Journal of Conflict Resolution, 44*(4), 523.

Dickinson, D. L. (2004). Bargaining outcomes with double-offer arbitration. *Experimental Economics, 8*, 145–156.

Dickinson, D. L., & Hunnicutt, L. (2005). Does fact finding promote settlement? Theory and a test. *Economic Inquiry, 43*(2), 401–417.

Dubler, N. N., & Liebman, C. B. (2004). Bioethics: Mediating conflict in the hospital environment. *Dispute Resolution Journal, 59*(2), 32–39.

Edelman, P. B. (1984). Institutionalizing dispute resolution alternatives. *Justice System Journal,* 9, 134–149.

Elangovan, A. R. (1995). Managerial third-party dispute intervention: A prescriptive model of strategy selection. *Academy of Management Review, 20,* 800–830.

Elkouri, F., Elkouri, E. A., Goggin, E. P., & Volz, M. M. (1997). *How arbitration works* (5th ed.). Washington, DC: BNA Books.

Feuille, P. (1975). Final offer arbitration and the chilling effect. *Industrial Relations, 14,* 302–310.

Folger, R. (1977). Distributive and procedural justice: Combine impact of "voice" and improvement on experienced inequity. *Journal of Personality and Social Psychology, 35,* 108–119.

Hebdon, R. (1996). Public sector dispute resolution in transition. In: D. Belman, M. Gunderson & D. Hyatt (Eds), *Public sector employment in a time of transition* (pp. 85–125). Madison, WI: Industrial Relations Research Association.

Hofstede, G. (1980). *Culture's consequences: International differences in work-related values.* Beverly Hills, CA: Sage.

James, K. (1993). The social context of organizational justice: Cultural, intergroup, and structural effects on justice behaviors and perceptions. In: R. Cropanzano (Ed.), *Justice in the workplace* (pp. 21–50). Hillsdale, NJ: Erlbaum.

Kagel, J. (1976). Comment. In: H. Anderson (Ed.), *New techniques in labor dispute resolution* (pp. 185–190). Washington, DC: BNA Books.

Kim, N. H., Wall, J. A., Sohn, D. W., & Kim, J. S. (1993). Community and industrial mediation in South Korea. *Journal of Conflict Resolution, 37*(2), 361–381.

Kolb, D. M. (1985). *The mediators.* Cambridge, MA: MIT Press.

Kressel, K., & Pruitt, D. G. (1985). Themes in the mediation of social conflict. *Journal of Social Issues, 41,* 179–198.

Kressel, K., & Pruitt, D. G. (Eds). (1989). *Mediation Research.* San Francisco, CA: Jossey-Bass.

Kochan, T. A. (1980). *Collective bargaining and industrial relations.* Homewood, IL: Richard D. Irwin.

LaTour, S. (1978). Determinants of participant and observer satisfaction with adversary and inquisitorial modes of adjudication. *Journal of Personality and Social Psychology, 36,* 1531 1545.

Leung, K. (1987). Some determinants of reactions to procedural models for conflict resolution: A cross-national study. *Journal of Personality and Social Psychology, 53*(5), 898–908.

Leung, K. (1997). Negotiation and reward allocations across cultures. In: P. C. Earley & M. Erez (Eds), *New perspectives in I/O psychology* (pp. 640–675). San Francisco, CA: Jossey-Bass.

Leung, K., Au, Y. F., Fernandez-Dols, J. M., & Iwawaki, S. (1992). Preference for methods of conflict processing in two collectivist cultures. *International Journal of Psychology, 27*(2), 195–209.

Leung, K., & Stephan, W. G. (1998). Perceptions of injustice in intercultural relations. *Applied and Preventative Psychology, 7,* 195–205.

Leung, K., & Tong, K. K. (2004). Justice across cultures: A three-stage model for intercultural negotiation. In: M. J. Gelfand & J. M. Brett (Eds), *Negotiation: Theoretical advances and cross-cultural perspectives* (pp. 313–333). Stanford, CA: Stanford University Press.

Lewicki, R. J., Saunders, D. M., & Minton, J. W. (1999). *Negotiation* (3rd ed.). New York: Irwin McGraw-Hill.

Lewicki, R. J., & Sheppard, B. H. (1985). Choosing how to intervene: Factors affecting the use of process and outcome control in third party dispute resolution. *Journal of Occupational Behavior, 6,* 49–64.

Lewicki, R. J., Weiss, S., & Lewin, D. (1992). Models of conflict, negotiation and third party intervention: A review and synthesis. *Journal of Organizational Behavior, 13,* 209–252.

Lind, E. A., & Early, P. C. (1992). Procedural justice and culture. *International Journal of Psychology, 27*(2), 227–242.

Lind, E. A., Lissak, R. L. K., & Conlon, D. E. (1983). Decision control and process control effects on procedural fairness judgments. *Journal of Personality and Social Psychology, 59,* 952–959.

Lind, E. A., Erickson, B. E., Friedland, N., & Dickenberger, N. (1978). Reactions to procedural models for adjudicative conflict resolution: A cross national study. *Journal of Conflict Resolution, 22,* 318–341.

Lind, E. A., & Tyler, T. R. (1988). *The social psychology of procedural justice.* New York: Plenum.

Lissak, R. I., & Sheppard, B. H. (1983). Beyond fairness: The criterion problem in research in dispute intervention. *Journal of Applied Social Psychology, 13,* 45–65.

Lytle, A. L., Brett, J. M., Barsness, Z., Tinsley, C. H., & Janssens, M. (1995). A para digm for quantitative cross-cultural research in organizational behavior. In: B. M. Staw & L. L. Cummings (Eds), *Research in organizational behavior* (Vol. 17, pp. 167–214). Greenwich, CT: JAI Press.

McAndrew, I. (2003). Final offer arbitration: A New Zealand variation. *Industrial Relations, 42*(4), 736–744.

McEwen, C. A., & Maiman, R. J. (1989). Mediation in small claims court: Consensual processes and outcomes. In: K. Kressel & D. G. Pruitt (Eds), *Mediation research* (pp. 53–67). San Francisco, CA: Jossey-Bass.

McGillicuddy, N. B., Welton, G. L., & Pruitt, D. G. (1987). Third-party intervention: A field experiment comparing three different models. *Journal of Personality and Social Psychology, 53,* 104.

McGrath, J. E. (1966). A social psychological approach to the study of negotiation. In: R. V. Bowers (Ed.), *Studies on behavior in organizations: A research symposium* (pp. 101–134). Athens, GA: University of Georgia Press.

Mansor, N. (1998). Managing conflict in Malaysia: Cultural and economic influences. In: K. Leung & D. Tjosvold (Eds), *Conflict management in the Asian Pacific* (pp. 147–166). New York: Wiley.

Meyer, J. F. (2002). It is a gift from the creator to keep us in harmony: Original (vs. alternative) dispute resolution on the Navajo Nation. *International Journal of Public Administration, 25*(11), 1379–1401.

Meyer, J. P., Gemmell, J. M., & Irving, P. G. (1997). Evaluating the management of interpersonal conflict in organizations: A factor-analytic study of outcome criteria. *Revue Canadienne des Sciences de L'Administration, 14,* 1–13.

Montero, J. P. (2005). A model of final offer arbitration in regulation. *Journal of Regulatory Economics, 28*(1), 23–46.

Moore, C. W. (2003). *The mediation process: Practical strategies for resolving conflict* (3rd ed.). San Francisco, CA: Jossey Bass.

Morris, M., & Leung, K. (2000). Justice for all? Progress in research on cultural variation in the psychology of distributive and procedural justice. *Applied Psychology: An International Review, 49*(1), 100–132.

Olson, C. A. (1988). Dispute resolution in the public sector. In: B. Aaron, J. M. Najita & J.L. Stern (Eds), *Public-sector bargaining* (2nd ed., pp. 160–188). Washington, DC: Bureau of National Affairs, Inc.

Olson, C. A., & Rau, B. L. (1997). Learning from interest arbitration: The nest round. *Industrial and Labor Relations Review, 50*, 237–251.

Peerenboom, R., & Scanlon, K. (2005). An untapped dispute resolution option. *The China Business Review, 32*(4), 36–41.

Pierce, R. S., Pruitt, D. G., & Czaja, S. J. (1993). Complaint-respondent differences in procedural choice. *International Journal of Conflict Management, 4*, 199–222.

Podd, A. (1997). NASD discloses disciplinary measures. *Wall Street Journal*, January 27, B7.

Polland, H. (1973). Mediation-arbitration: A trade union view. *Monthly Labor Review*, September, 63–65.

Pruitt, D. G. (1981). *Negotiation behavior*. New York: Academic Press.

Pruitt, D. G., & Johnson, D. F. (1970). Mediation as an aid to face-saving in negotiation. *Journal of Personality and Social Psychology, 14*, 239–246.

Pucci, A. N. (2005). Arbitration in Brazil: Foreign investment and the new Brazilian approach to arbitration. *Dispute Resolution Journal, 60*(1), 82–87.

Robertson, B. (1991, June). *The arb-med process: How it works and why?* Unpublished manuscript. Addressed to the IMSSA National Conference.

Roongrengsuke, S., & Chansuthus, D. (1998). Conflict management in Thailand. In: K. Leung & D. Tjosvold (Eds), *Conflict management in the Asian Pacific* (pp. 147–166). New York: Wiley.

Ross, W. H. (2005). Should "Night Baseball" arbitration be used in lieu of public-sector strikes? Psychological considerations and suggestions for research. *Journal of Collective Negotiations in the Public Sector, 31*(1), 45–70.

Ross, W. H., & Conlon, D. E. (2000). Hybrid forms of third party dispute resolution: Theoretical implications of combining mediation and arbitration. *Academy of Management Review, 25*, 416–427.

Ross, W. H., Conlon, D. E., & Lind, E. A. (1990). The mediator as leader: Effects of behavioral style and deadline certainty on negotiator behavior. *Group and Organization Studies, 15*, 105–124.

Rudin, J. (2002). Aboriginal alternative dispute resolution in Canada – A case study. *International Journal of Public Administration, 25*(11), 1403–1426.

Sacks, M. A., Reichert, K. S., & Proffitt, W. (1999). Broadening the evaluation of dispute resolution: Context and relationships over time. *Negotiation Journal, 15*(4), 339–345.

Schneider, B. V. H. (1988). Public-sector labor legislation – An evolutionary analysis. In: B. Aaron, J. M. Najita & J. L. Stern (Eds), *Public-sector bargaining* (2nd ed., pp. 189–228). Washington, DC: Bureau of National Affairs, Inc.

Schwartz, S. (1994). Beyond individualism/collectivism: New cultural dimensions of values. In: H. C. Triandis, U. Kim & G. Yoon (Eds), *Individualism and collectivism*. London: Sage.

Schwartz, S., & Bilsky, W. (1990). Toward a universal theory of the content and structure of values. *Journal of Personality and Social Psychology, 58*, 878–891.

Serrin, W. (1983). Jersey arbitration law: Why unions tend to win. *New York Times*, November 19, 28.

Sheppard, B. H. (1983). Managers as inquisitors: Some lessons from the law. In: M.H. Bazerman & R. J. Lewicki (Eds), *Negotiating in organizations* (pp. 193–213). Beverly Hills, CA: Sage.

Sheppard, B. H. (1984). Third party conflict intervention: A procedural framework. In: B. M. Staw & L. L. Cummings (Eds), *Research in organizational behavior* (Vol. 6, pp. 141–190). Greenwich, CT: JAI Press.

Sheppard, B. H. (1985). Justice is no simple matter: Case for elaborating our model of procedural fairness. *Journal of Personality and Social Psychology, 49*, 953–962.

Slaikeu, K. A. (1996). *When push comes to shove: A practical guide to mediating disputes.* San Francisco, CA: Jossey-Bass.

Montaqu-Smith, N. (1998). Arbitration gets designer. *International Commercial Litigation, 30*, 14–21.

Starke, F. A., & Notz, W. W. (1981). Pre- and post-intervention effects of conventional vs. final offer arbitration. *Academy of Management Journal, 24*, 832–850.

Stevens, C. M. (1966). Is compulsory arbitration compatible with bargaining? *Industrial Relations, 5*, 38–50.

Stokes, G. (1999). Solomon's wisdom: An early analysis of the effects of the police and fire interest arbitration reform act in New Jersey. *Journal of Collective Negotiations in the Public Sector, 28*, 219–231.

Thibaut, J., & Walker, L. (1975). *Procedural justice: A psychological analysis.* Hillsdale, NJ: Lawrence Erlbaum.

Thibault, J., & Walker, L. (1978). A theory of procedure. *California Law Review, 66*, 541–566.

Thomas, K. W. (1992). Conflict and negotiation processes in organizations. In: M. D. Dunnette & L. M. Hough (Eds), *Handbook of industrial and organizational psychology* (2nd ed., Vol. 3, pp. 651–717). Palo Alto, CA: Consulting Psychologists Press.

Thomas, K. W., Jamieson, D. W., & Moore, R. K. (1978). Conflict and collaboration: Some concluding observations. *California Management Review, 21*, 91–95.

Tinsley, C. H. (1997). Understanding conflict in a Chinese cultural context. In: R. Bies, R.J. Lewicki & B. Sheppard (Eds), *Research on negotiations in organizations* (pp. 209–225). Beverly Hills, CA: Sage.

Tinsley, C. H. (1998). Models of conflict resolution in Japanese, German, and American cultures. *Journal of Applied Psychology, 83*, 316–323.

Tinsley, C. H. (2001). How we get to yes: Predicting the constellation of strategies used across cultures to negotiate conflict. *Journal of Applied Psychology, 86*, 583–593.

Tinsley, C. H. (2004). Culture and conflict: Enlarging our dispute resolution framework. In: M.J. Gelfand & J. M. Brett (Eds), *Negotiation: Theoretical advances and cross-cultural perspectives* (pp. 193–212). Stanford, CA: Stanford University Press.

Triandis, H. C. (1995). *Individualism and collectivism.* Boulder, CO: Westview Press.

Tse, D. K., Francis, J., & Walls, J. (1994). Cultural differences in conducting intra- and inter-cultural negotiation: A Sino-Canadian comparison. *Journal of International Business Studies, 25*, 537–555.

Ury, W. L., Brett, J. M., & Goldberg, S. B. (1988). *Getting disputes resolved.* San Francisco, CA: Jossey- Bass.

Van de Kragt, A. J. C., Stark, F. A., Notz, W. W., & Boschman, I. (1989). Double final offer arbitration: Does it work as intended? Paper presented at the second biannual conference of the International Association for Conflict Management, Athens GA, June 11–14.

Walker, L., LaTour, S., Lind, E. A., & Thibaut, J. (1974). Reactions of participants and observers to modes of adjudication. *Journal of Applied Social Psychology, 4*, 295–310.

Wall, J. A., & Blum, M. (1991). Community mediation in the People's Republic of China. *Journal of Conflict Resolution, 35*(1), 3–20.

Wall, J. A., Blum, M., & Callister, R. R. (1999). Malaysian community mediation. *Journal of Conflict Resolution, 43*(3), 343–365.

Wall, J. A., Stark, J. B., & Standifer, R. L. (2001). Mediation: A current review and theory development. *Journal of Conflict Resolution, 45*, 370–391.

Woo, K. T. (1999). Court-connected mediation in Korea. *Dispute Resolution Journal, 54*(2), 36–41.

Yang, K. S. (1993). Chinese social orientation: An integrative analysis. In: L. Y. Cheng, F.M.C. Cheung & C. N. Chen (Eds), *Psychotherapy for the Chinese: Selected Papers from the First International Conference*. Hong Kong: The Chinese University of Hong Kong.

Zack, A. M. (2003). The quest for finality in airline disputes: The case for arb-med. *Dispute Resolution Journal, 58*(4), 34–38.

ABOUT THE AUTHORS

Fred R. Blass is an Assistant in Management at Florida State University. He received a Ph.D. in Management from Florida State University, and before joining the faculty at Florida State, served on the Department of Management faculty at the United States Air Force Academy. Blass has research interests in power and influence in organizations and organizational socialization. He has published his research in such journals as *Human Resource Management* and *The Leadership Quarterly*. Also, he has presented his research at both national and regional professional conferences.

Donald E. Conlon is the Eli Broad Professor of Management and Chairperson of the Department of Management at the Eli Broad College of Business at Michigan State University. He received his Ph.D. in business administration from the University of Illinois at Urbana-Champaign. His research focuses on organizational justice, conflict and negotiation, managerial decision-making, and the effects of context on customer perceptions of service exchanges. Recent publications have appeared in the *Academy of Management Journal*, *Journal of Applied Psychology*, and the *International Journal of Conflict Management*.

Russell Cropanzano is the Brien Lesk Professor of Organizational Behavior at the University of Arizona's Eller College of Management. He received his Ph.D. from Purdue University. Dr. Cropanzano's primary research areas include perceptions of organizational justice as well as on the experience and impact of workplace emotion. He has edited four books, presented over 60 papers, and published roughly 80 scholarly articles and chapters. In addition, he is a co-author (with Robert Folger) of the book *Organizational Justice and Human Resources Management*, which won the 1998 Book Award from the International Association of Conflict Management. Dr. Cropanzano was also a winner of the 2000 Outstanding Paper Award from the *Consulting Psychology Journal*. He is currently editor of the *Journal of Management*, a fellow in the Society for Industrial/Organizational Psychology, and Representative-at-Large for the Organizational Behavior Division of the Academy of Management.

Gerald R. Ferris is the Francis Eppes Professor of Management and Professor of Psychology at Florida State University. He received a Ph.D. in Business Administration from the University of Illinois at Urbana-Champaign. Ferris has research interests in the areas of social influence and effectiveness processes in organizations, and the role of reputation in organizations, and he is the author of articles published in such journals as the *Journal of Applied Psychology, Organizational Behavior and Human Decision Processes, Personnel Psychology, Academy of Management Journal, Academy of Management Review*, and the *Journal of Organizational Behavior*. He served as Editor of the annual research series, *Research in Personnel and Human Resources Management* from its inception in 1983 until 2003. Ferris was the recipient of the Heneman Career Achievement Award, from the Human Resource Division of the Academy of Management, in 2001.

Aparna Joshi is Assistant Professor of Industrial Relations and Human Resources at the University of Illinois, Urbana-Champaign. She conducts research in the area of work team diversity, global and distributed teams, team social capital and cross-cultural issues in HR. Her research appears in *Academy of Management Review, Journal of Applied Psychology, Journal of Organizational Behavior, Journal of Management, Personnel Psychology, Journal of World Business, Journal of International Human Resource Management*, and the *International Handbook of Work and Organizational Psychology*. She has taught courses on Performance Management, Training and Development, Managing Workplace Diversity and Strategic Human Resource Management.

Mary Dana Laird is a Ph.D. candidate in Management at Florida State University. Her current research interests include organizational politics perceptions, personal reputation, supervisor–subordinate relationships, and feedback in the performance evaluation process. She has published her research in the *Handbook of Organizational Politics*, and *Human Resource Management Review*, and she has presented several papers at professional conferences.

Anne L. Lytle is a Senior Lecturer in Organizational Behavior at the Australian Graduate School of Management at the University of New South Wales, Australia. She received her Ph.D. in Organizational Behavior from the Kellogg Graduate School of Management, Northwestern University. Her research, teaching, and consulting focuses on negotiation, conflict management, influence, and leadership. Her publications have appeared in *Academy of Management Journal, Negotiation Journal, Journal of Applied Social Psychology*, and *Research in Organizational Behavior.*

Christopher J. Meyer is an Assistant Professor in the Hankamer School of Business at Baylor University. He received his Ph.D. in management from Michigan State University. His research interests lie mainly in the area of human motivation. Specifically, his research focuses on the impact of such motivational forces as perceptions of fairness, emotions and power on negotiated organizational outcomes or the structure of negotiation – i.e., third parties or coalitions in negotiation. Meyer's research has been published in the *Academy of Management Journal*, the *Journal of Applied Psychology*, and the *Journal of the American Veterinary Medical Association.* In addition, Meyer's work has been published in the *Handbook of Organizational Justice* and the *Handbook of Negotiation and Culture.*

Christopher Robert is an Assistant Professor in the Department of Management with a joint appointment in the Department of Psychological Sciences at the University of Missouri, Columbia. He received his Ph.D. in Industrial and Organizational Psychology from the University of Illinois at Urbana-Champaign in 1998. His primary research interests involve cross-cultural and international management issues, including the influence of culture on management practices and organizational outcomes, and cross-cultural methodology and measurement issues. He is also interested in small group interaction, negotiation and conflict, and most recently in humor and culture. His research has appeared in journals such as the *Journal of Applied Psychology, Organizational Behavior and Human Decision Processes, Journal of Management*, and *Personnel Psychology.*

Hyuntak Roh is a doctoral student in Labor and Industrial Relations at University of Illinois at Urbana-Champaign. He received master's degree in Human Resources and Industrial Relations from the same institution and has a B.A. in psychology from Yonsei University, Seoul, Korea. His principal research interests include workforce diversity, global teams, and employee turnover. Prior to his academic career, he has worked for Towers Perrin and Samsung Economic Research Institute in Korea.

Dianna L. Stone is a Professor of Management at the University of Texas at San Antonio. She received her Ph.D. from Purdue University. Her research focuses on a number of issues including diversity in organizations, the influence of culture on human resources practices, stigmas in organizations, electronic human resources management (eHR), information privacy, and reactions to selection techniques. She is a Fellow of the American Psychological Association and the Society for Industrial and Organizational Psychology. The results of her research have been published in such outlets as the *Journal of Applied Psychology*, the *Academy of Management Review, Personnel Psychology, Organizational Behavior and Human Decision Processes, Human Resources Management Review*, the *Journal of Management*, and the *Journal of Applied Social Psychology*. She has recently edited two books on electronic human resources management (i.e., *The Brave New World of eHR*, and *Advances in Human Performance and Cognitive Engineering Research*). She also serves on the editorial boards of *Human Resources Management Review, Human Resources Management*, and an Associate Editor of *The Business Journal of Hispanic Research*.

Eugene F. Stone-Romero received his Ph.D. from the University of California-Irvine and is a Professor of Management at the University of Texas at San Antonio. He is a Fellow of the Society for Industrial and Organizational Psychology, the Association for Psychological Science, and the American Psychological Association. The results of his research have appeared in such outlets as the *Journal of Applied Psychology, Organizational Behavior and Human Performance, Personnel Psychology, Journal of Vocational Behavior, Academy of Management Journal, Journal of Management, Educational and Psychological Measurement, Journal of Educational Psychology, International Review of Industrial and Organizational Psychology, Research in Personnel and Human Resources Management, Applied Psychology: An International Review*, and the *Journal of Applied Social Psychology*. He is also the author of numerous book chapters dealing with issues germane to the related fields of human resources management, industrial and organizational psychology, organizational behavior, and applied social psychology. Finally, he is the author of a book titled *Research Methods in Organizational Behavior*, and the co-author of a book titled *Job Satisfaction: How People Feel About Their Jobs and How It Affects Their Performance*.

Michael C. Sturman is an Associate Professor at Cornell University's School of Hotel Administration, and is the Kenneth and Marjorie Blanchard Professor of Human Resources. There, he teaches undergraduate, graduate, and executive education courses on human resource management, compensation, and cost–benefit analysis. His current research focuses on the prediction of individual job performance over time, the influence of compensation systems, and the impact of human resource management on organizational performance. He has published both research-oriented and practitioner-oriented papers in such journals as the *Journal of Applied Psychology, Academy of Management Journal, Personnel Psychology, Journal of Management, Cornell Hotel and Restaurant Administration Quarterly, International Journal of Hospitality Management, Lodging Magazine, Lodging HR, A.A.H.O.A. Hospitality, HR.Com,* and *The American Compensation Association Journal.* Michael holds a Ph.D., M.S., and B.S. from Cornell University's School of Industrial and Labor Relations, and is a Senior Professional of Human Resources as certified by the Society for Human Resource Management.

Harold W. Willaby is a Ph.D. student in psychology at the University of Sydney. He holds a Masters of Business Administration degree from the Australian Graduate School of Management. His primary research interest is decision making under conditions of uncertainty.

Thomas A. Wright, formerly a Professor of Organizational Behavior at the University of Nevada, Reno, is now the Jon Wefald Leadership Chair in Business Administration and a Professor of Management at Kansas State University. He received his Ph.D. from the University of California, Berkeley. Similar to the Claude Rains character from the classic movie, Casablanca, he has published his work in many of the "usual suspects" including the *Academy of Management Review, Journal of Applied Psychology, Psychometrika, Academy of Management Executive, Journal of Organizational Behavior, Journal of Management, Journal of Occupational Health Psychology, Organizational Dynamics*, and the *Journal of Management Inquiry.* The highlight of his professional career has been publishing a number of articles on business ethics with his late father, Vincent P. Wright.

Wan Yan is currently a Ph.D. candidate at the University of Missouri, Columbia, in the Department of Management. Her research interests include cultural differences in emotion management and the meaning of work. She was born in the People's Republic of China, and holds a Master's degree in Agricultural Economics from University of Missouri, Columbia. She worked for Colgate Palmolive and Deutsche Bank, China, before pursuing degrees in the United States. Wan knows a lot of good jokes.

Robert Zinko is Assistant Professor of Management at East Carolina University. He received a Ph.D. in Management at Florida State University. His main area of research interest is personal reputation as it relates to other aspects of social influence processes in organizations. He has published in such journals as *Journal of Applied Psychology, Organizational Dynamics, Human Resource Management Review*, and *The Leadership Quarterly*. Also, he has presented his research at both national and regional professional conferences.

SET UP A CONTINUATION ORDER TODAY!

Did you know that you can set up a continuation order on all Elsevier-JAI series and have each new volume sent directly to you upon publication? For details on how to set up a **continuation order**, contact your nearest regional sales office listed below.

To view related series in Business & Management, please visit:

www.elsevier.com/businessandmanagement

The Americas
Customer Service Department
11830 Westline Industrial Drive
St. Louis, MO 63146
USA
US customers:
Tel: +1 800 545 2522 (Toll-free number)
Fax: +1 800 535 9935
For Customers outside US:
Tel: +1 800 460 3110 (Toll-free number).
Fax: +1 314 453 7095
usbkinfo@elsevier.com

Europe, Middle East & Africa
Customer Service Department
Linacre House
Jordan Hill
Oxford OX2 8DP
UK
Tel: +44 (0) 1865 474140
Fax: +44 (0) 1865 474141
eurobkinfo@elsevier.com

Japan
Customer Service Department
2F Higashi Azabu, 1 Chome Bldg
1-9-15 Higashi Azabu, Minato-ku
Tokyo 106-0044
Japan
Tel: +81 3 3589 6370
Fax: +81 3 3589 6371
books@elsevierjapan.com

APAC
Customer Service Department
3 Killiney Road #08-01
Winsland House I
Singapore 239519
Tel: +65 6349 0222
Fax: +65 6733 1510
asiainfo@elsevier.com

Australia & New Zealand
Customer Service Department
30-52 Smidmore Street
Marrickville, New South Wales 2204
Australia
Tel: +61 (02) 9517 8999
Fax: +61 (02) 9517 2249
service@elsevier.com.au

30% Discount for Authors on All Books!

A 30% discount is available to Elsevier book and journal contributors on all books (except multi-volume reference works).

To claim your discount, full payment is required with your order, which must be sent directly to the publisher at the nearest regional sales office above.